Tina's Groove

by Rina Piccolo

**Andrews McMeel
Publishing**

Kansas City

06 07 08 09 10 VON 10 9 8 7 6 5 4 3 2 1

ISBN-13: 978-0-7407-5697-9
ISBN-10: 0-7407-5697-4

Library of Congress Control Number: 2005935667

www.tinasgroove.com

www.andrewsmcmeel.com

——— **ATTENTION: SCHOOLS AND BUSINESSES** ———

Andrews McMeel books are available at quantity discounts with bulk purchase for educational, business, or sales promotional use. For information, please write to: Special Sales Department, Andrews McMeel Publishing, LLC, 4520 Main Street, Kansas City, Missouri 64111.

For Brendan

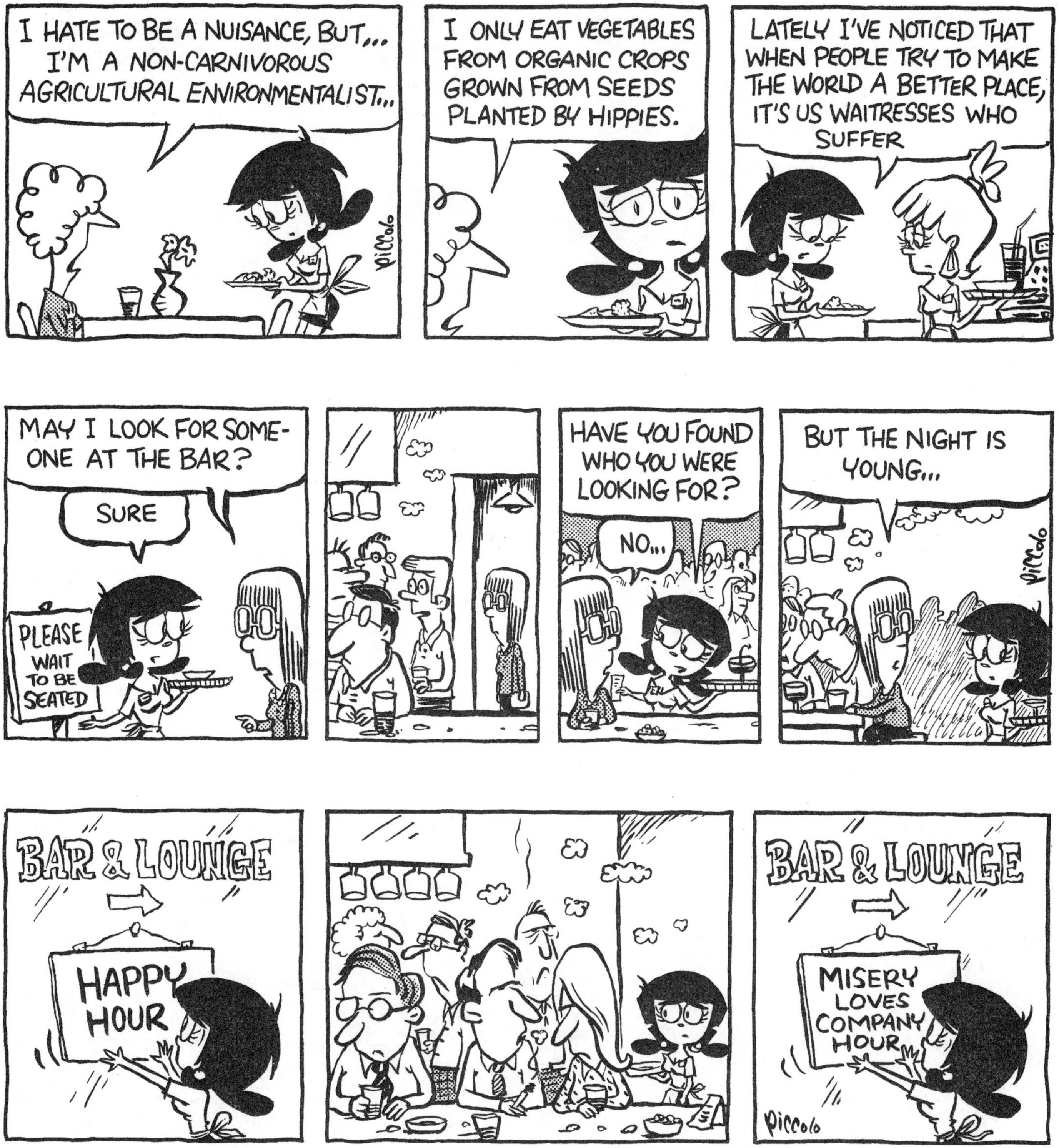
I HATE TO BE A NUISANCE, BUT,.. I'M A NON-CARNIVOROUS AGRICULTURAL ENVIRONMENTALIST...
I ONLY EAT VEGETABLES FROM ORGANIC CROPS GROWN FROM SEEDS PLANTED BY HIPPIES.
LATELY I'VE NOTICED THAT WHEN PEOPLE TRY TO MAKE THE WORLD A BETTER PLACE, IT'S US WAITRESSES WHO SUFFER
MAY I LOOK FOR SOME-ONE AT THE BAR?
SURE
PLEASE WAIT TO BE SEATED
HAVE YOU FOUND WHO YOU WERE LOOKING FOR?
NO...
BUT THE NIGHT IS YOUNG...
BAR & LOUNGE
HAPPY HOUR
BAR & LOUNGE
MISERY LOVES COMPANY HOUR

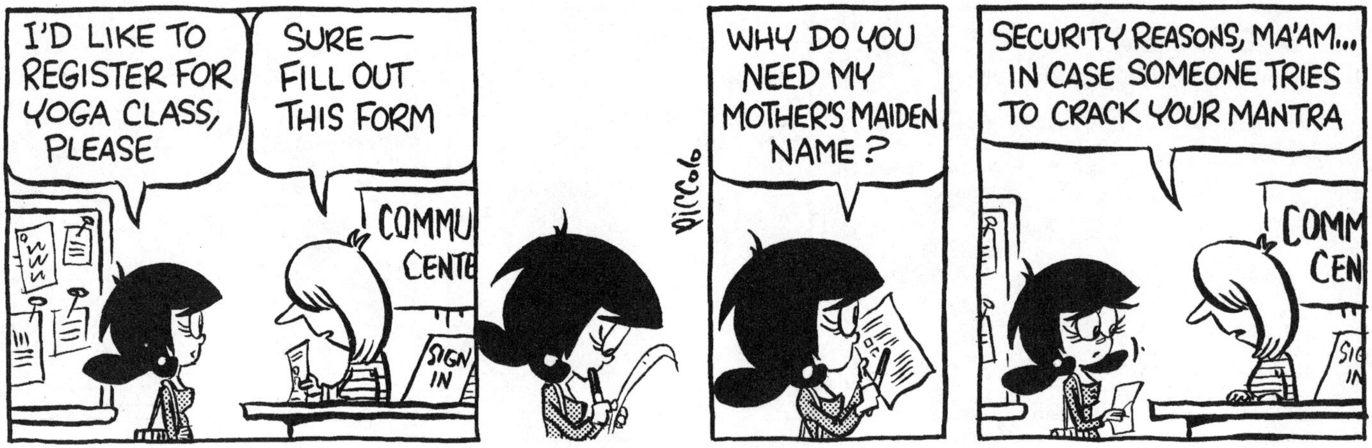
I'D LIKE TO REGISTER FOR YOGA CLASS, PLEASE
SURE— FILL OUT THIS FORM
COMMU CENTE
SIGN IN
PICCOLO
WHY DO YOU NEED MY MOTHER'S MAIDEN NAME?
SECURITY REASONS, MA'AM... IN CASE SOMEONE TRIES TO CRACK YOUR MANTRA
COMM CEN

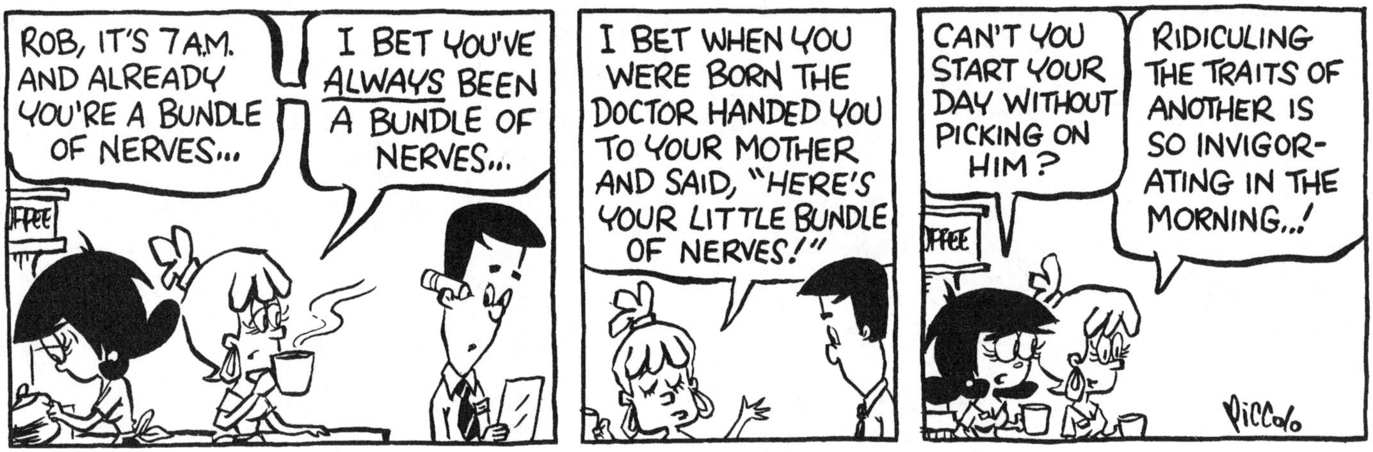
ROB, IT'S 7 A.M. AND ALREADY YOU'RE A BUNDLE OF NERVES...
I BET YOU'VE ALWAYS BEEN A BUNDLE OF NERVES...
I BET WHEN YOU WERE BORN THE DOCTOR HANDED YOU TO YOUR MOTHER AND SAID, "HERE'S YOUR LITTLE BUNDLE OF NERVES!"
CAN'T YOU START YOUR DAY WITHOUT PICKING ON HIM?
RIDICULING THE TRAITS OF ANOTHER IS SO INVIGOR-ATING IN THE MORNING...!
PICCOLO

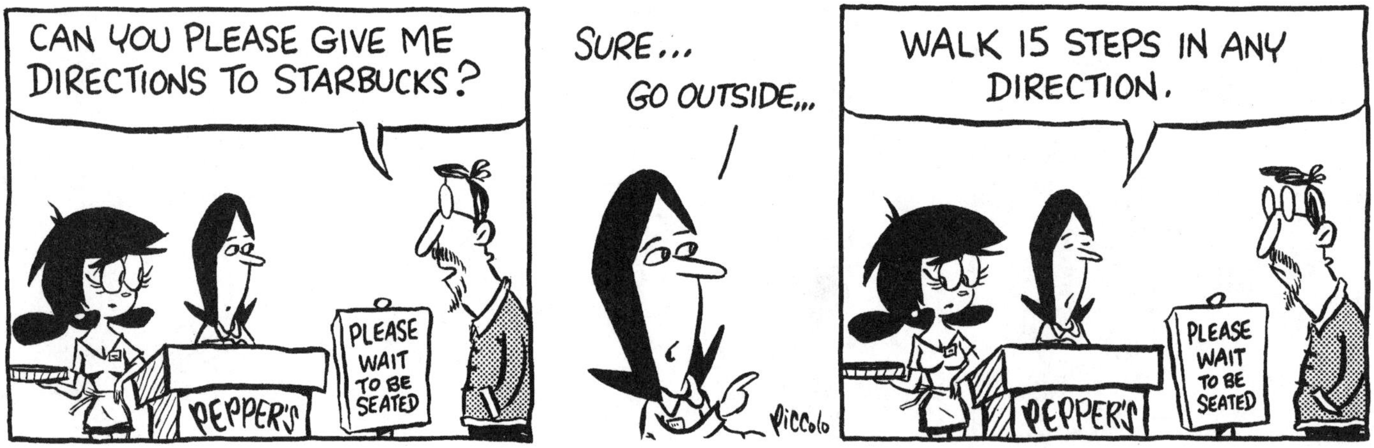
CAN YOU PLEASE GIVE ME DIRECTIONS TO STARBUCKS?
PLEASE WAIT TO BE SEATED
PEPPER'S
SURE...
GO OUTSIDE...
PICCOLO
WALK 15 STEPS IN ANY DIRECTION.
PLEASE WAIT TO BE SEATED
PEPPER'S

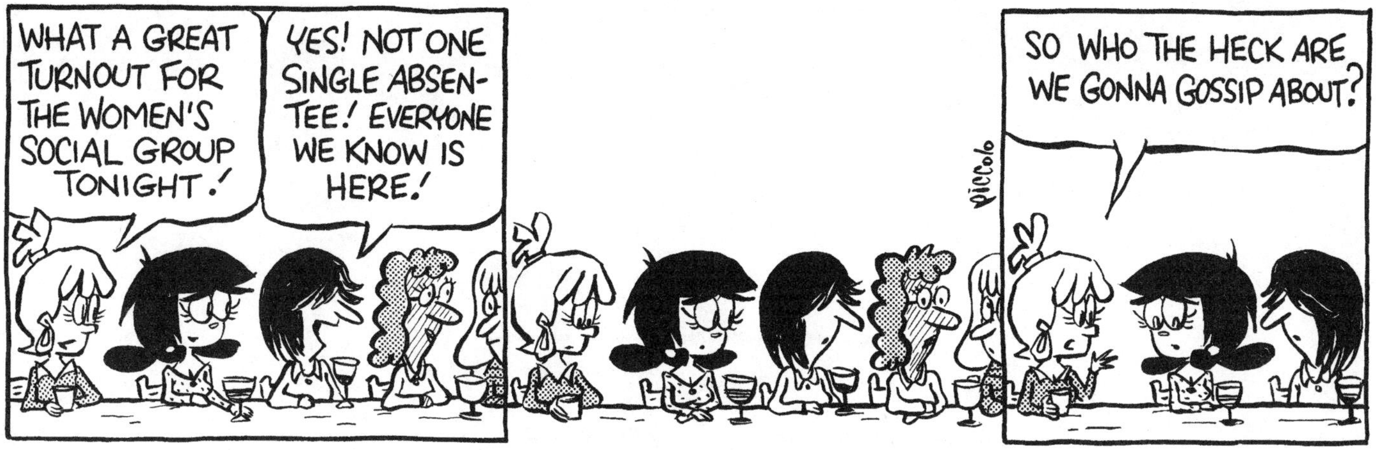

WHAT A GREAT TURNOUT FOR THE WOMEN'S SOCIAL GROUP TONIGHT!
YES! NOT ONE SINGLE ABSENTEE! EVERYONE WE KNOW IS HERE!
SO WHO THE HECK ARE WE GONNA GOSSIP ABOUT?

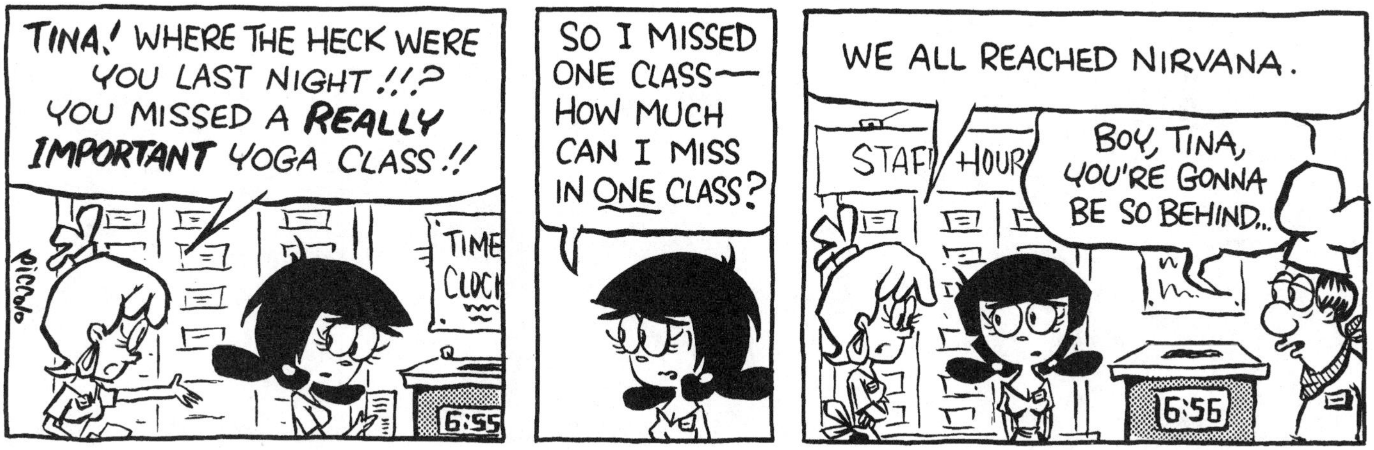

TINA! WHERE THE HECK WERE YOU LAST NIGHT!!? YOU MISSED A **REALLY IMPORTANT** YOGA CLASS!!
TIME
6:55
SO I MISSED ONE CLASS— HOW MUCH CAN I MISS IN ONE CLASS?
WE ALL REACHED NIRVANA.
BOY, TINA, YOU'RE GONNA BE SO BEHIND...
6:56

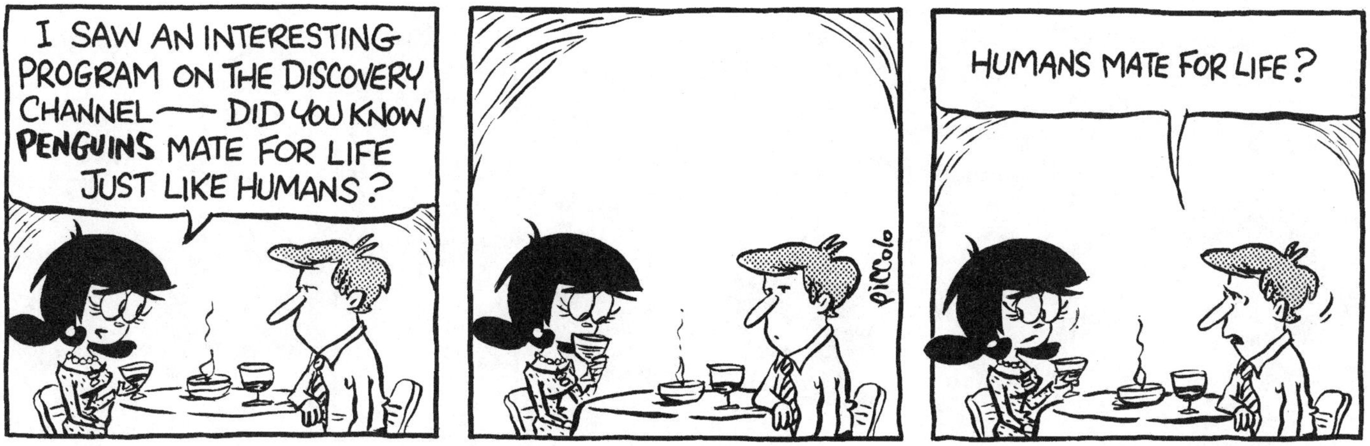

I SAW AN INTERESTING PROGRAM ON THE DISCOVERY CHANNEL— DID YOU KNOW **PENGUINS** MATE FOR LIFE JUST LIKE HUMANS?
HUMANS MATE FOR LIFE?

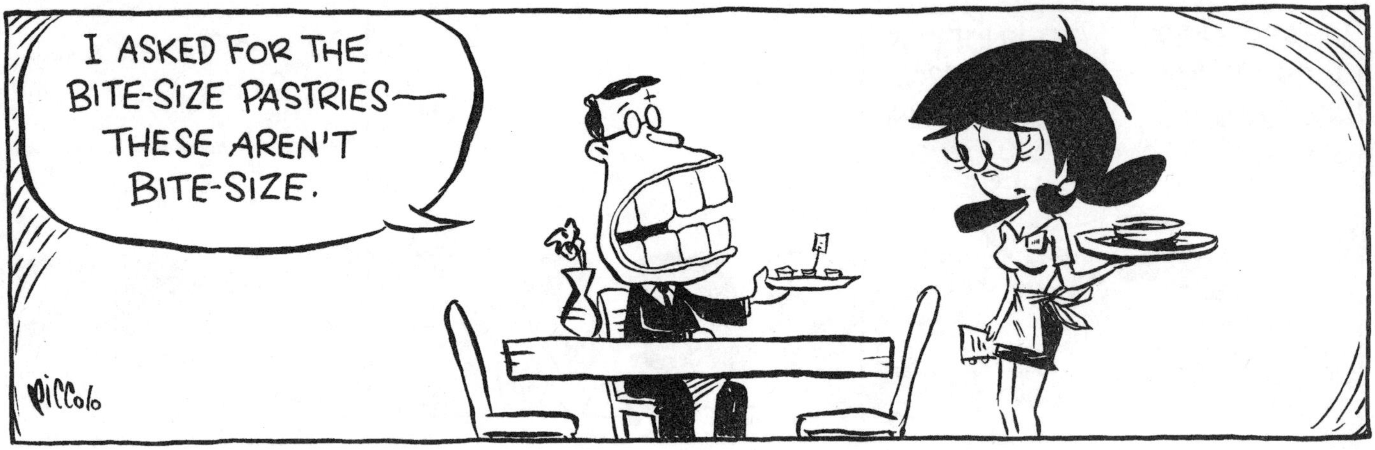
I ASKED FOR THE BITE-SIZE PASTRIES— THESE AREN'T BITE-SIZE.

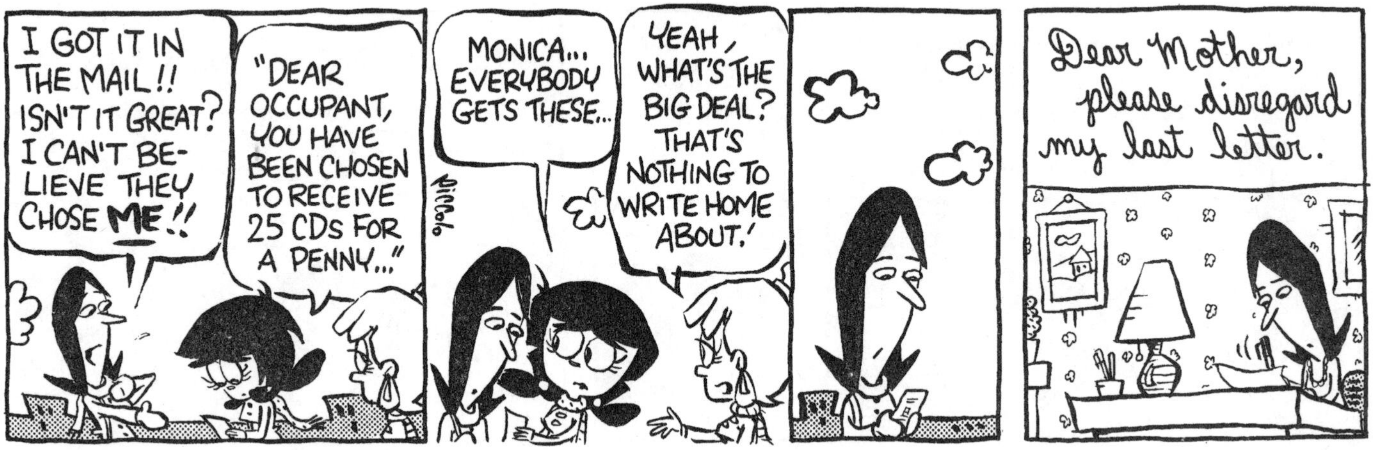
I GOT IT IN THE MAIL!! ISN'T IT GREAT? I CAN'T BELIEVE THEY CHOSE **ME**!!
"DEAR OCCUPANT, YOU HAVE BEEN CHOSEN TO RECEIVE 25 CDs FOR A PENNY..."
MONICA... EVERYBODY GETS THESE...
YEAH, WHAT'S THE BIG DEAL? THAT'S NOTHING TO WRITE HOME ABOUT.
Dear Mother, please disregard my last letter.

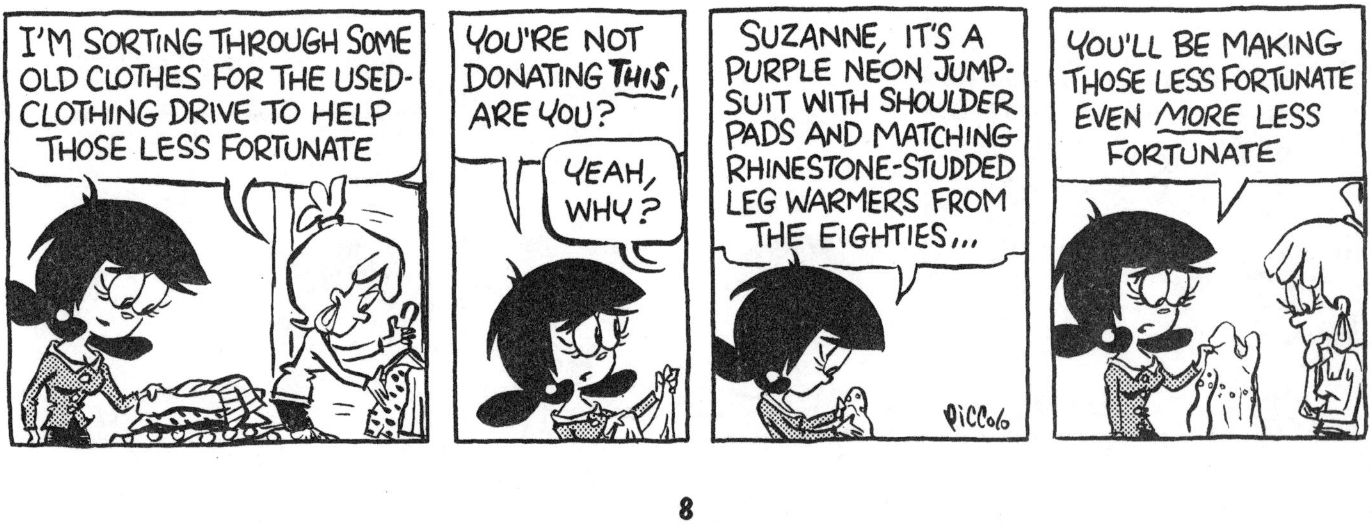
I'M SORTING THROUGH SOME OLD CLOTHES FOR THE USED-CLOTHING DRIVE TO HELP THOSE LESS FORTUNATE
YOU'RE NOT DONATING **THIS**, ARE YOU?
YEAH, WHY?
SUZANNE, IT'S A PURPLE NEON JUMP-SUIT WITH SHOULDER PADS AND MATCHING RHINESTONE-STUDDED LEG WARMERS FROM THE EIGHTIES...
YOU'LL BE MAKING THOSE LESS FORTUNATE EVEN MORE LESS FORTUNATE

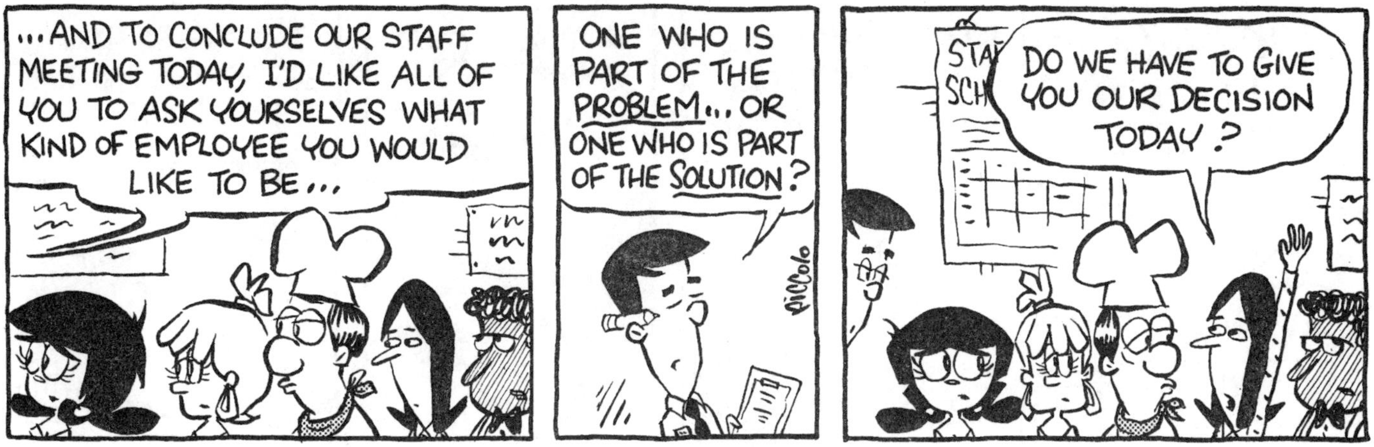
...AND TO CONCLUDE OUR STAFF MEETING TODAY, I'D LIKE ALL OF YOU TO ASK YOURSELVES WHAT KIND OF EMPLOYEE YOU WOULD LIKE TO BE...
ONE WHO IS PART OF THE PROBLEM... OR ONE WHO IS PART OF THE SOLUTION?
PICCOLO
DO WE HAVE TO GIVE YOU OUR DECISION TODAY?

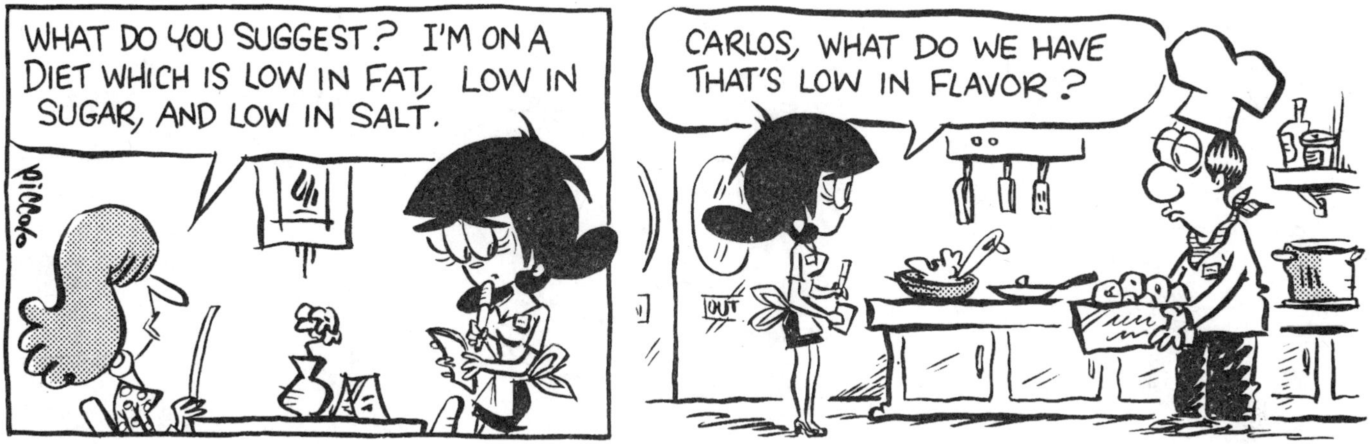
WHAT DO YOU SUGGEST? I'M ON A DIET WHICH IS LOW IN FAT, LOW IN SUGAR, AND LOW IN SALT.
PICCOLO
CARLOS, WHAT DO WE HAVE THAT'S LOW IN FLAVOR?
OUT

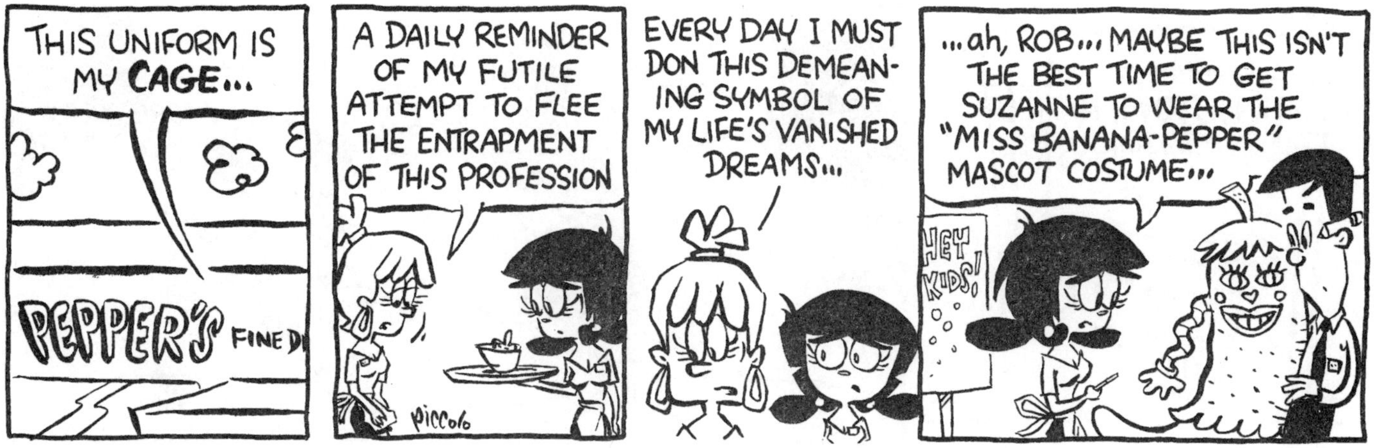
THIS UNIFORM IS MY **CAGE**...
PEPPER'S FINE DI
A DAILY REMINDER OF MY FUTILE ATTEMPT TO FLEE THE ENTRAPMENT OF THIS PROFESSION
PICCOLO
EVERY DAY I MUST DON THIS DEMEANING SYMBOL OF MY LIFE'S VANISHED DREAMS...
...ah, ROB... MAYBE THIS ISN'T THE BEST TIME TO GET SUZANNE TO WEAR THE "MISS BANANA-PEPPER" MASCOT COSTUME...
HEY KIDS!

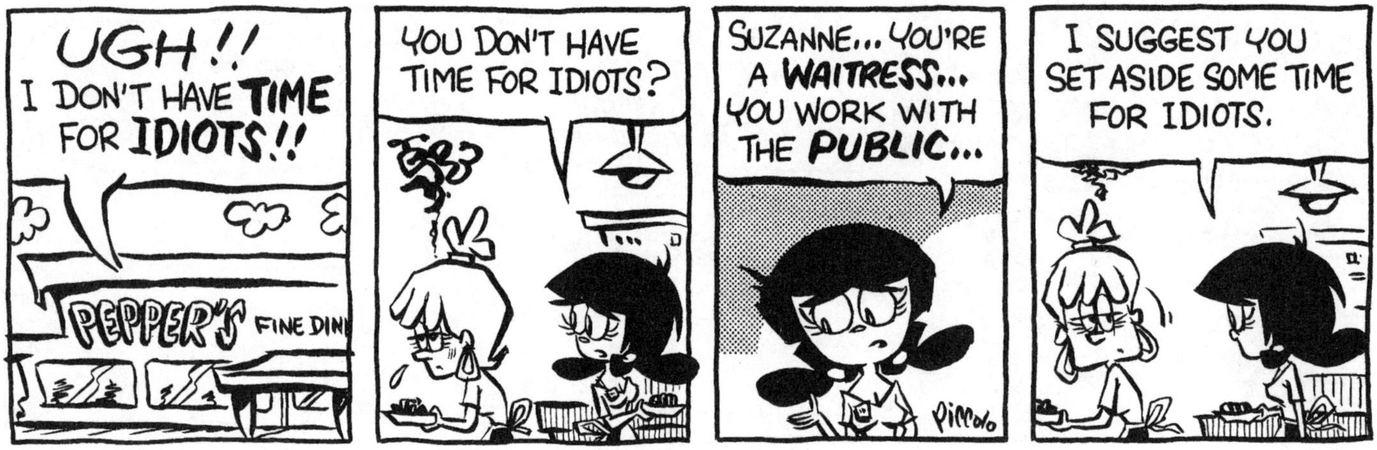
UGH!! I DON'T HAVE TIME FOR IDIOTS!!
PEPPER'S FINE DINI
YOU DON'T HAVE TIME FOR IDIOTS?
SUZANNE... YOU'RE A WAITRESS... YOU WORK WITH THE PUBLIC...
Piccolo
I SUGGEST YOU SET ASIDE SOME TIME FOR IDIOTS.

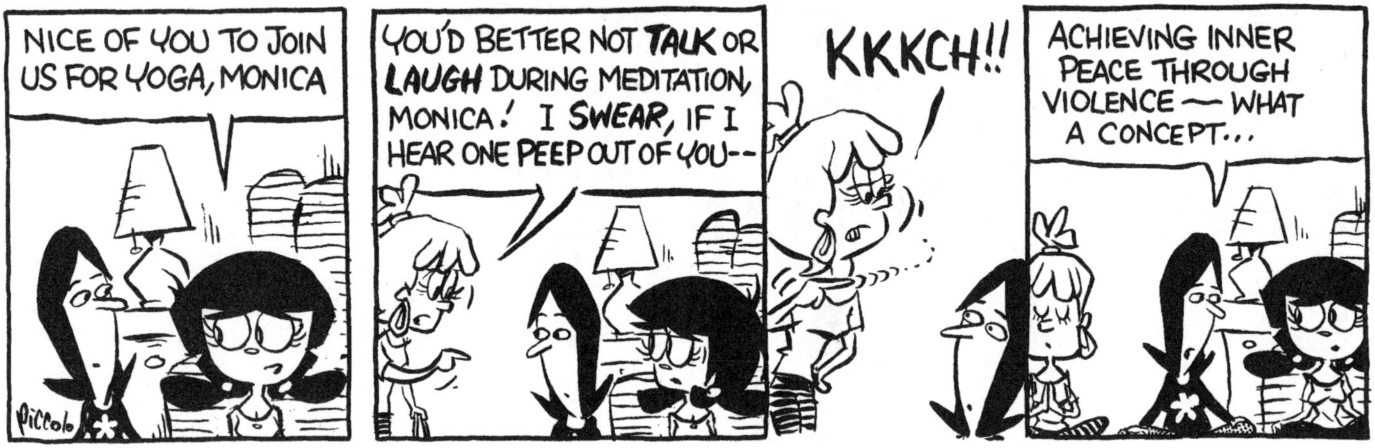
NICE OF YOU TO JOIN US FOR YOGA, MONICA
Piccolo
YOU'D BETTER NOT TALK OR LAUGH DURING MEDITATION, MONICA! I SWEAR, IF I HEAR ONE PEEP OUT OF YOU--
KKKCH!!
ACHIEVING INNER PEACE THROUGH VIOLENCE — WHAT A CONCEPT...

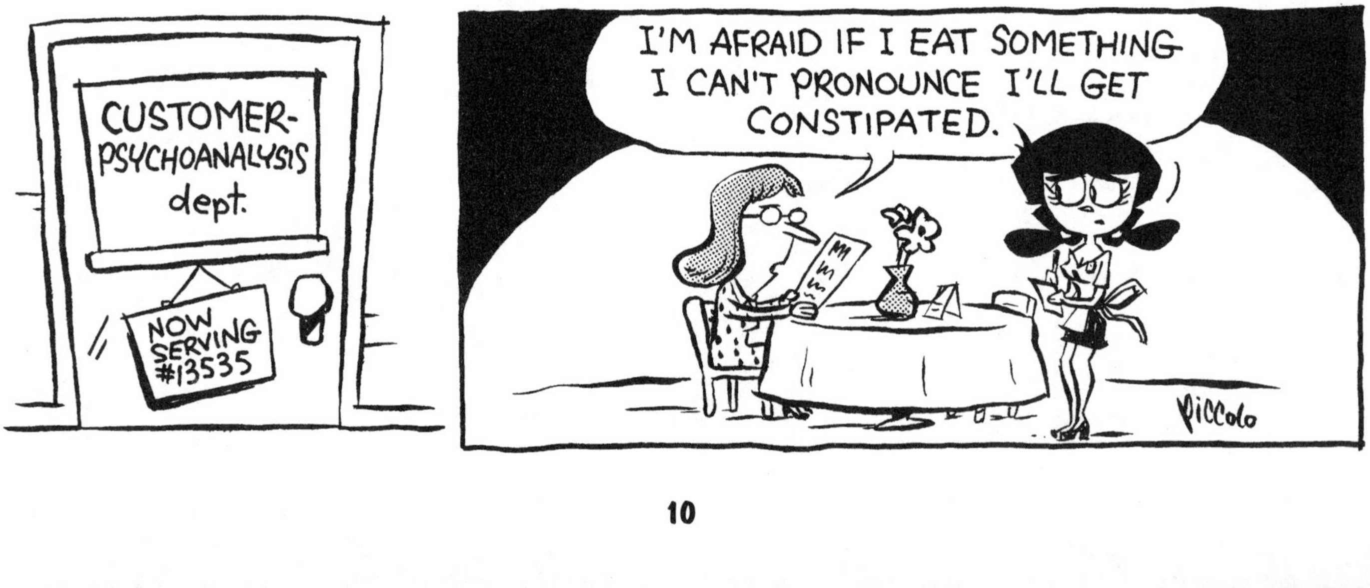
CUSTOMER-PSYCHOANALYSIS dept.
NOW SERVING #13535
I'M AFRAID IF I EAT SOMETHING I CAN'T PRONOUNCE I'LL GET CONSTIPATED.
Piccolo

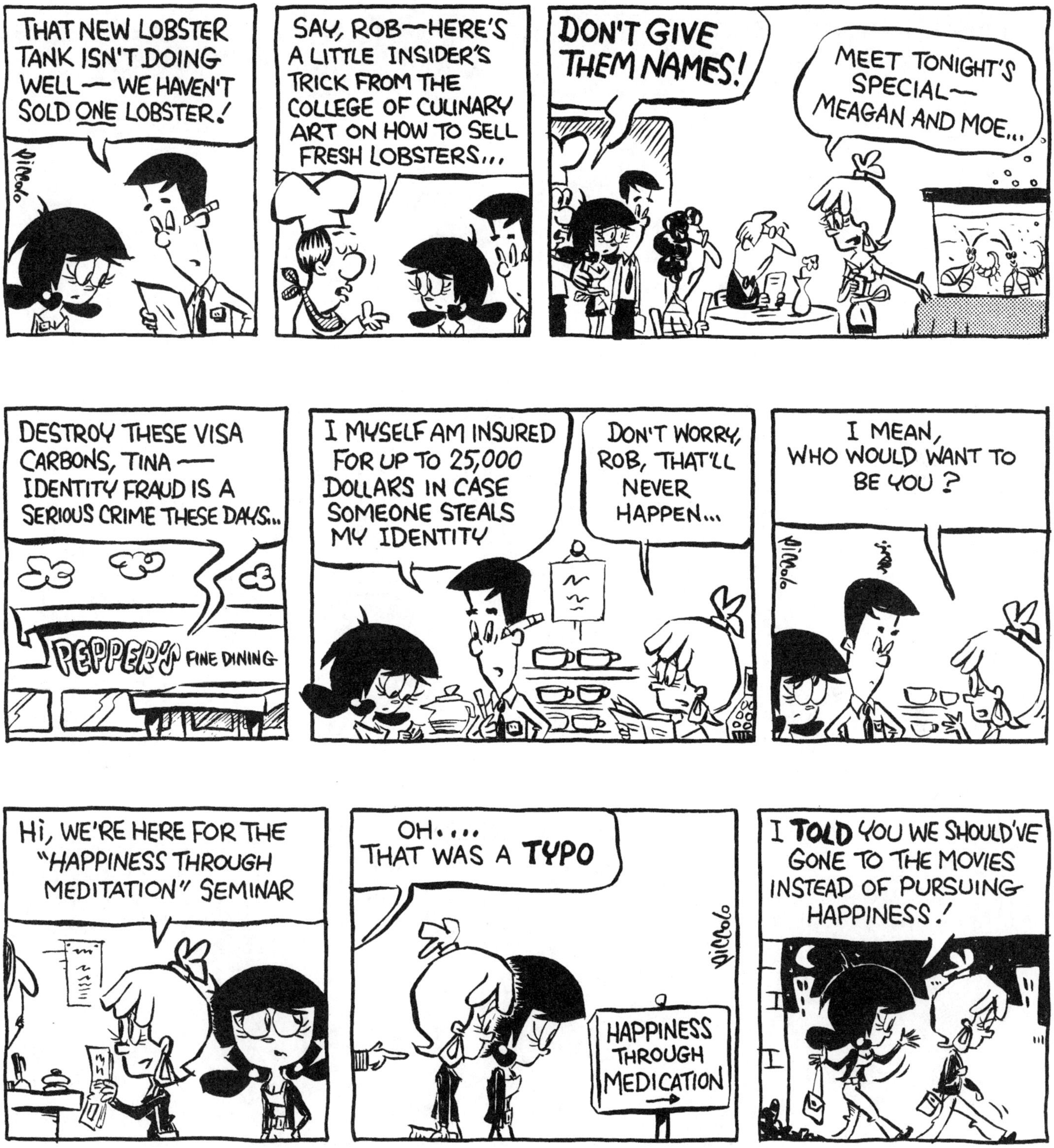
THAT NEW LOBSTER TANK ISN'T DOING WELL— WE HAVEN'T SOLD ONE LOBSTER!
SAY, ROB—HERE'S A LITTLE INSIDER'S TRICK FROM THE COLLEGE OF CULINARY ART ON HOW TO SELL FRESH LOBSTERS...
DON'T GIVE THEM NAMES!
MEET TONIGHT'S SPECIAL— MEAGAN AND MOE...
DESTROY THESE VISA CARBONS, TINA— IDENTITY FRAUD IS A SERIOUS CRIME THESE DAYS...
PEPPER'S FINE DINING
I MYSELF AM INSURED FOR UP TO 25,000 DOLLARS IN CASE SOMEONE STEALS MY IDENTITY
DON'T WORRY, ROB, THAT'LL NEVER HAPPEN...
I MEAN, WHO WOULD WANT TO BE YOU?
Hi, WE'RE HERE FOR THE "HAPPINESS THROUGH MEDITATION" SEMINAR
OH.... THAT WAS A TYPO
HAPPINESS THROUGH MEDICATION
I TOLD YOU WE SHOULD'VE GONE TO THE MOVIES INSTEAD OF PURSUING HAPPINESS!

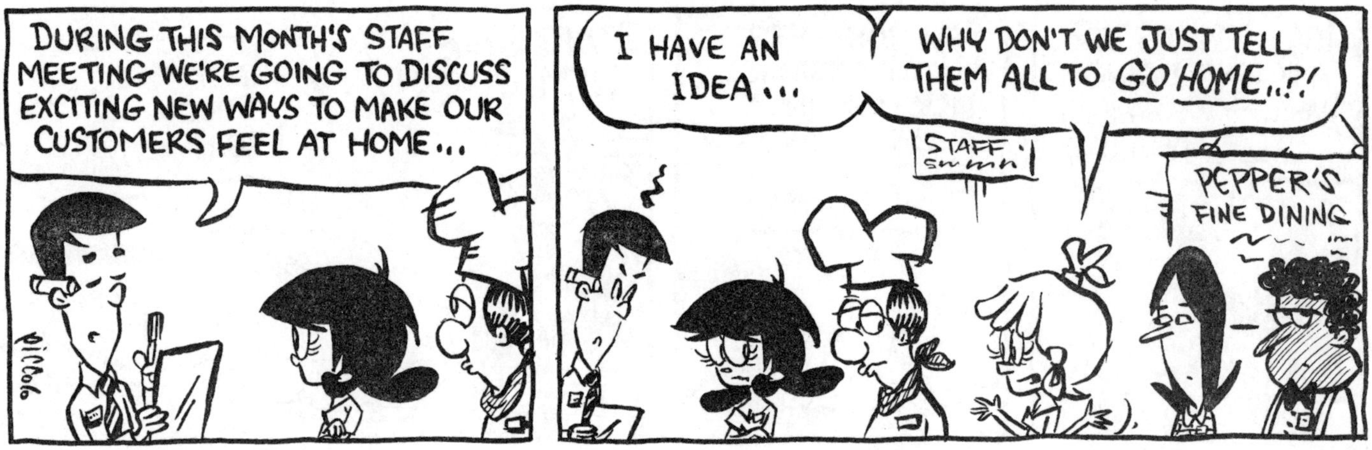
DURING THIS MONTH'S STAFF MEETING WE'RE GOING TO DISCUSS EXCITING NEW WAYS TO MAKE OUR CUSTOMERS FEEL AT HOME...
PICCOLO
I HAVE AN IDEA...
WHY DON'T WE JUST TELL THEM ALL TO GO HOME..?!
STAFF
PEPPER'S FINE DINING

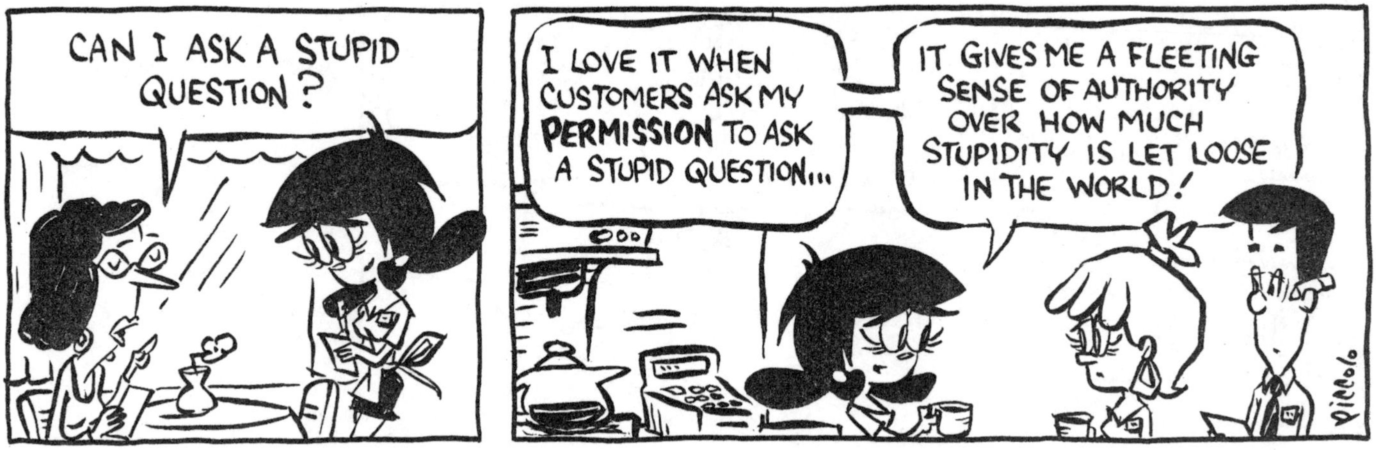
CAN I ASK A STUPID QUESTION?
I LOVE IT WHEN CUSTOMERS ASK MY **PERMISSION** TO ASK A STUPID QUESTION...
IT GIVES ME A FLEETING SENSE OF AUTHORITY OVER HOW MUCH STUPIDITY IS LET LOOSE IN THE WORLD!
PICCOLO

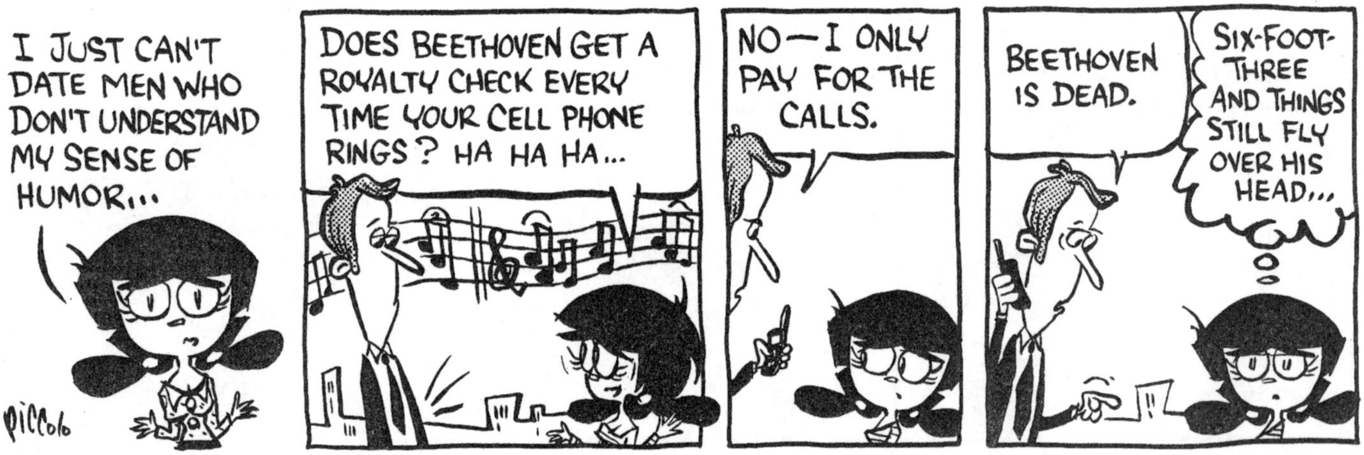
I JUST CAN'T DATE MEN WHO DON'T UNDERSTAND MY SENSE OF HUMOR...
PICCOLO
DOES BEETHOVEN GET A ROYALTY CHECK EVERY TIME YOUR CELL PHONE RINGS? HA HA HA...
NO—I ONLY PAY FOR THE CALLS.
BEETHOVEN IS DEAD.
SIX-FOOT-THREE AND THINGS STILL FLY OVER HIS HEAD...

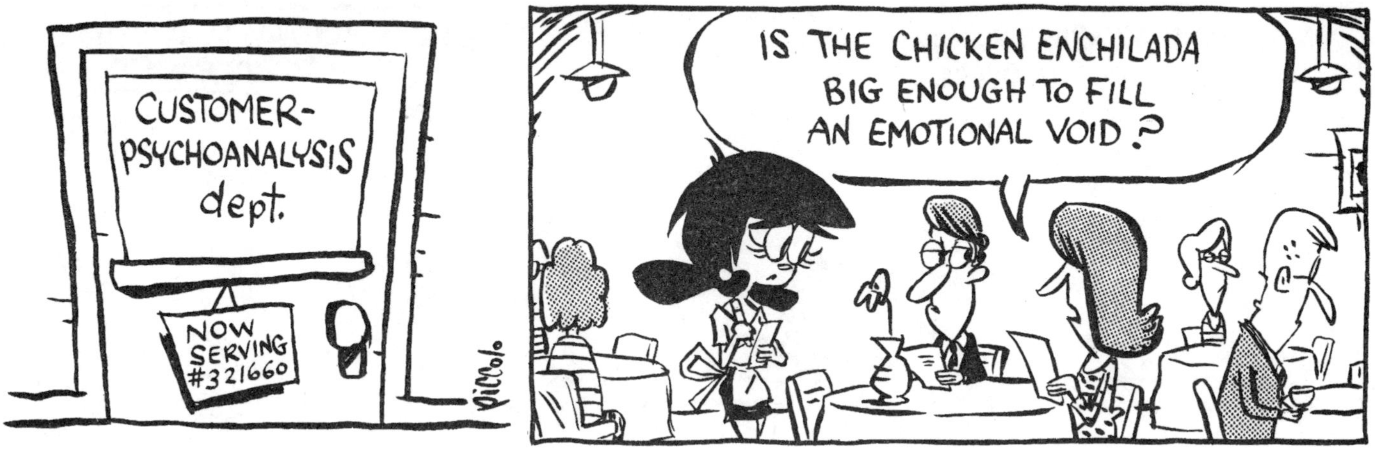
CUSTOMER-PSYCHOANALYSIS dept.
NOW SERVING #321660
IS THE CHICKEN ENCHILADA BIG ENOUGH TO FILL AN EMOTIONAL VOID?
Piccolo

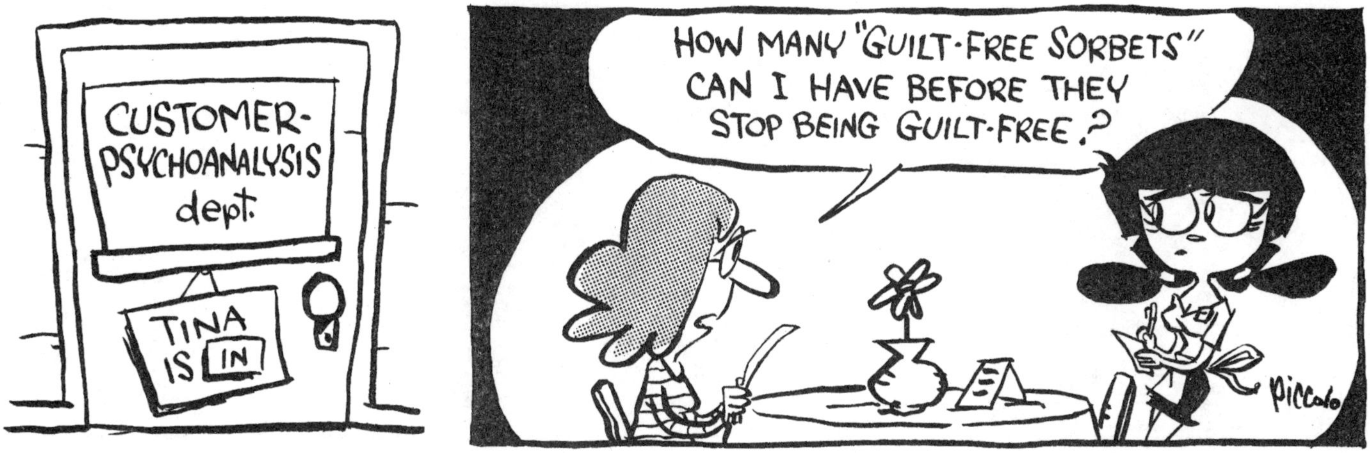
CUSTOMER-PSYCHOANALYSIS dept.
TINA IS IN
HOW MANY "GUILT-FREE SORBETS" CAN I HAVE BEFORE THEY STOP BEING GUILT-FREE?
Piccolo

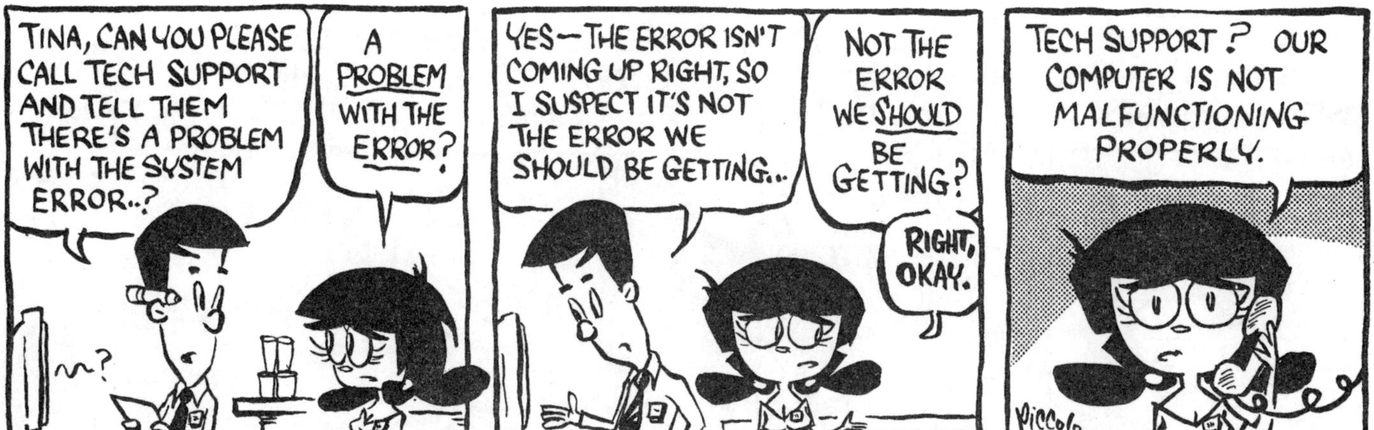
TINA, CAN YOU PLEASE CALL TECH SUPPORT AND TELL THEM THERE'S A PROBLEM WITH THE SYSTEM ERROR..?
A PROBLEM WITH THE ERROR?
YES—THE ERROR ISN'T COMING UP RIGHT, SO I SUSPECT IT'S NOT THE ERROR WE SHOULD BE GETTING...
NOT THE ERROR WE SHOULD BE GETTING?
RIGHT, OKAY.
TECH SUPPORT? OUR COMPUTER IS NOT MALFUNCTIONING PROPERLY.
Piccolo

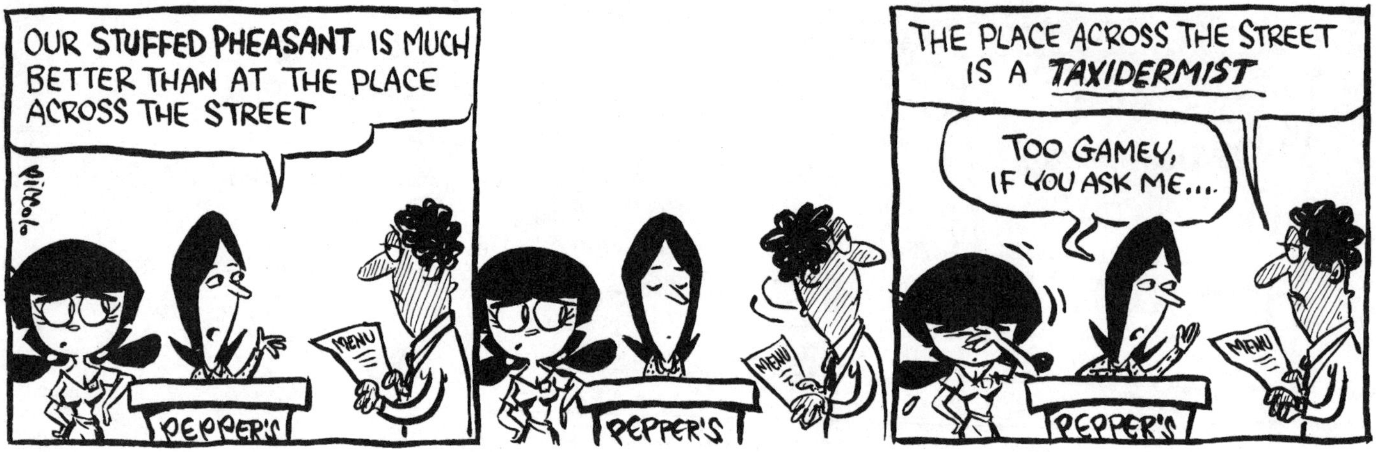
OUR STUFFED PHEASANT IS MUCH BETTER THAN AT THE PLACE ACROSS THE STREET
MENU
PEPPER'S
THE PLACE ACROSS THE STREET IS A TAXIDERMIST
TOO GAMEY, IF YOU ASK ME...

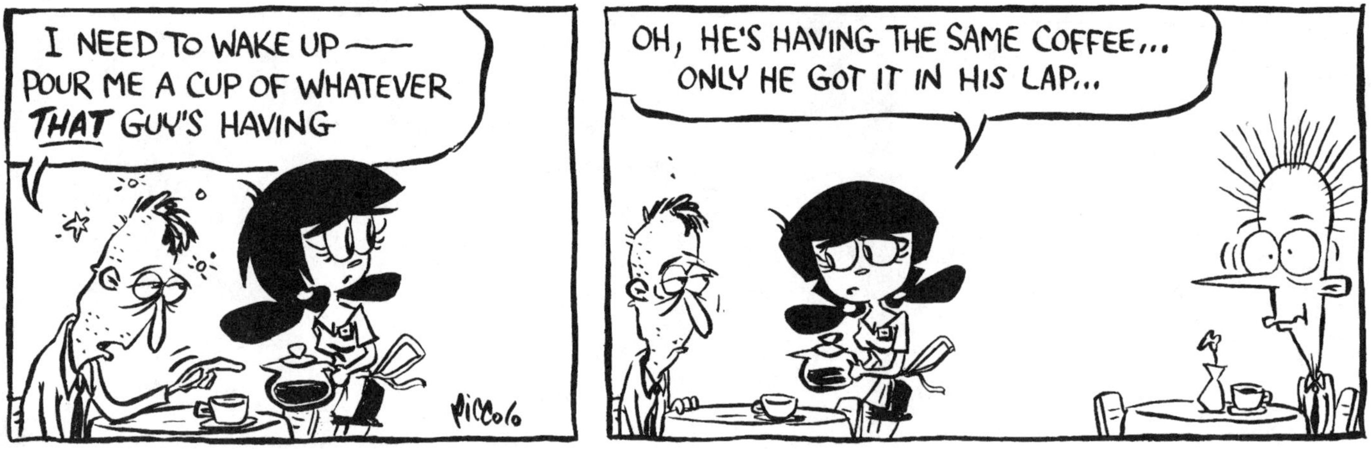
I NEED TO WAKE UP—— POUR ME A CUP OF WHATEVER THAT GUY'S HAVING
OH, HE'S HAVING THE SAME COFFEE... ONLY HE GOT IT IN HIS LAP...

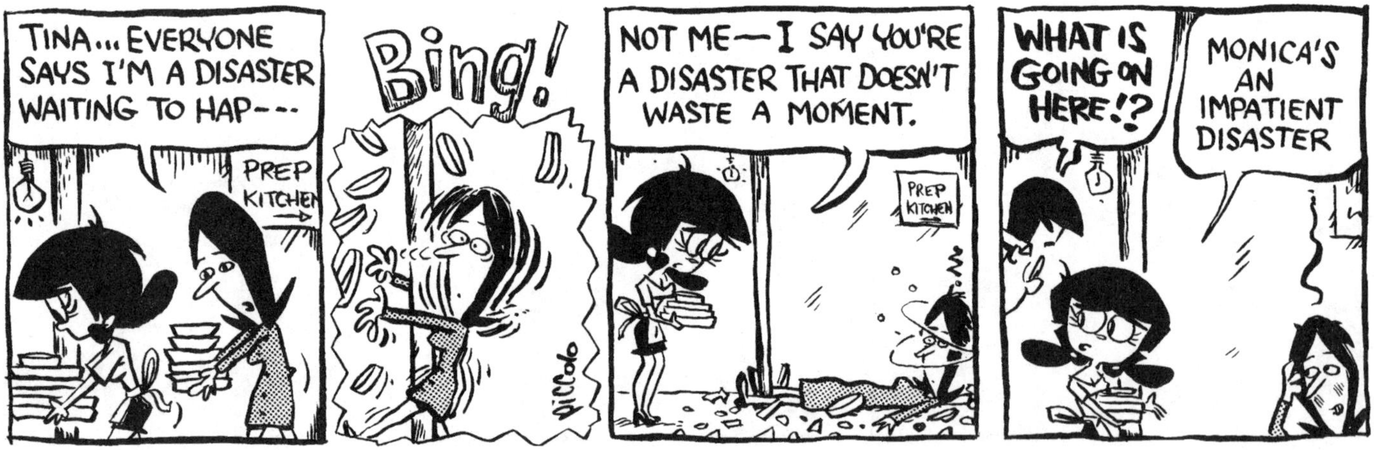
TINA... EVERYONE SAYS I'M A DISASTER WAITING TO HAP---
PREP KITCHEN
Bing!
NOT ME—I SAY YOU'RE A DISASTER THAT DOESN'T WASTE A MOMENT.
WHAT IS GOING ON HERE!?
MONICA'S AN IMPATIENT DISASTER

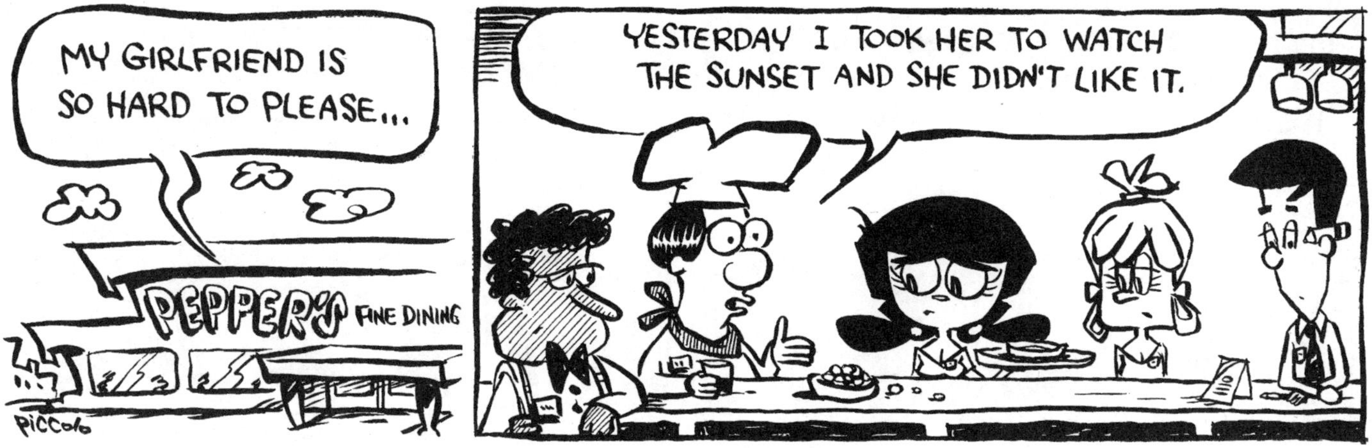
MY GIRLFRIEND IS SO HARD TO PLEASE...
PEPPER'S FINE DINING
YESTERDAY I TOOK HER TO WATCH THE SUNSET AND SHE DIDN'T LIKE IT.

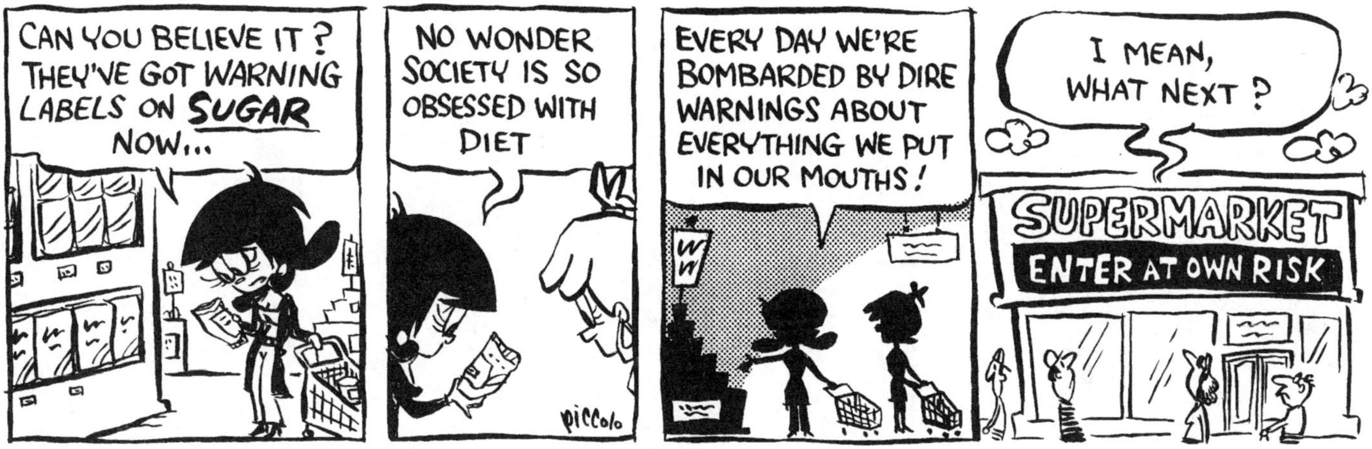
CAN YOU BELIEVE IT? THEY'VE GOT WARNING LABELS ON SUGAR NOW...
NO WONDER SOCIETY IS SO OBSESSED WITH DIET
EVERY DAY WE'RE BOMBARDED BY DIRE WARNINGS ABOUT EVERYTHING WE PUT IN OUR MOUTHS!
I MEAN, WHAT NEXT?
SUPERMARKET
ENTER AT OWN RISK

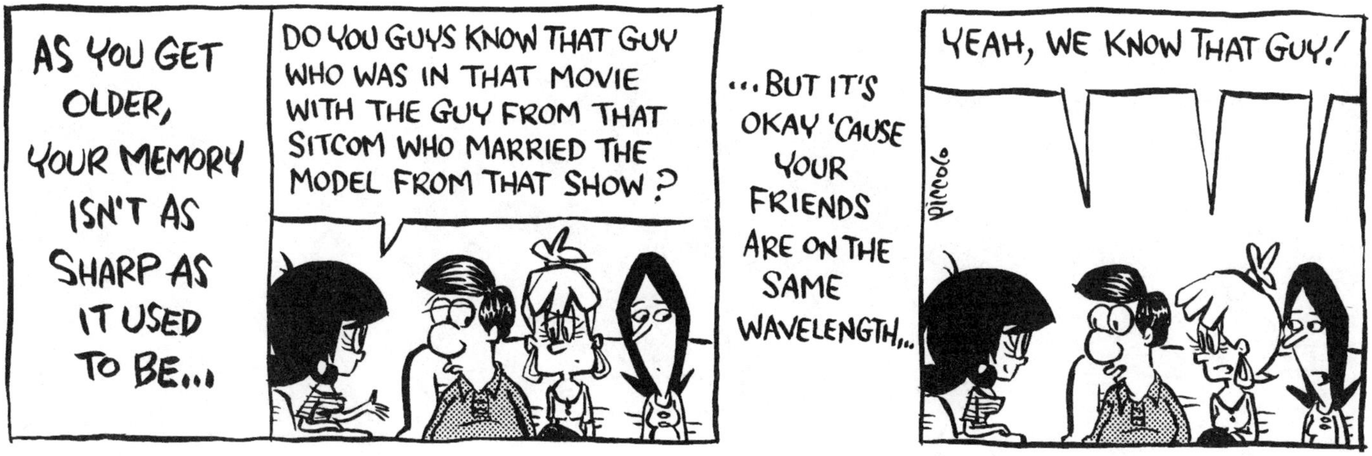
AS YOU GET OLDER, YOUR MEMORY ISN'T AS SHARP AS IT USED TO BE...
DO YOU GUYS KNOW THAT GUY WHO WAS IN THAT MOVIE WITH THE GUY FROM THAT SITCOM WHO MARRIED THE MODEL FROM THAT SHOW?
...BUT IT'S OKAY 'CAUSE YOUR FRIENDS ARE ON THE SAME WAVELENGTH...
YEAH, WE KNOW THAT GUY!

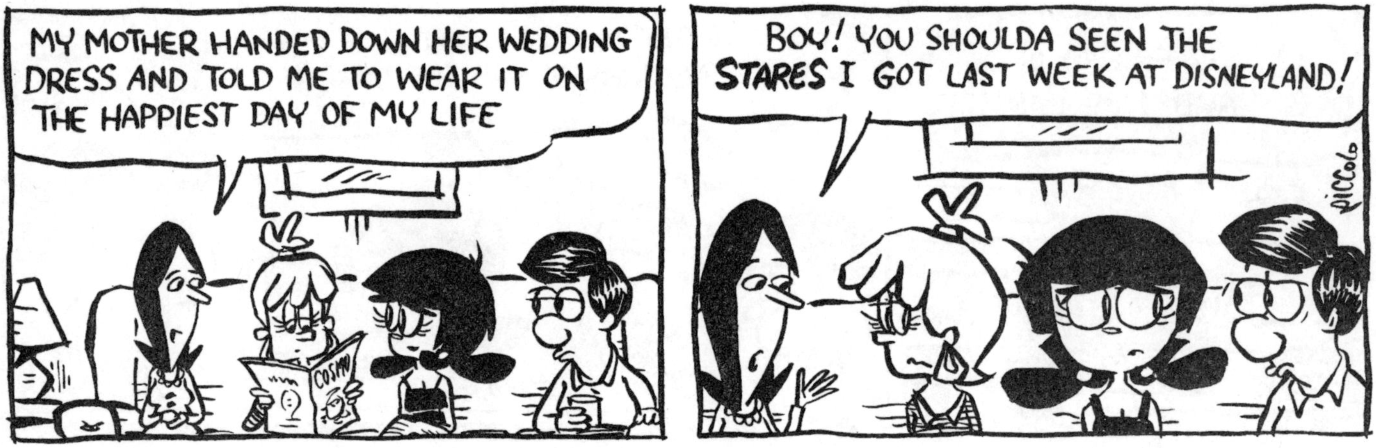
MY MOTHER HANDED DOWN HER WEDDING DRESS AND TOLD ME TO WEAR IT ON THE HAPPIEST DAY OF MY LIFE
COSMO
BOY! YOU SHOULDA SEEN THE STARES I GOT LAST WEEK AT DISNEYLAND!
PICCOLO

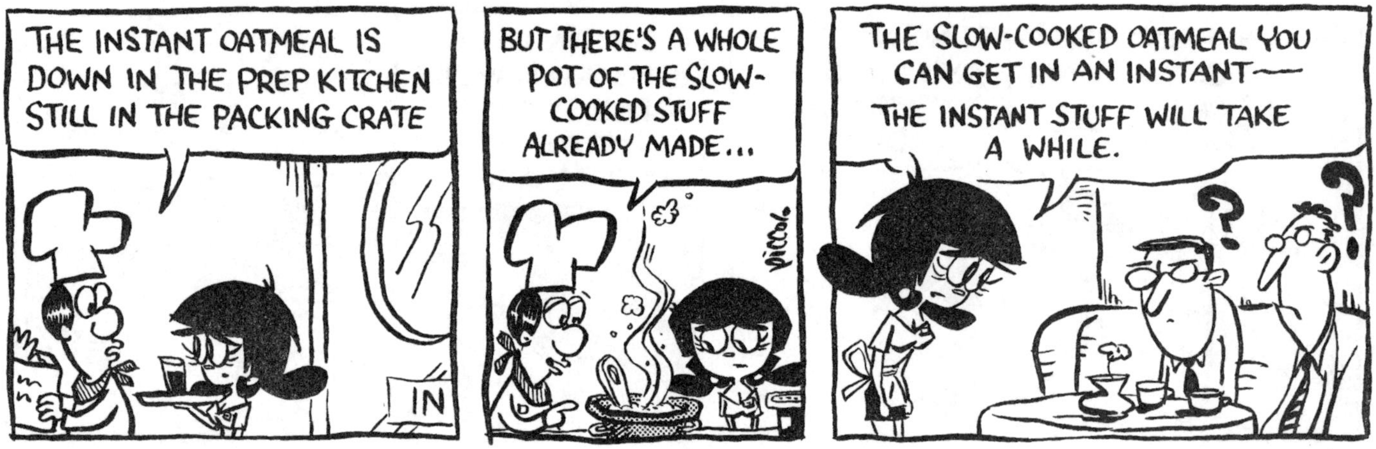
THE INSTANT OATMEAL IS DOWN IN THE PREP KITCHEN STILL IN THE PACKING CRATE
IN
BUT THERE'S A WHOLE POT OF THE SLOW-COOKED STUFF ALREADY MADE...
PICCOLO
THE SLOW-COOKED OATMEAL YOU CAN GET IN AN INSTANT—
THE INSTANT STUFF WILL TAKE A WHILE.

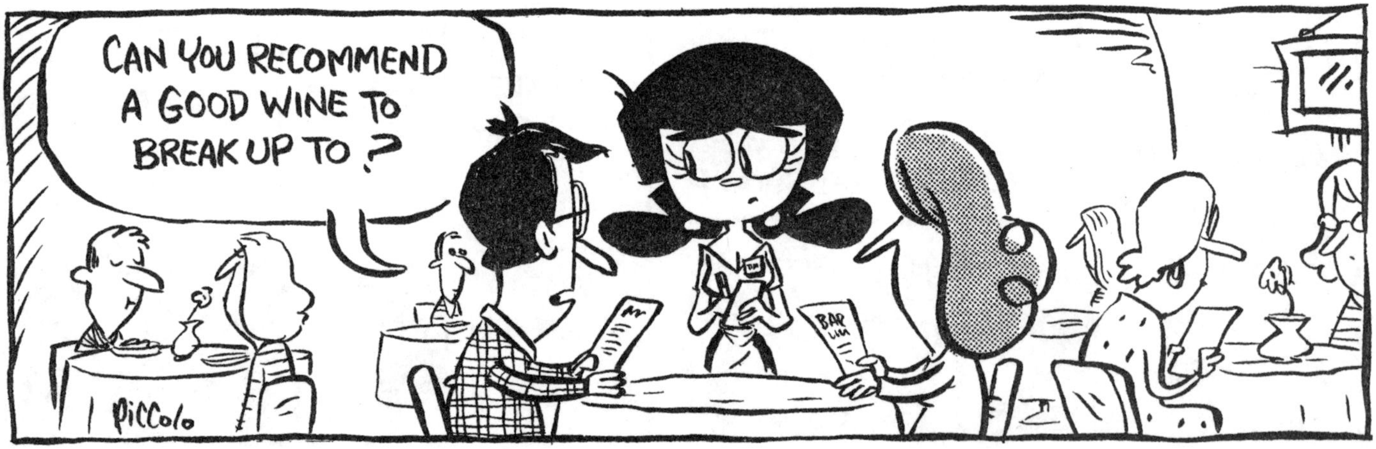
CAN YOU RECOMMEND A GOOD WINE TO BREAK UP TO?
BAR
PICCOLO

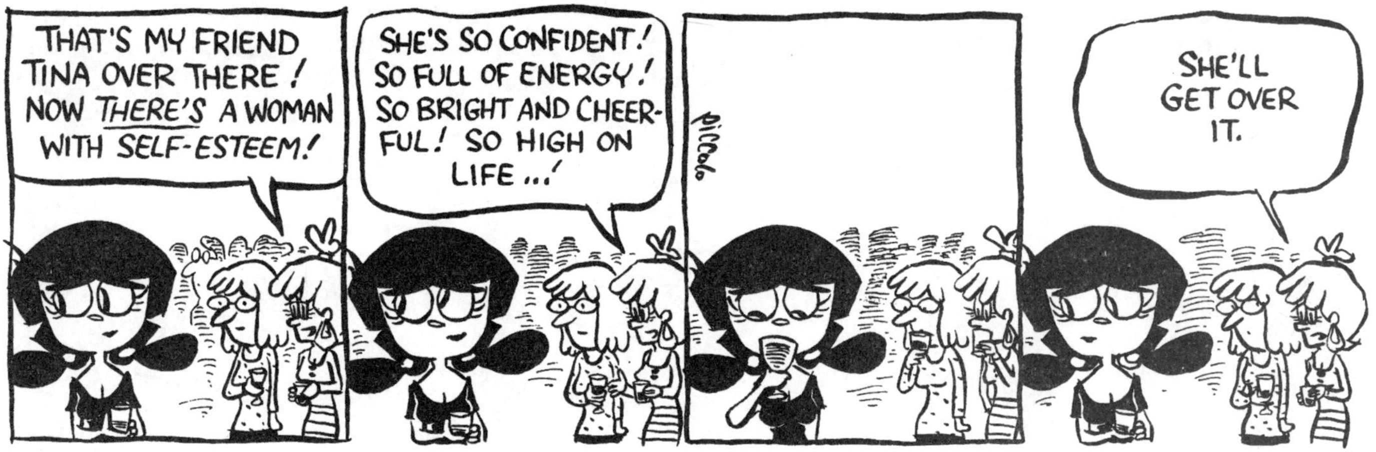
THAT'S MY FRIEND TINA OVER THERE! NOW THERE'S A WOMAN WITH SELF-ESTEEM!
SHE'S SO CONFIDENT! SO FULL OF ENERGY! SO BRIGHT AND CHEER-FUL! SO HIGH ON LIFE...!
Piccolo
SHE'LL GET OVER IT.

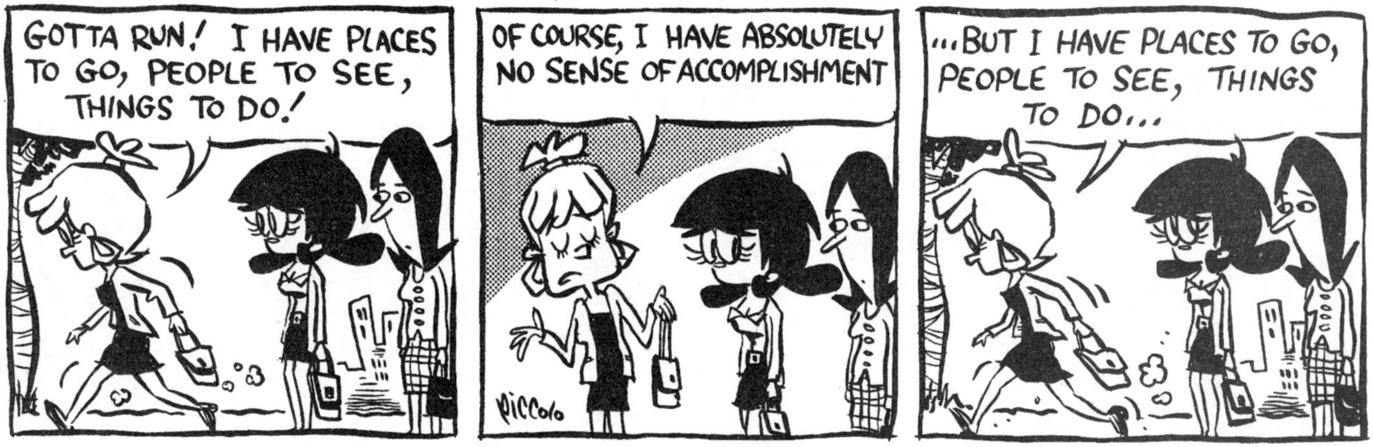
GOTTA RUN! I HAVE PLACES TO GO, PEOPLE TO SEE, THINGS TO DO!
OF COURSE, I HAVE ABSOLUTELY NO SENSE OF ACCOMPLISHMENT
Piccolo
...BUT I HAVE PLACES TO GO, PEOPLE TO SEE, THINGS TO DO...

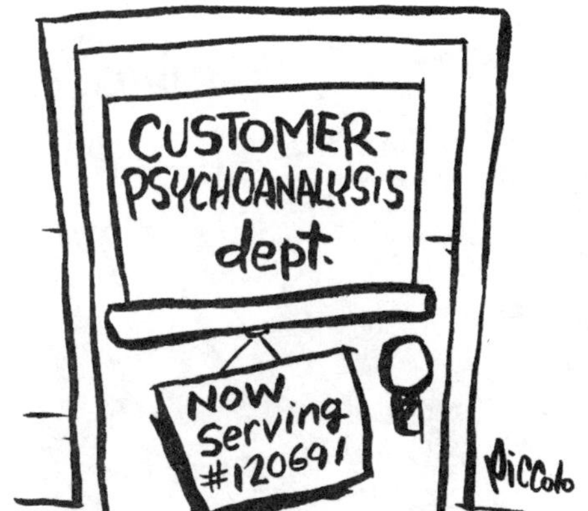
CUSTOMER-PSYCHOANALYSIS dept.
NOW Serving #120691
Piccolo

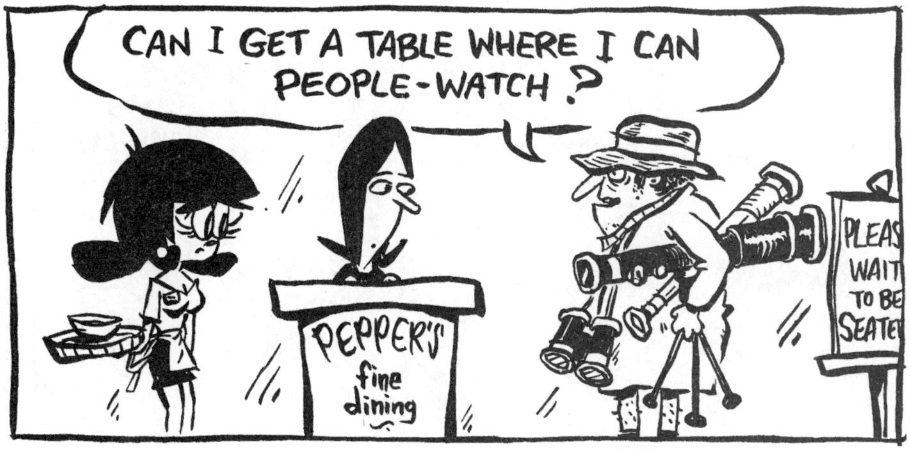
CAN I GET A TABLE WHERE I CAN PEOPLE-WATCH?
PEPPER'S fine dining

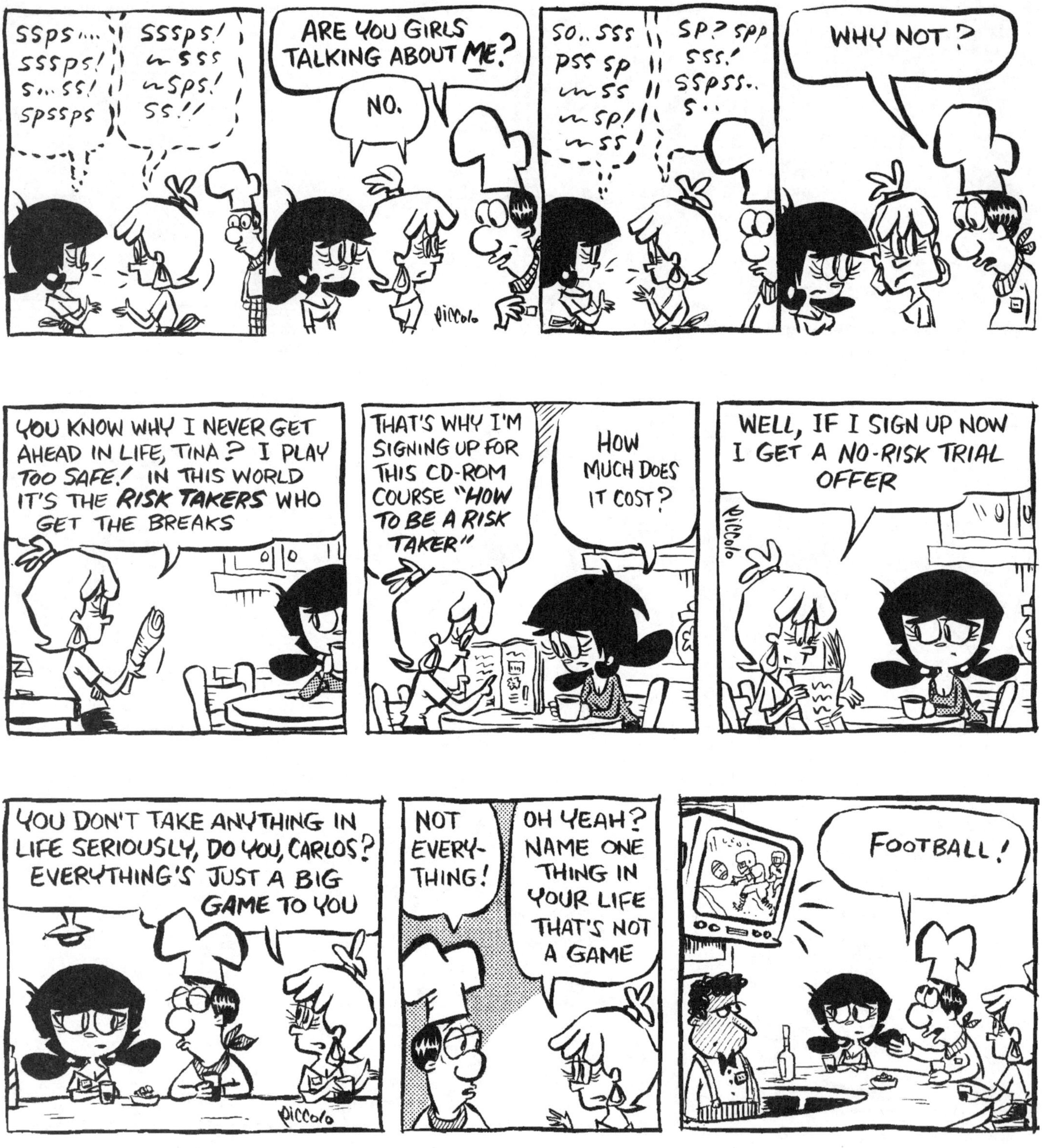
SSPS.... SSSPS! S...SS! SPSSPS
SSSPS! ~SSS ~SPS! SS!!
ARE YOU GIRLS TALKING ABOUT ME?
NO.
SO.. SSS PSS SP ~SS ~SP! ~SS
SP? SPP SSS! SSPSS.. S..
WHY NOT?
YOU KNOW WHY I NEVER GET AHEAD IN LIFE, TINA? I PLAY TOO SAFE! IN THIS WORLD IT'S THE RISK TAKERS WHO GET THE BREAKS
THAT'S WHY I'M SIGNING UP FOR THIS CD-ROM COURSE "HOW TO BE A RISK TAKER"
HOW MUCH DOES IT COST?
WELL, IF I SIGN UP NOW I GET A NO-RISK TRIAL OFFER
YOU DON'T TAKE ANYTHING IN LIFE SERIOUSLY, DO YOU, CARLOS? EVERYTHING'S JUST A BIG GAME TO YOU
NOT EVERY-THING!
OH YEAH? NAME ONE THING IN YOUR LIFE THAT'S NOT A GAME
FOOTBALL!

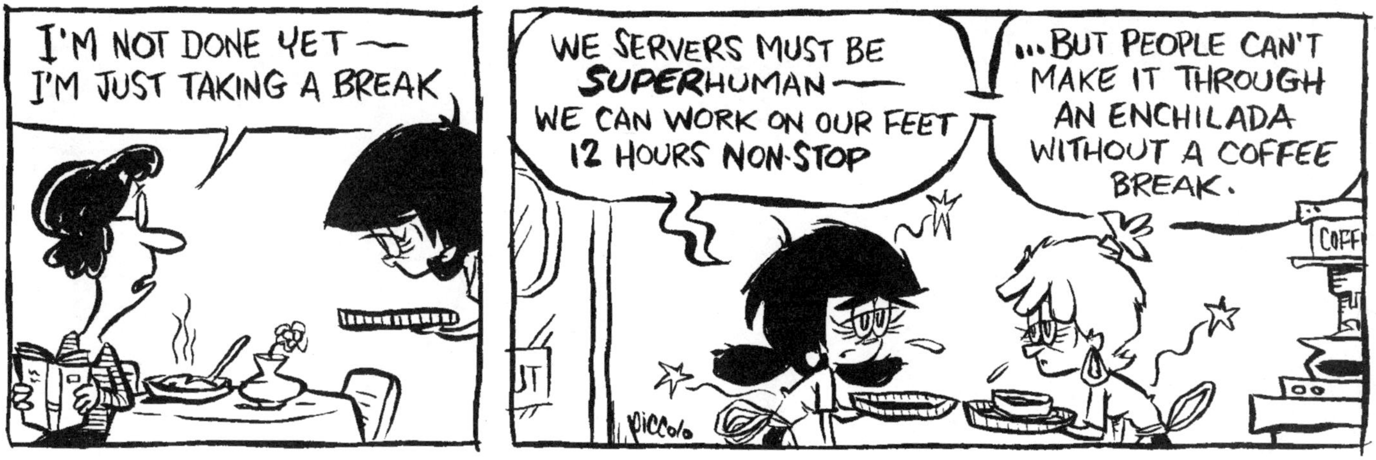
I'M NOT DONE YET — I'M JUST TAKING A BREAK
WE SERVERS MUST BE SUPERHUMAN — WE CAN WORK ON OUR FEET 12 HOURS NON-STOP
...BUT PEOPLE CAN'T MAKE IT THROUGH AN ENCHILADA WITHOUT A COFFEE BREAK.
piccolo

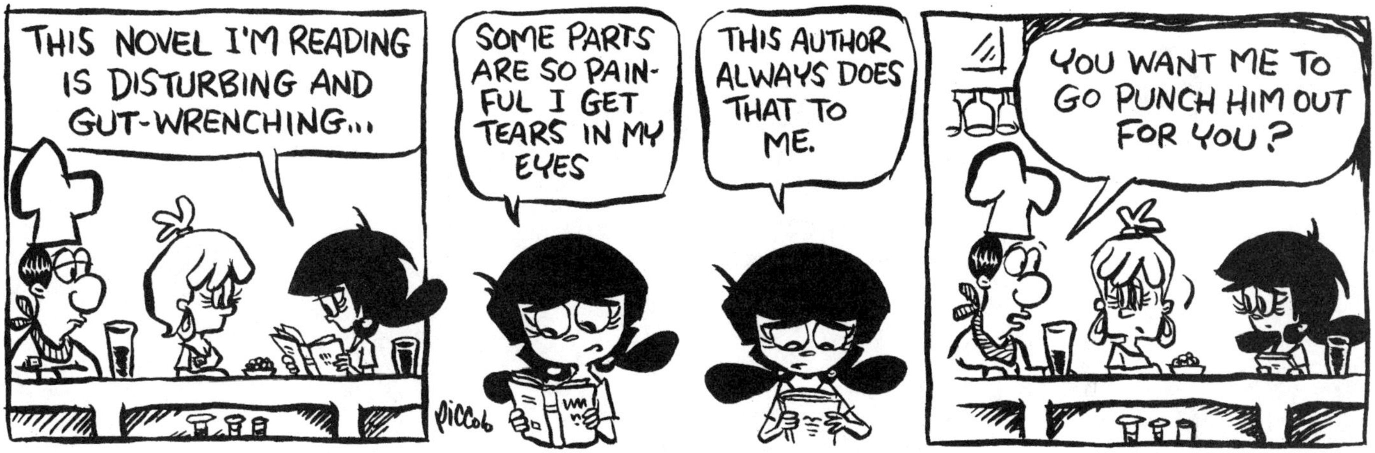
THIS NOVEL I'M READING IS DISTURBING AND GUT-WRENCHING...
SOME PARTS ARE SO PAIN-FUL I GET TEARS IN MY EYES
THIS AUTHOR ALWAYS DOES THAT TO ME.
YOU WANT ME TO GO PUNCH HIM OUT FOR YOU?
piccolo

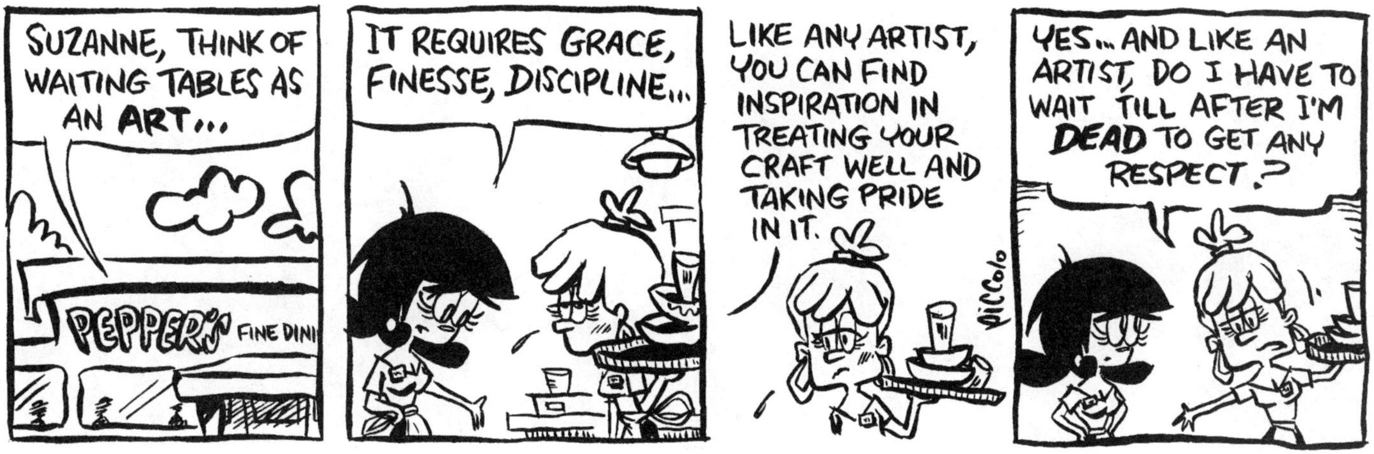
SUZANNE, THINK OF WAITING TABLES AS AN ART...
PEPPER'S
FINE DINI
IT REQUIRES GRACE, FINESSE, DISCIPLINE...
LIKE ANY ARTIST, YOU CAN FIND INSPIRATION IN TREATING YOUR CRAFT WELL AND TAKING PRIDE IN IT.
YES... AND LIKE AN ARTIST, DO I HAVE TO WAIT TILL AFTER I'M DEAD TO GET ANY RESPECT?
piccolo

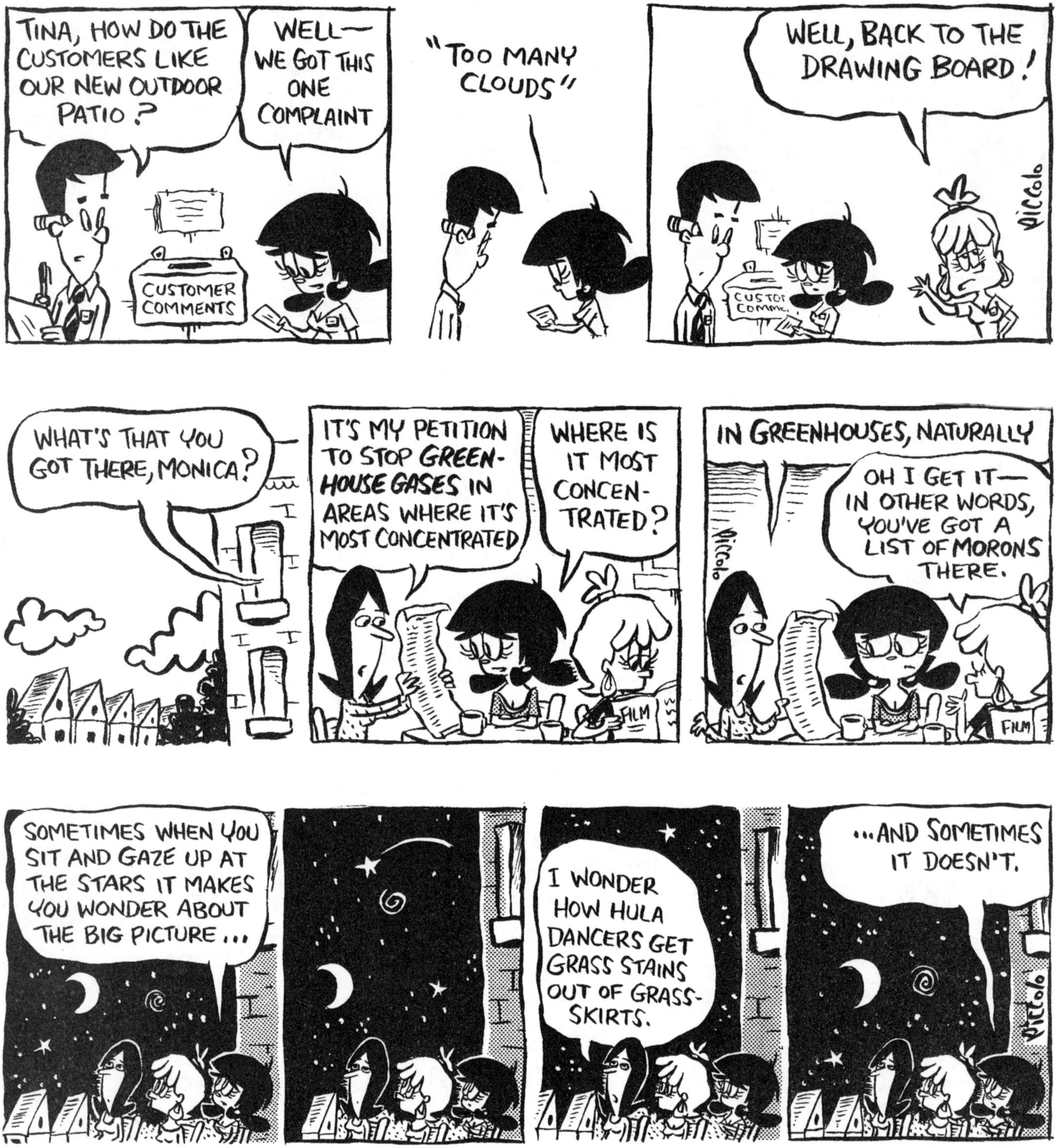
TINA, HOW DO THE CUSTOMERS LIKE OUR NEW OUTDOOR PATIO?
WELL— WE GOT THIS ONE COMPLAINT
CUSTOMER COMMENTS
"TOO MANY CLOUDS"
WELL, BACK TO THE DRAWING BOARD!
piccolo
WHAT'S THAT YOU GOT THERE, MONICA?
IT'S MY PETITION TO STOP GREEN-HOUSE GASES IN AREAS WHERE IT'S MOST CONCENTRATED
WHERE IS IT MOST CONCEN-TRATED?
FILM
IN GREENHOUSES, NATURALLY
OH I GET IT— IN OTHER WORDS, YOU'VE GOT A LIST OF MORONS THERE.
piccolo
FILM
SOMETIMES WHEN YOU SIT AND GAZE UP AT THE STARS IT MAKES YOU WONDER ABOUT THE BIG PICTURE...
I WONDER HOW HULA DANCERS GET GRASS STAINS OUT OF GRASS-SKIRTS.
...AND SOMETIMES IT DOESN'T.
piccolo

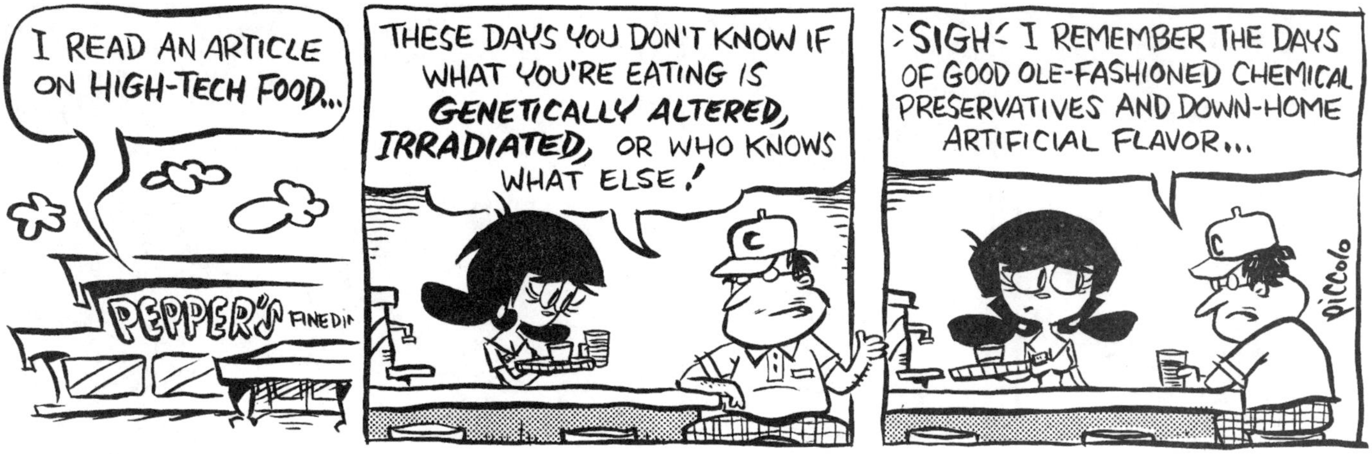
I READ AN ARTICLE ON HIGH-TECH FOOD...
PEPPER'S FINE DI
THESE DAYS YOU DON'T KNOW IF WHAT YOU'RE EATING IS GENETICALLY ALTERED, IRRADIATED, OR WHO KNOWS WHAT ELSE!
>SIGH< I REMEMBER THE DAYS OF GOOD OLE-FASHIONED CHEMICAL PRESERVATIVES AND DOWN-HOME ARTIFICIAL FLAVOR...
PICCOLO

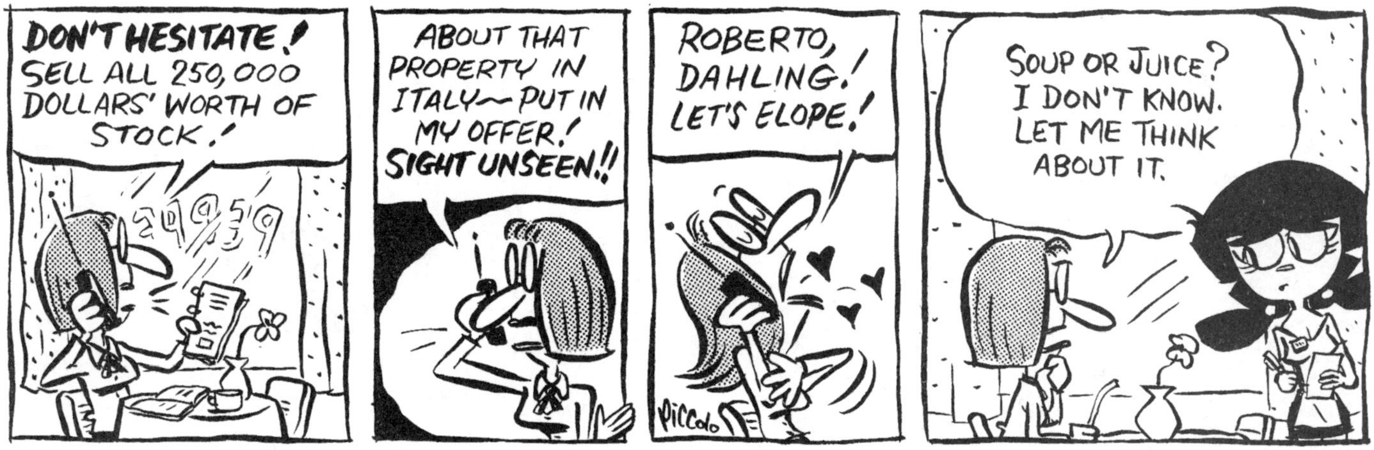
DON'T HESITATE! SELL ALL 250,000 DOLLARS' WORTH OF STOCK!
ABOUT THAT PROPERTY IN ITALY—PUT IN MY OFFER! SIGHT UNSEEN!!
ROBERTO, DAHLING! LET'S ELOPE!
PICCOLO
SOUP OR JUICE? I DON'T KNOW. LET ME THINK ABOUT IT.

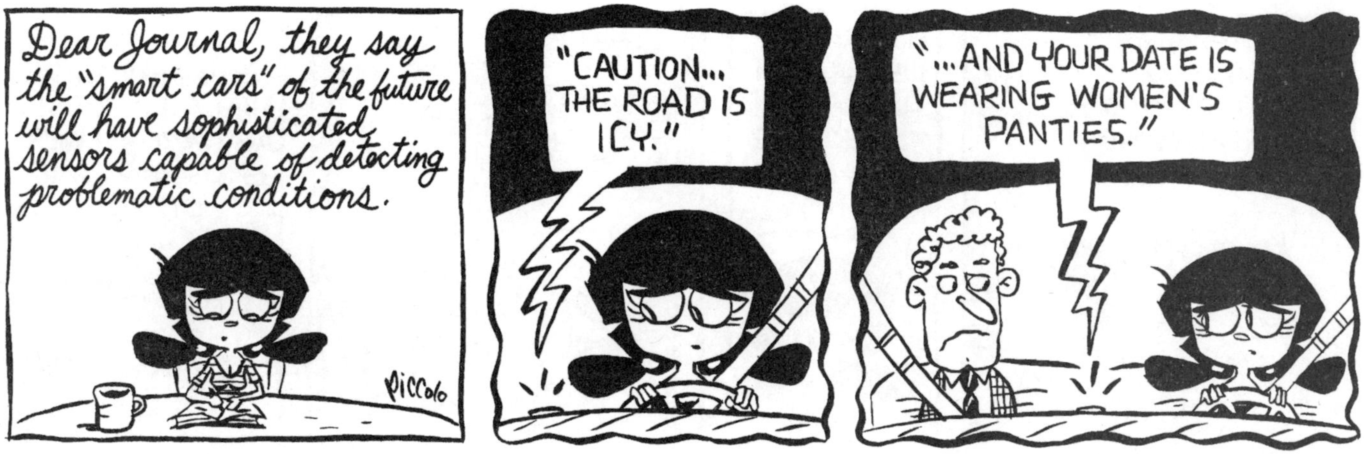
Dear Journal, they say the "smart cars" of the future will have sophisticated sensors capable of detecting problematic conditions.
PICCOLO
"CAUTION... THE ROAD IS ICY."
"...AND YOUR DATE IS WEARING WOMEN'S PANTIES."

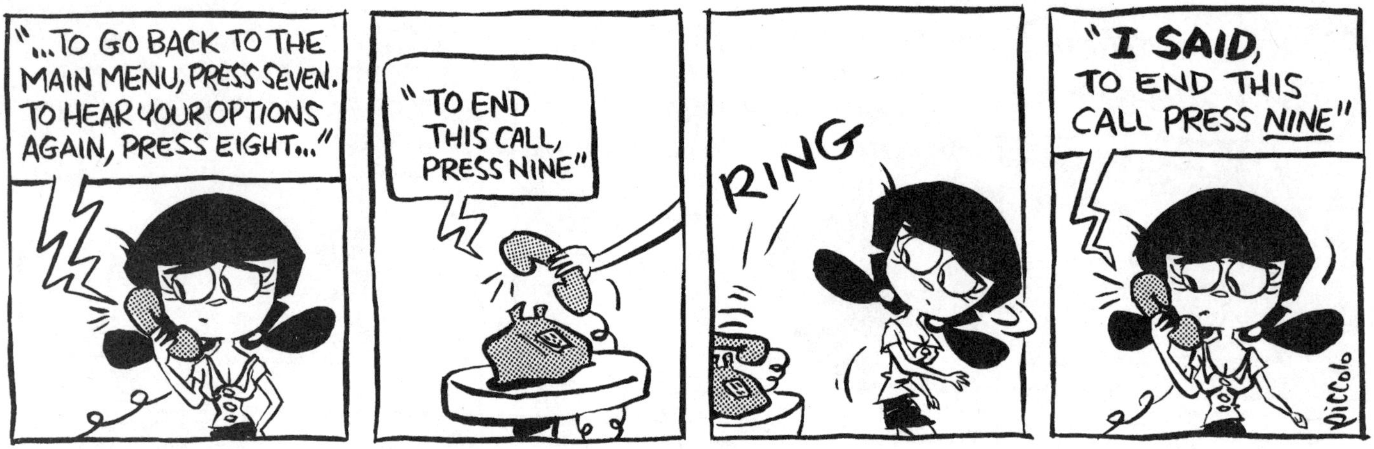
"...TO GO BACK TO THE MAIN MENU, PRESS SEVEN. TO HEAR YOUR OPTIONS AGAIN, PRESS EIGHT..."
"TO END THIS CALL, PRESS NINE"
RING
"I SAID, TO END THIS CALL PRESS NINE"
PICCOLO

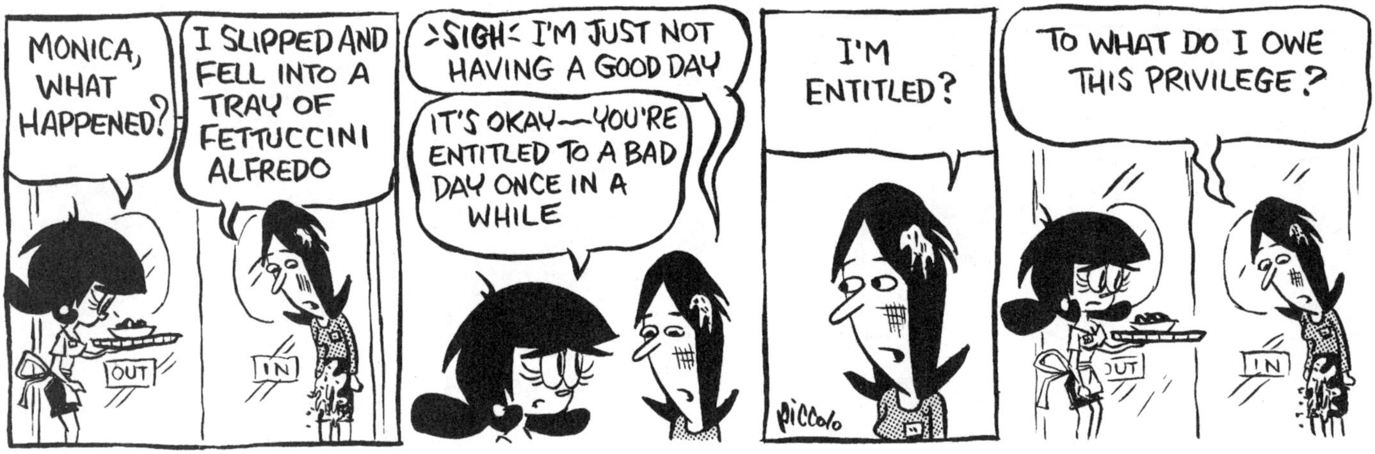
MONICA, WHAT HAPPENED?
I SLIPPED AND FELL INTO A TRAY OF FETTUCCINI ALFREDO
OUT
IN
>SIGH< I'M JUST NOT HAVING A GOOD DAY
IT'S OKAY—YOU'RE ENTITLED TO A BAD DAY ONCE IN A WHILE
I'M ENTITLED?
PICCOLO
TO WHAT DO I OWE THIS PRIVILEGE?
OUT
IN

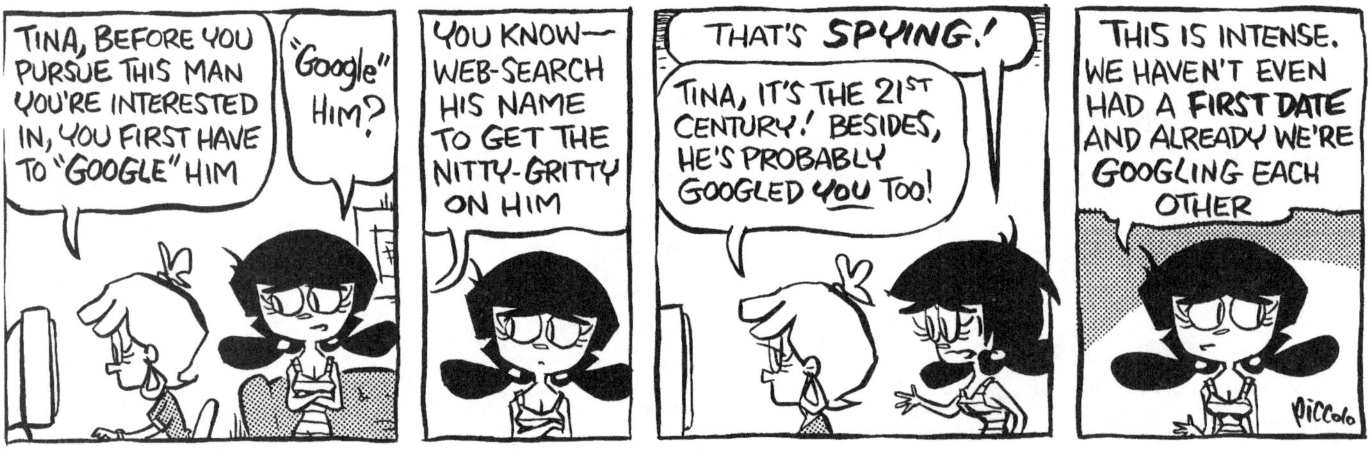
TINA, BEFORE YOU PURSUE THIS MAN YOU'RE INTERESTED IN, YOU FIRST HAVE TO "GOOGLE" HIM
"Google" HIM?
YOU KNOW—WEB-SEARCH HIS NAME TO GET THE NITTY-GRITTY ON HIM
THAT'S SPYING!
TINA, IT'S THE 21ST CENTURY! BESIDES, HE'S PROBABLY GOOGLED YOU TOO!
THIS IS INTENSE. WE HAVEN'T EVEN HAD A FIRST DATE AND ALREADY WE'RE GOOGLING EACH OTHER
PICCOLO

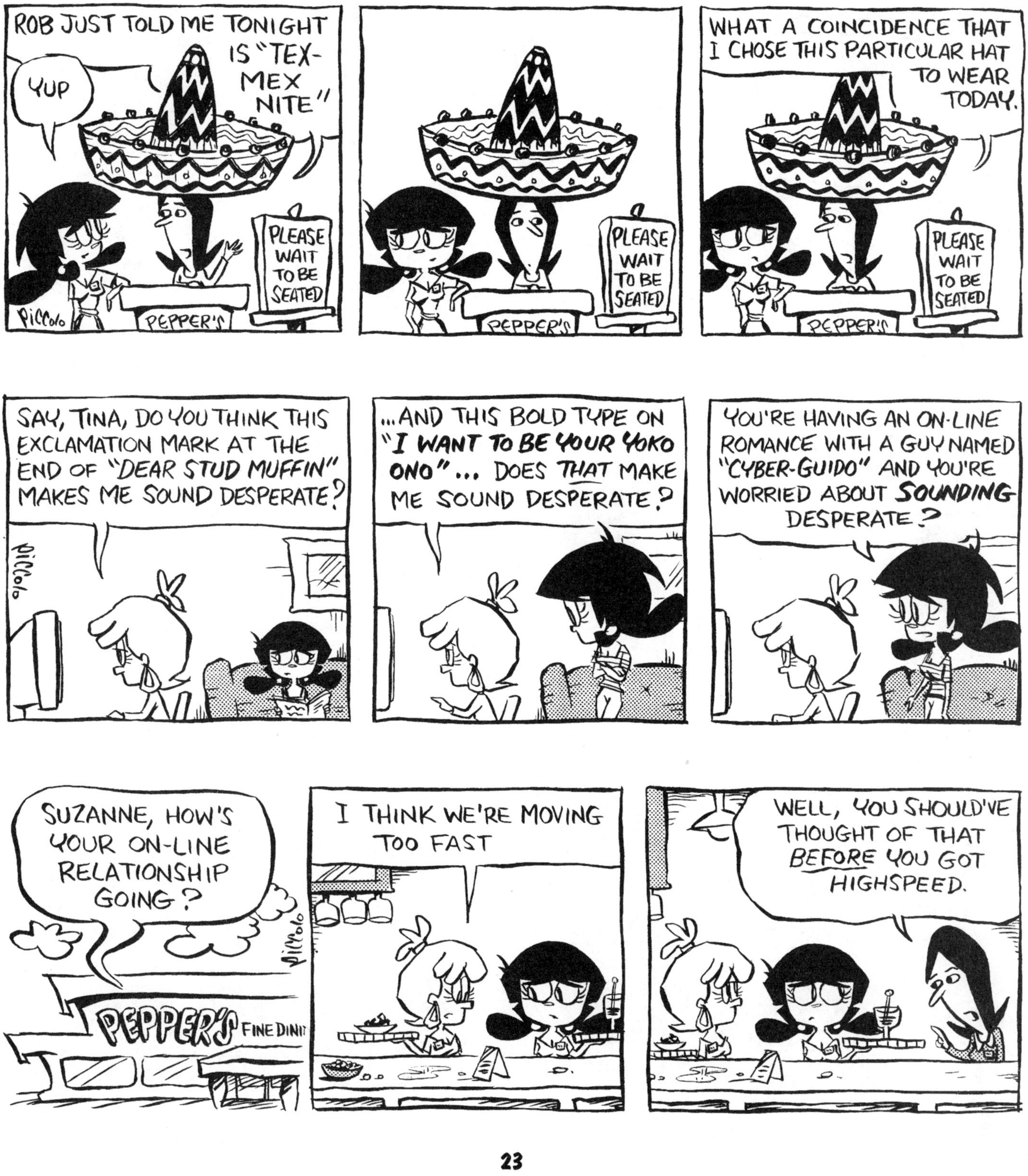
ROB JUST TOLD ME TONIGHT IS "TEX-MEX NITE"
YUP
PLEASE WAIT TO BE SEATED
PEPPER'S
PICCOLO
WHAT A COINCIDENCE THAT I CHOSE THIS PARTICULAR HAT TO WEAR TODAY.
SAY, TINA, DO YOU THINK THIS EXCLAMATION MARK AT THE END OF "DEAR STUD MUFFIN" MAKES ME SOUND DESPERATE?
...AND THIS BOLD TYPE ON "I WANT TO BE YOUR YOKO ONO" ... DOES THAT MAKE ME SOUND DESPERATE?
YOU'RE HAVING AN ON-LINE ROMANCE WITH A GUY NAMED "CYBER-GUIDO" AND YOU'RE WORRIED ABOUT SOUNDING DESPERATE?
SUZANNE, HOW'S YOUR ON-LINE RELATIONSHIP GOING?
PEPPER'S FINE DINI
I THINK WE'RE MOVING TOO FAST
WELL, YOU SHOULD'VE THOUGHT OF THAT BEFORE YOU GOT HIGHSPEED.

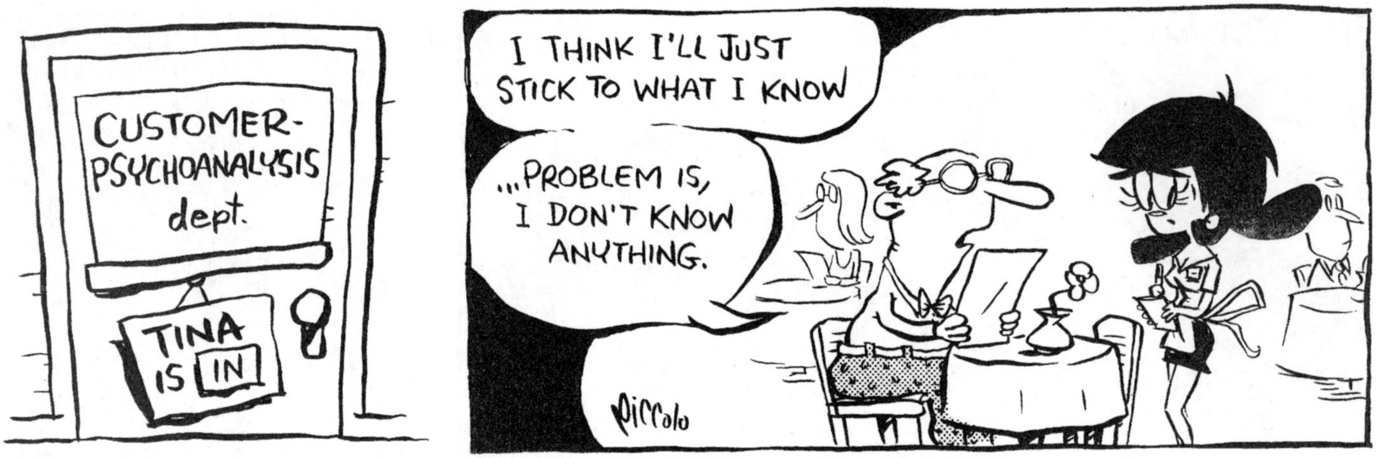
CUSTOMER-PSYCHOANALYSIS dept.
TINA IS IN
I THINK I'LL JUST STICK TO WHAT I KNOW
...PROBLEM IS, I DON'T KNOW ANYTHING.

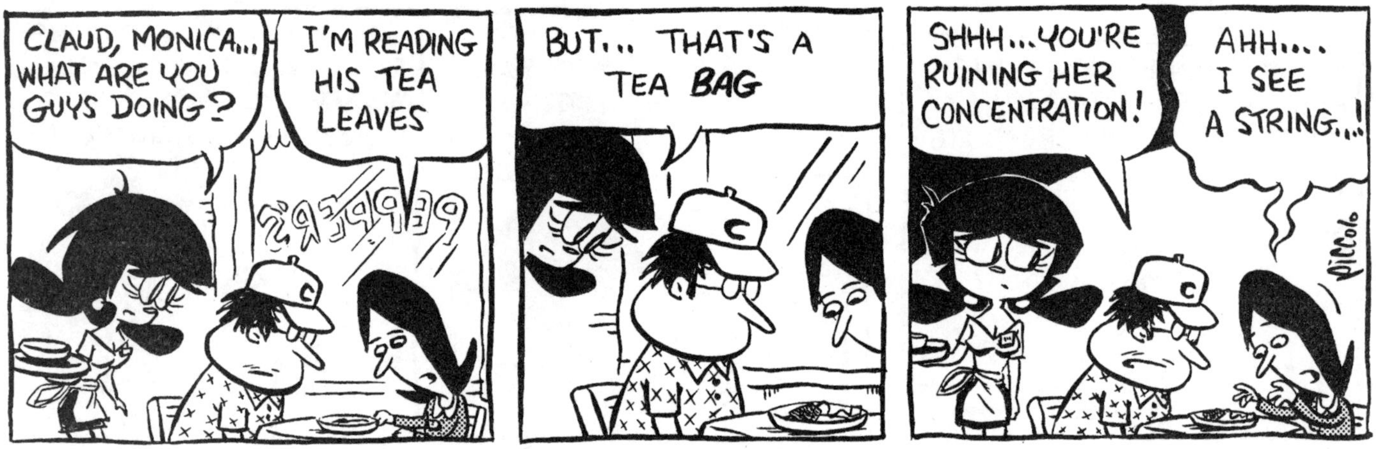
CLAUD, MONICA... WHAT ARE YOU GUYS DOING?
I'M READING HIS TEA LEAVES
BUT... THAT'S A TEA BAG
SHHH...YOU'RE RUINING HER CONCENTRATION!
AHH.... I SEE A STRING...!

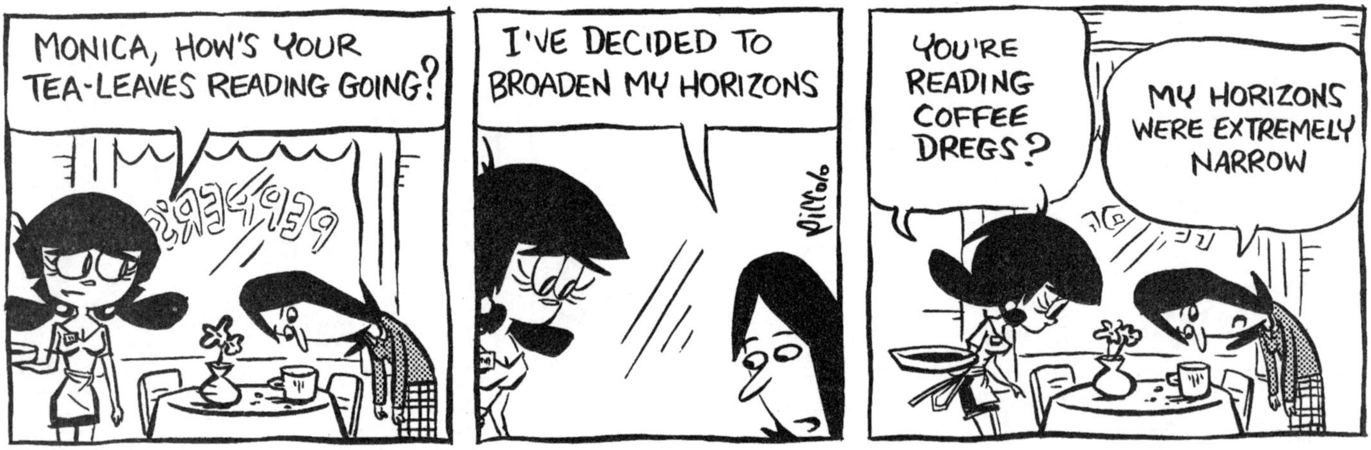
MONICA, HOW'S YOUR TEA-LEAVES READING GOING?
I'VE DECIDED TO BROADEN MY HORIZONS
YOU'RE READING COFFEE DREGS?
MY HORIZONS WERE EXTREMELY NARROW

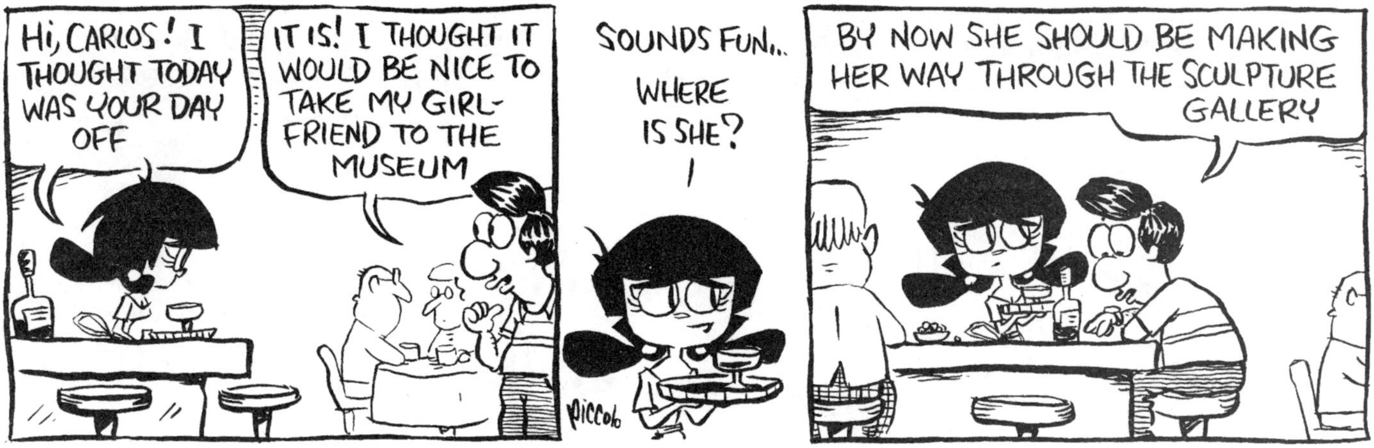
Hi, CARLOS! I THOUGHT TODAY WAS YOUR DAY OFF
IT IS! I THOUGHT IT WOULD BE NICE TO TAKE MY GIRL-FRIEND TO THE MUSEUM
SOUNDS FUN...
WHERE IS SHE?
BY NOW SHE SHOULD BE MAKING HER WAY THROUGH THE SCULPTURE GALLERY
Piccolo

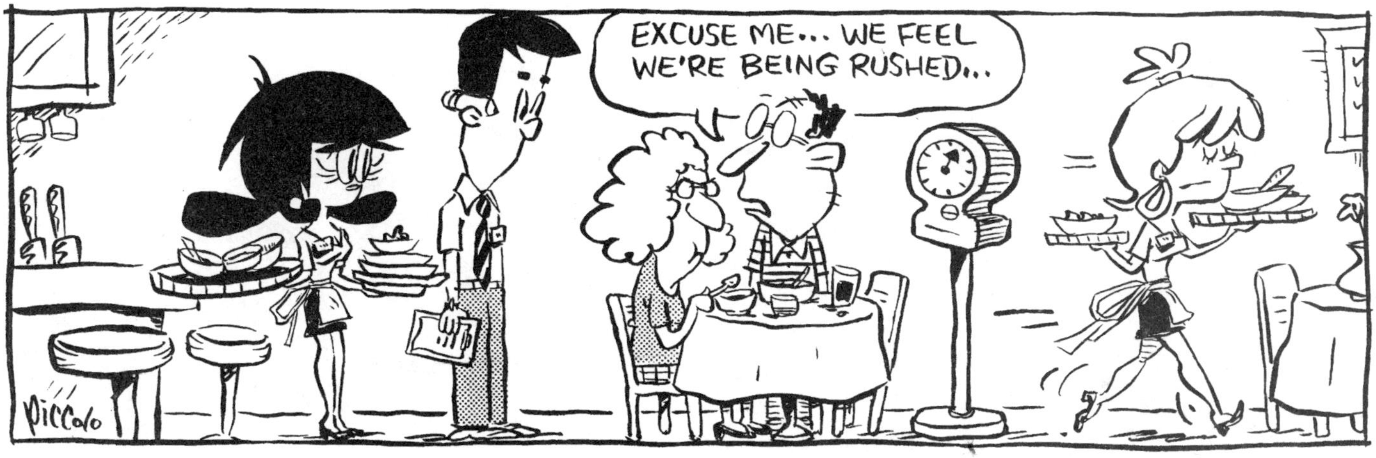
EXCUSE ME... WE FEEL WE'RE BEING RUSHED...
Piccolo

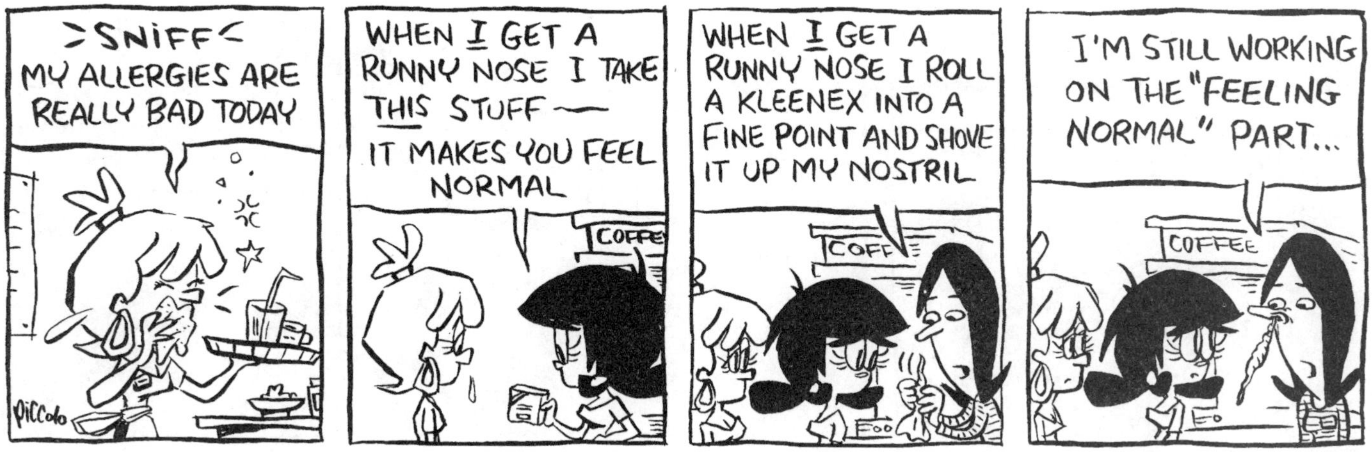
>SNIFF<
MY ALLERGIES ARE REALLY BAD TODAY
WHEN I GET A RUNNY NOSE I TAKE THIS STUFF —
IT MAKES YOU FEEL NORMAL
WHEN I GET A RUNNY NOSE I ROLL A KLEENEX INTO A FINE POINT AND SHOVE IT UP MY NOSTRIL
I'M STILL WORKING ON THE "FEELING NORMAL" PART...
COFFEE
Piccolo

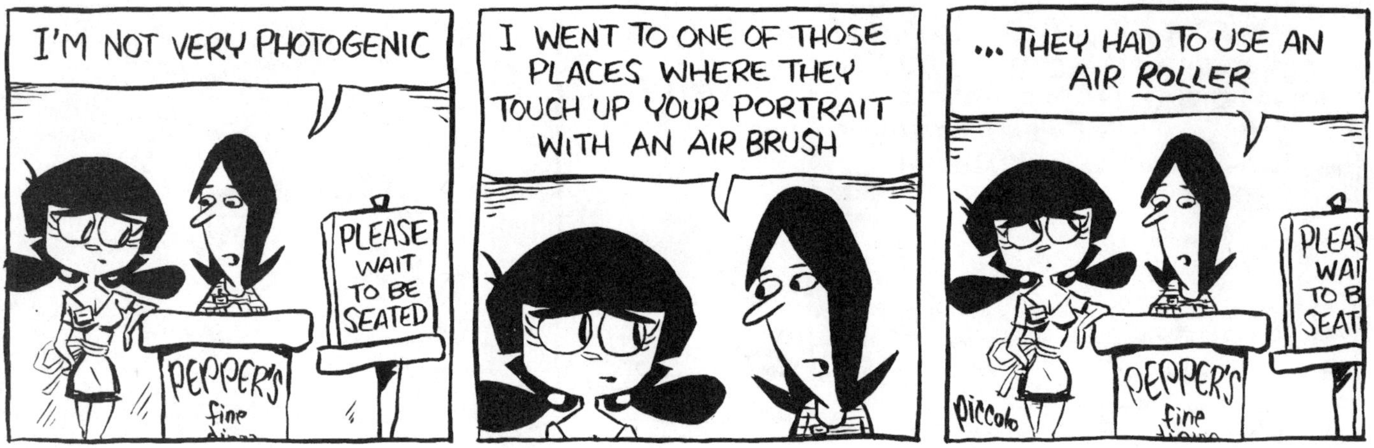
I'M NOT VERY PHOTOGENIC
PLEASE WAIT TO BE SEATED
PEPPER'S fine
I WENT TO ONE OF THOSE PLACES WHERE THEY TOUCH UP YOUR PORTRAIT WITH AN AIR BRUSH
... THEY HAD TO USE AN AIR ROLLER
PEPPER'S fine
piccolo

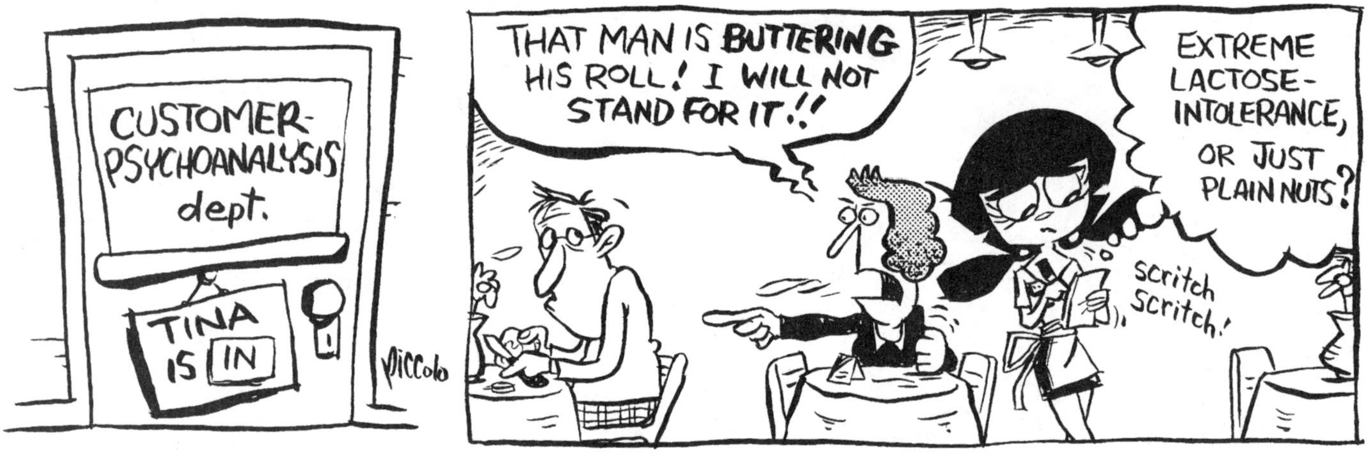
CUSTOMER-PSYCHOANALYSIS dept.
TINA IS IN
piccolo
THAT MAN IS BUTTERING HIS ROLL! I WILL NOT STAND FOR IT!!
EXTREME LACTOSE-INTOLERANCE, OR JUST PLAIN NUTS?
scritch scritch!

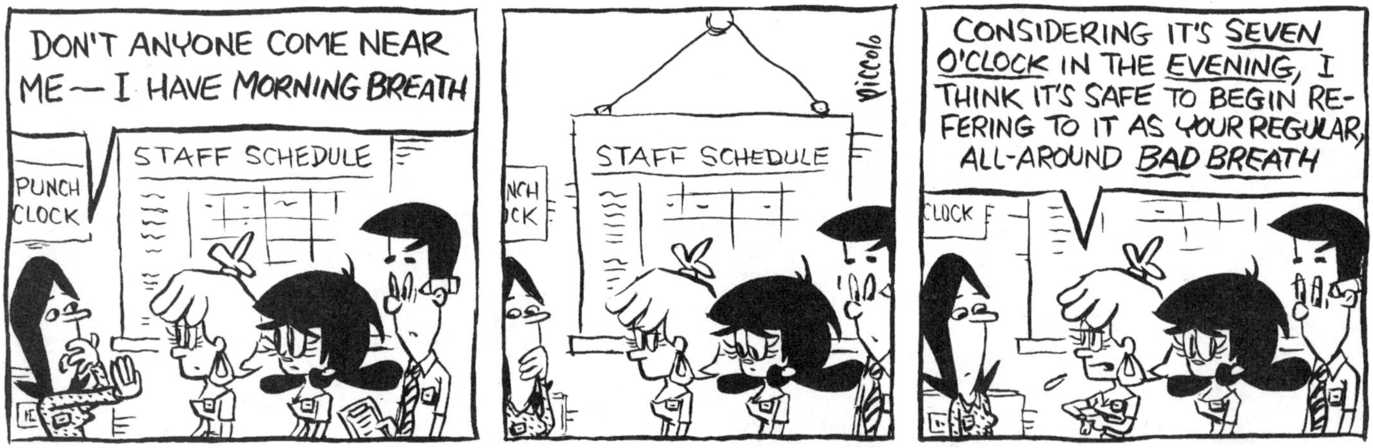
DON'T ANYONE COME NEAR ME—I HAVE MORNING BREATH
PUNCH CLOCK
STAFF SCHEDULE
piccolo
STAFF SCHEDULE
CONSIDERING IT'S SEVEN O'CLOCK IN THE EVENING, I THINK IT'S SAFE TO BEGIN REFERING TO IT AS YOUR REGULAR, ALL-AROUND BAD BREATH
CLOCK

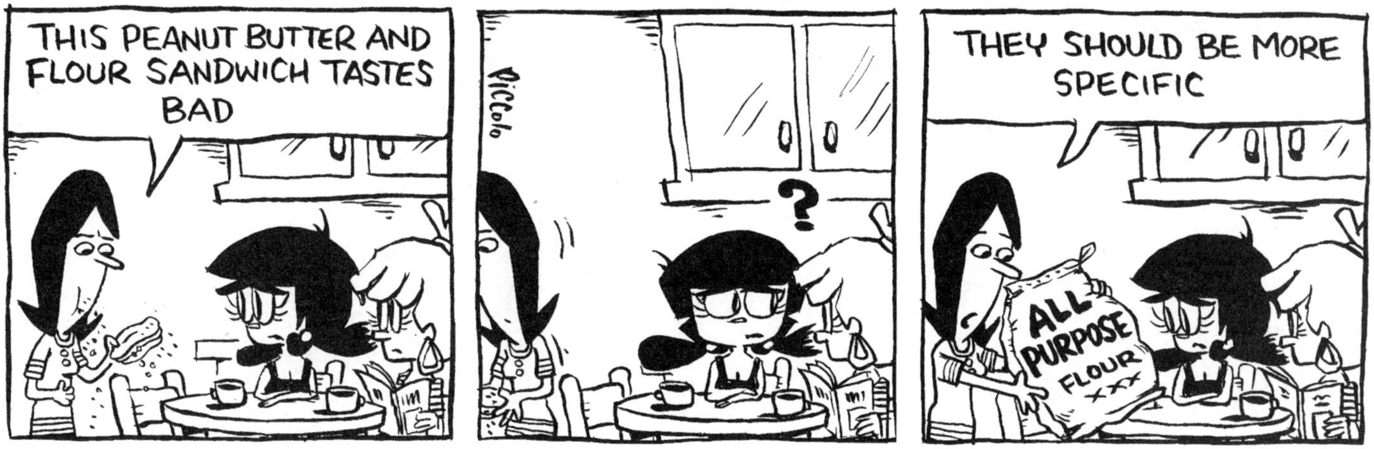
THIS PEANUT BUTTER AND FLOUR SANDWICH TASTES BAD
?
ALL PURPOSE FLOUR XXX
THEY SHOULD BE MORE SPECIFIC

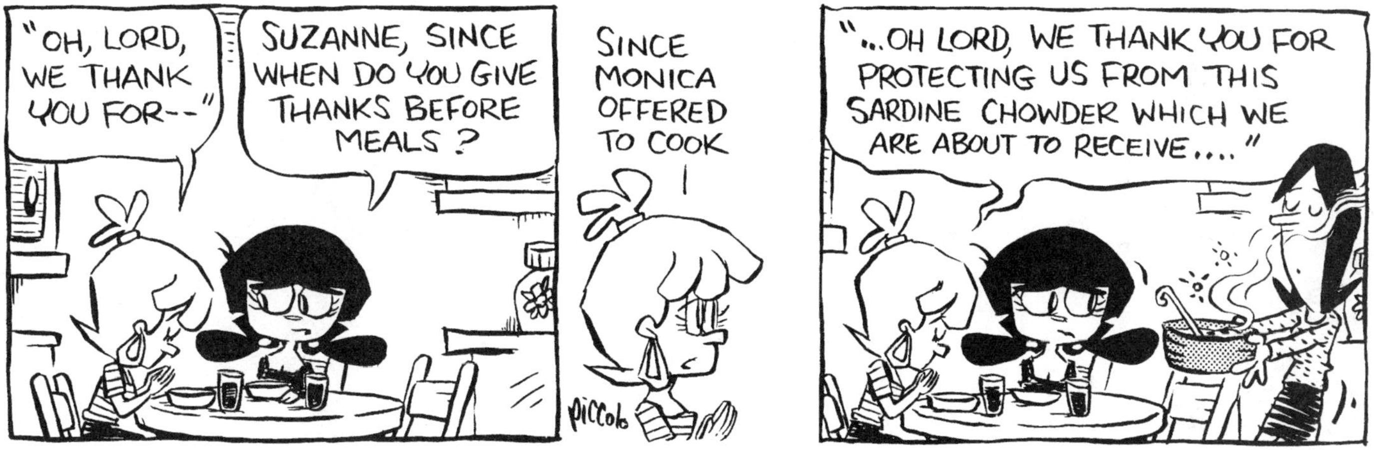
"OH, LORD, WE THANK YOU FOR--"
SUZANNE, SINCE WHEN DO YOU GIVE THANKS BEFORE MEALS?
SINCE MONICA OFFERED TO COOK
"...OH LORD, WE THANK YOU FOR PROTECTING US FROM THIS SARDINE CHOWDER WHICH WE ARE ABOUT TO RECEIVE...."

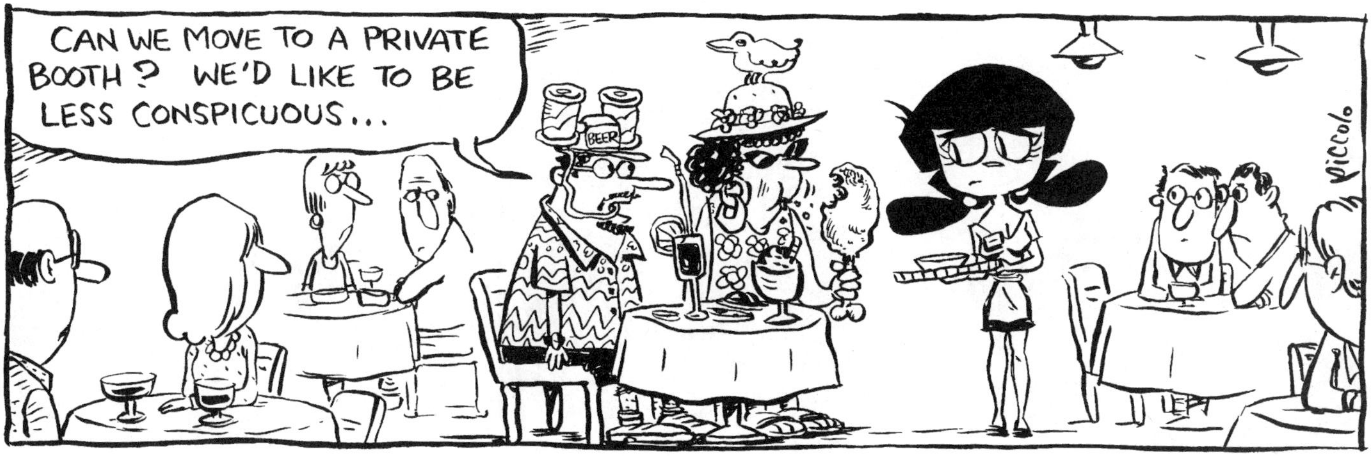
CAN WE MOVE TO A PRIVATE BOOTH? WE'D LIKE TO BE LESS CONSPICUOUS...
BEER

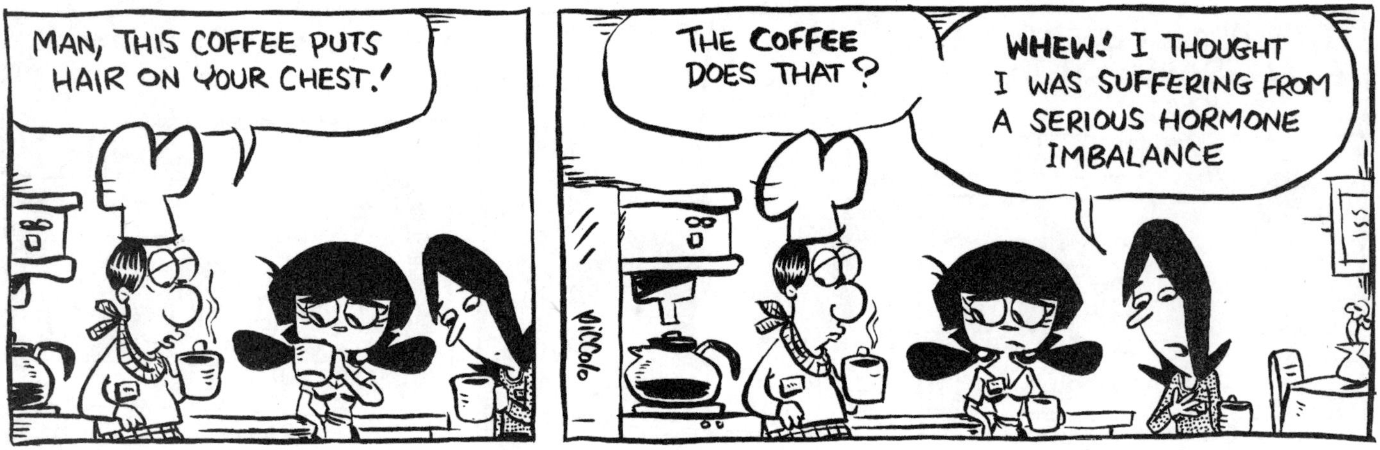
MAN, THIS COFFEE PUTS HAIR ON YOUR CHEST!
THE **COFFEE** DOES THAT?
WHEW! I THOUGHT I WAS SUFFERING FROM A SERIOUS HORMONE IMBALANCE
PICCOLO

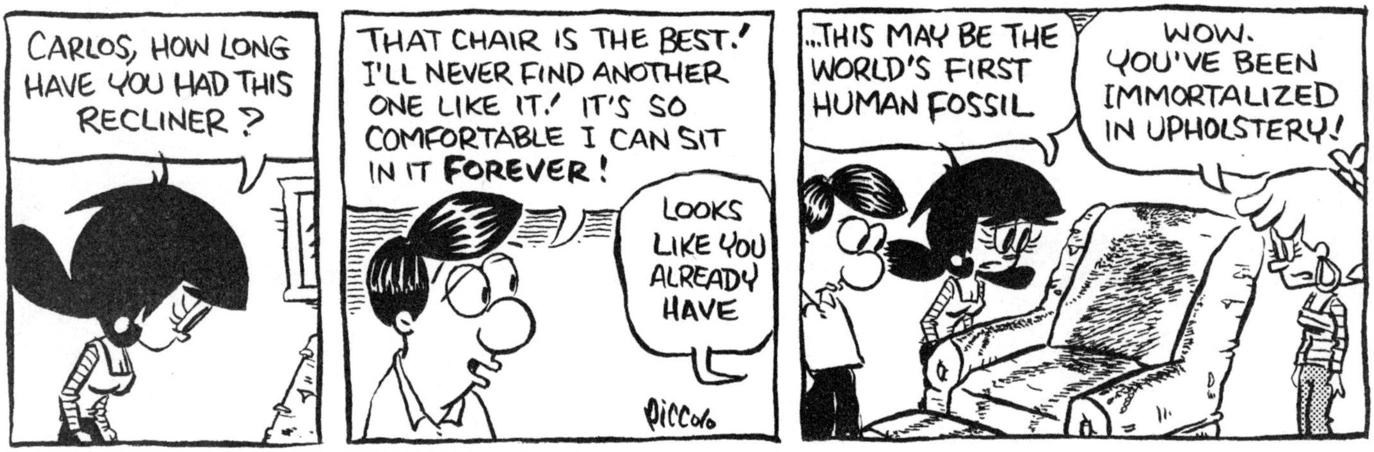
CARLOS, HOW LONG HAVE YOU HAD THIS RECLINER?
THAT CHAIR IS THE BEST! I'LL NEVER FIND ANOTHER ONE LIKE IT! IT'S SO COMFORTABLE I CAN SIT IN IT **FOREVER**!
LOOKS LIKE YOU ALREADY HAVE
PICCOLO
...THIS MAY BE THE WORLD'S FIRST HUMAN FOSSIL
WOW. YOU'VE BEEN IMMORTALIZED IN UPHOLSTERY!

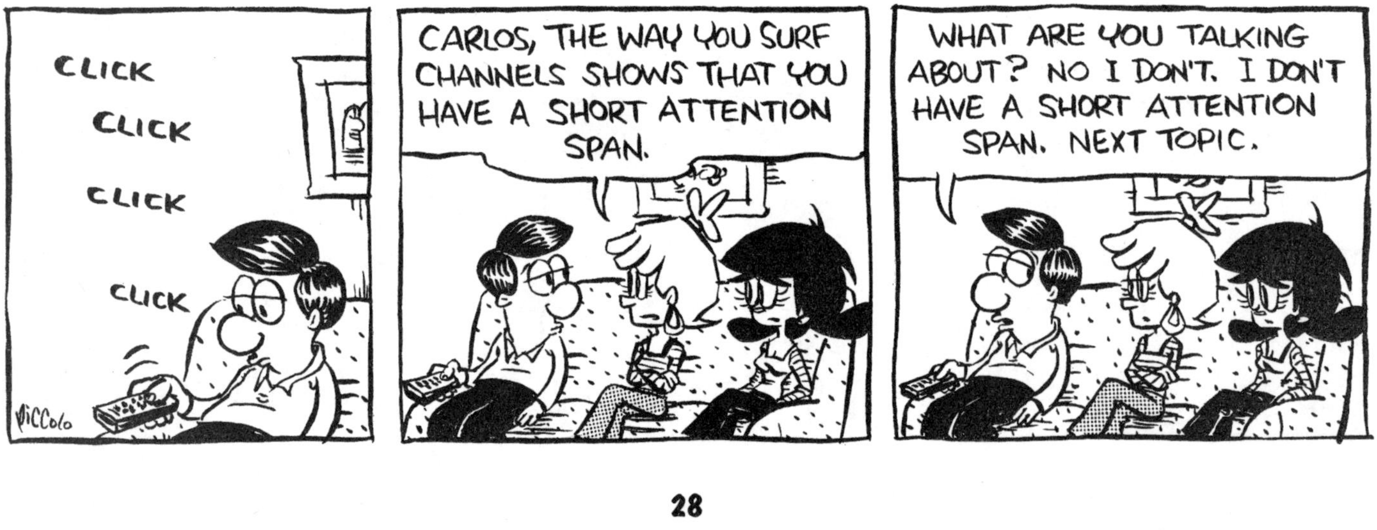
CLICK
CLICK
CLICK
CLICK
PICCOLO
CARLOS, THE WAY YOU SURF CHANNELS SHOWS THAT YOU HAVE A SHORT ATTENTION SPAN.
WHAT ARE YOU TALKING ABOUT? NO I DON'T. I DON'T HAVE A SHORT ATTENTION SPAN. NEXT TOPIC.

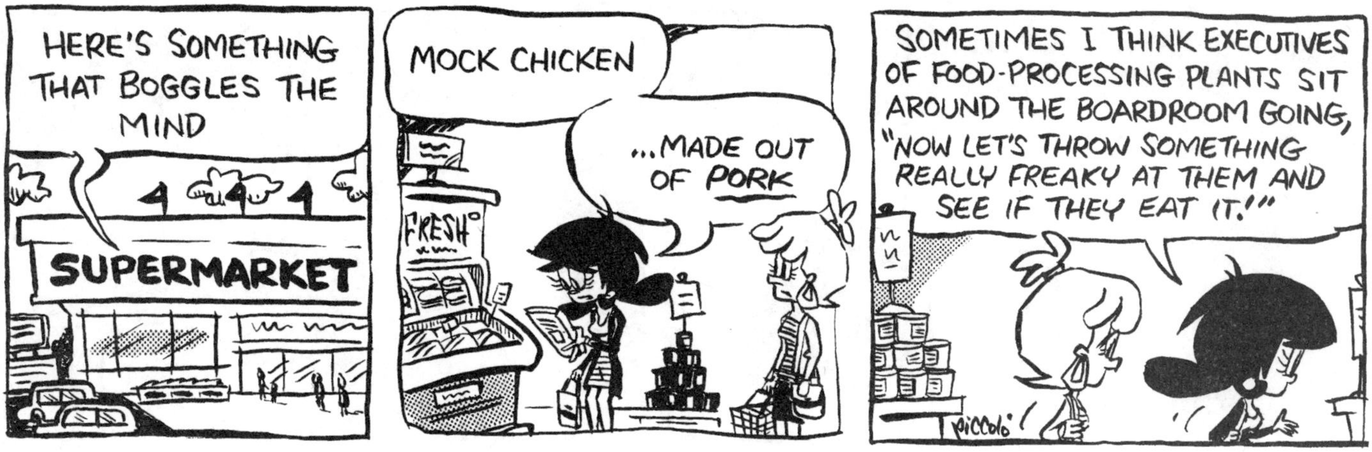
HERE'S SOMETHING THAT BOGGLES THE MIND
SUPERMARKET
MOCK CHICKEN
...MADE OUT OF PORK
FRESH
SOMETIMES I THINK EXECUTIVES OF FOOD-PROCESSING PLANTS SIT AROUND THE BOARDROOM GOING, "NOW LET'S THROW SOMETHING REALLY FREAKY AT THEM AND SEE IF THEY EAT IT!"
piccolo

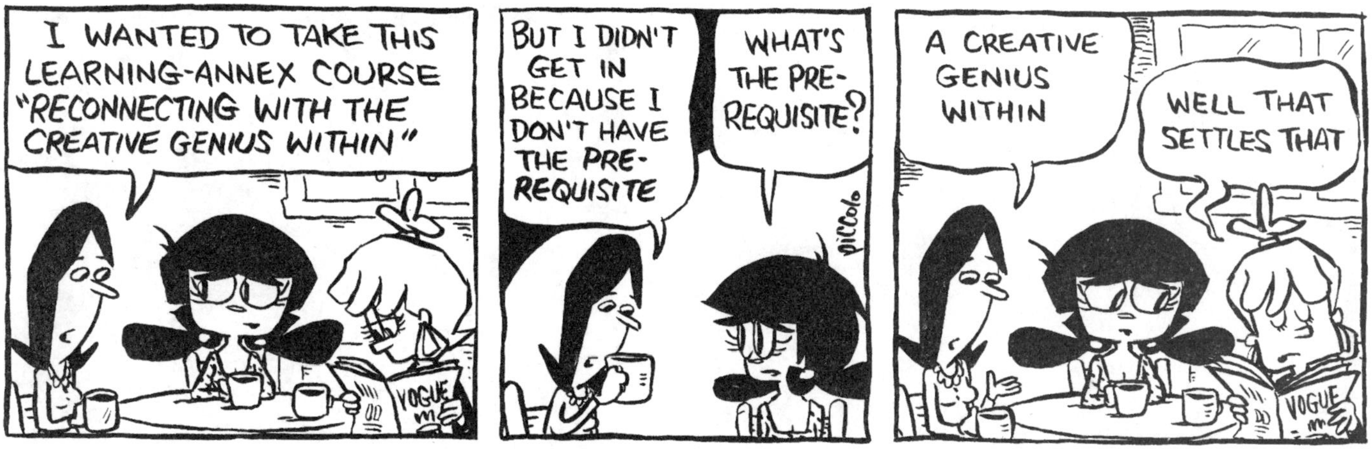
I WANTED TO TAKE THIS LEARNING-ANNEX COURSE "RECONNECTING WITH THE CREATIVE GENIUS WITHIN"
VOGUE
BUT I DIDN'T GET IN BECAUSE I DON'T HAVE THE PRE-REQUISITE
WHAT'S THE PRE-REQUISITE?
piccolo
A CREATIVE GENIUS WITHIN
WELL THAT SETTLES THAT
VOGUE

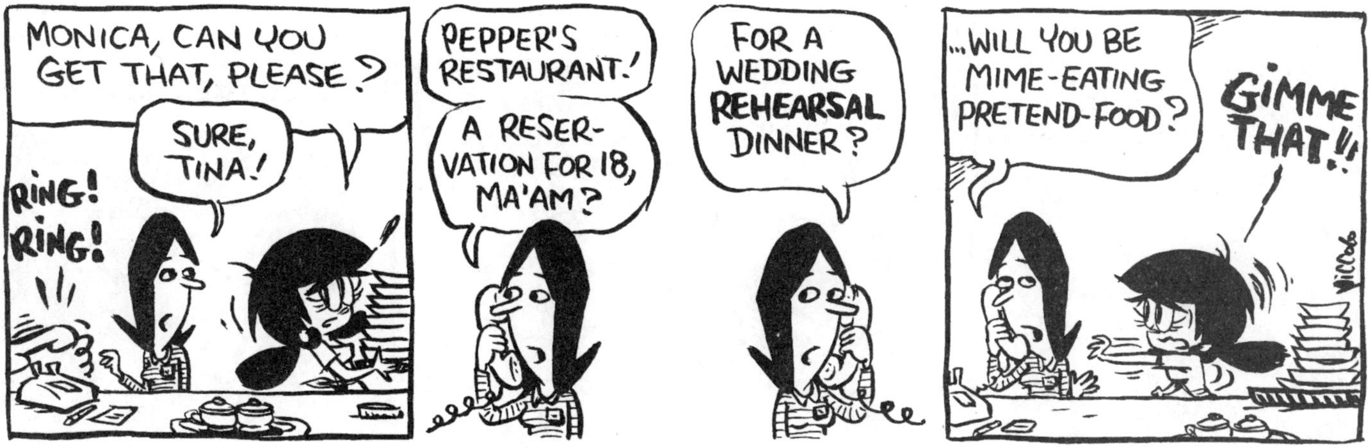
MONICA, CAN YOU GET THAT, PLEASE?
SURE, TINA!
RING! RING!
PEPPER'S RESTAURANT!
A RESER-VATION FOR 18, MA'AM?
FOR A WEDDING REHEARSAL DINNER?
...WILL YOU BE MIME-EATING PRETEND-FOOD?
GIMME THAT!!
piccolo

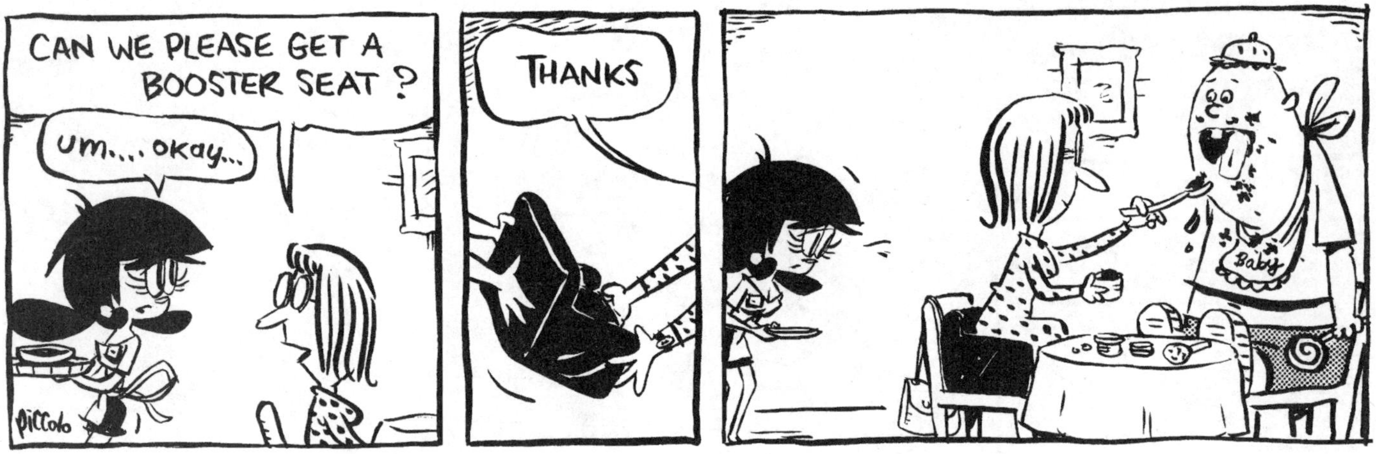
CAN WE PLEASE GET A BOOSTER SEAT ?
um.... okay...
piccolo
THANKS
Baby

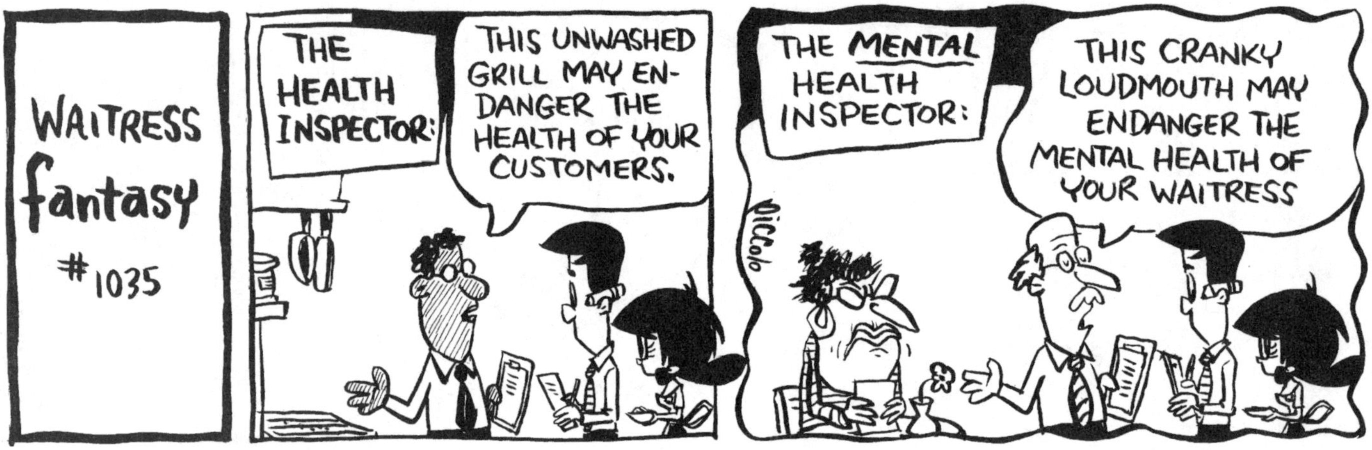
WAITRESS fantasy #1035
THE HEALTH INSPECTOR:
THIS UNWASHED GRILL MAY EN-DANGER THE HEALTH OF YOUR CUSTOMERS.
THE MENTAL HEALTH INSPECTOR:
THIS CRANKY LOUDMOUTH MAY ENDANGER THE MENTAL HEALTH OF YOUR WAITRESS
piccolo

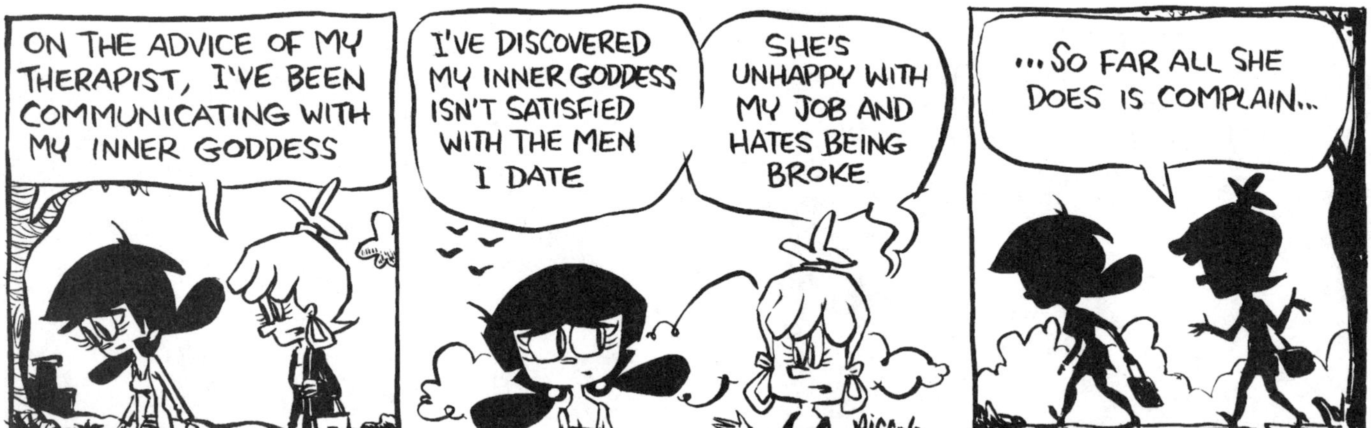
ON THE ADVICE OF MY THERAPIST, I'VE BEEN COMMUNICATING WITH MY INNER GODDESS
I'VE DISCOVERED MY INNER GODDESS ISN'T SATISFIED WITH THE MEN I DATE
SHE'S UNHAPPY WITH MY JOB AND HATES BEING BROKE
piccolo
...SO FAR ALL SHE DOES IS COMPLAIN...

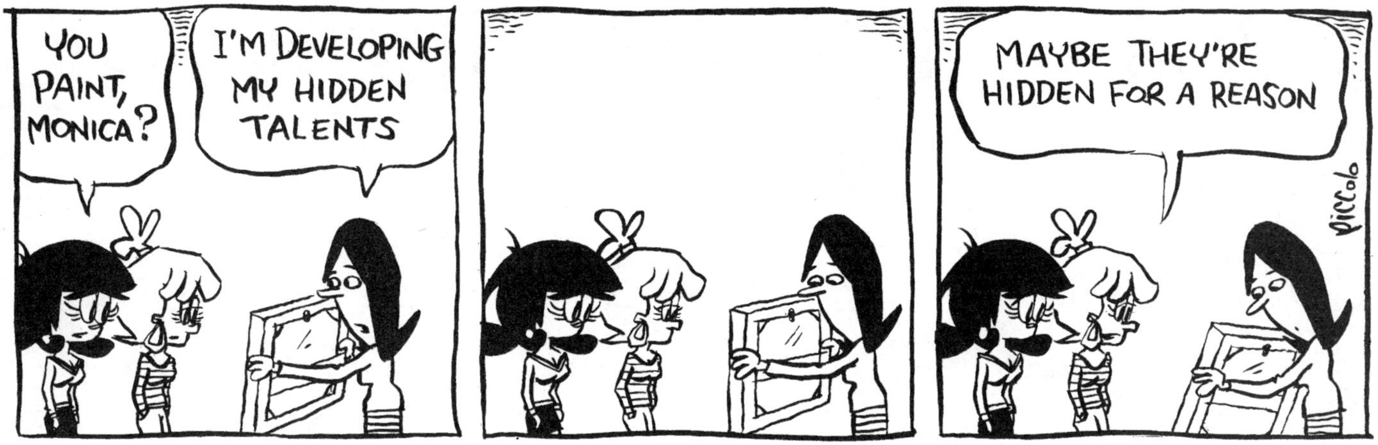
YOU PAINT, MONICA?
I'M DEVELOPING MY HIDDEN TALENTS
MAYBE THEY'RE HIDDEN FOR A REASON
Piccolo

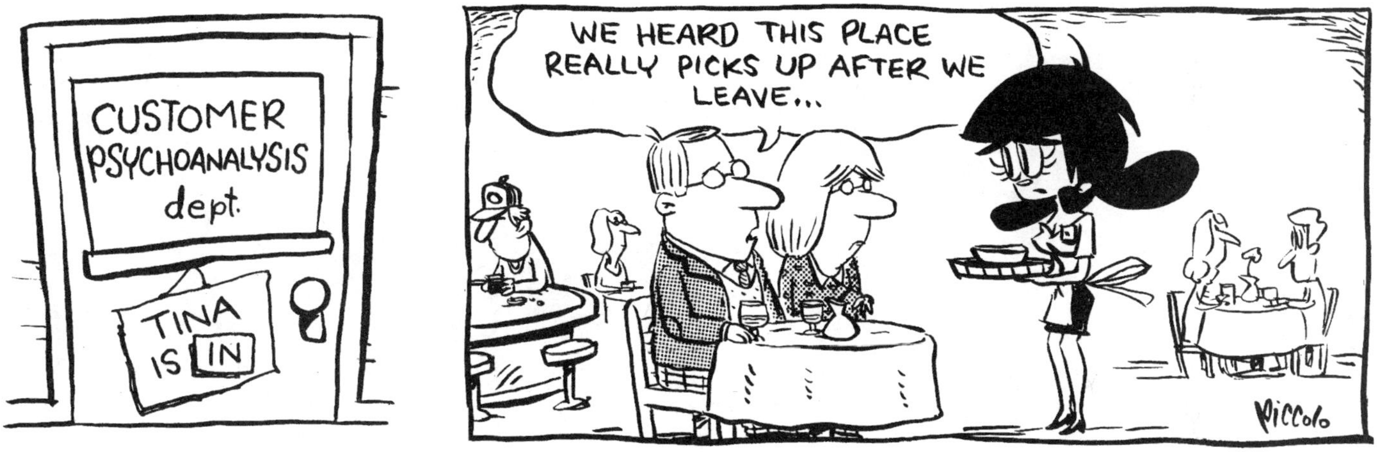
CUSTOMER PSYCHOANALYSIS dept.
TINA IS IN
WE HEARD THIS PLACE REALLY PICKS UP AFTER WE LEAVE...
Piccolo

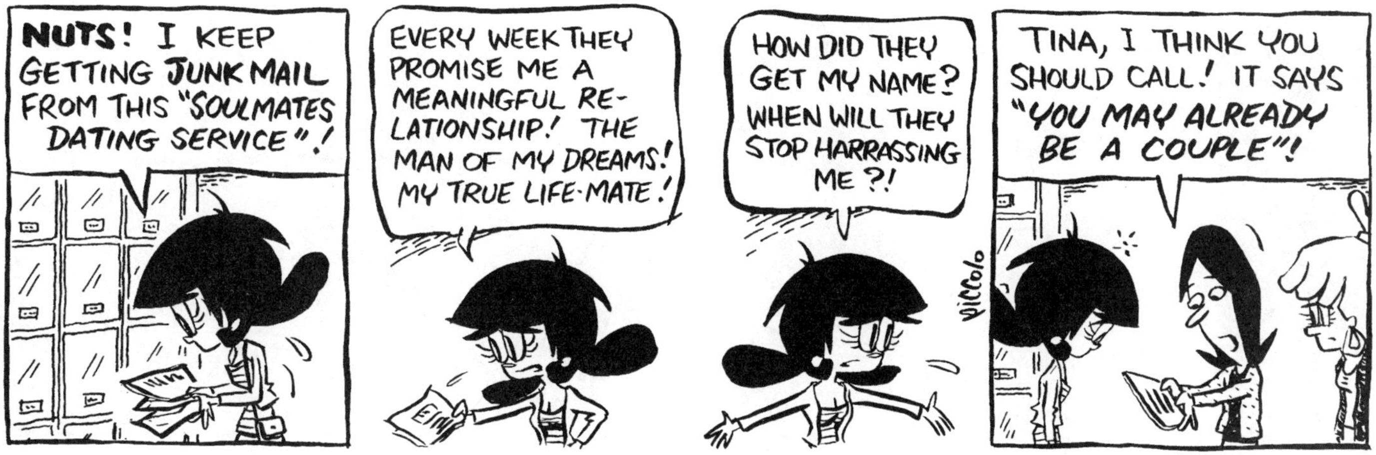
NUTS! I KEEP GETTING JUNK MAIL FROM THIS "SOULMATES DATING SERVICE"!
EVERY WEEK THEY PROMISE ME A MEANINGFUL RE-LATIONSHIP! THE MAN OF MY DREAMS! MY TRUE LIFE-MATE!
HOW DID THEY GET MY NAME? WHEN WILL THEY STOP HARRASSING ME?!
Piccolo
TINA, I THINK YOU SHOULD CALL! IT SAYS "YOU MAY ALREADY BE A COUPLE"!

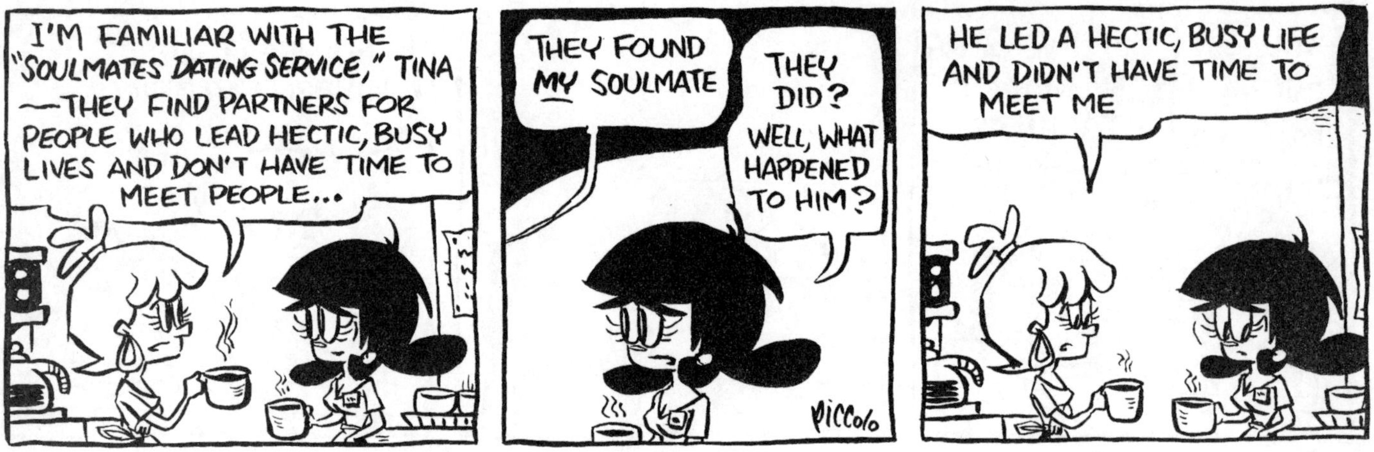
I'M FAMILIAR WITH THE "SOULMATES DATING SERVICE," TINA —THEY FIND PARTNERS FOR PEOPLE WHO LEAD HECTIC, BUSY LIVES AND DON'T HAVE TIME TO MEET PEOPLE...
THEY FOUND MY SOULMATE
THEY DID? WELL, WHAT HAPPENED TO HIM?
PICCOLO
HE LED A HECTIC, BUSY LIFE AND DIDN'T HAVE TIME TO MEET ME

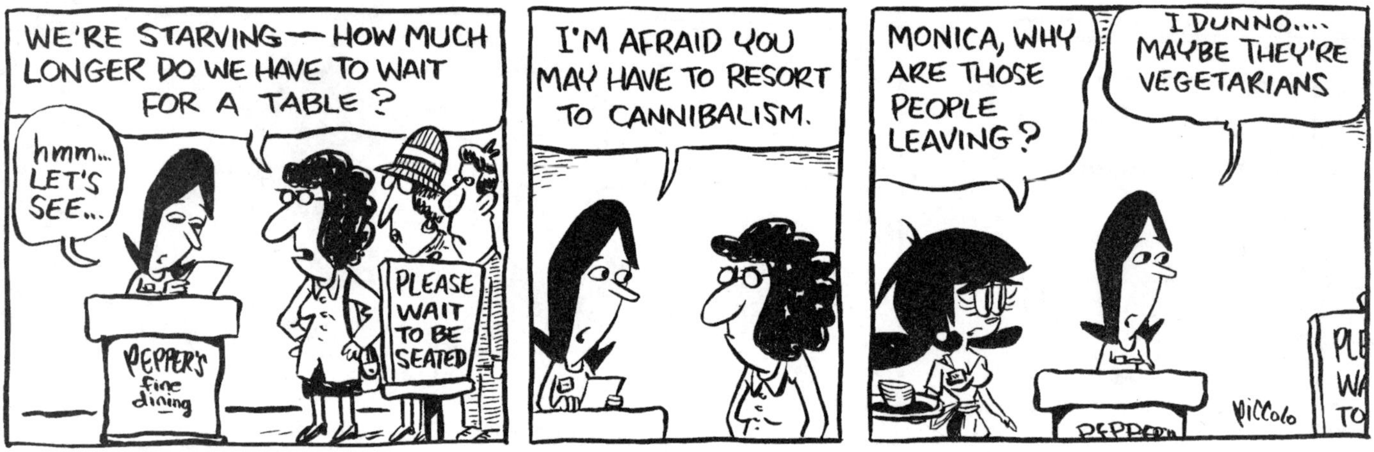
WE'RE STARVING— HOW MUCH LONGER DO WE HAVE TO WAIT FOR A TABLE?
hmm... LET'S SEE...
PEPPER'S fine dining
PLEASE WAIT TO BE SEATED
I'M AFRAID YOU MAY HAVE TO RESORT TO CANNIBALISM.
MONICA, WHY ARE THOSE PEOPLE LEAVING?
I DUNNO.... MAYBE THEY'RE VEGETARIANS
PICCOLO

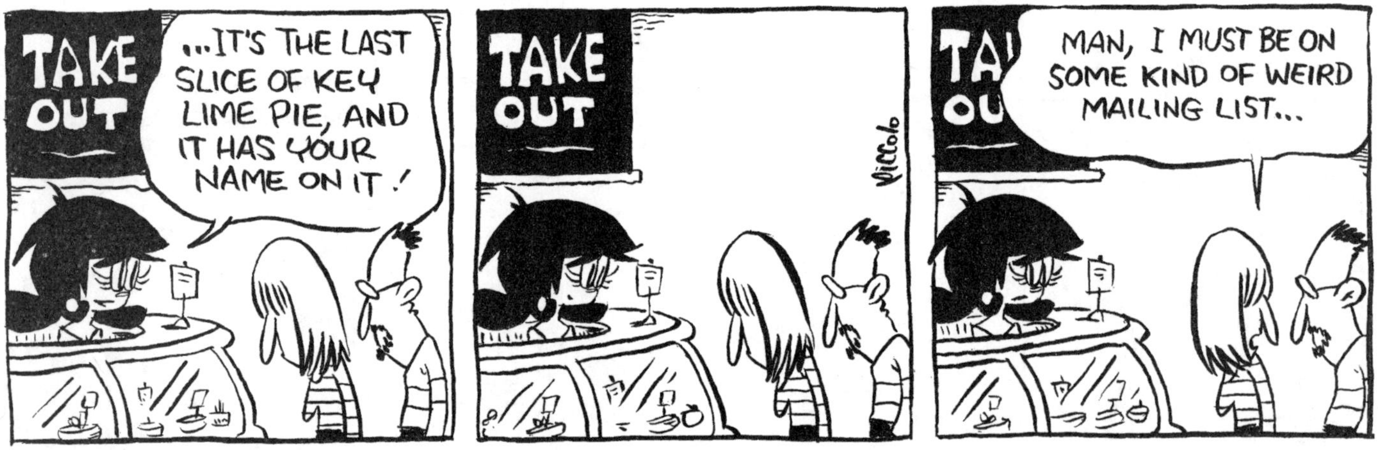
TAKE OUT
...IT'S THE LAST SLICE OF KEY LIME PIE, AND IT HAS YOUR NAME ON IT!
TAKE OUT
PICCOLO
MAN, I MUST BE ON SOME KIND OF WEIRD MAILING LIST...

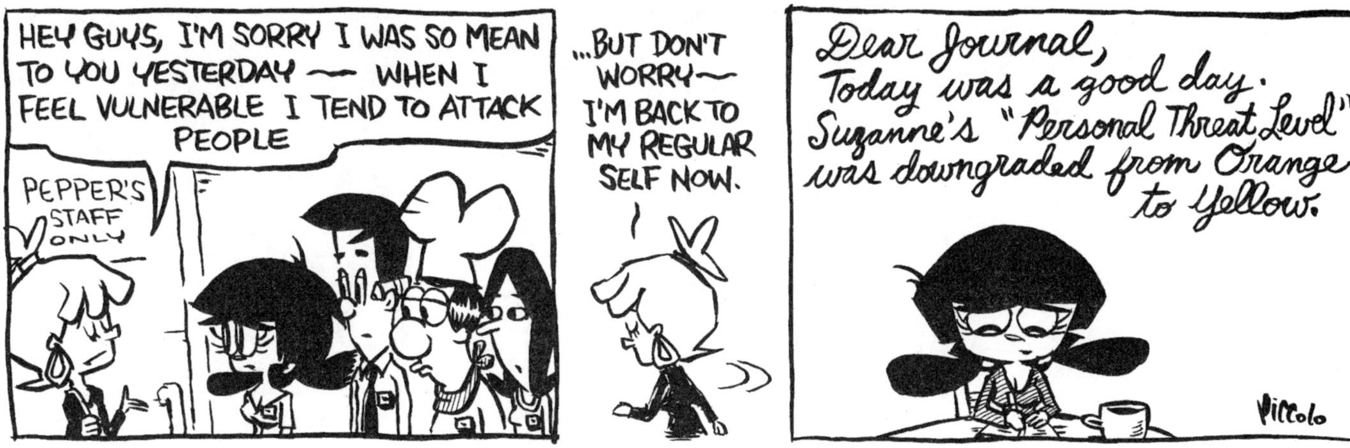
HEY GUYS, I'M SORRY I WAS SO MEAN TO YOU YESTERDAY — WHEN I FEEL VULNERABLE I TEND TO ATTACK PEOPLE
PEPPER'S STAFF ONLY
...BUT DON'T WORRY— I'M BACK TO MY REGULAR SELF NOW.
Dear Journal,
Today was a good day.
Suzanne's "Personal Threat Level" was downgraded from Orange to Yellow.
Piccolo

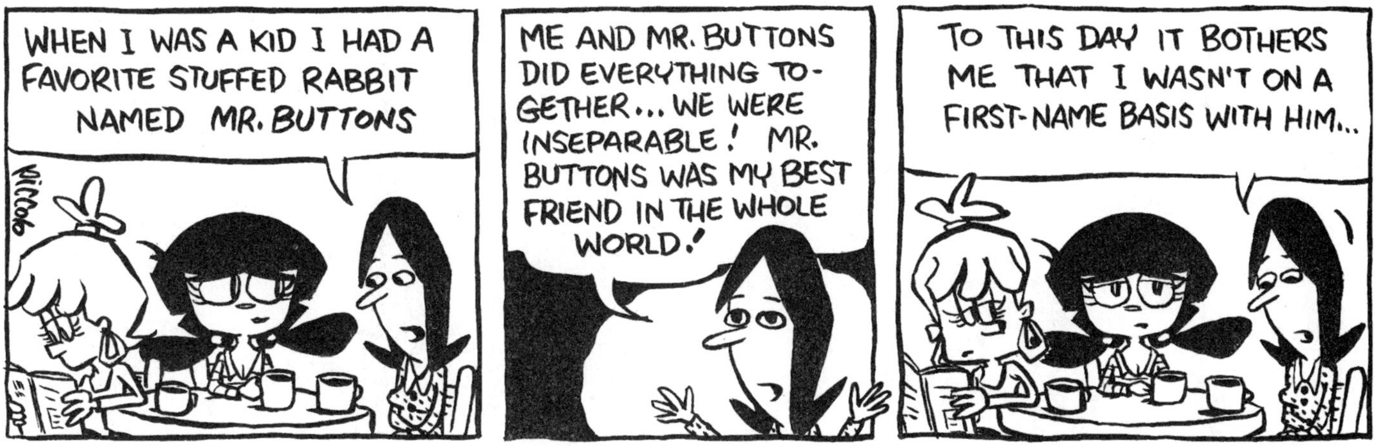
WHEN I WAS A KID I HAD A FAVORITE STUFFED RABBIT NAMED MR. BUTTONS
Piccolo
ME AND MR. BUTTONS DID EVERYTHING TOGETHER... WE WERE INSEPARABLE! MR. BUTTONS WAS MY BEST FRIEND IN THE WHOLE WORLD!
TO THIS DAY IT BOTHERS ME THAT I WASN'T ON A FIRST-NAME BASIS WITH HIM...

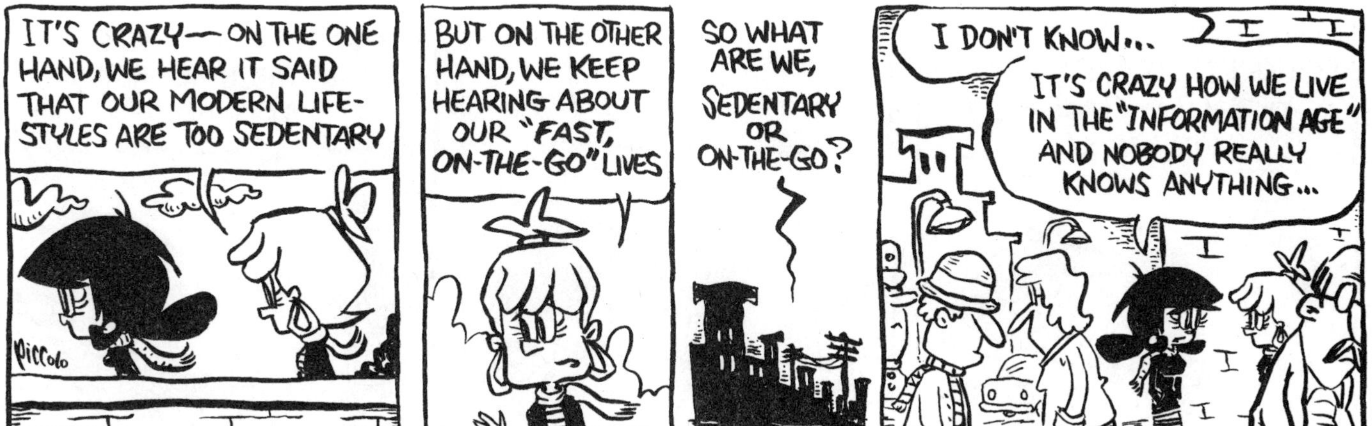
IT'S CRAZY— ON THE ONE HAND, WE HEAR IT SAID THAT OUR MODERN LIFESTYLES ARE TOO SEDENTARY
Piccolo
BUT ON THE OTHER HAND, WE KEEP HEARING ABOUT OUR "FAST, ON-THE-GO" LIVES
SO WHAT ARE WE, SEDENTARY OR ON-THE-GO?
I DON'T KNOW...
IT'S CRAZY HOW WE LIVE IN THE "INFORMATION AGE" AND NOBODY REALLY KNOWS ANYTHING...

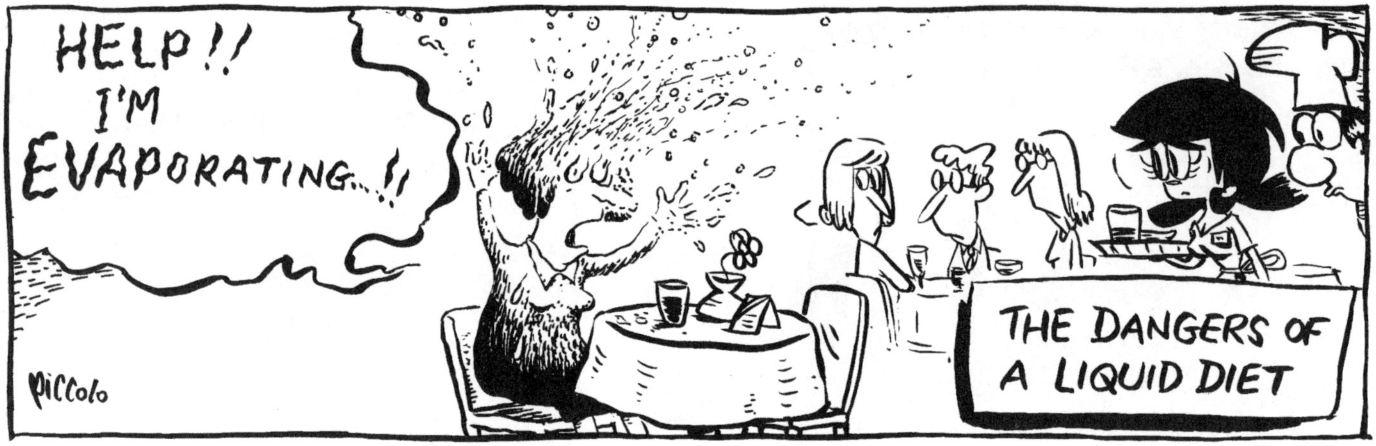
HELP!! I'M EVAPORATING...!!
THE DANGERS OF A LIQUID DIET
piccolo

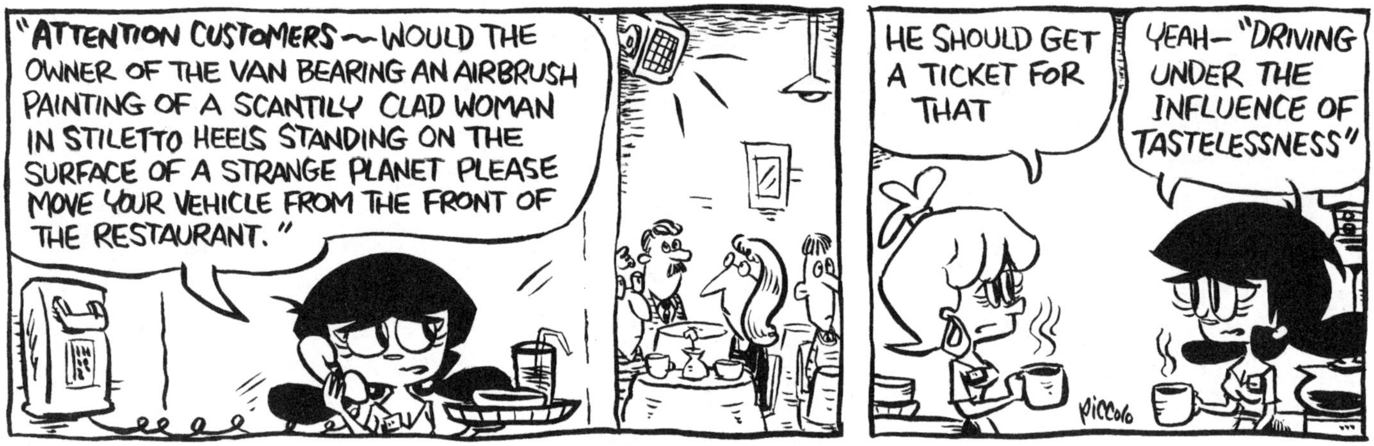
"ATTENTION CUSTOMERS ~ WOULD THE OWNER OF THE VAN BEARING AN AIRBRUSH PAINTING OF A SCANTILY CLAD WOMAN IN STILETTO HEELS STANDING ON THE SURFACE OF A STRANGE PLANET PLEASE MOVE YOUR VEHICLE FROM THE FRONT OF THE RESTAURANT."
HE SHOULD GET A TICKET FOR THAT
YEAH– "DRIVING UNDER THE INFLUENCE OF TASTELESSNESS"
piccolo

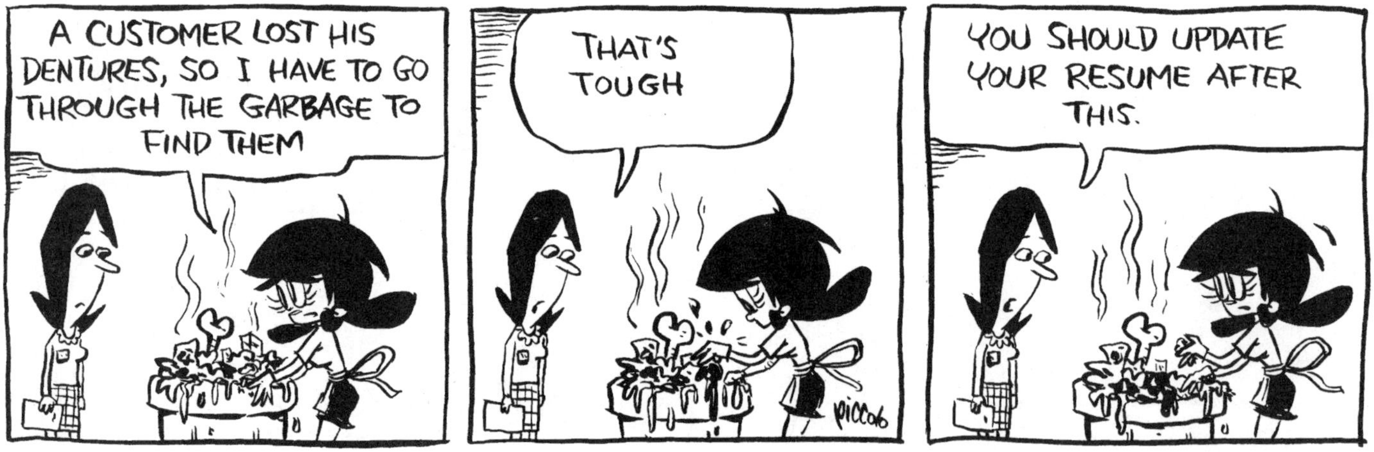
A CUSTOMER LOST HIS DENTURES, SO I HAVE TO GO THROUGH THE GARBAGE TO FIND THEM
THAT'S TOUGH
YOU SHOULD UPDATE YOUR RESUME AFTER THIS.
piccolo

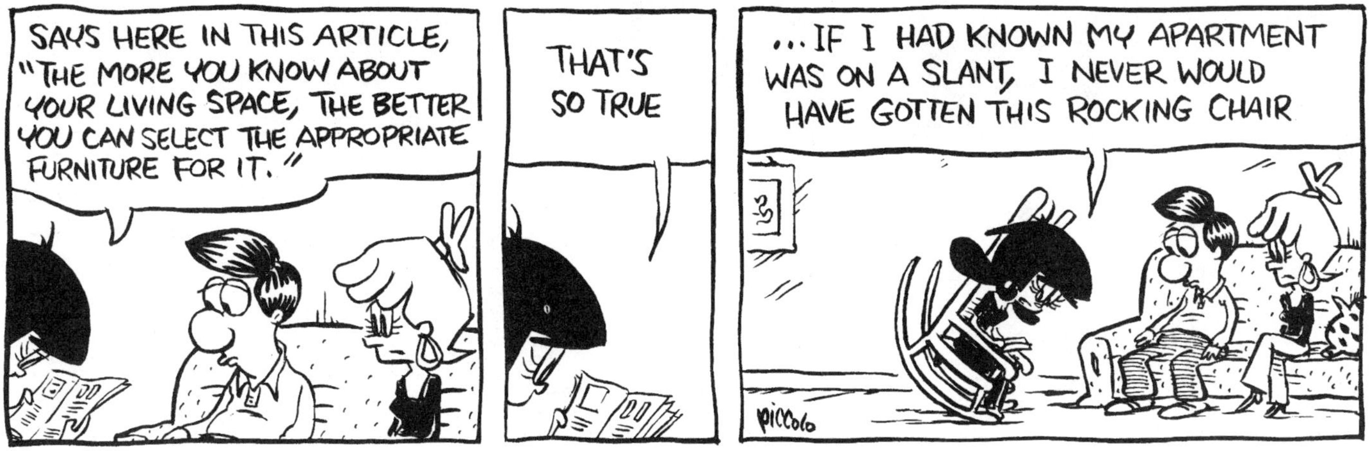
SAYS HERE IN THIS ARTICLE, "THE MORE YOU KNOW ABOUT YOUR LIVING SPACE, THE BETTER YOU CAN SELECT THE APPROPRIATE FURNITURE FOR IT."
THAT'S SO TRUE
...IF I HAD KNOWN MY APARTMENT WAS ON A SLANT, I NEVER WOULD HAVE GOTTEN THIS ROCKING CHAIR
piccolo

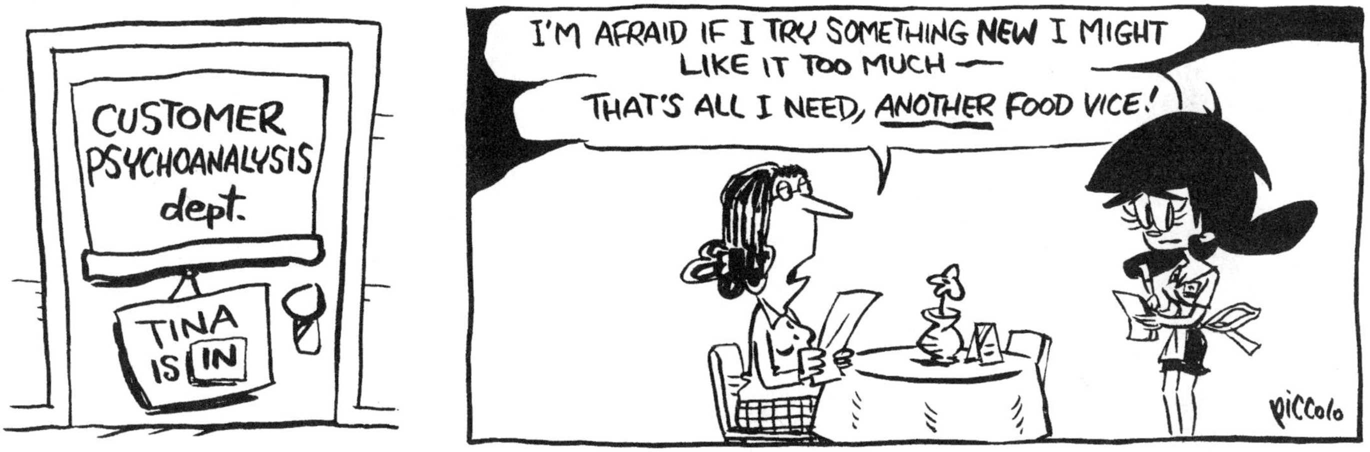
CUSTOMER PSYCHOANALYSIS dept.
TINA IS IN
I'M AFRAID IF I TRY SOMETHING NEW I MIGHT LIKE IT TOO MUCH — THAT'S ALL I NEED, ANOTHER FOOD VICE!
piccolo

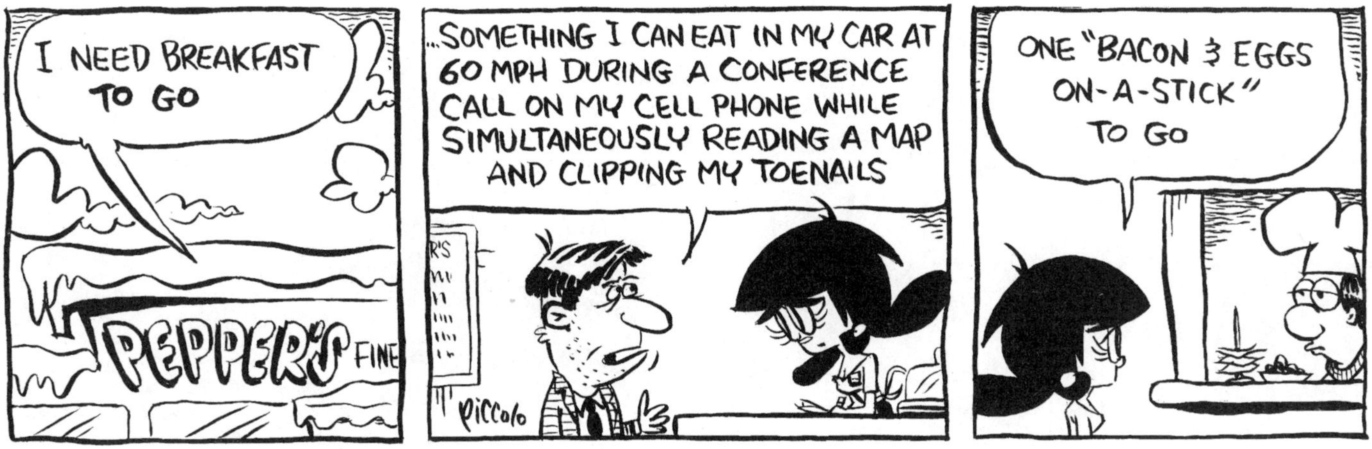
I NEED BREAKFAST TO GO
PEPPER'S FINE
...SOMETHING I CAN EAT IN MY CAR AT 60 MPH DURING A CONFERENCE CALL ON MY CELL PHONE WHILE SIMULTANEOUSLY READING A MAP AND CLIPPING MY TOENAILS
piccolo
ONE "BACON & EGGS ON-A-STICK" TO GO

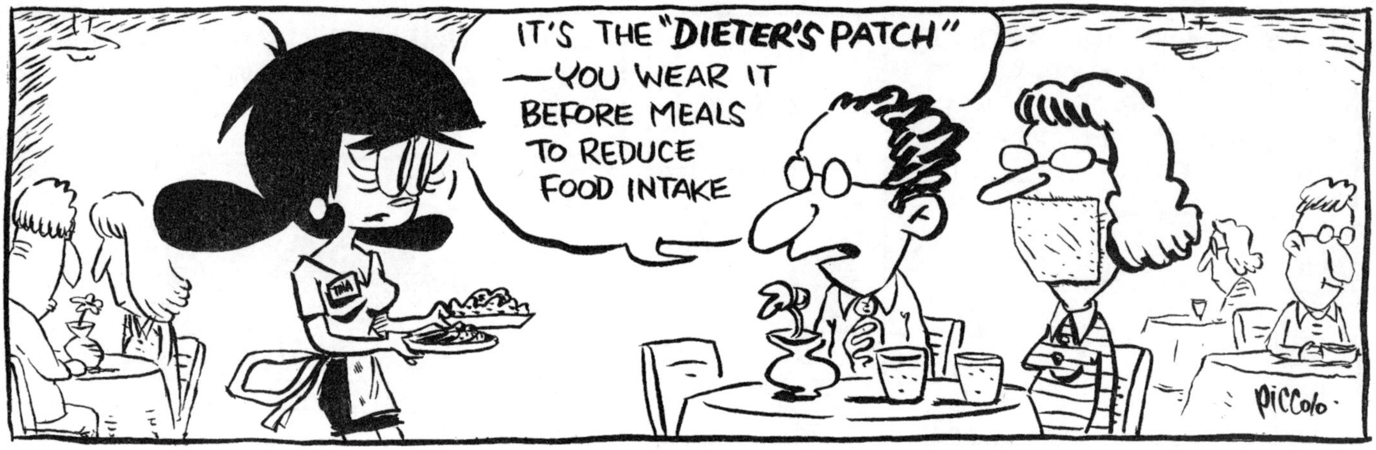
IT'S THE "DIETER'S PATCH" —YOU WEAR IT BEFORE MEALS TO REDUCE FOOD INTAKE
TINA
PICCOLO

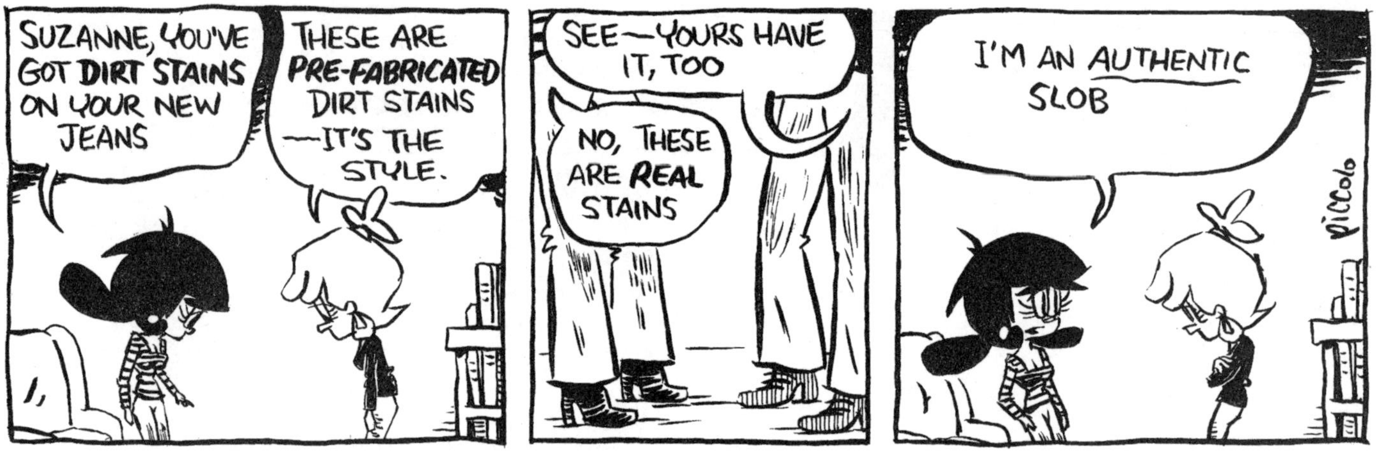
SUZANNE, YOU'VE GOT DIRT STAINS ON YOUR NEW JEANS
THESE ARE PRE-FABRICATED DIRT STAINS —IT'S THE STYLE.
SEE—YOURS HAVE IT, TOO
NO, THESE ARE REAL STAINS
I'M AN AUTHENTIC SLOB
PICCOLO

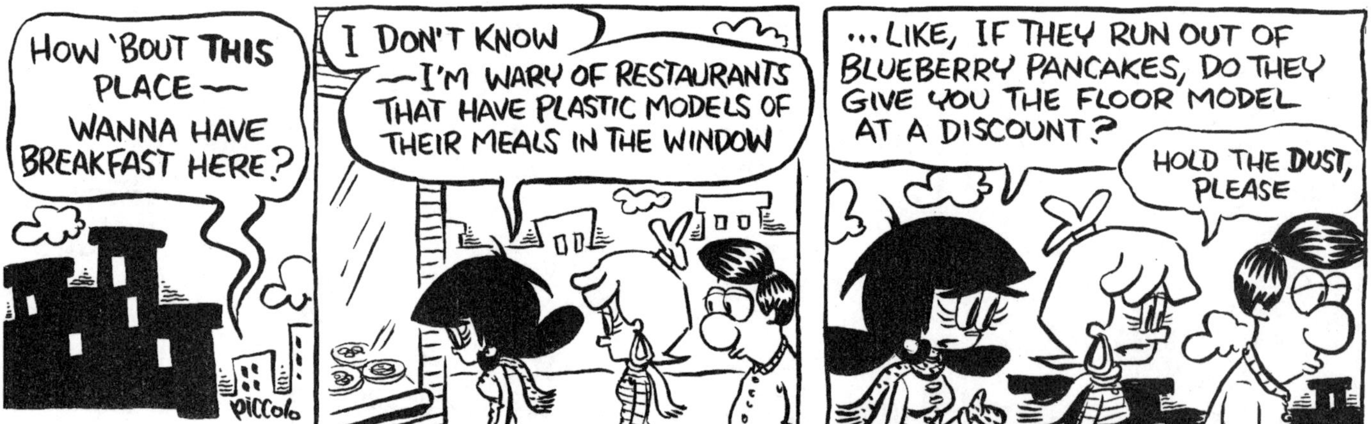
HOW 'BOUT THIS PLACE— WANNA HAVE BREAKFAST HERE?
PICCOLO
I DON'T KNOW
—I'M WARY OF RESTAURANTS THAT HAVE PLASTIC MODELS OF THEIR MEALS IN THE WINDOW
...LIKE, IF THEY RUN OUT OF BLUEBERRY PANCAKES, DO THEY GIVE YOU THE FLOOR MODEL AT A DISCOUNT?
HOLD THE DUST, PLEASE

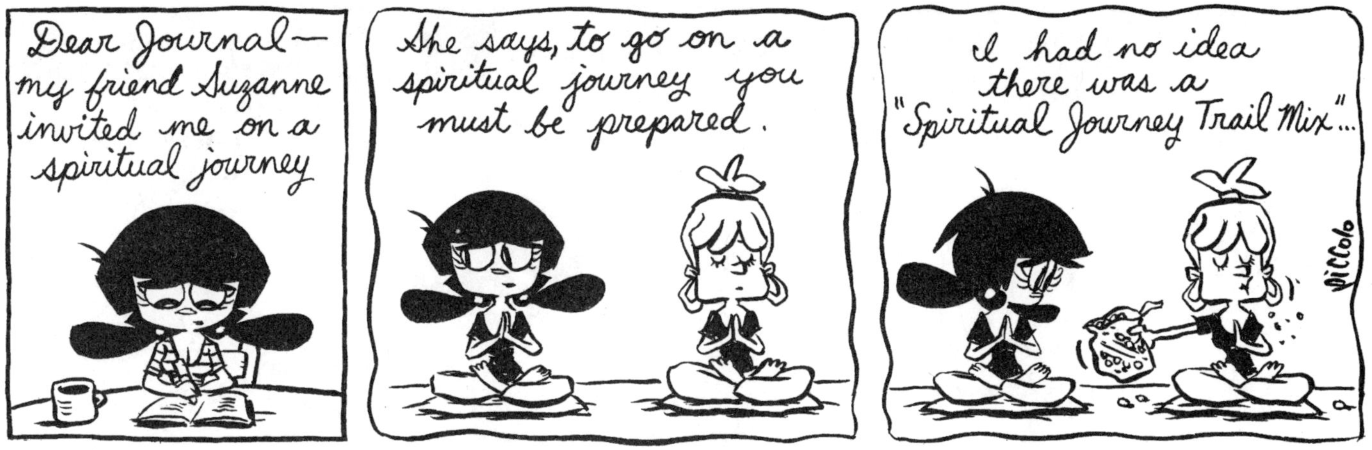
Dear Journal— my friend Suzanne invited me on a spiritual journey
She says, to go on a spiritual journey you must be prepared.
I had no idea there was a "Spiritual Journey Trail Mix"...
Piccolo

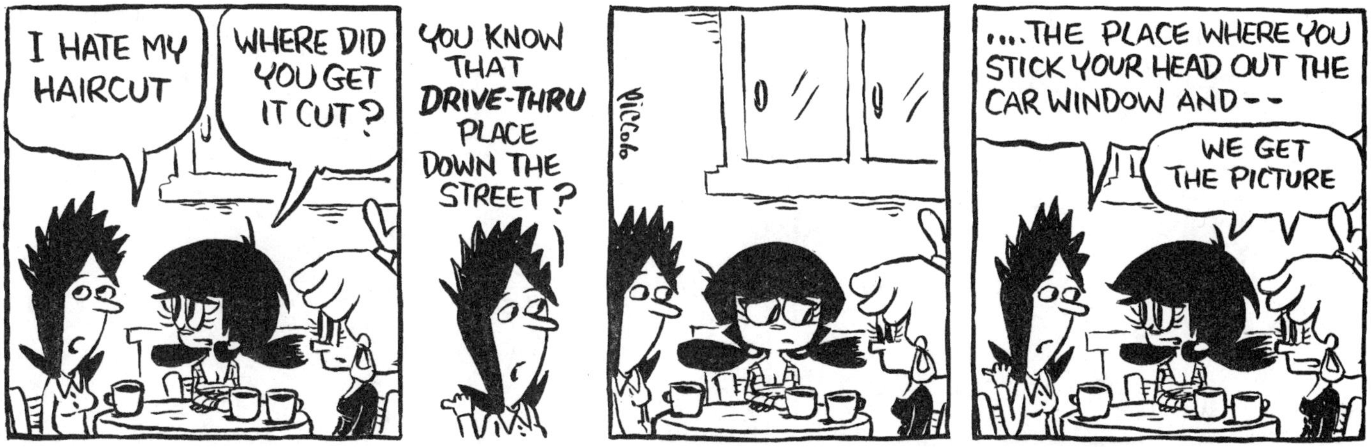
I HATE MY HAIRCUT
WHERE DID YOU GET IT CUT?
YOU KNOW THAT DRIVE-THRU PLACE DOWN THE STREET?
Piccolo
...THE PLACE WHERE YOU STICK YOUR HEAD OUT THE CAR WINDOW AND--
WE GET THE PICTURE

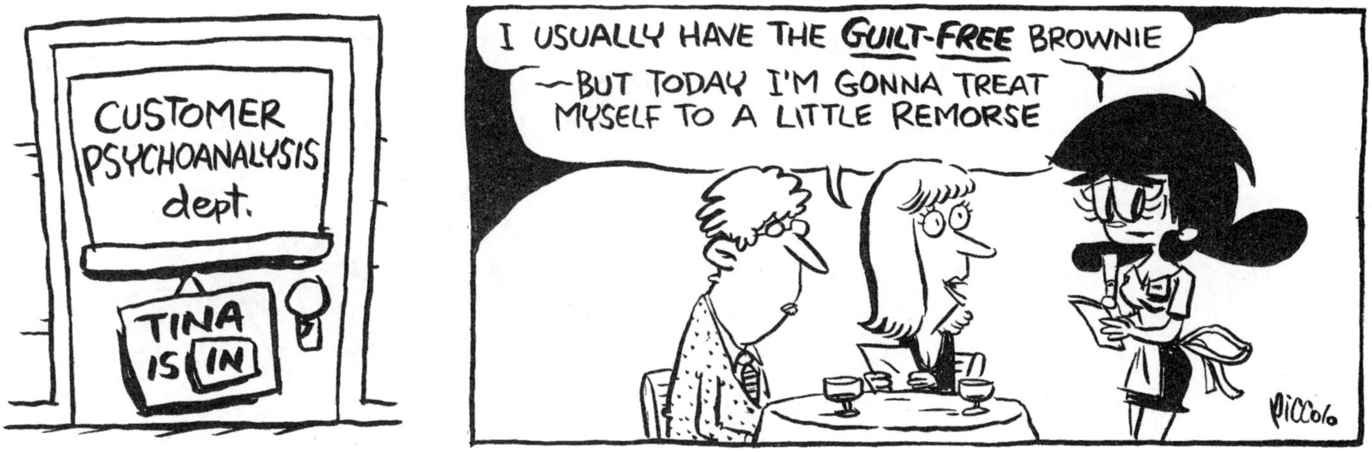
CUSTOMER PSYCHOANALYSIS dept.
TINA IS IN
I USUALLY HAVE THE GUILT-FREE BROWNIE
—BUT TODAY I'M GONNA TREAT MYSELF TO A LITTLE REMORSE
Piccolo

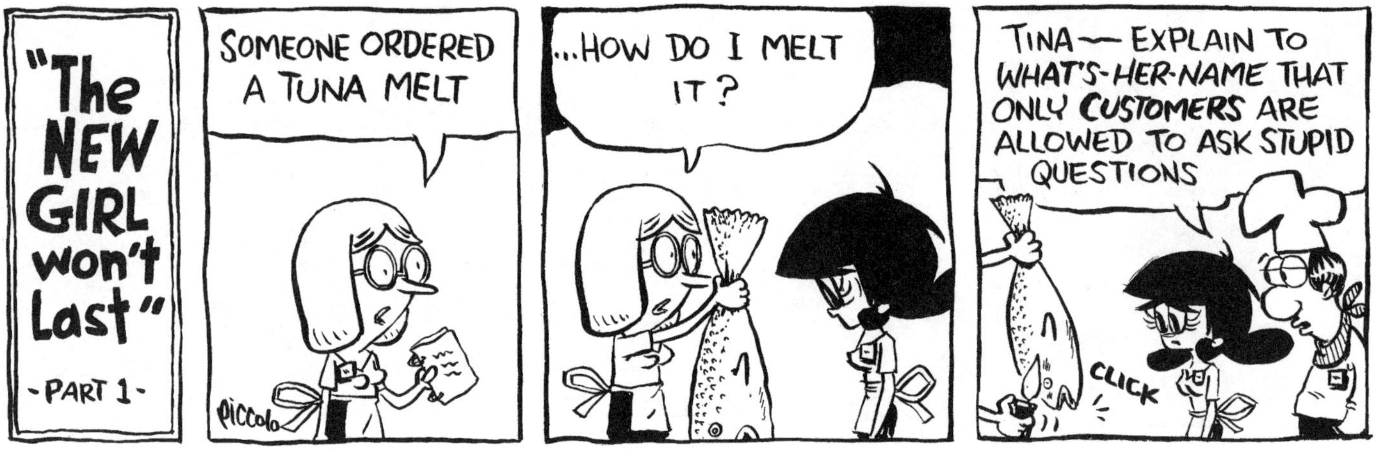
"The NEW GIRL won't Last"
-PART 1-
SOMEONE ORDERED A TUNA MELT
PICCOLO
...HOW DO I MELT IT?
TINA — EXPLAIN TO WHAT'S-HER-NAME THAT ONLY CUSTOMERS ARE ALLOWED TO ASK STUPID QUESTIONS
CLICK

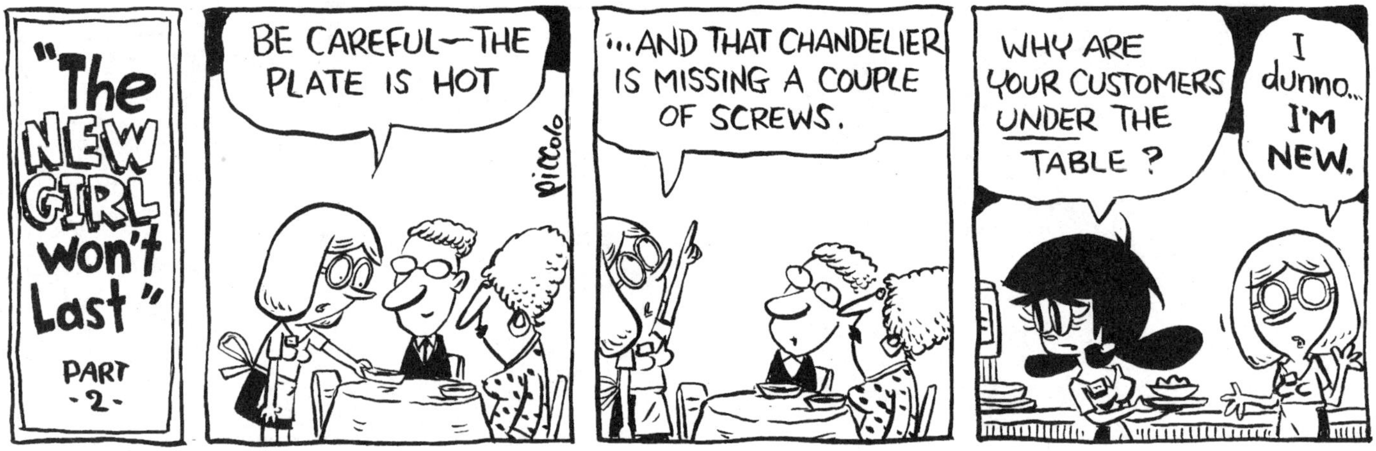
"The NEW GIRL won't Last"
PART -2-
BE CAREFUL — THE PLATE IS HOT
PICCOLO
...AND THAT CHANDELIER IS MISSING A COUPLE OF SCREWS.
WHY ARE YOUR CUSTOMERS UNDER THE TABLE?
I dunno... I'M NEW.

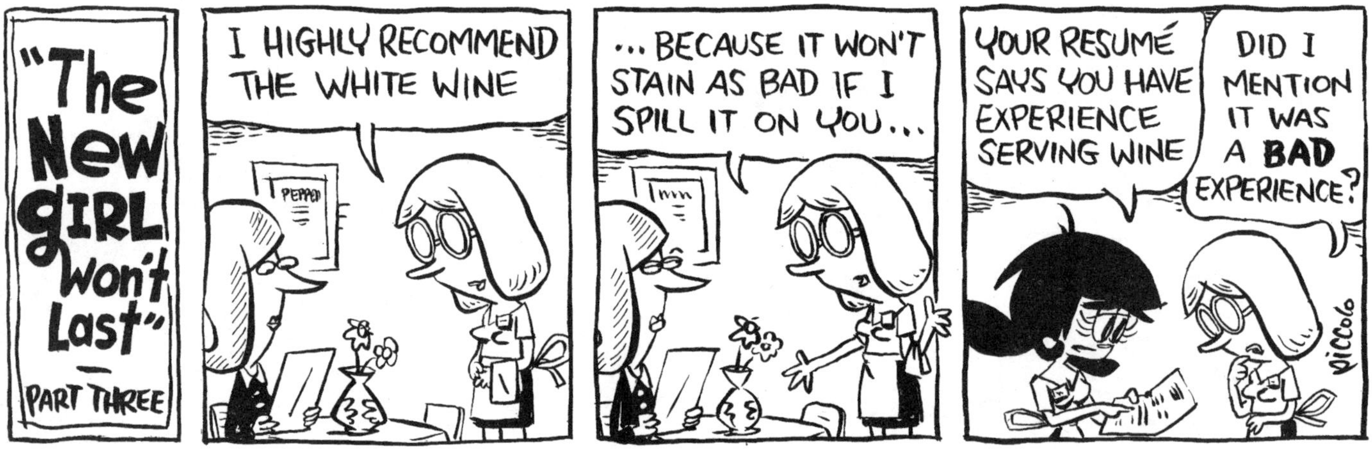
"The New GIRL won't Last"
PART THREE
I HIGHLY RECOMMEND THE WHITE WINE
PEPPER
...BECAUSE IT WON'T STAIN AS BAD IF I SPILL IT ON YOU...
YOUR RESUMÉ SAYS YOU HAVE EXPERIENCE SERVING WINE
DID I MENTION IT WAS A BAD EXPERIENCE?
PICCOLO

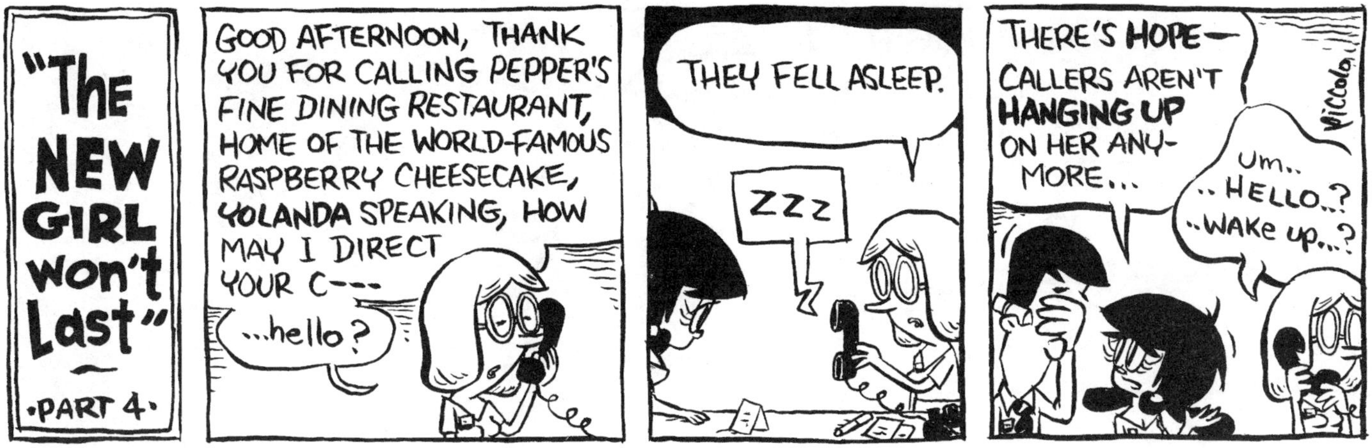
"The NEW GIRL won't Last"
•PART 4•
GOOD AFTERNOON, THANK YOU FOR CALLING PEPPER'S FINE DINING RESTAURANT, HOME OF THE WORLD-FAMOUS RASPBERRY CHEESECAKE, YOLANDA SPEAKING, HOW MAY I DIRECT YOUR C---
...hello?
THEY FELL ASLEEP.
ZZZ
THERE'S HOPE— CALLERS AREN'T HANGING UP ON HER ANY-MORE...
Um.. ..HELLO..? ..WAKE UP...?
Piccolo

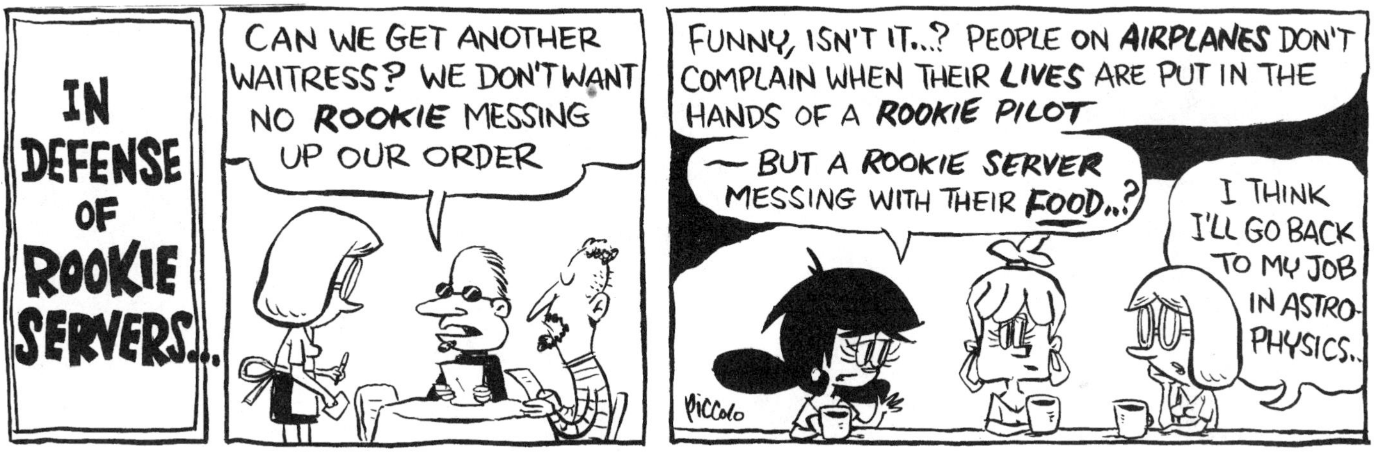
IN DEFENSE OF ROOKIE SERVERS...
CAN WE GET ANOTHER WAITRESS? WE DON'T WANT NO ROOKIE MESSING UP OUR ORDER
FUNNY, ISN'T IT...? PEOPLE ON AIRPLANES DON'T COMPLAIN WHEN THEIR LIVES ARE PUT IN THE HANDS OF A ROOKIE PILOT
—BUT A ROOKIE SERVER MESSING WITH THEIR FOOD..?
I THINK I'LL GO BACK TO MY JOB IN ASTRO-PHYSICS..
Piccolo

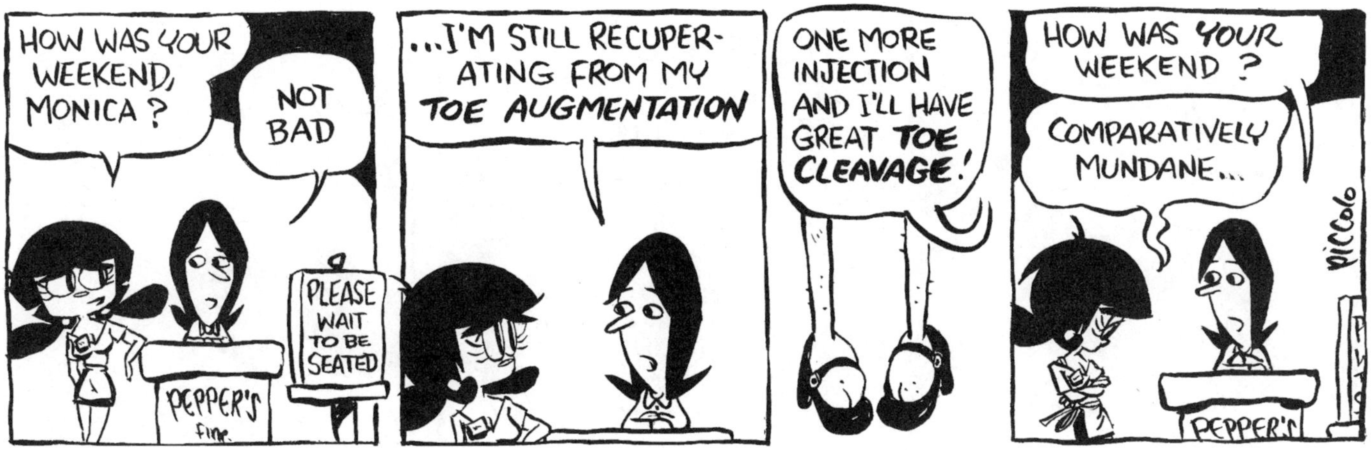
HOW WAS YOUR WEEKEND, MONICA?
NOT BAD
PLEASE WAIT TO BE SEATED
PEPPER'S Fine
...I'M STILL RECUPER-ATING FROM MY TOE AUGMENTATION
ONE MORE INJECTION AND I'LL HAVE GREAT TOE CLEAVAGE!
HOW WAS YOUR WEEKEND?
COMPARATIVELY MUNDANE...
PEPPER'S
Piccolo

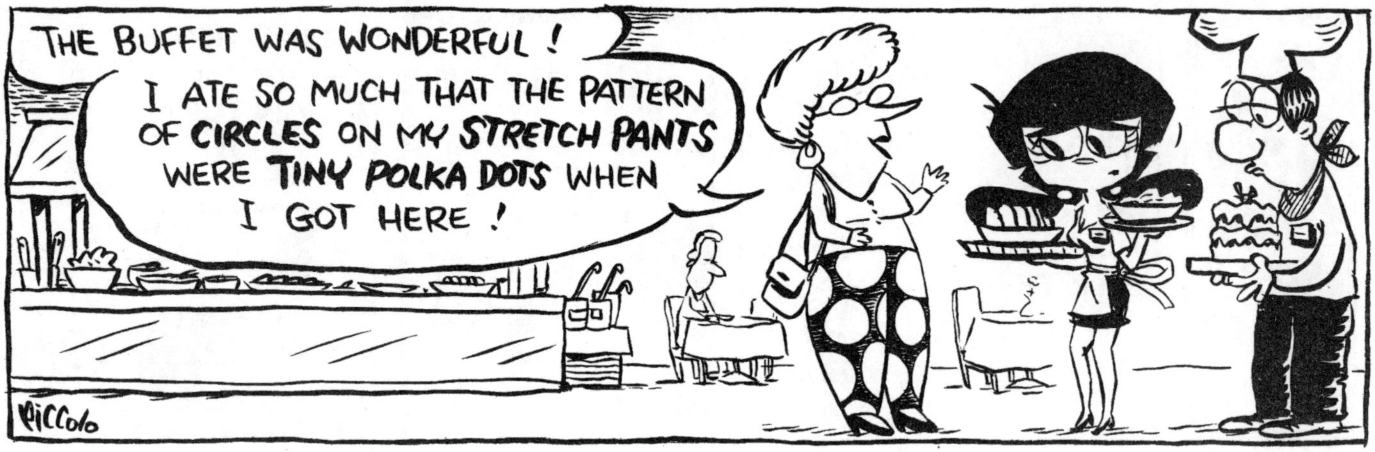
THE BUFFET WAS WONDERFUL !
I ATE SO MUCH THAT THE PATTERN OF CIRCLES ON MY STRETCH PANTS WERE TINY POLKA DOTS WHEN I GOT HERE !
Piccolo

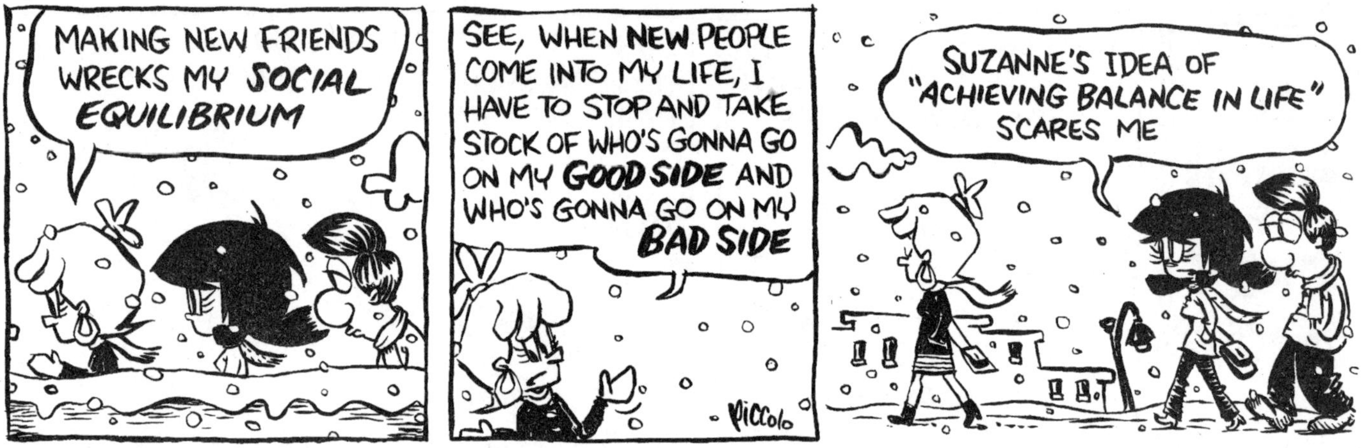
MAKING NEW FRIENDS WRECKS MY SOCIAL EQUILIBRIUM
SEE, WHEN NEW PEOPLE COME INTO MY LIFE, I HAVE TO STOP AND TAKE STOCK OF WHO'S GONNA GO ON MY GOOD SIDE AND WHO'S GONNA GO ON MY BAD SIDE
Piccolo
SUZANNE'S IDEA OF "ACHIEVING BALANCE IN LIFE" SCARES ME

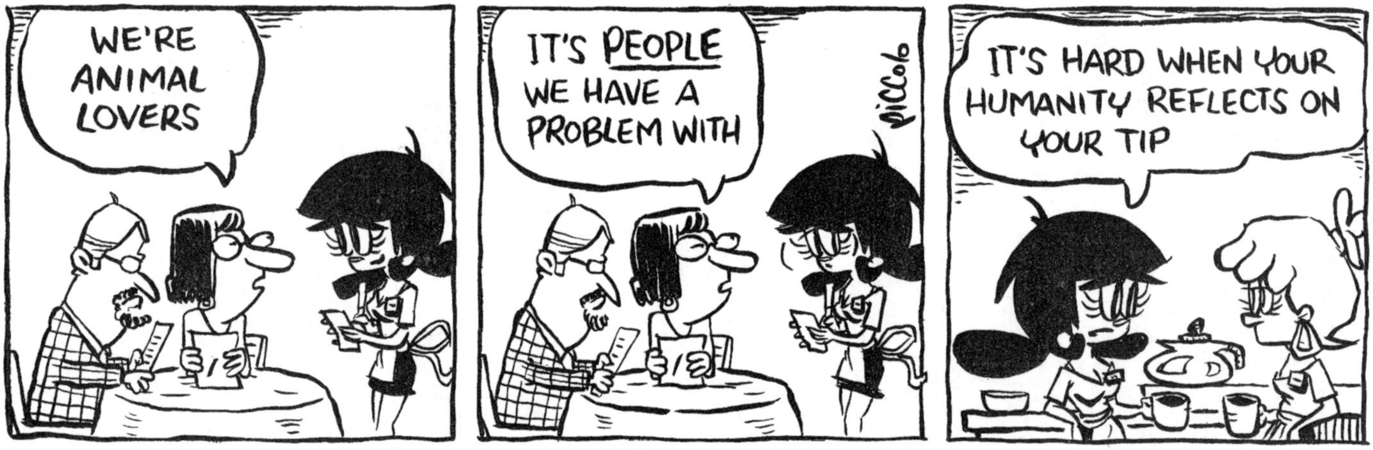
WE'RE ANIMAL LOVERS
IT'S PEOPLE WE HAVE A PROBLEM WITH
Piccolo
IT'S HARD WHEN YOUR HUMANITY REFLECTS ON YOUR TIP

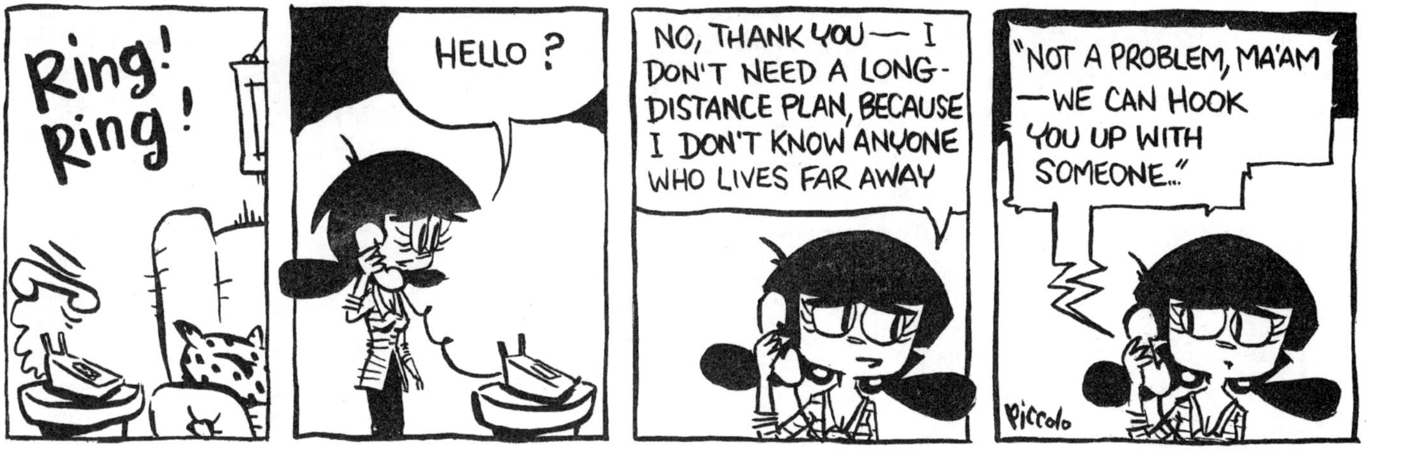
Ring! Ring!
HELLO ?
NO, THANK YOU — I DON'T NEED A LONG-DISTANCE PLAN, BECAUSE I DON'T KNOW ANYONE WHO LIVES FAR AWAY
"NOT A PROBLEM, MA'AM —WE CAN HOOK YOU UP WITH SOMEONE..."
Piccolo

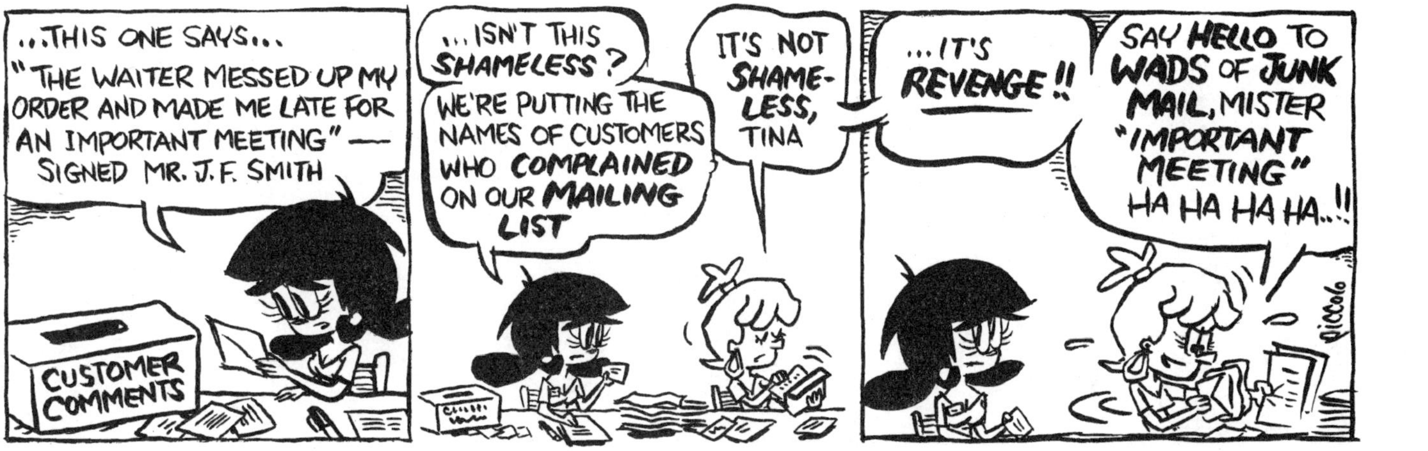
...THIS ONE SAYS... "THE WAITER MESSED UP MY ORDER AND MADE ME LATE FOR AN IMPORTANT MEETING" — SIGNED MR. J.F. SMITH
CUSTOMER COMMENTS
...ISN'T THIS SHAMELESS?
WE'RE PUTTING THE NAMES OF CUSTOMERS WHO COMPLAINED ON OUR MAILING LIST
IT'S NOT SHAMELESS, TINA
...IT'S REVENGE!!
SAY HELLO TO WADS OF JUNK MAIL, MISTER "IMPORTANT MEETING" HA HA HA HA..!!
Piccolo

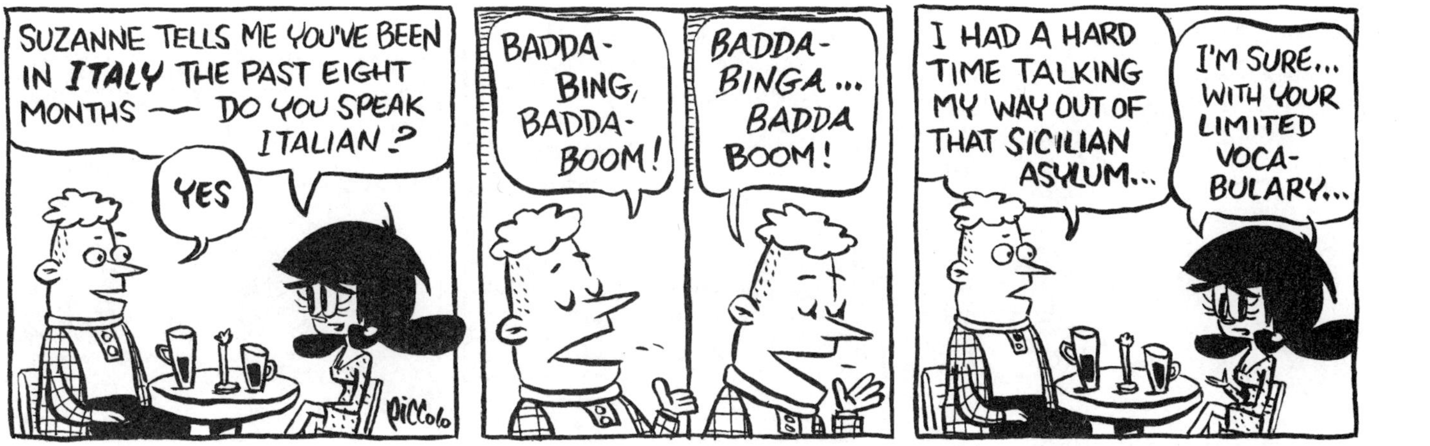
SUZANNE TELLS ME YOU'VE BEEN IN ITALY THE PAST EIGHT MONTHS — DO YOU SPEAK ITALIAN?
YES
Piccolo
BADDA-BING, BADDA-BOOM!
BADDA-BINGA... BADDA BOOM!
I HAD A HARD TIME TALKING MY WAY OUT OF THAT SICILIAN ASYLUM...
I'M SURE... WITH YOUR LIMITED VOCA-BULARY...

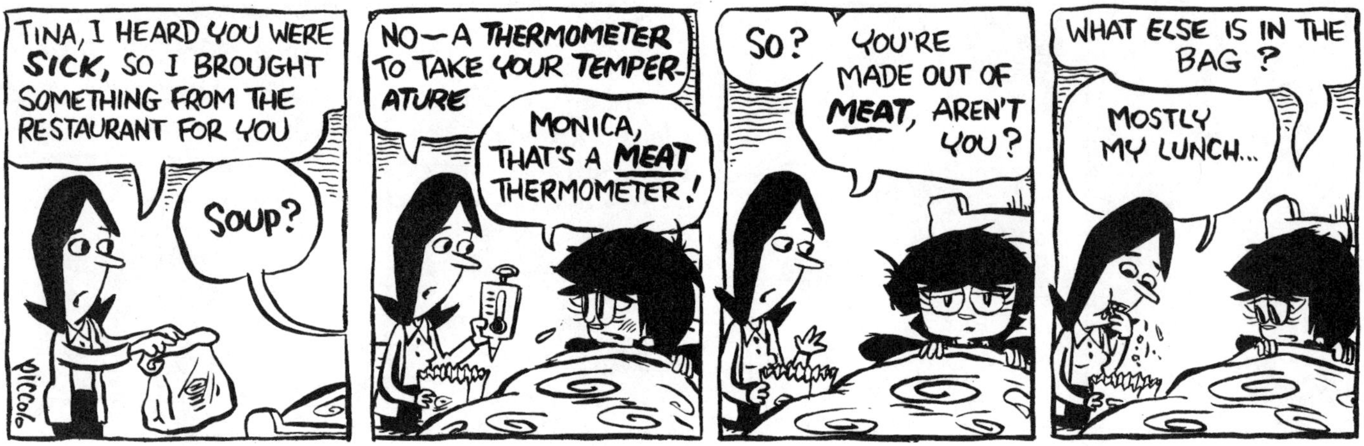
TINA, I HEARD YOU WERE SICK, SO I BROUGHT SOMETHING FROM THE RESTAURANT FOR YOU
SOUP?
NO— A THERMOMETER TO TAKE YOUR TEMPERATURE
MONICA, THAT'S A MEAT THERMOMETER!
SO?
YOU'RE MADE OUT OF MEAT, AREN'T YOU?
WHAT ELSE IS IN THE BAG?
MOSTLY MY LUNCH...
PICCOLO

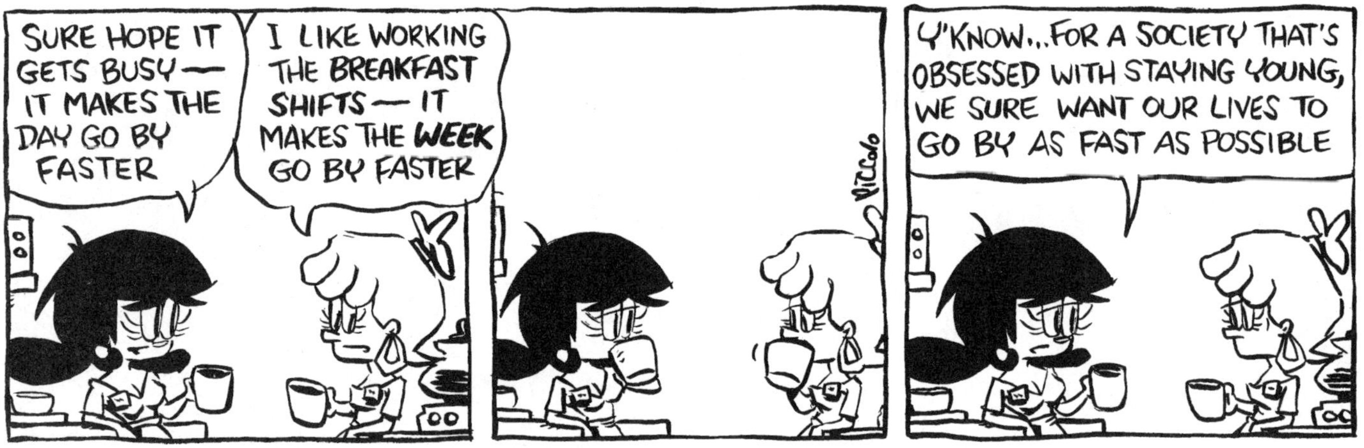
SURE HOPE IT GETS BUSY— IT MAKES THE DAY GO BY FASTER
I LIKE WORKING THE BREAKFAST SHIFTS— IT MAKES THE WEEK GO BY FASTER
PICCOLO
Y'KNOW...FOR A SOCIETY THAT'S OBSESSED WITH STAYING YOUNG, WE SURE WANT OUR LIVES TO GO BY AS FAST AS POSSIBLE

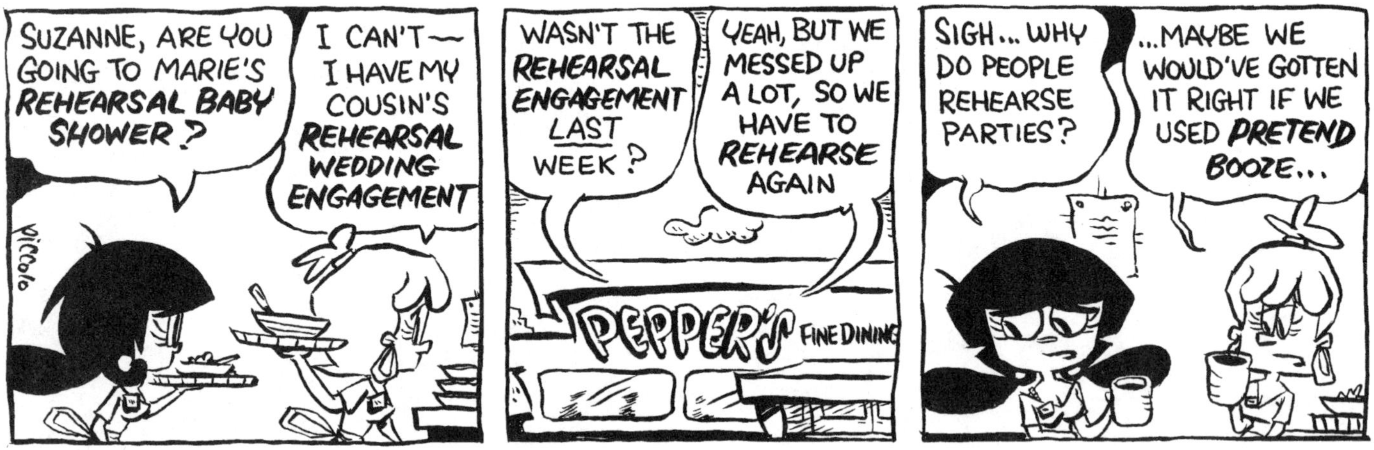
SUZANNE, ARE YOU GOING TO MARIE'S REHEARSAL BABY SHOWER?
I CAN'T— I HAVE MY COUSIN'S REHEARSAL WEDDING ENGAGEMENT
PICCOLO
WASN'T THE REHEARSAL ENGAGEMENT LAST WEEK?
YEAH, BUT WE MESSED UP A LOT, SO WE HAVE TO REHEARSE AGAIN
PEPPER'S FINE DINING
SIGH... WHY DO PEOPLE REHEARSE PARTIES?
...MAYBE WE WOULD'VE GOTTEN IT RIGHT IF WE USED PRETEND BOOZE...

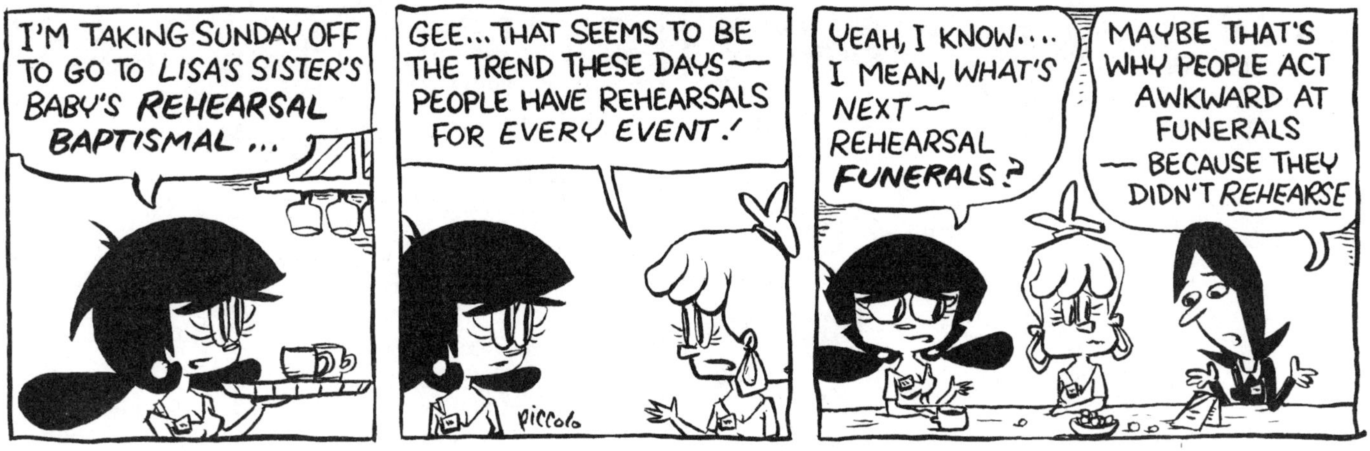
I'M TAKING SUNDAY OFF TO GO TO LISA'S SISTER'S BABY'S REHEARSAL BAPTISMAL ...
GEE... THAT SEEMS TO BE THE TREND THESE DAYS — PEOPLE HAVE REHEARSALS FOR EVERY EVENT!
piccolo
YEAH, I KNOW.... I MEAN, WHAT'S NEXT — REHEARSAL FUNERALS?
MAYBE THAT'S WHY PEOPLE ACT AWKWARD AT FUNERALS — BECAUSE THEY DIDN'T REHEARSE

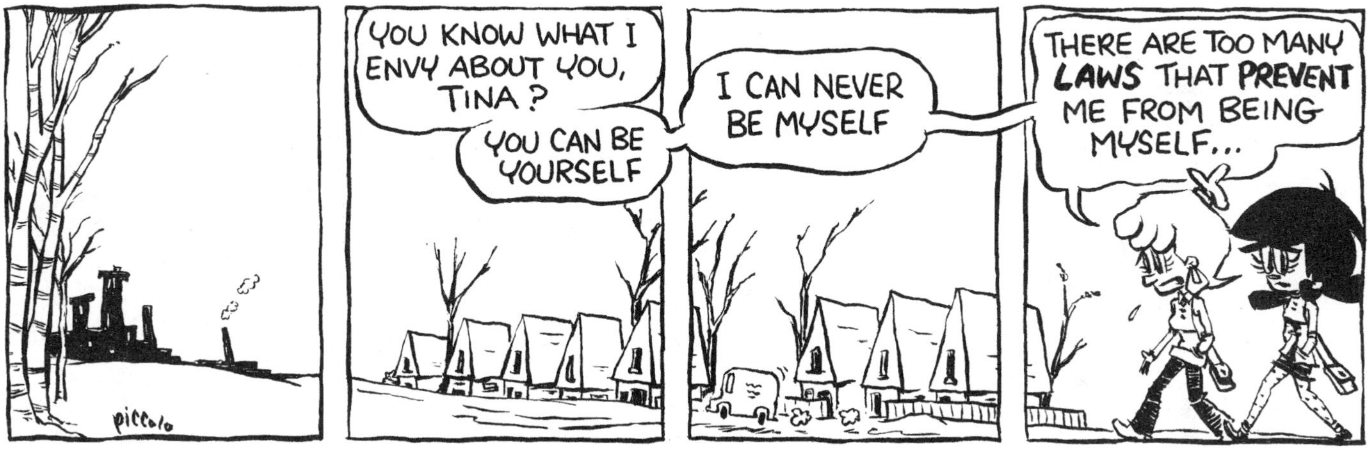
piccolo
YOU KNOW WHAT I ENVY ABOUT YOU, TINA?
YOU CAN BE YOURSELF
I CAN NEVER BE MYSELF
THERE ARE TOO MANY LAWS THAT PREVENT ME FROM BEING MYSELF...

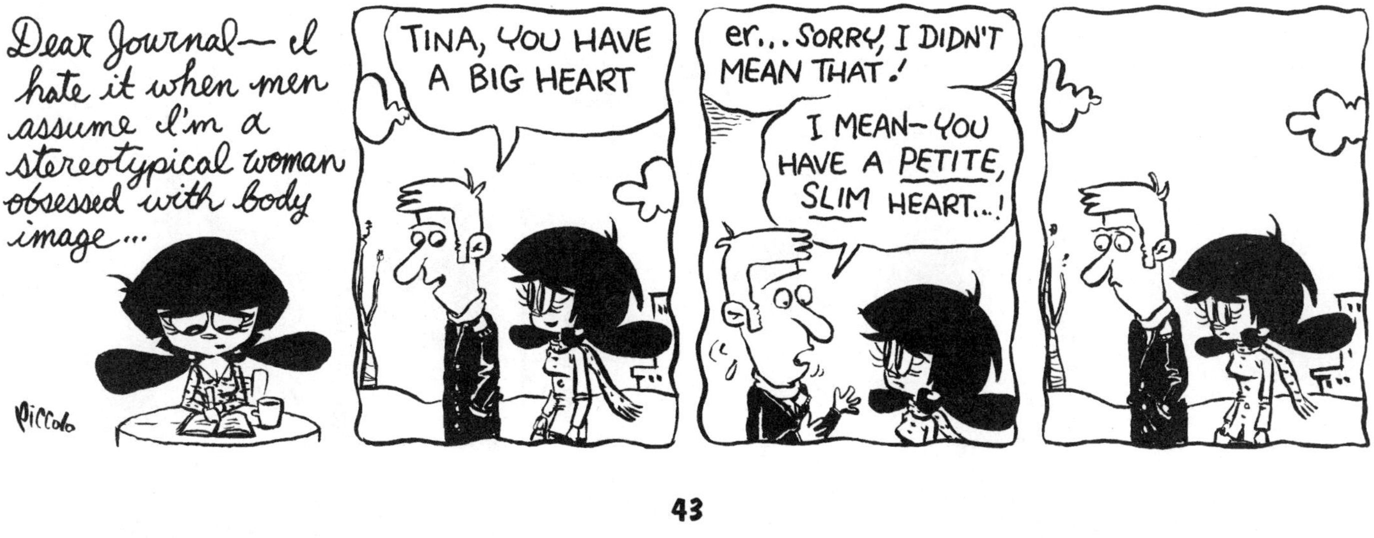
Dear Journal— I hate it when men assume I'm a stereotypical woman obsessed with body image...
piccolo
TINA, YOU HAVE A BIG HEART
er... SORRY, I DIDN'T MEAN THAT!
I MEAN— YOU HAVE A PETITE, SLIM HEART...!

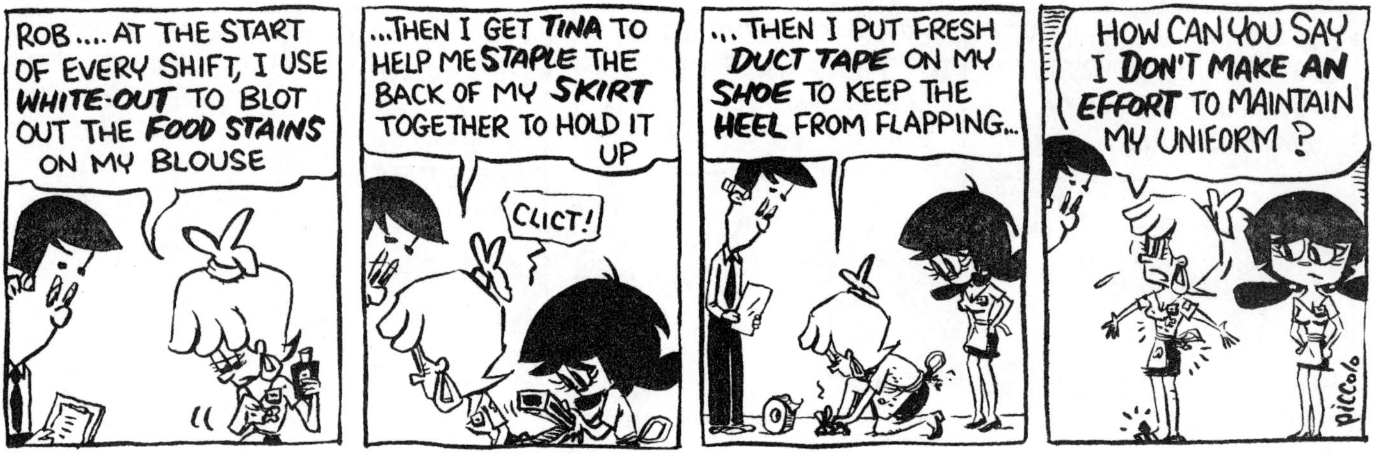
ROB.... AT THE START OF EVERY SHIFT, I USE WHITE-OUT TO BLOT OUT THE FOOD STAINS ON MY BLOUSE
...THEN I GET TINA TO HELP ME STAPLE THE BACK OF MY SKIRT TOGETHER TO HOLD IT UP
CLICT!
...THEN I PUT FRESH DUCT TAPE ON MY SHOE TO KEEP THE HEEL FROM FLAPPING...
HOW CAN YOU SAY I DON'T MAKE AN EFFORT TO MAINTAIN MY UNIFORM ?
piccolo

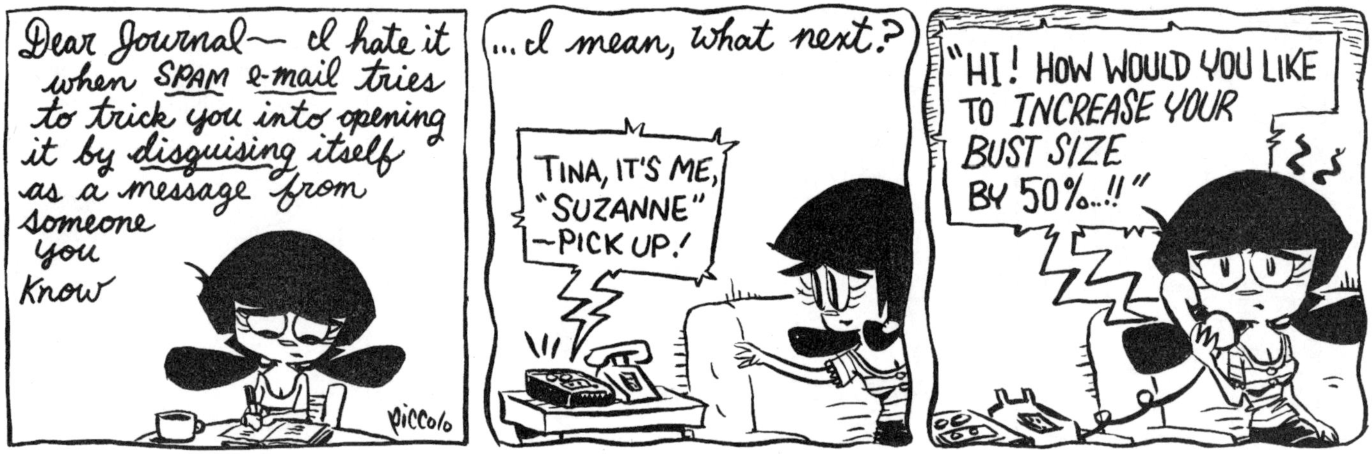
Dear Journal— I hate it when SPAM e-mail tries to trick you into opening it by disguising itself as a message from someone you know
piccolo
...I mean, what next?
TINA, IT'S ME, "SUZANNE" —PICK UP!
"HI! HOW WOULD YOU LIKE TO INCREASE YOUR BUST SIZE BY 50%...!!"

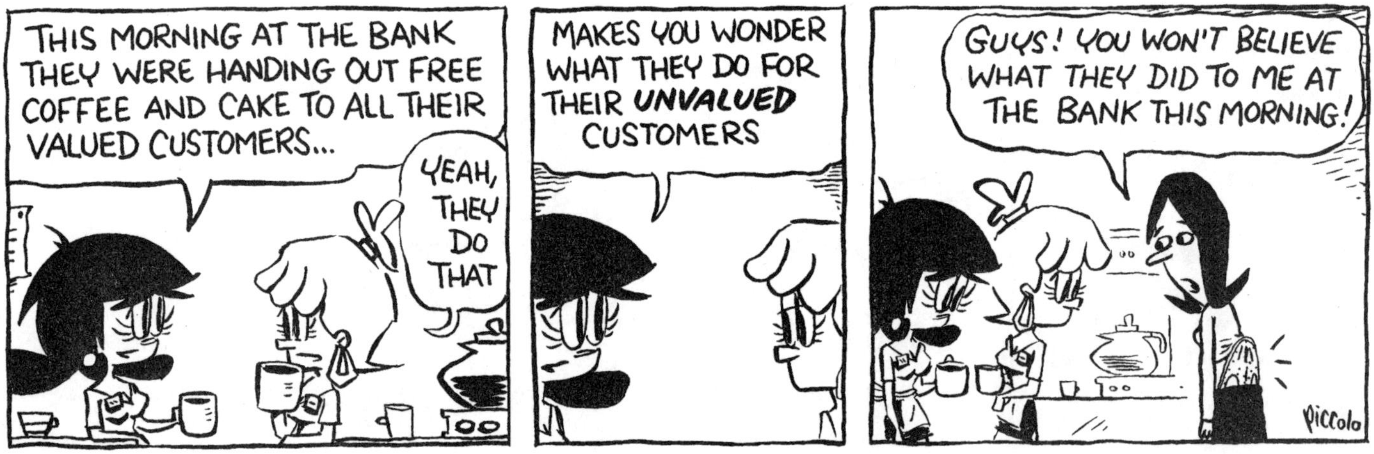
THIS MORNING AT THE BANK THEY WERE HANDING OUT FREE COFFEE AND CAKE TO ALL THEIR VALUED CUSTOMERS...
YEAH, THEY DO THAT
MAKES YOU WONDER WHAT THEY DO FOR THEIR UNVALUED CUSTOMERS
GUYS! YOU WON'T BELIEVE WHAT THEY DID TO ME AT THE BANK THIS MORNING!
piccolo

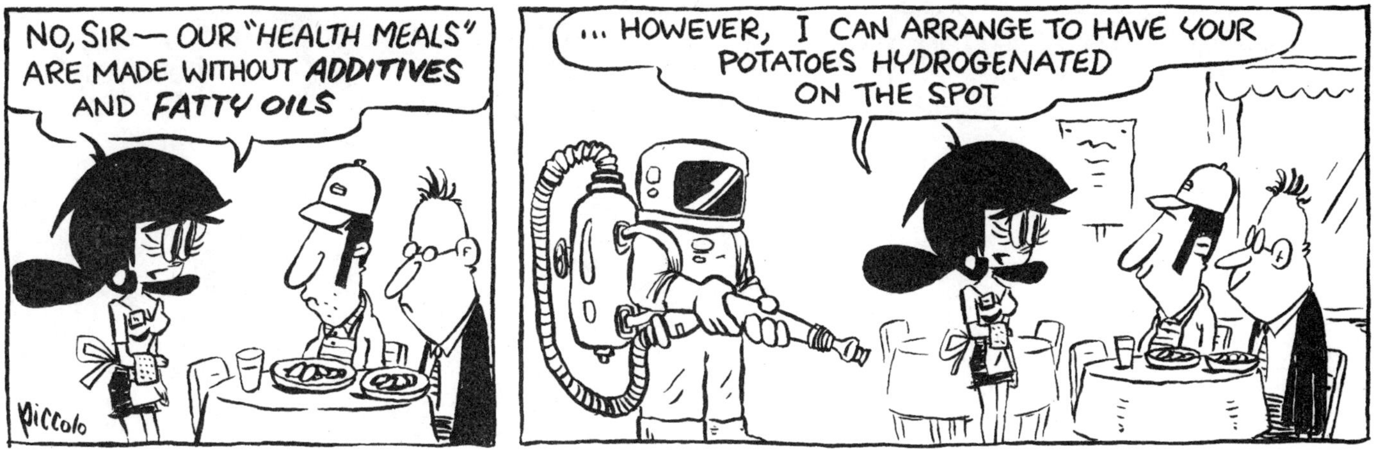
NO, SIR — OUR "HEALTH MEALS" ARE MADE WITHOUT ***ADDITIVES*** AND ***FATTY OILS***
piccolo
... HOWEVER, I CAN ARRANGE TO HAVE YOUR POTATOES HYDROGENATED ON THE SPOT

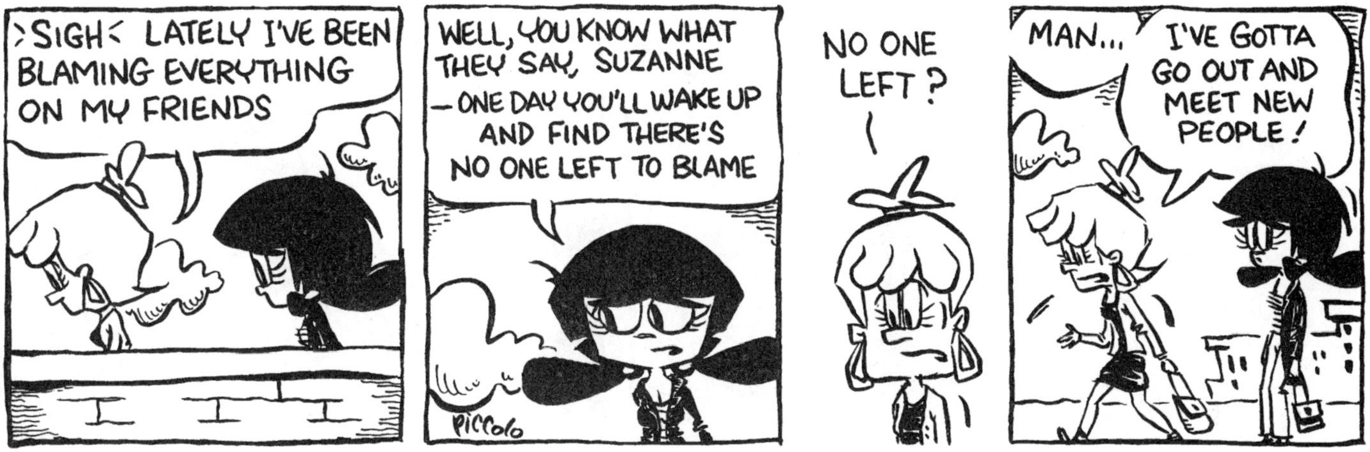
>SIGH< LATELY I'VE BEEN BLAMING EVERYTHING ON MY FRIENDS
WELL, YOU KNOW WHAT THEY SAY, SUZANNE — ONE DAY YOU'LL WAKE UP AND FIND THERE'S NO ONE LEFT TO BLAME
piccolo
NO ONE LEFT ?
MAN...
I'VE GOTTA GO OUT AND MEET NEW PEOPLE !

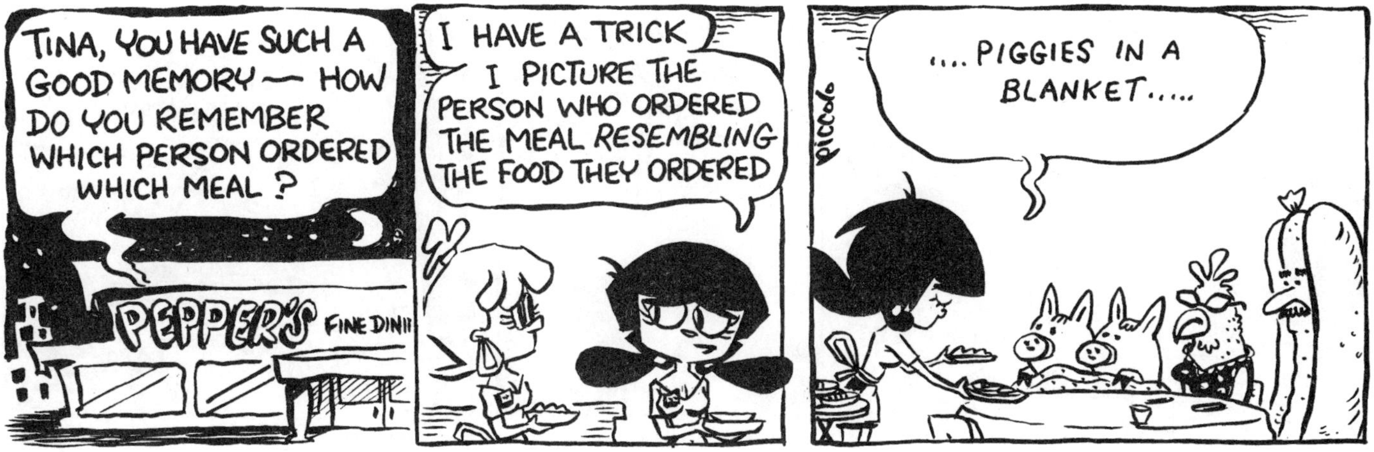
TINA, YOU HAVE SUCH A GOOD MEMORY — HOW DO YOU REMEMBER WHICH PERSON ORDERED WHICH MEAL ?
PEPPER'S
FINE DINI
I HAVE A TRICK
I PICTURE THE PERSON WHO ORDERED THE MEAL *RESEMBLING* THE FOOD THEY ORDERED
piccolo
.... PIGGIES IN A BLANKET.....

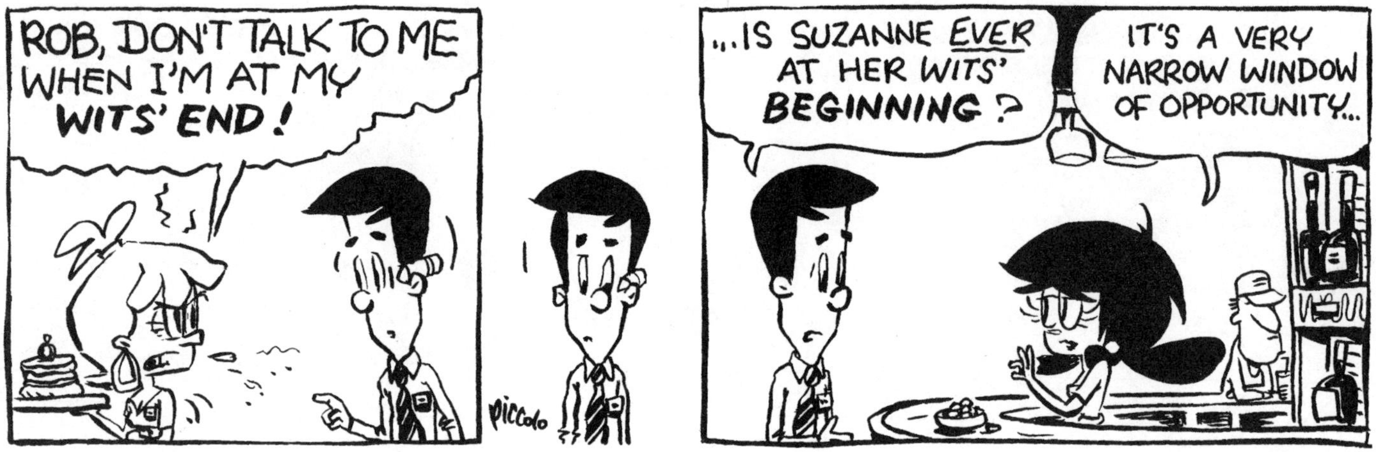
ROB, DON'T TALK TO ME WHEN I'M AT MY **WITS' END!**
...IS SUZANNE EVER AT HER WITS' **BEGINNING?**
IT'S A VERY NARROW WINDOW OF OPPORTUNITY...

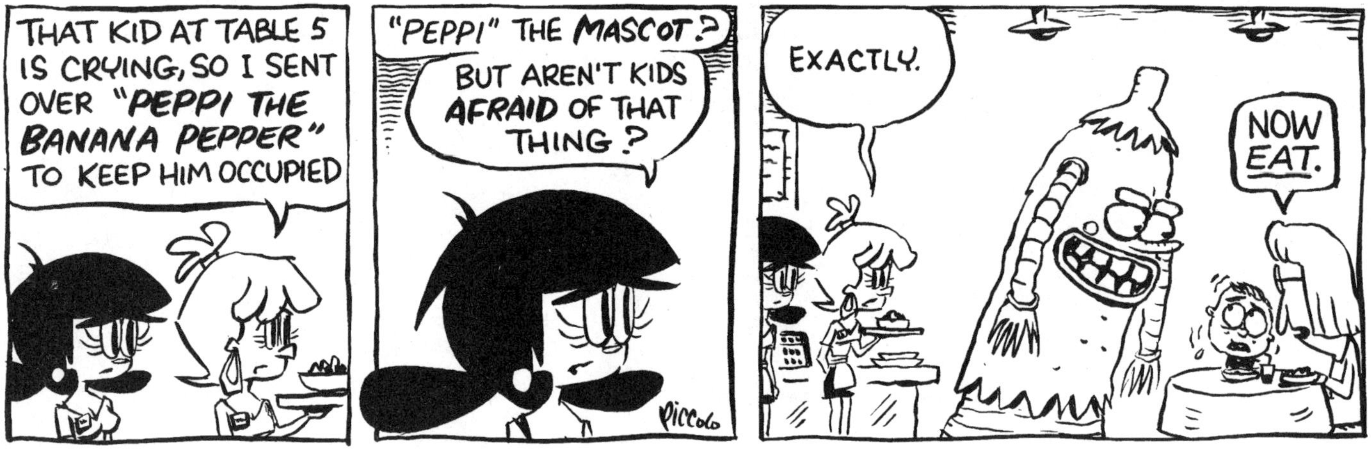
THAT KID AT TABLE 5 IS CRYING, SO I SENT OVER **"PEPPI THE BANANA PEPPER"** TO KEEP HIM OCCUPIED
"PEPPI" THE **MASCOT?**
BUT AREN'T KIDS **AFRAID** OF THAT THING?
EXACTLY.
NOW EAT.

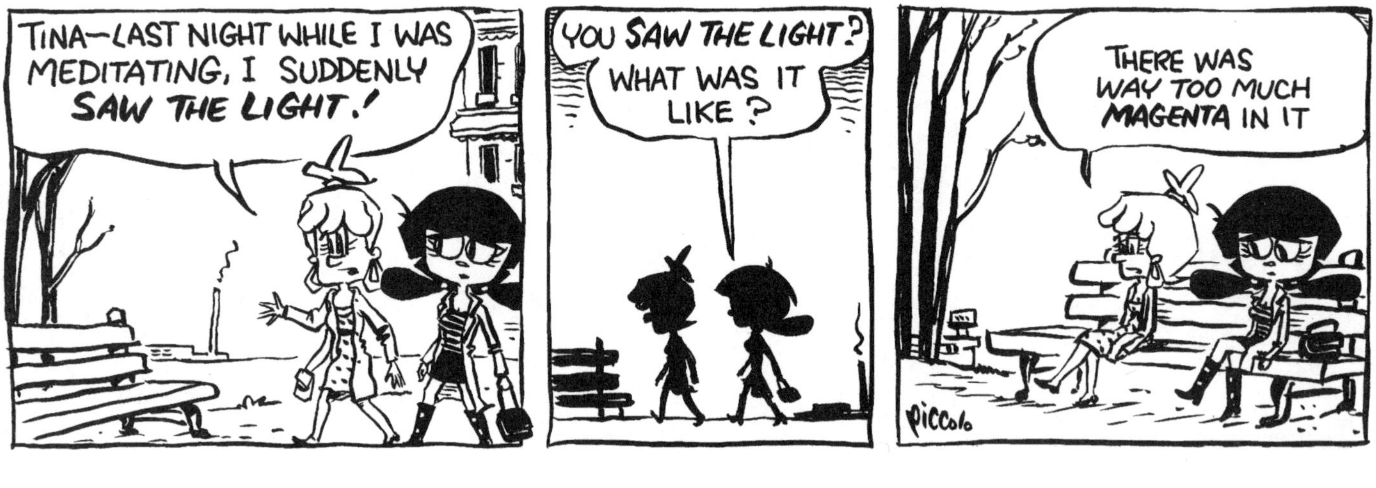
TINA—LAST NIGHT WHILE I WAS MEDITATING, I SUDDENLY **SAW THE LIGHT!**
YOU **SAW THE LIGHT?**
WHAT WAS IT LIKE?
THERE WAS WAY TOO MUCH **MAGENTA** IN IT

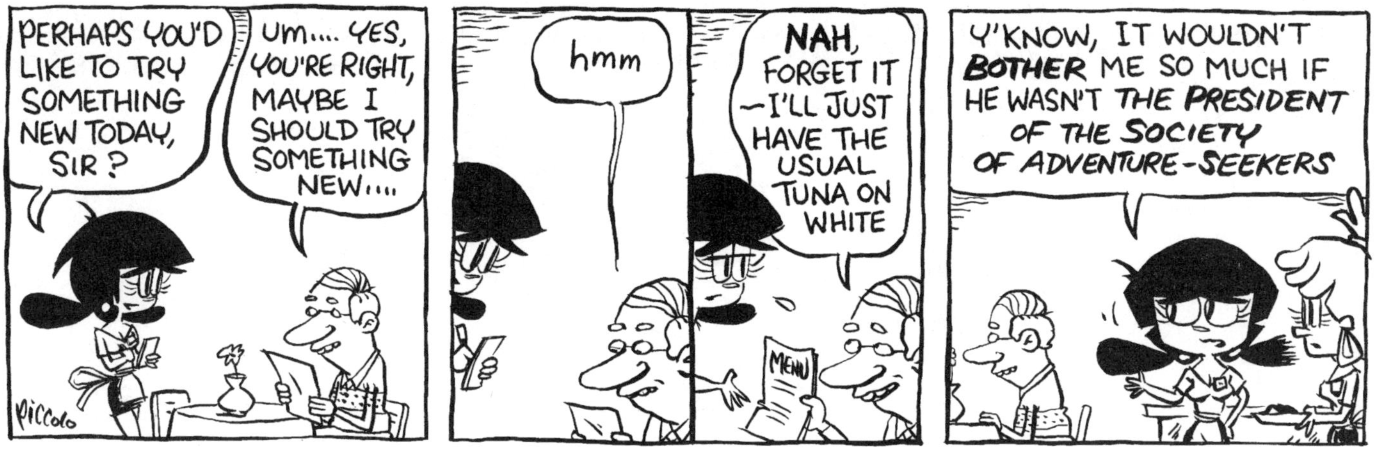
PERHAPS YOU'D LIKE TO TRY SOMETHING NEW TODAY, SIR?
UM.... YES, YOU'RE RIGHT, MAYBE I SHOULD TRY SOMETHING NEW....
Piccolo
hmm
NAH, FORGET IT —I'LL JUST HAVE THE USUAL TUNA ON WHITE
MENU
Y'KNOW, IT WOULDN'T **BOTHER** ME SO MUCH IF HE WASN'T ***THE PRESIDENT OF THE SOCIETY OF ADVENTURE-SEEKERS***

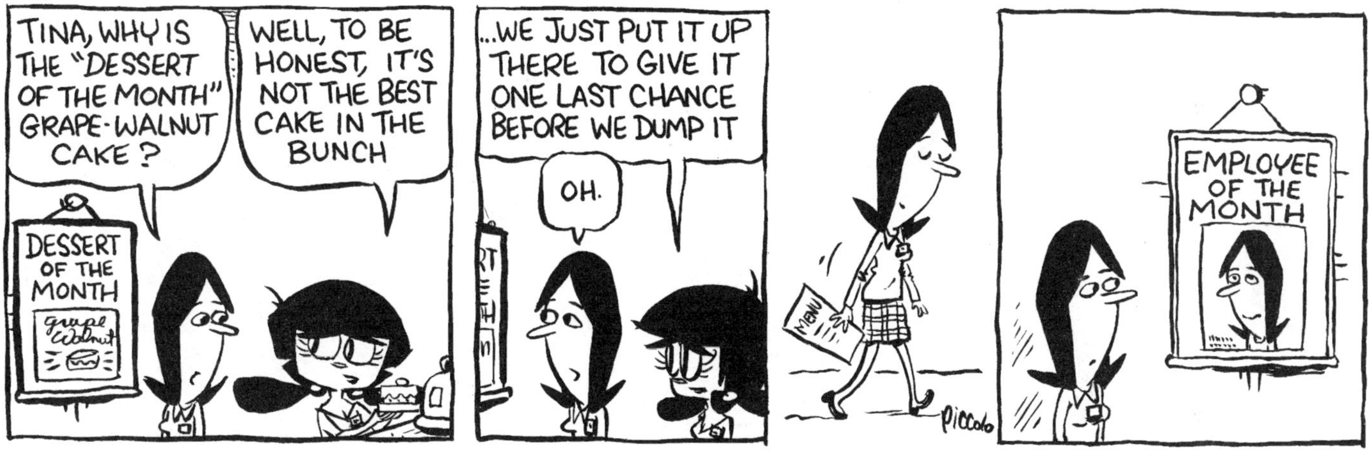
TINA, WHY IS THE "DESSERT OF THE MONTH" GRAPE-WALNUT CAKE?
WELL, TO BE HONEST, IT'S NOT THE BEST CAKE IN THE BUNCH
DESSERT OF THE MONTH
grape Walnut
...WE JUST PUT IT UP THERE TO GIVE IT ONE LAST CHANCE BEFORE WE DUMP IT
OH.
MENU
Piccolo
EMPLOYEE OF THE MONTH

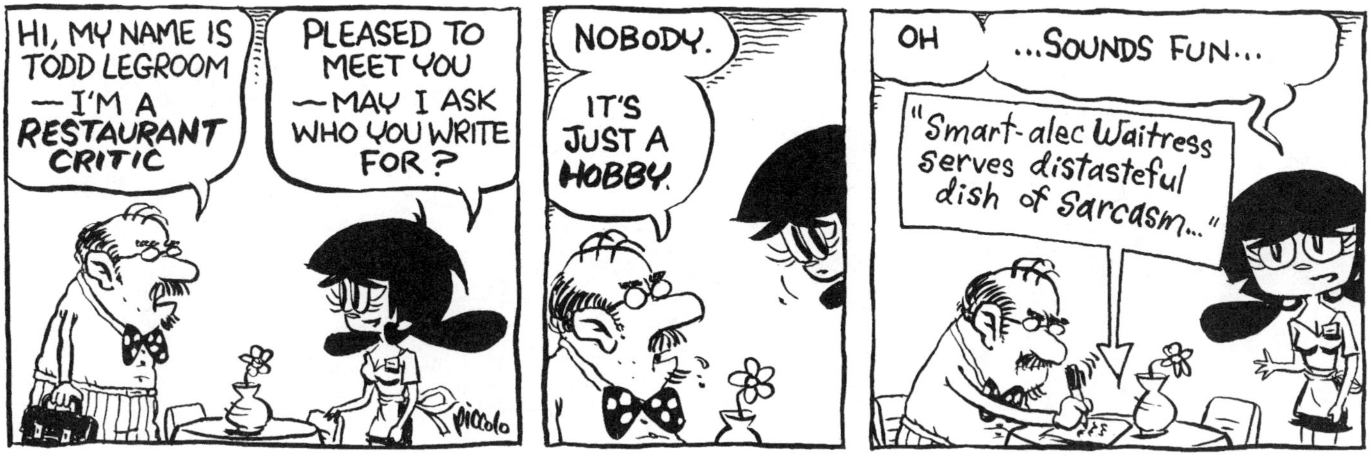
HI, MY NAME IS TODD LEGROOM —I'M A **RESTAURANT CRITIC**
PLEASED TO MEET YOU —MAY I ASK WHO YOU WRITE FOR?
Piccolo
NOBODY.
IT'S JUST A **HOBBY**.
OH
...SOUNDS FUN...
"Smart-alec Waitress serves distasteful dish of sarcasm..."

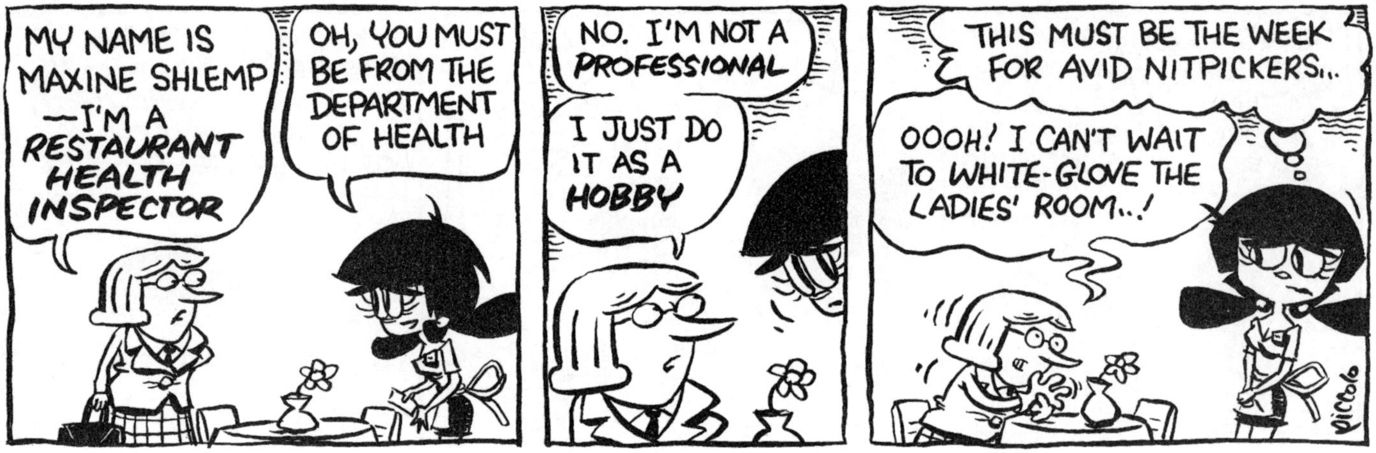
MY NAME IS MAXINE SHLEMP —I'M A **RESTAURANT HEALTH INSPECTOR**
OH, YOU MUST BE FROM THE DEPARTMENT OF HEALTH
NO. I'M NOT A **PROFESSIONAL**
I JUST DO IT AS A **HOBBY**
THIS MUST BE THE WEEK FOR AVID NITPICKERS...
OOOH! I CAN'T WAIT TO WHITE-GLOVE THE LADIES' ROOM..!
PICCOLO

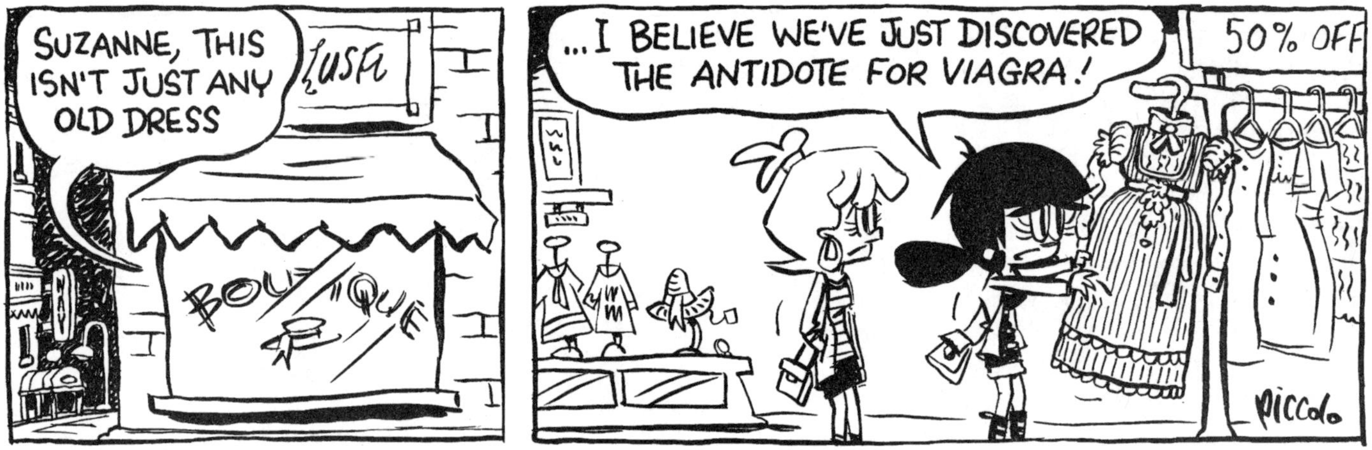
SUZANNE, THIS ISN'T JUST ANY OLD DRESS
...I BELIEVE WE'VE JUST DISCOVERED THE ANTIDOTE FOR VIAGRA!
50% OFF
PICCOLO

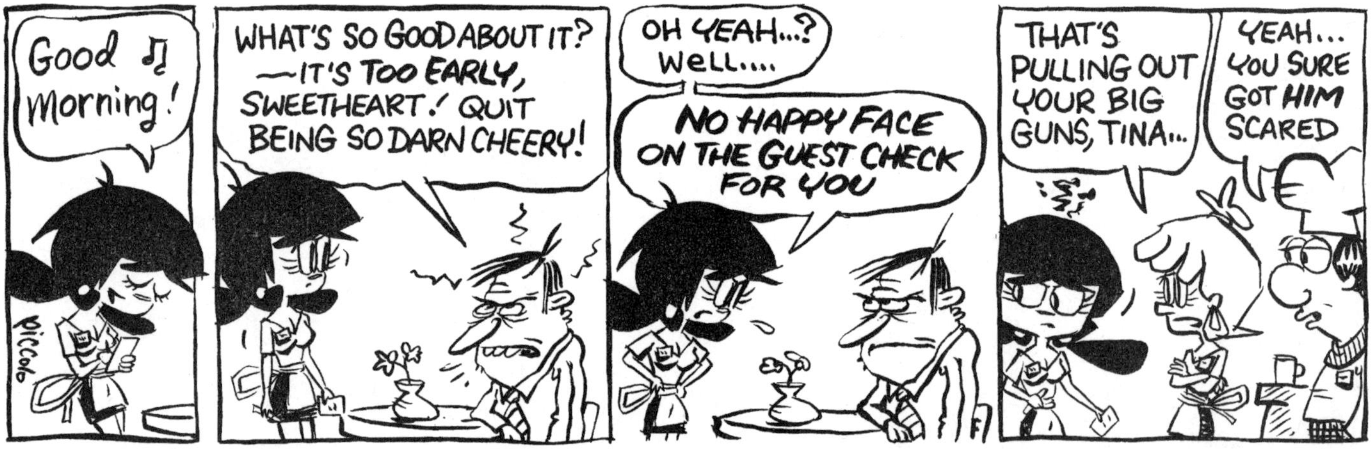
Good ♫ Morning!
PICCOLO
WHAT'S SO GOOD ABOUT IT? —IT'S **TOO EARLY**, SWEETHEART! QUIT BEING SO DARN CHEERY!
OH YEAH...? WELL....
NO HAPPY FACE ON THE GUEST CHECK FOR YOU
THAT'S PULLING OUT YOUR BIG GUNS, TINA...
YEAH... YOU SURE GOT **HIM** SCARED

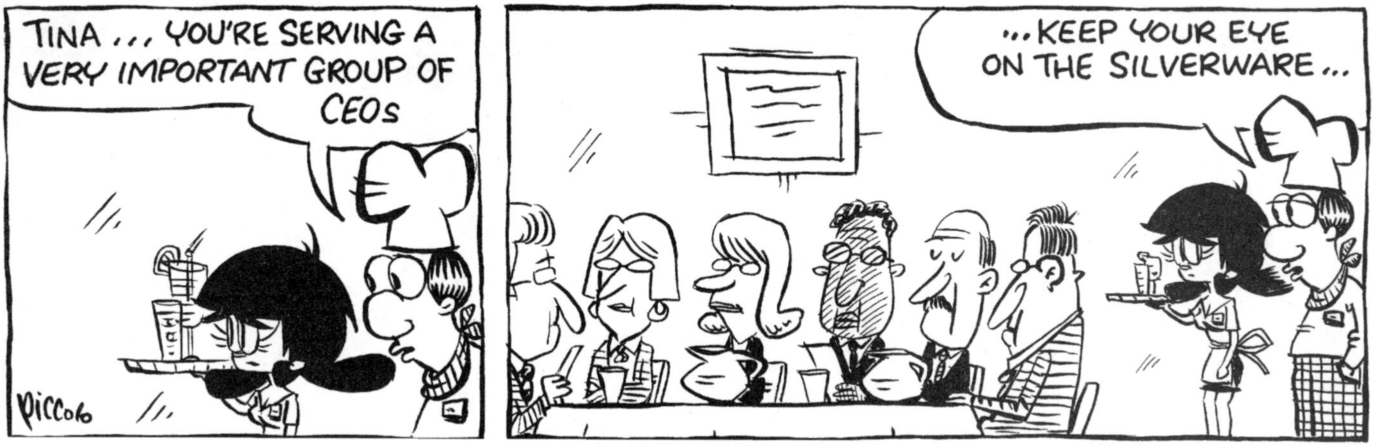
TINA ... YOU'RE SERVING A VERY IMPORTANT GROUP OF CEOs
...KEEP YOUR EYE ON THE SILVERWARE...

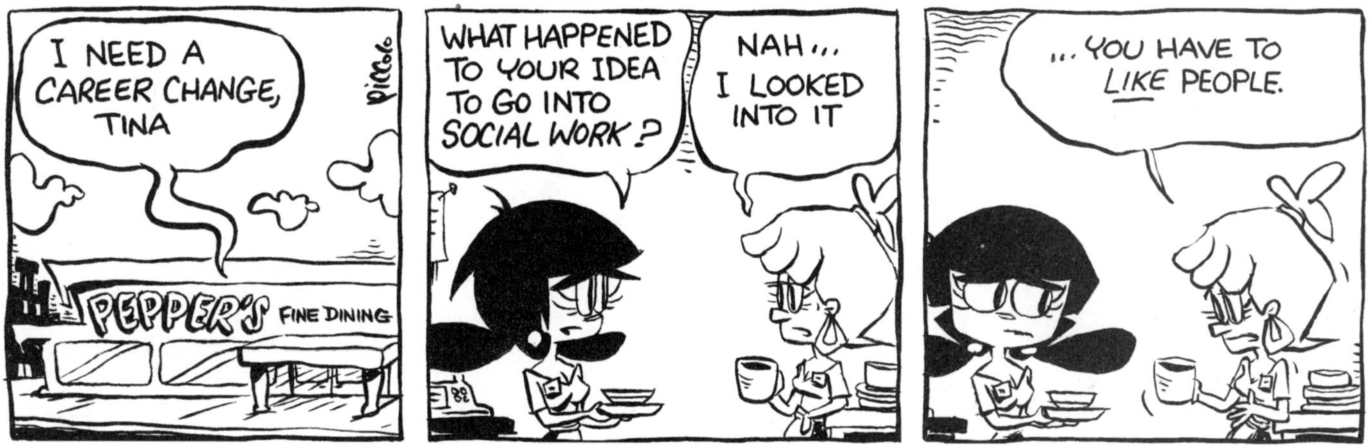
I NEED A CAREER CHANGE, TINA
PEPPER'S FINE DINING
WHAT HAPPENED TO YOUR IDEA TO GO INTO SOCIAL WORK ?
NAH... I LOOKED INTO IT
...YOU HAVE TO LIKE PEOPLE.

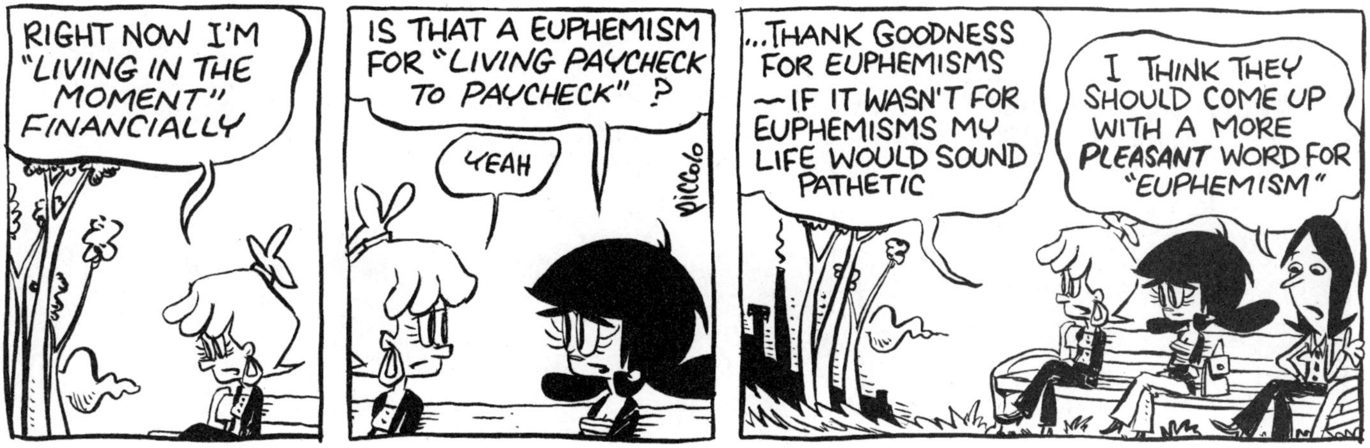
RIGHT NOW I'M "LIVING IN THE MOMENT" FINANCIALLY
IS THAT A EUPHEMISM FOR "LIVING PAYCHECK TO PAYCHECK" ?
YEAH
...THANK GOODNESS FOR EUPHEMISMS —IF IT WASN'T FOR EUPHEMISMS MY LIFE WOULD SOUND PATHETIC
I THINK THEY SHOULD COME UP WITH A MORE PLEASANT WORD FOR "EUPHEMISM"

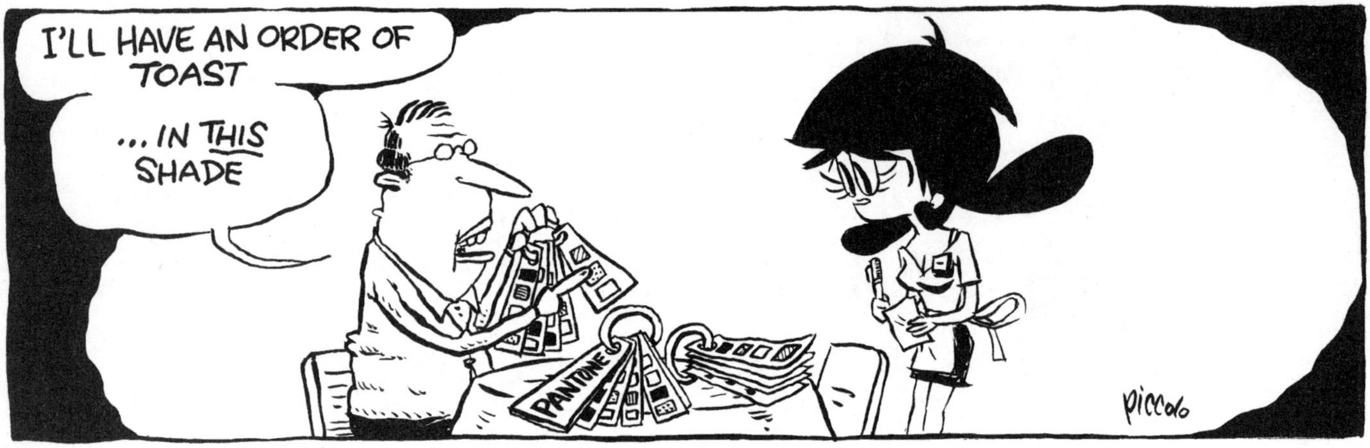
I'LL HAVE AN ORDER OF TOAST
...IN THIS SHADE
PANTONE
piccolo

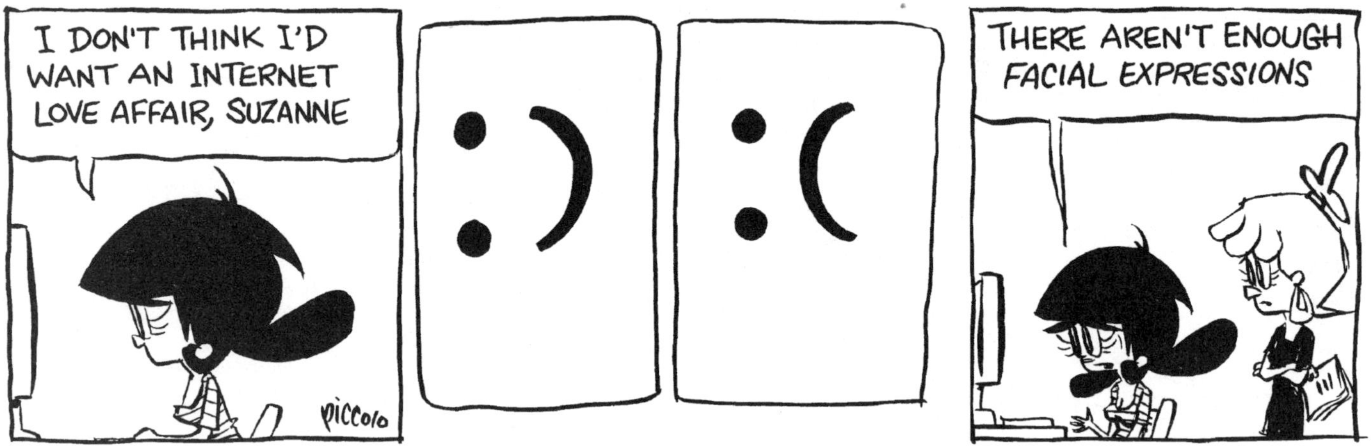
I DON'T THINK I'D WANT AN INTERNET LOVE AFFAIR, SUZANNE
:)
:(
THERE AREN'T ENOUGH FACIAL EXPRESSIONS
piccolo

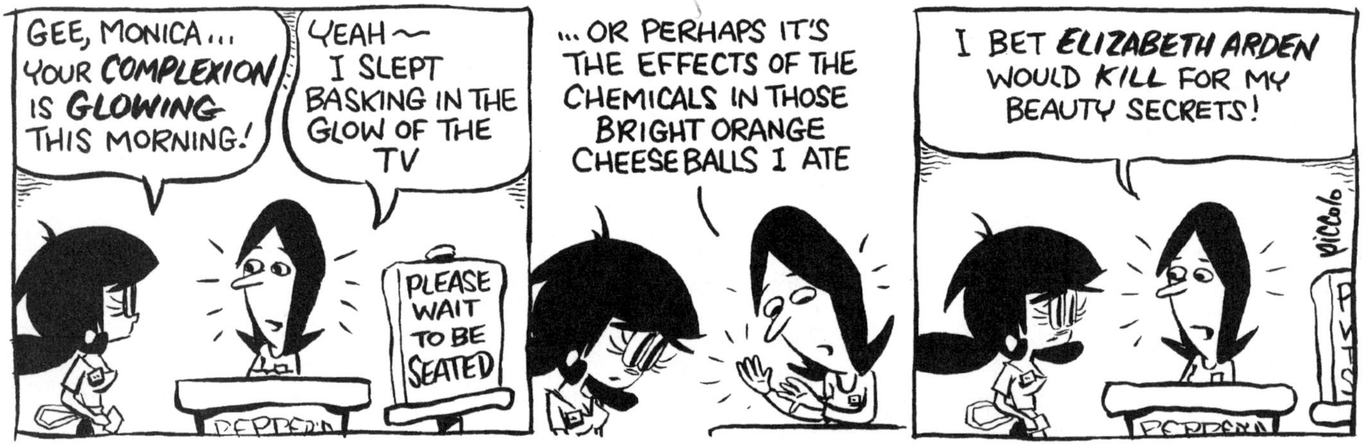
GEE, MONICA... YOUR COMPLEXION IS GLOWING THIS MORNING!
YEAH ~ I SLEPT BASKING IN THE GLOW OF THE TV
PLEASE WAIT TO BE SEATED
...OR PERHAPS IT'S THE EFFECTS OF THE CHEMICALS IN THOSE BRIGHT ORANGE CHEESEBALLS I ATE
I BET ELIZABETH ARDEN WOULD KILL FOR MY BEAUTY SECRETS!
piccolo

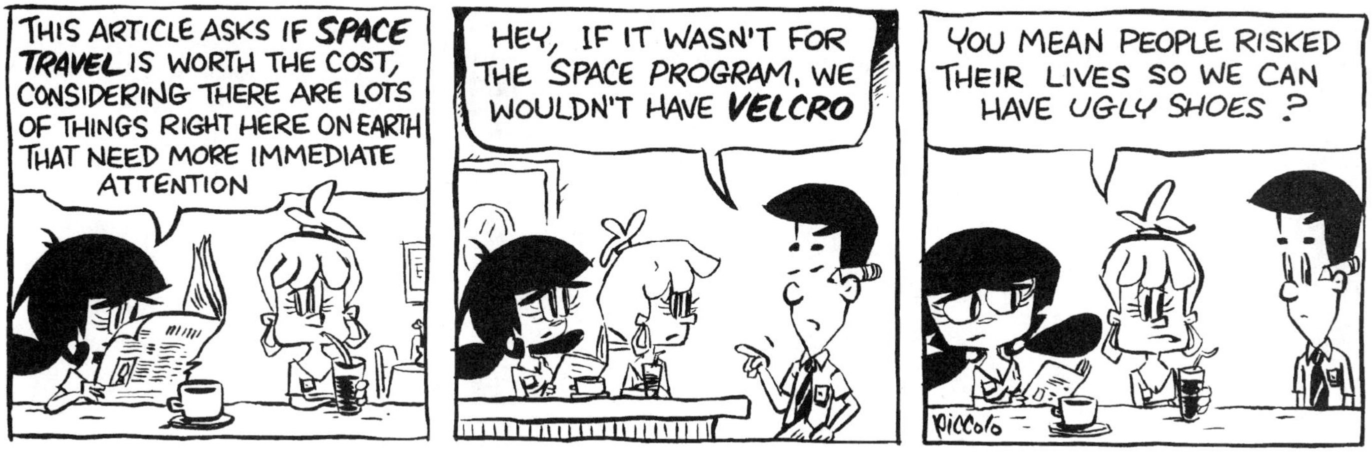
THIS ARTICLE ASKS IF SPACE TRAVEL IS WORTH THE COST, CONSIDERING THERE ARE LOTS OF THINGS RIGHT HERE ON EARTH THAT NEED MORE IMMEDIATE ATTENTION
HEY, IF IT WASN'T FOR THE SPACE PROGRAM, WE WOULDN'T HAVE VELCRO
YOU MEAN PEOPLE RISKED THEIR LIVES SO WE CAN HAVE UGLY SHOES ?
Piccolo

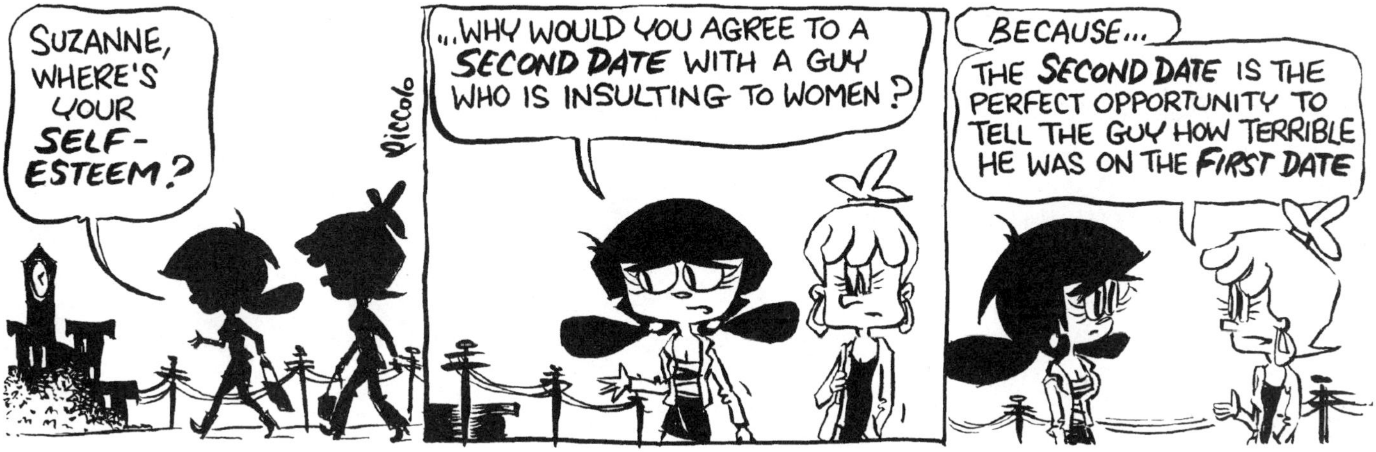
SUZANNE, WHERE'S YOUR SELF-ESTEEM ?
Piccolo
...WHY WOULD YOU AGREE TO A SECOND DATE WITH A GUY WHO IS INSULTING TO WOMEN ?
BECAUSE...
THE SECOND DATE IS THE PERFECT OPPORTUNITY TO TELL THE GUY HOW TERRIBLE HE WAS ON THE FIRST DATE

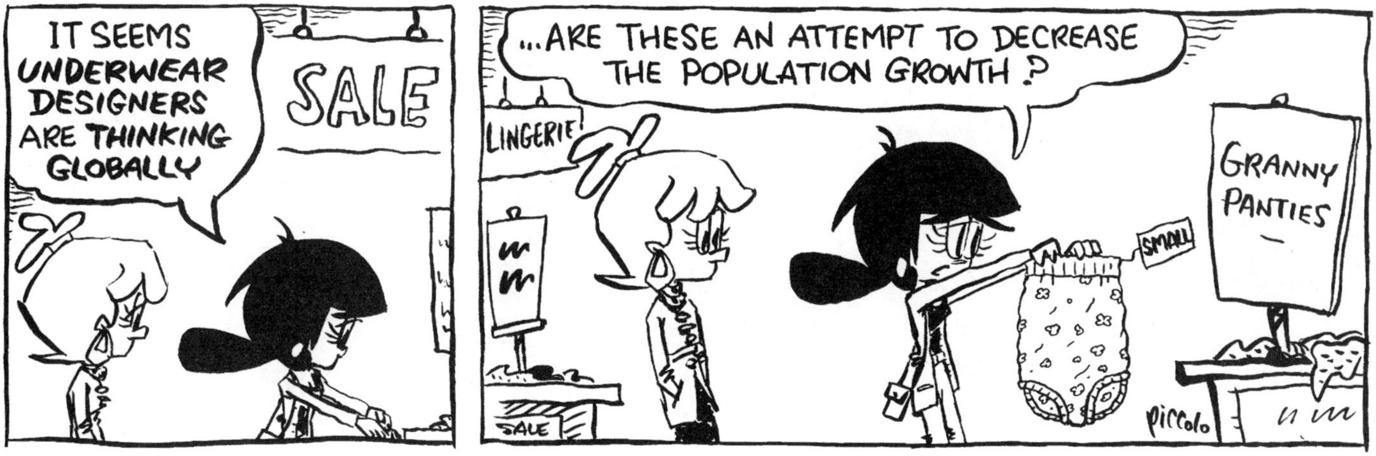
IT SEEMS UNDERWEAR DESIGNERS ARE THINKING GLOBALLY
SALE
...ARE THESE AN ATTEMPT TO DECREASE THE POPULATION GROWTH ?
LINGERIE
GRANNY PANTIES
SMALL
SALE
Piccolo

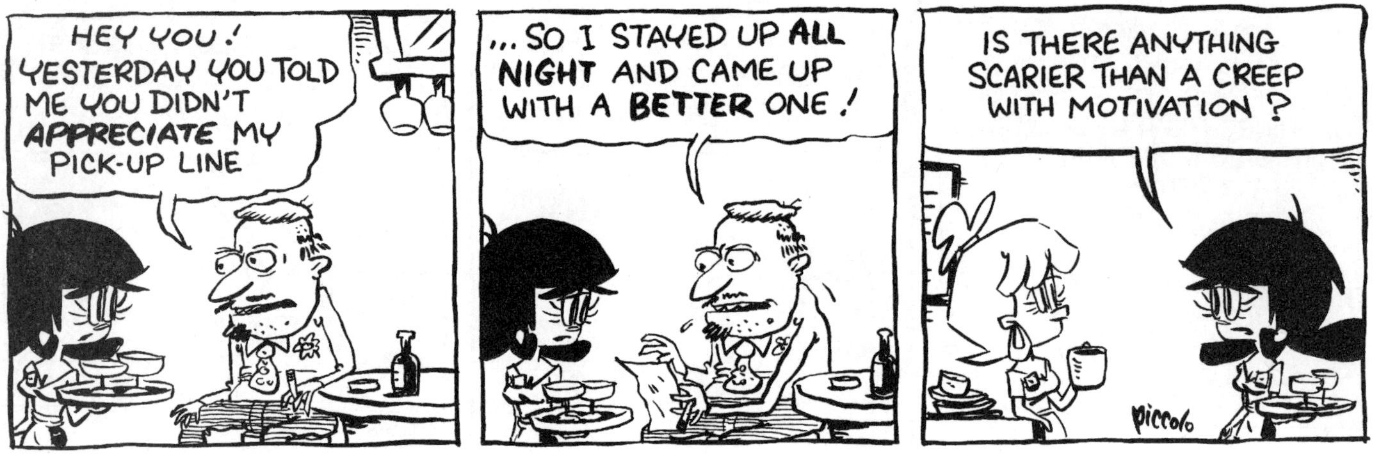
HEY YOU! YESTERDAY YOU TOLD ME YOU DIDN'T **APPRECIATE** MY PICK-UP LINE
...SO I STAYED UP **ALL NIGHT** AND CAME UP WITH A **BETTER** ONE!
IS THERE ANYTHING SCARIER THAN A CREEP WITH MOTIVATION?
piccolo

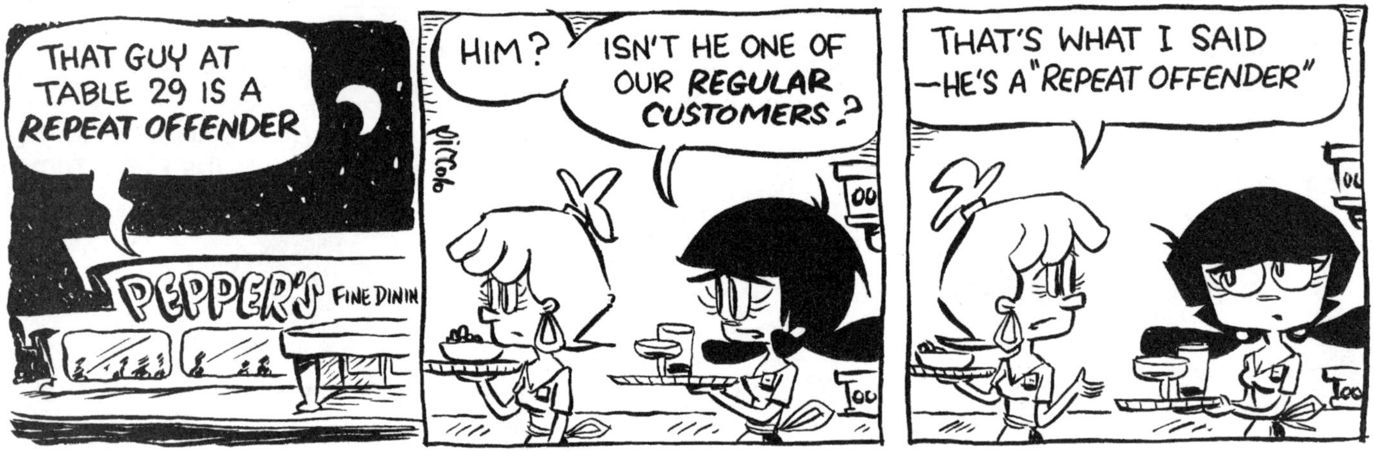
THAT GUY AT TABLE 29 IS A **REPEAT OFFENDER**
PEPPER'S
FINE DININ
piccolo
HIM?
ISN'T HE ONE OF OUR **REGULAR CUSTOMERS**?
THAT'S WHAT I SAID —HE'S A "REPEAT OFFENDER"

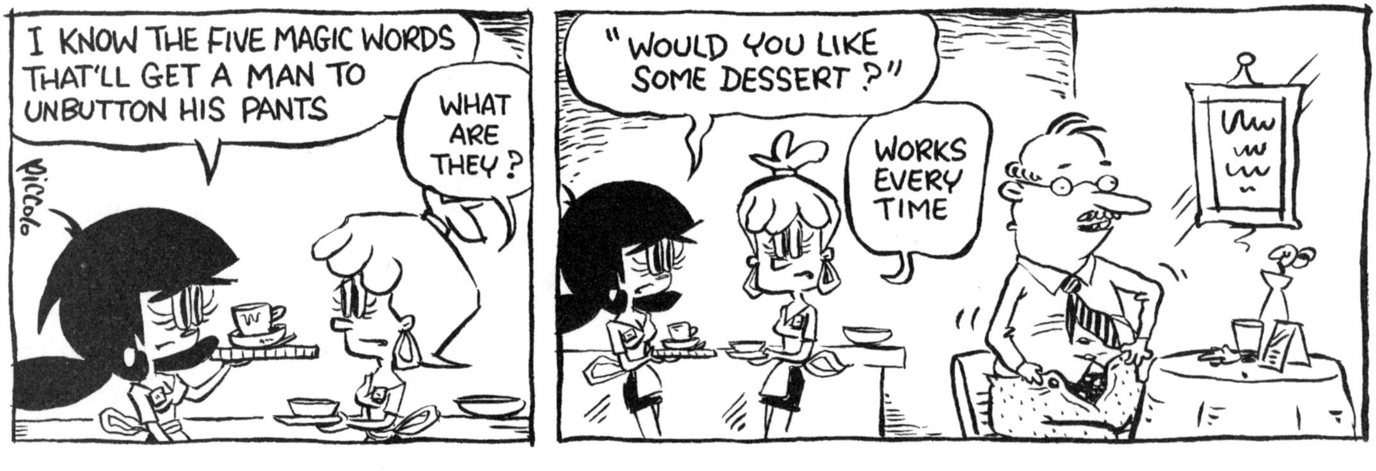
I KNOW THE FIVE MAGIC WORDS THAT'LL GET A MAN TO UNBUTTON HIS PANTS
WHAT ARE THEY?
piccolo
"WOULD YOU LIKE SOME DESSERT?"
WORKS EVERY TIME

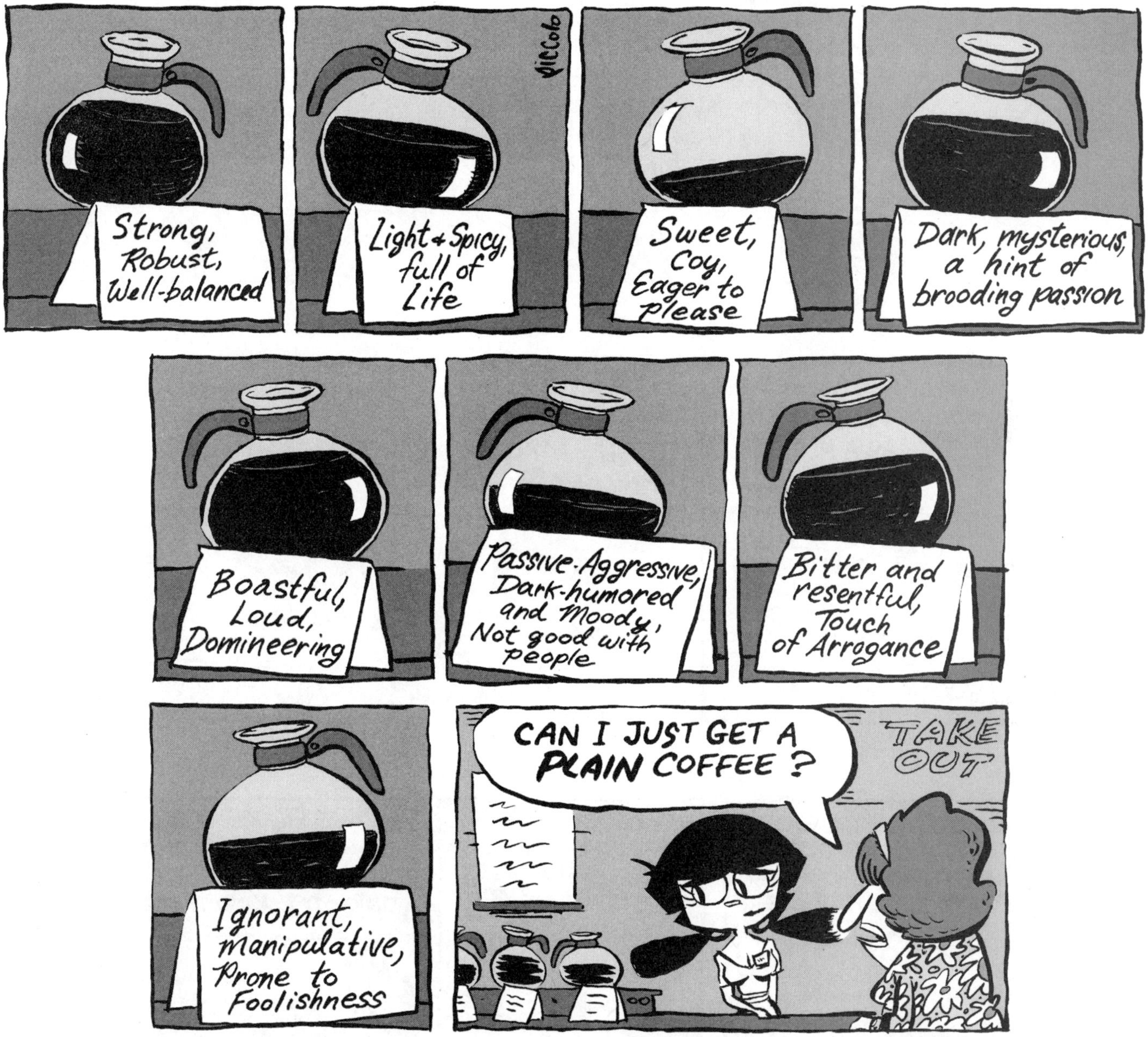

Piccolo
Strong, Robust, Well-balanced
Light & Spicy, full of Life
Sweet, Coy, Eager to please
Dark, mysterious, a hint of brooding passion
Boastful, Loud, Domineering
Passive-Aggressive, Dark-humored and Moody, Not good with people
Bitter and resentful, Touch of Arrogance
Ignorant, manipulative, Prone to Foolishness
TAKE OUT
CAN I JUST GET A PLAIN COFFEE ?

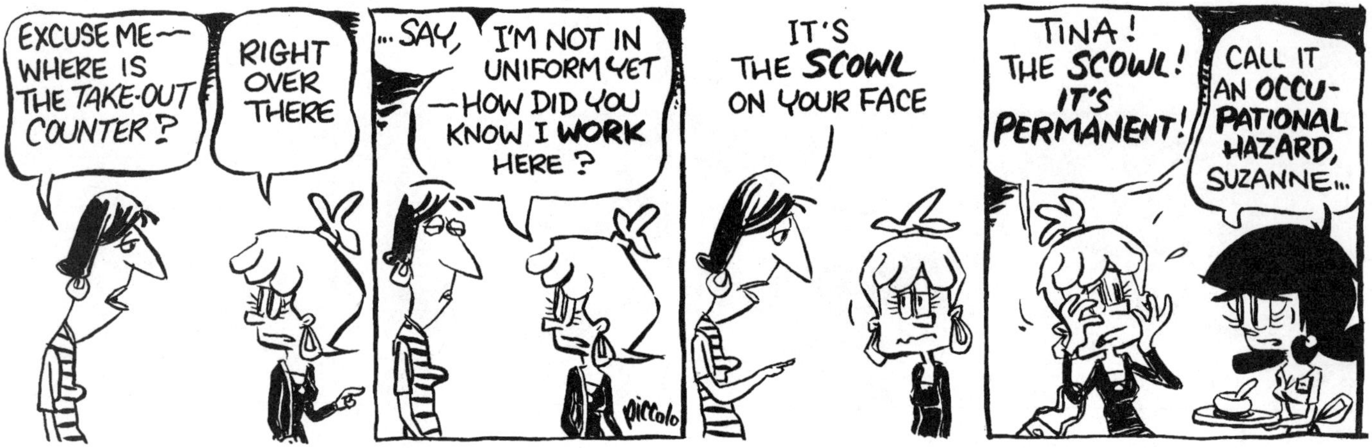
EXCUSE ME— WHERE IS THE TAKE-OUT COUNTER?
RIGHT OVER THERE
...SAY,
I'M NOT IN UNIFORM YET —HOW DID YOU KNOW I WORK HERE?
piccolo
IT'S THE SCOWL ON YOUR FACE
TINA! THE SCOWL! IT'S PERMANENT!
CALL IT AN OCCUPATIONAL HAZARD, SUZANNE...

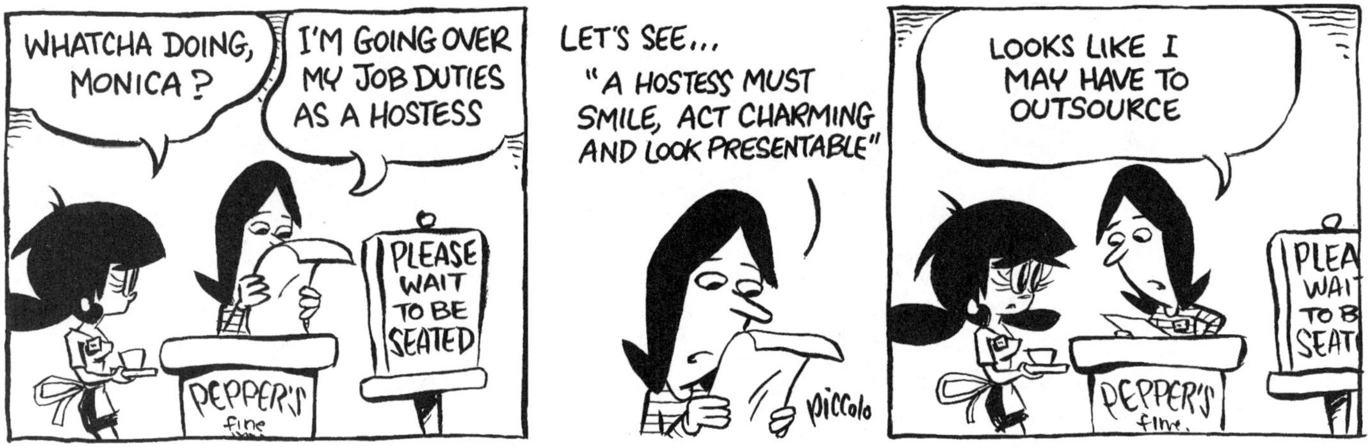
WHATCHA DOING, MONICA?
I'M GOING OVER MY JOB DUTIES AS A HOSTESS
PLEASE WAIT TO BE SEATED
PEPPER'S
LET'S SEE... "A HOSTESS MUST SMILE, ACT CHARMING AND LOOK PRESENTABLE"
piccolo
LOOKS LIKE I MAY HAVE TO OUTSOURCE

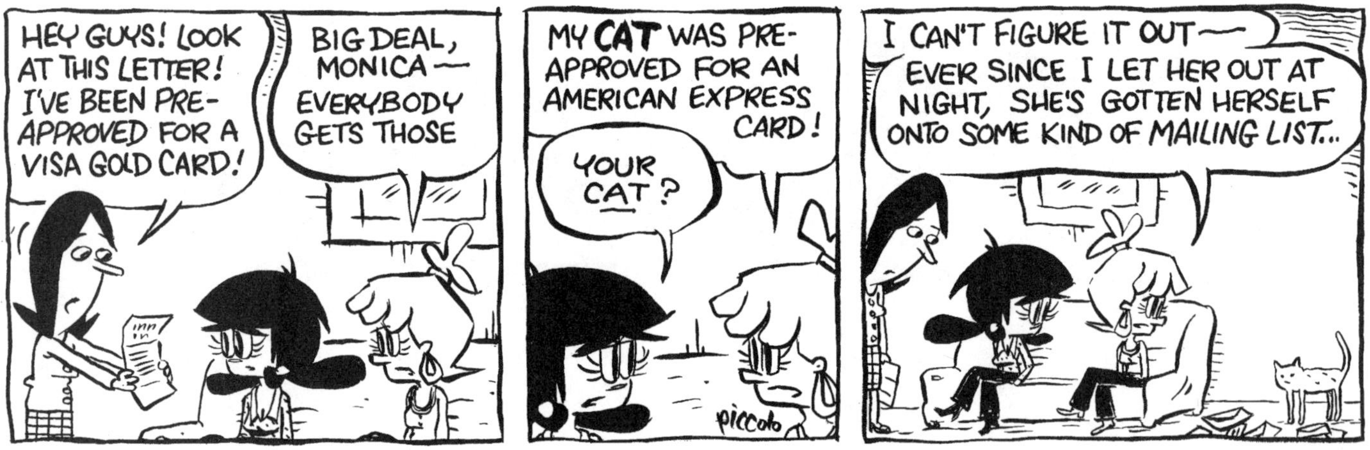
HEY GUYS! LOOK AT THIS LETTER! I'VE BEEN PRE-APPROVED FOR A VISA GOLD CARD!
BIG DEAL, MONICA— EVERYBODY GETS THOSE
MY CAT WAS PRE-APPROVED FOR AN AMERICAN EXPRESS CARD!
YOUR CAT?
piccolo
I CAN'T FIGURE IT OUT—
EVER SINCE I LET HER OUT AT NIGHT, SHE'S GOTTEN HERSELF ONTO SOME KIND OF MAILING LIST...

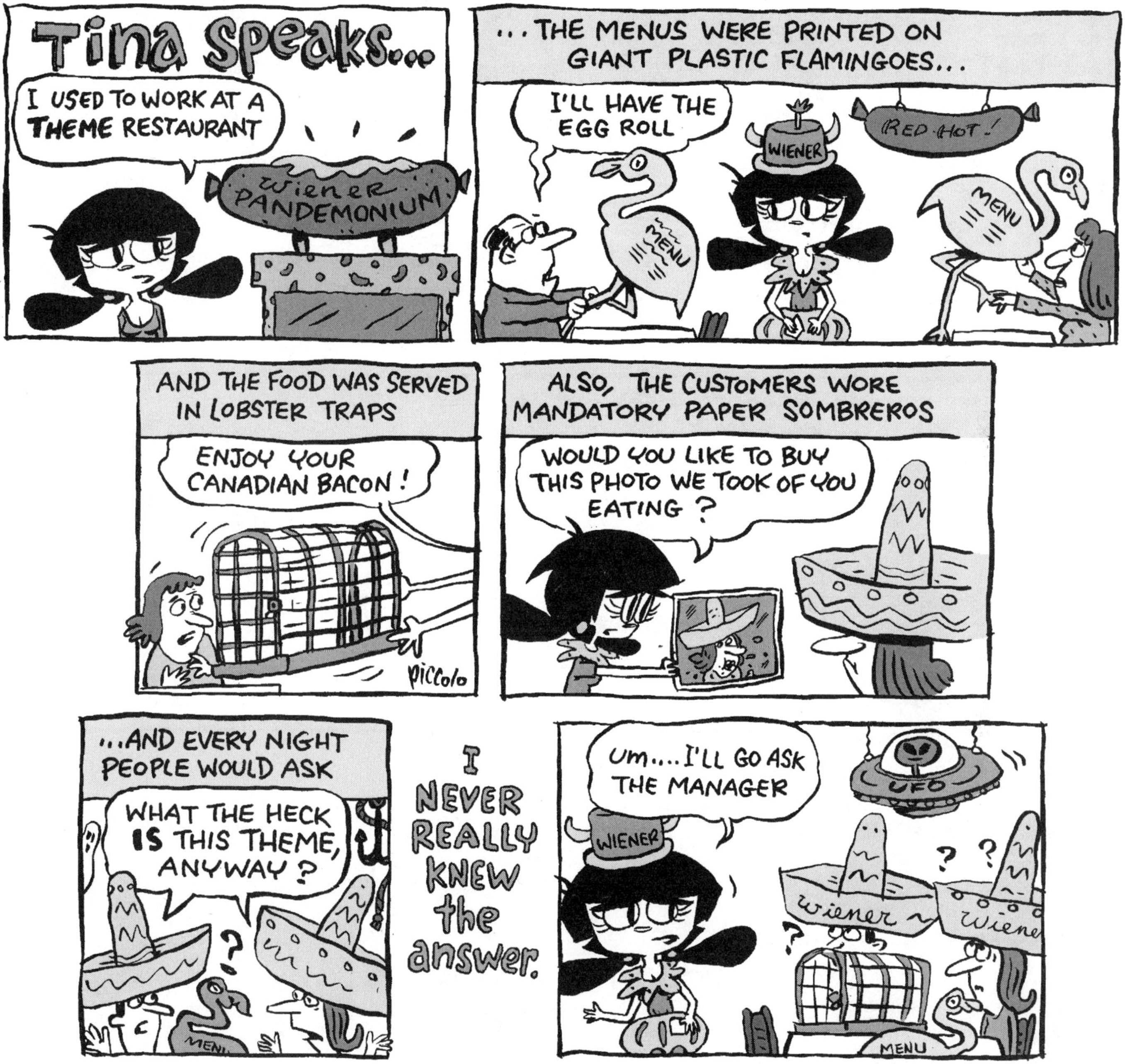
Tina speaks...
I USED TO WORK AT A THEME RESTAURANT
wiener PANDEMONIUM
...THE MENUS WERE PRINTED ON GIANT PLASTIC FLAMINGOES...
I'LL HAVE THE EGG ROLL
WIENER
RED HOT!
MENU
MENU
AND THE FOOD WAS SERVED IN LOBSTER TRAPS
ENJOY YOUR CANADIAN BACON!
piccolo
ALSO, THE CUSTOMERS WORE MANDATORY PAPER SOMBREROS
WOULD YOU LIKE TO BUY THIS PHOTO WE TOOK OF YOU EATING?
...AND EVERY NIGHT PEOPLE WOULD ASK
WHAT THE HECK IS THIS THEME, ANYWAY?
MENU
I NEVER REALLY KNEW the answer.
Um.... I'LL GO ASK THE MANAGER
UFO
WIENER
wiener
Wiener
MENU

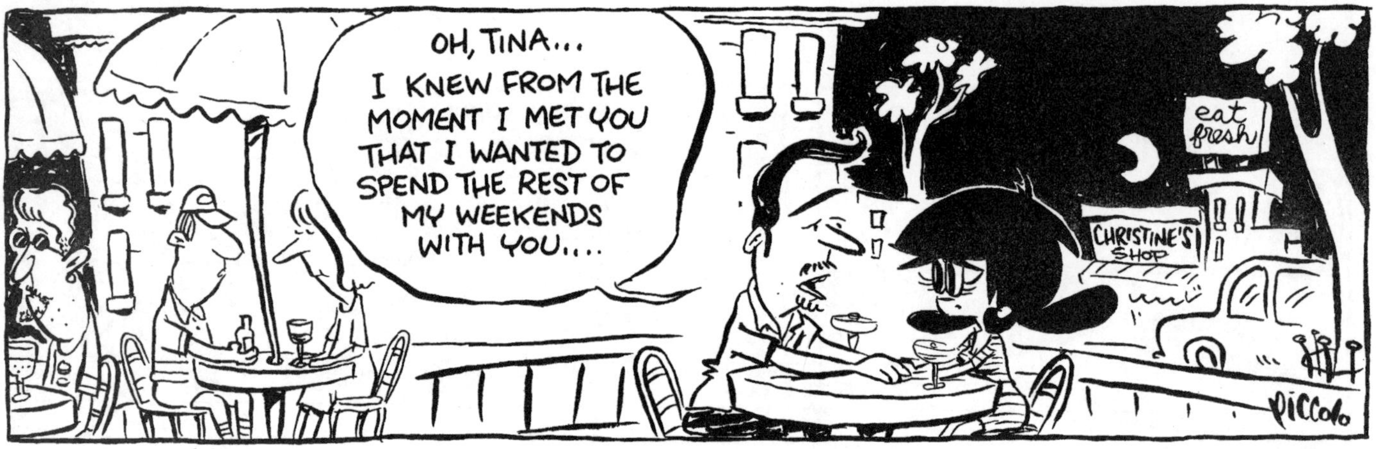
OH, TINA...
I KNEW FROM THE MOMENT I MET YOU THAT I WANTED TO SPEND THE REST OF MY WEEKENDS WITH YOU....
eat fresh
CHRISTINE'S SHOP
piccolo

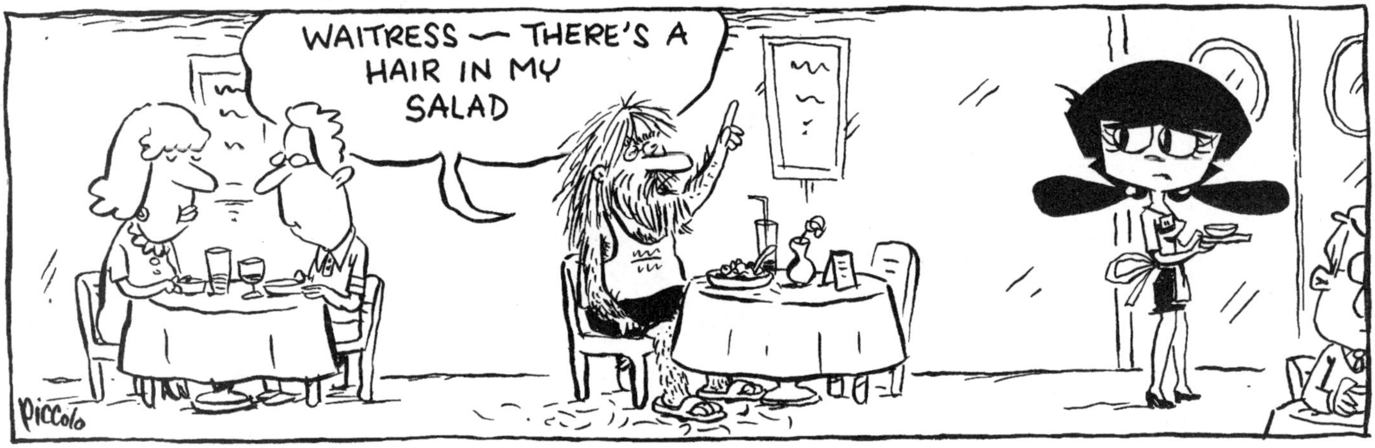
WAITRESS — THERE'S A HAIR IN MY SALAD
piccolo

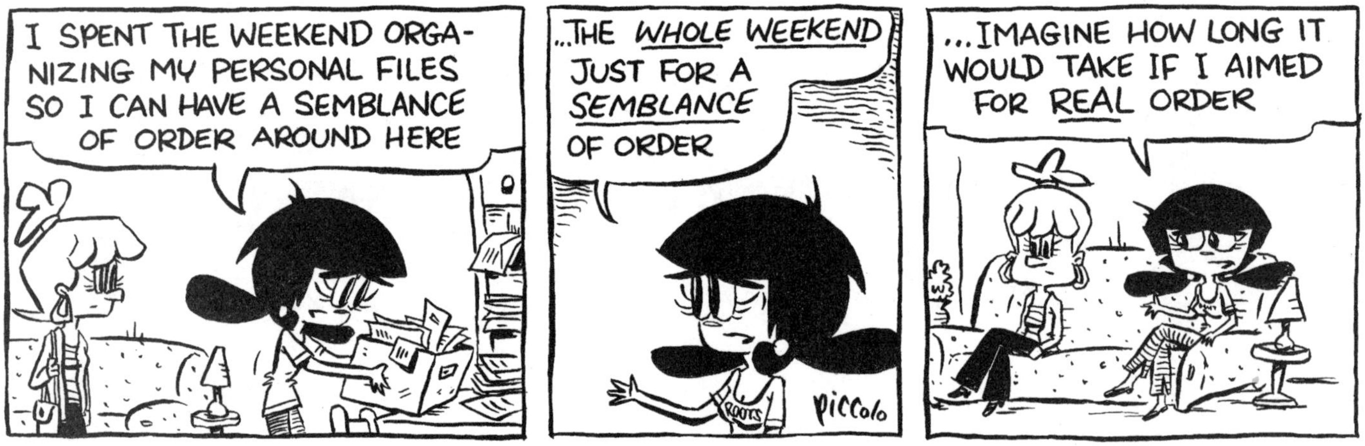
I SPENT THE WEEKEND ORGA-NIZING MY PERSONAL FILES SO I CAN HAVE A SEMBLANCE OF ORDER AROUND HERE
...THE WHOLE WEEKEND JUST FOR A SEMBLANCE OF ORDER
ROOTS
piccolo
...IMAGINE HOW LONG IT WOULD TAKE IF I AIMED FOR REAL ORDER

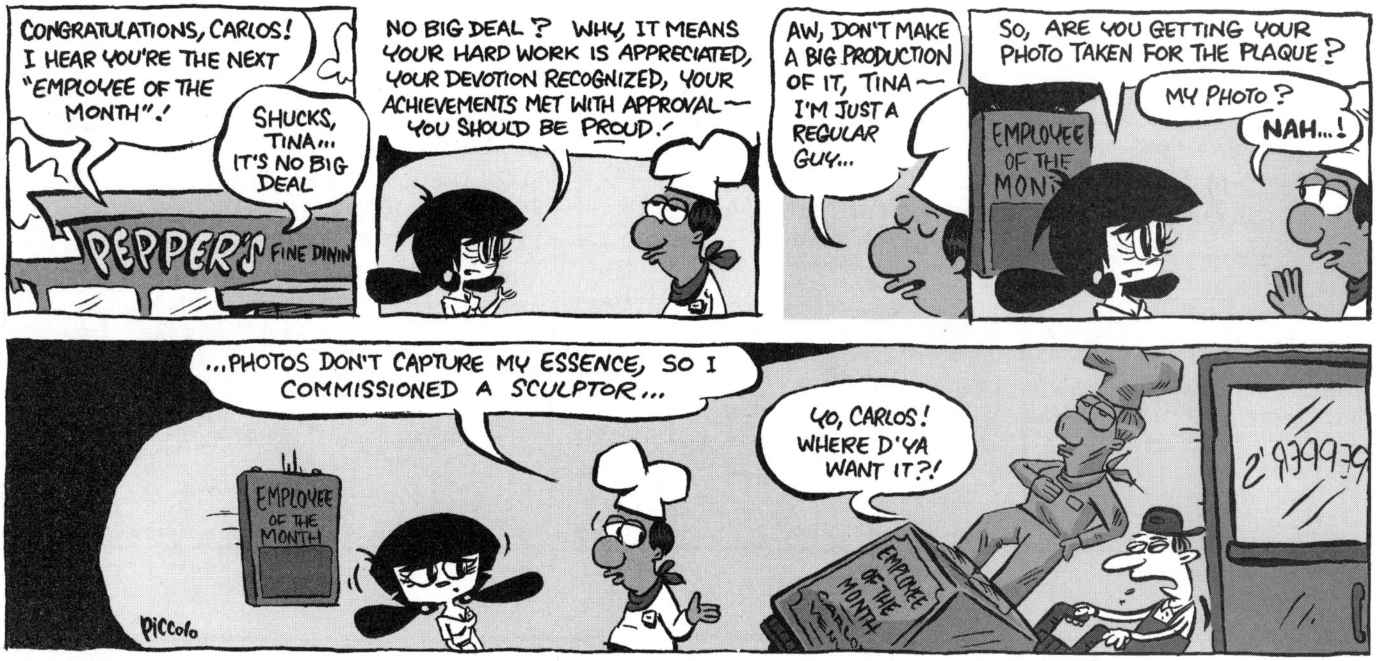
CONGRATULATIONS, CARLOS! I HEAR YOU'RE THE NEXT "EMPLOYEE OF THE MONTH"!
SHUCKS, TINA... IT'S NO BIG DEAL
PEPPER'S FINE DININ
NO BIG DEAL? WHY, IT MEANS YOUR HARD WORK IS APPRECIATED, YOUR DEVOTION RECOGNIZED, YOUR ACHIEVEMENTS MET WITH APPROVAL— YOU SHOULD BE PROUD!
AW, DON'T MAKE A BIG PRODUCTION OF IT, TINA— I'M JUST A REGULAR GUY...
SO, ARE YOU GETTING YOUR PHOTO TAKEN FOR THE PLAQUE?
MY PHOTO?
NAH...!
...PHOTOS DON'T CAPTURE MY ESSENCE, SO I COMMISSIONED A SCULPTOR...
YO, CARLOS! WHERE D'YA WANT IT?!
EMPLOYEE OF THE MONTH
PICCOLO

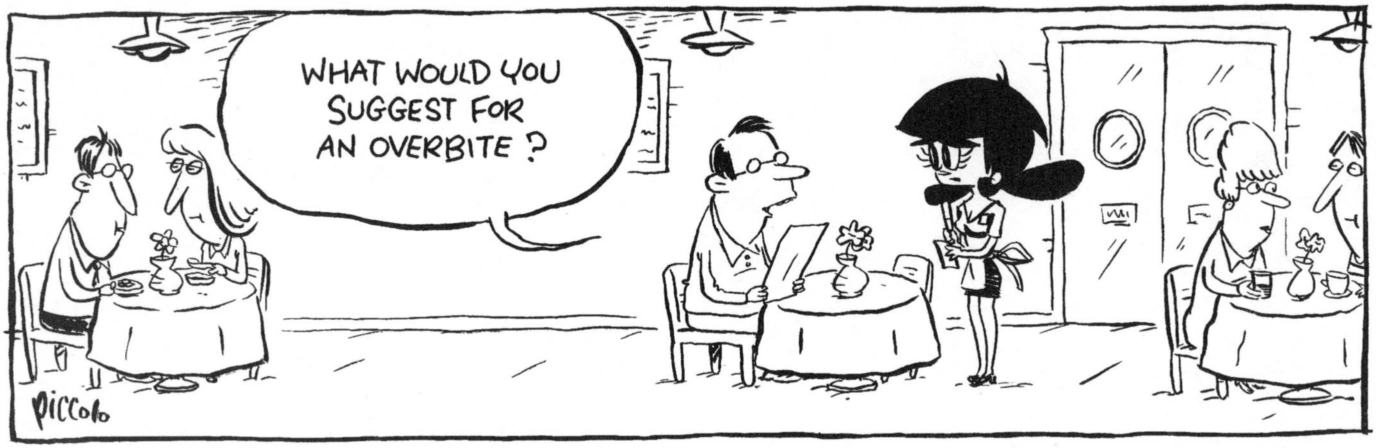
WHAT WOULD YOU SUGGEST FOR AN OVERBITE ?
PICCOLO

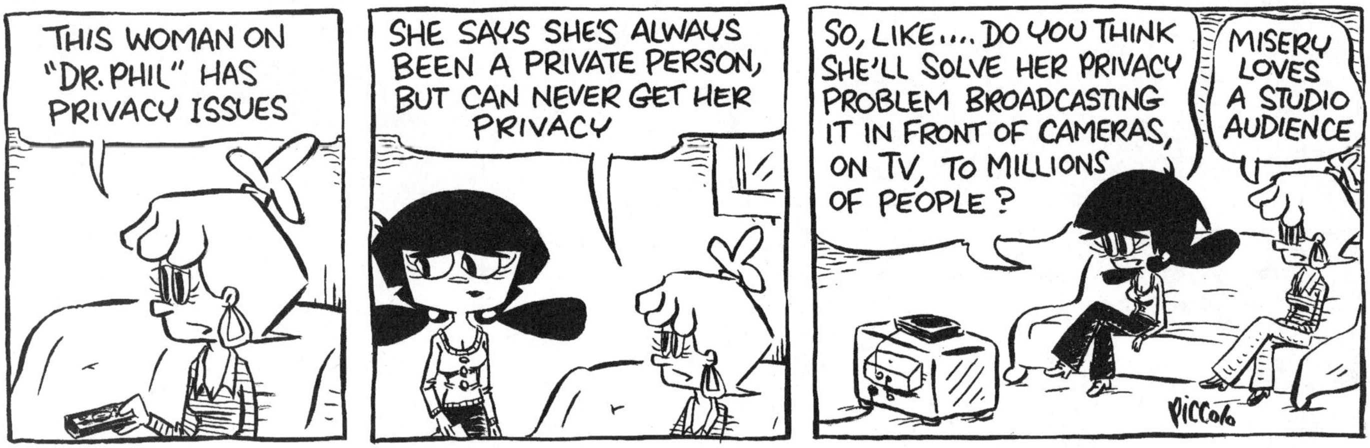
THIS WOMAN ON "DR. PHIL" HAS PRIVACY ISSUES
SHE SAYS SHE'S ALWAYS BEEN A PRIVATE PERSON, BUT CAN NEVER GET HER PRIVACY
SO, LIKE.... DO YOU THINK SHE'LL SOLVE HER PRIVACY PROBLEM BROADCASTING IT IN FRONT OF CAMERAS, ON TV, TO MILLIONS OF PEOPLE ?
MISERY LOVES A STUDIO AUDIENCE
PICCOLO

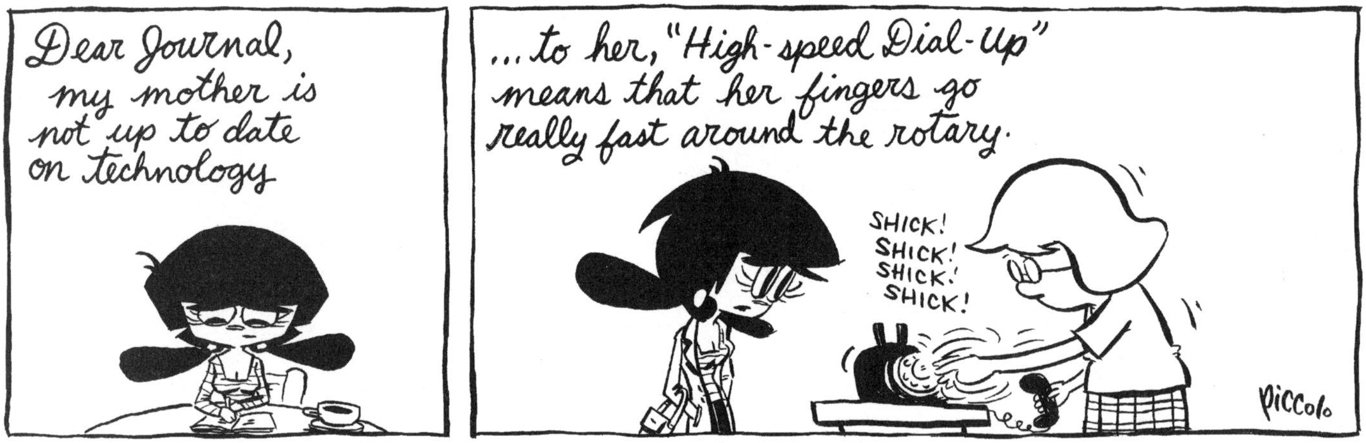
Dear Journal, my mother is not up to date on technology
...to her, "High-speed Dial-Up" means that her fingers go really fast around the rotary.
SHICK! SHICK! SHICK! SHICK!
PICCOLO

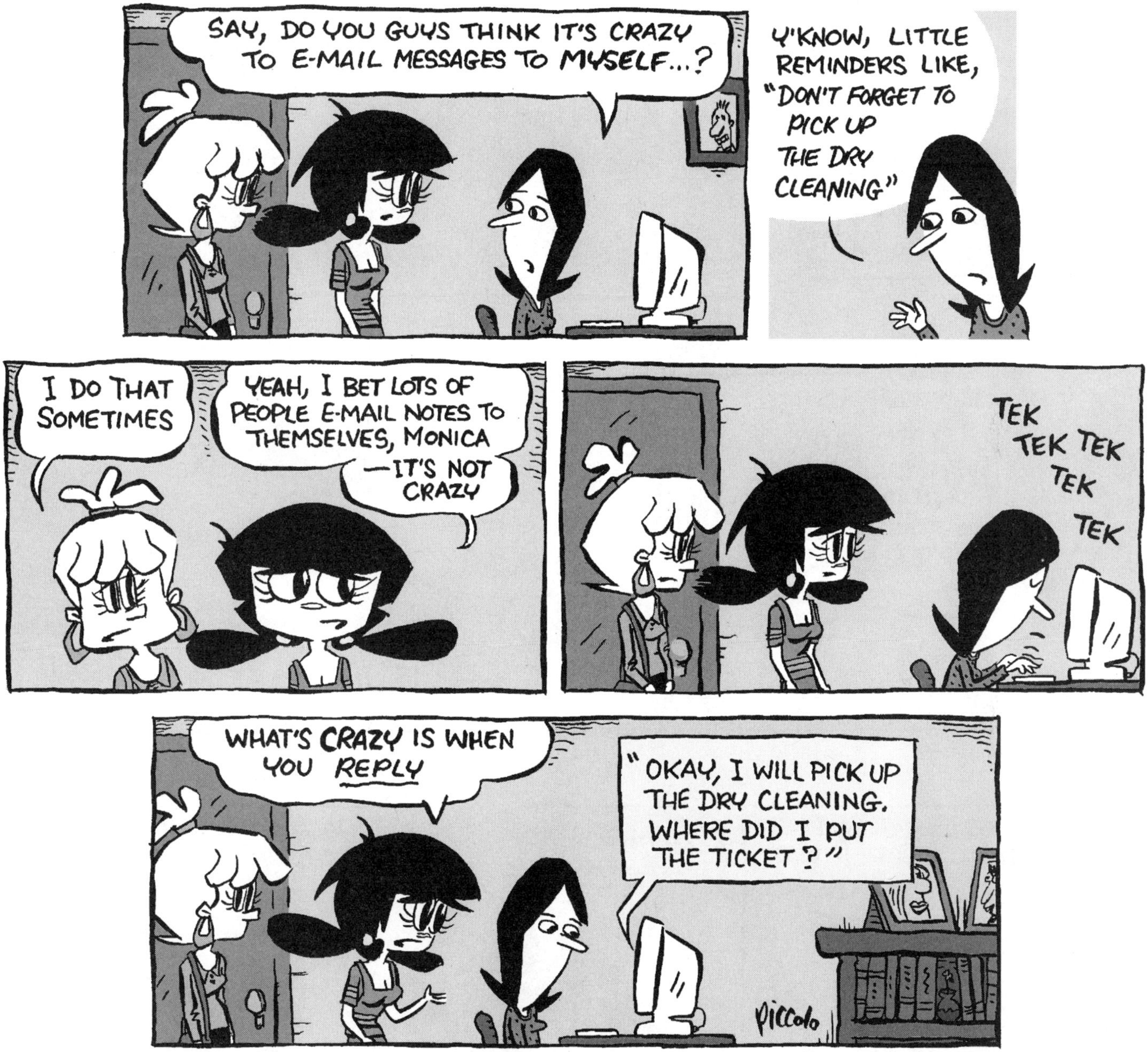
SAY, DO YOU GUYS THINK IT'S CRAZY TO E-MAIL MESSAGES TO MYSELF...?
Y'KNOW, LITTLE REMINDERS LIKE, "DON'T FORGET TO PICK UP THE DRY CLEANING"
I DO THAT SOMETIMES
YEAH, I BET LOTS OF PEOPLE E-MAIL NOTES TO THEMSELVES, MONICA
—IT'S NOT CRAZY
TEK TEK TEK TEK TEK
WHAT'S CRAZY IS WHEN YOU REPLY
"OKAY, I WILL PICK UP THE DRY CLEANING. WHERE DID I PUT THE TICKET?"
piccolo

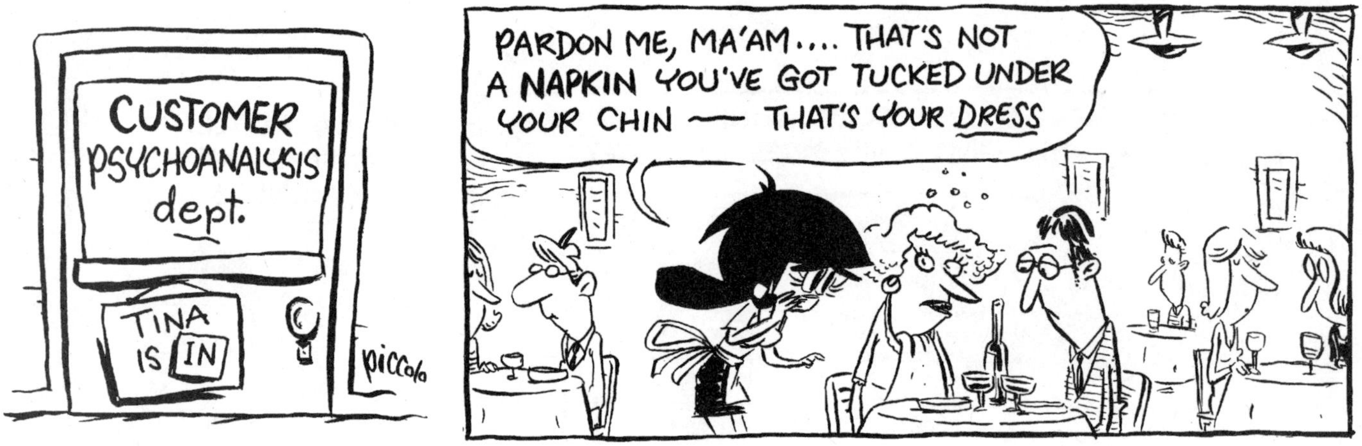
CUSTOMER PSYCHOANALYSIS dept.
TINA IS IN
piccolo
PARDON ME, MA'AM.... THAT'S NOT A NAPKIN YOU'VE GOT TUCKED UNDER YOUR CHIN — THAT'S YOUR DRESS

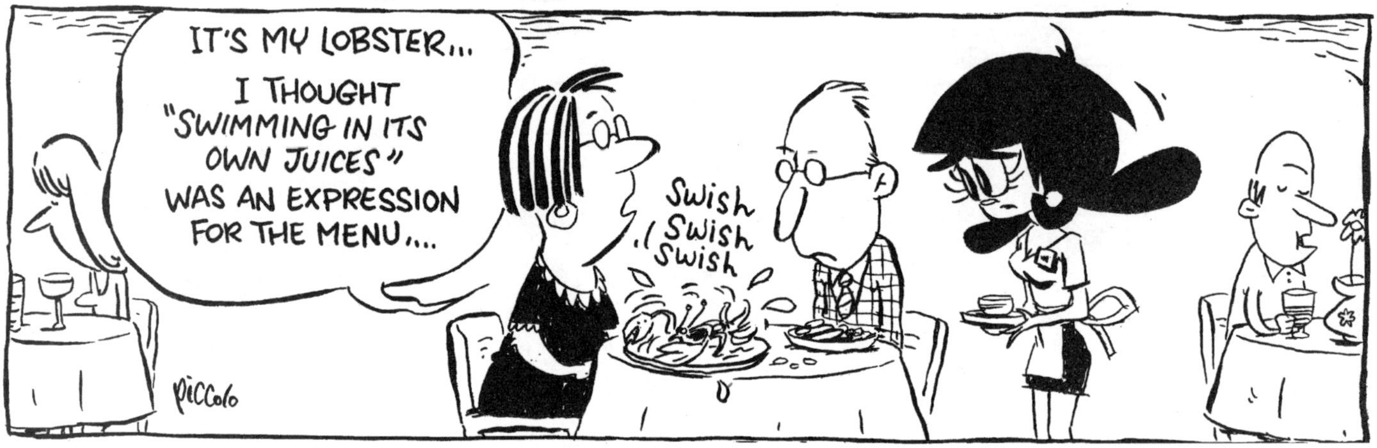
IT'S MY LOBSTER... I THOUGHT "SWIMMING IN ITS OWN JUICES" WAS AN EXPRESSION FOR THE MENU....
Swish Swish Swish
piccolo

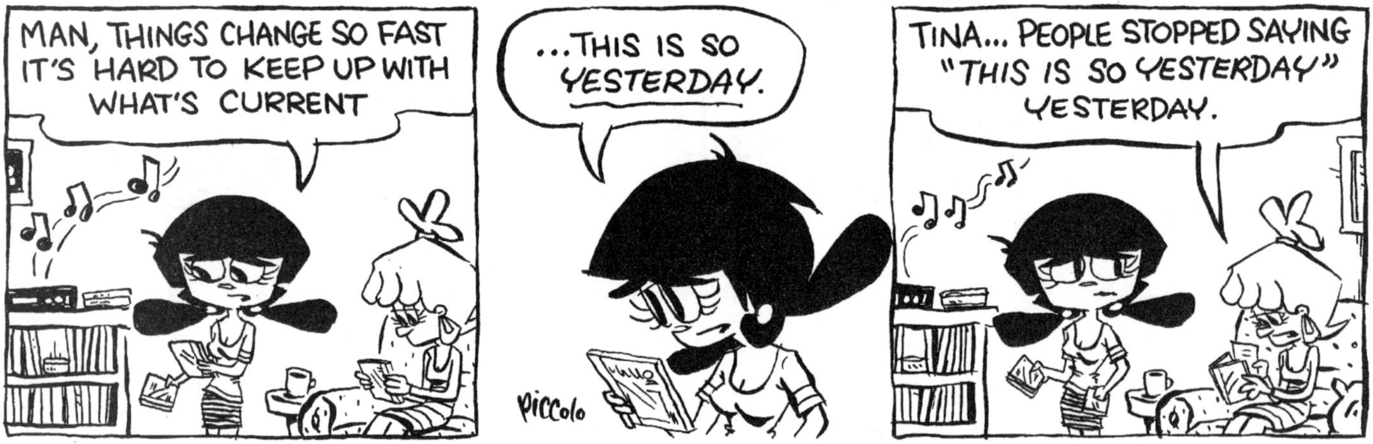
MAN, THINGS CHANGE SO FAST IT'S HARD TO KEEP UP WITH WHAT'S CURRENT
...THIS IS SO YESTERDAY.
piccolo
TINA... PEOPLE STOPPED SAYING "THIS IS SO YESTERDAY" YESTERDAY.

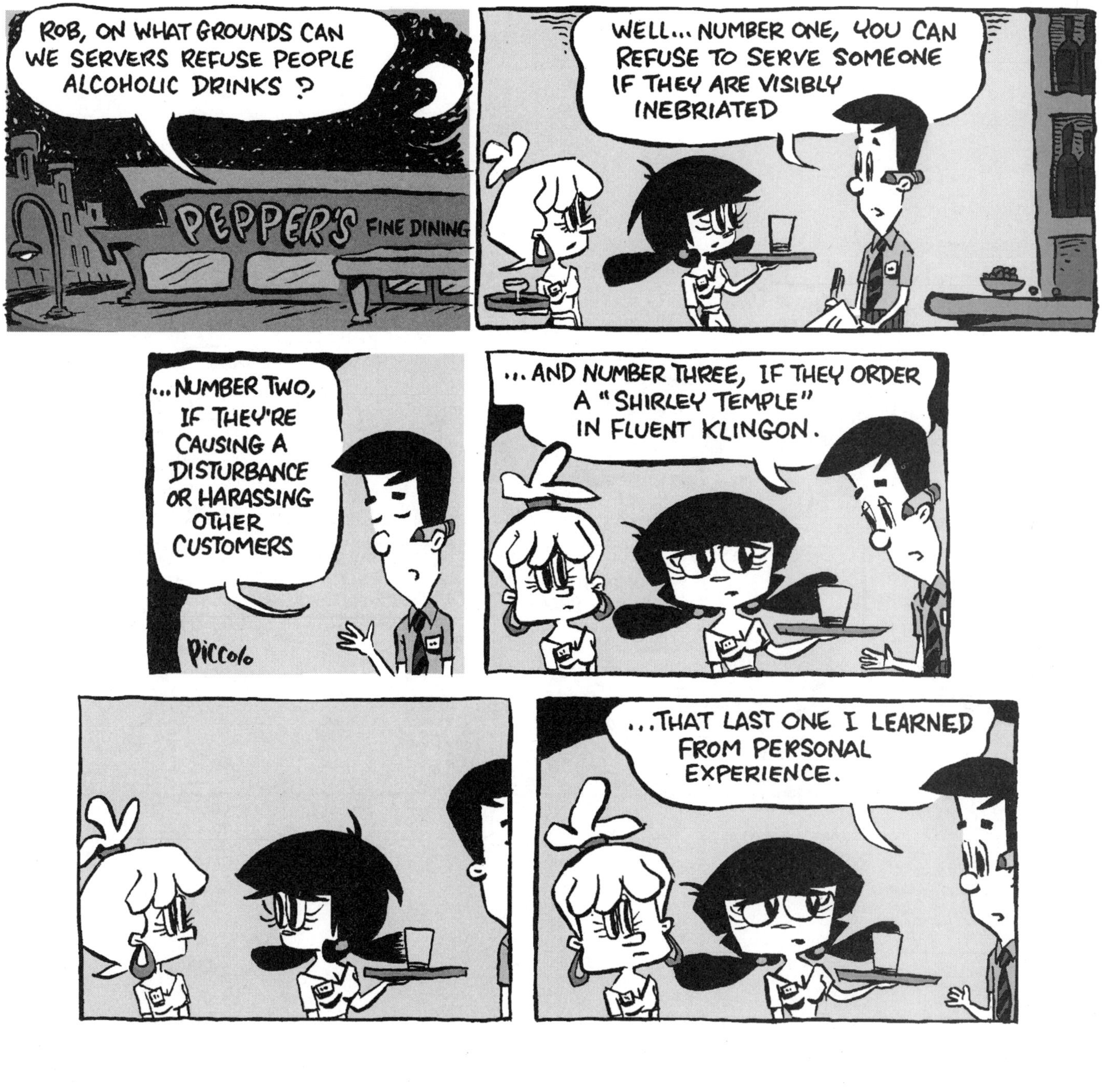
ROB, ON WHAT GROUNDS CAN WE SERVERS REFUSE PEOPLE ALCOHOLIC DRINKS ?
PEPPER'S FINE DINING
WELL... NUMBER ONE, YOU CAN REFUSE TO SERVE SOMEONE IF THEY ARE VISIBLY INEBRIATED
...NUMBER TWO, IF THEY'RE CAUSING A DISTURBANCE OR HARASSING OTHER CUSTOMERS
PICCOLO
...AND NUMBER THREE, IF THEY ORDER A "SHIRLEY TEMPLE" IN FLUENT KLINGON.
...THAT LAST ONE I LEARNED FROM PERSONAL EXPERIENCE.

Tina Speaks...
CELL PHONE COMPANIES SHOULD BILL PEOPLE ACCORDING TO THE QUALITY OF THEIR CONVERSATIONS...
IMAGINE A WORLD WHERE YOU CAN EAT IN PUBLIC WITHOUT HAVING TO HEAR A STRANGER'S TOENAIL REMOVAL STORY.
!
"THIS CALL MAY BE MONITORED FOR QUALITY..."
...wouldn't that be great...?
WHAT'S THIS "LOUDMOUTH FEE" ON MY CELL PHONE BILL?
I GOT CHARGED FOR PEDESTRIAN DIALOGUE AND VULGAR EXPLETIVES
I GIT CHARGED FOR BAD ENGLISH! I'S AIN'T GONNA TALK NO MO'.!
BILL
Piccolo

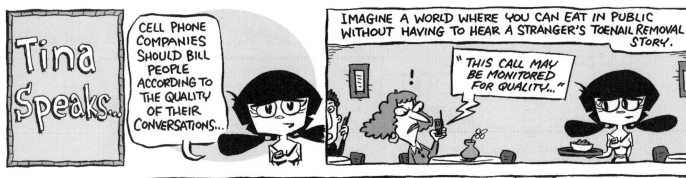

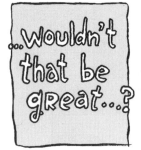

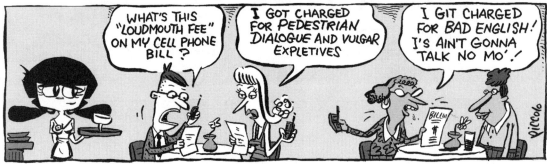

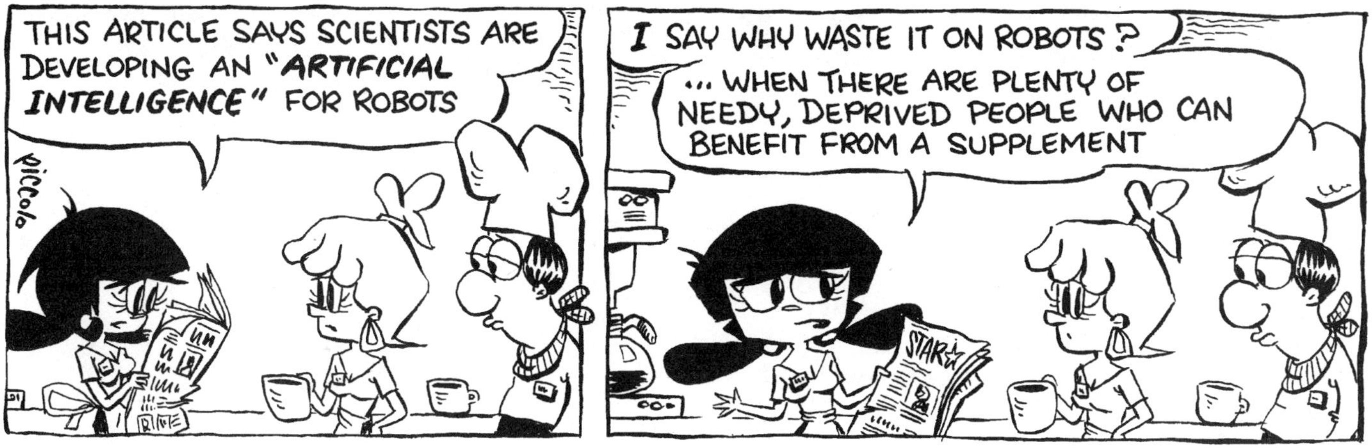
THIS ARTICLE SAYS SCIENTISTS ARE DEVELOPING AN "ARTIFICIAL INTELLIGENCE" FOR ROBOTS
piccolo
I SAY WHY WASTE IT ON ROBOTS?
... WHEN THERE ARE PLENTY OF NEEDY, DEPRIVED PEOPLE WHO CAN BENEFIT FROM A SUPPLEMENT
STAR

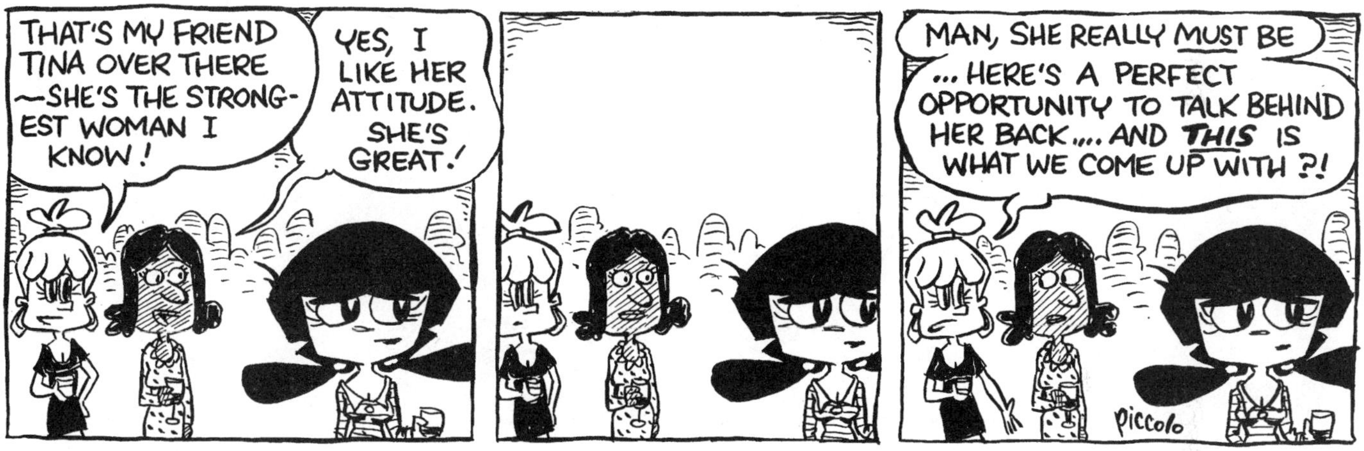
THAT'S MY FRIEND TINA OVER THERE —SHE'S THE STRONGEST WOMAN I KNOW!
YES, I LIKE HER ATTITUDE. SHE'S GREAT!
MAN, SHE REALLY MUST BE
... HERE'S A PERFECT OPPORTUNITY TO TALK BEHIND HER BACK.... AND THIS IS WHAT WE COME UP WITH?!
piccolo

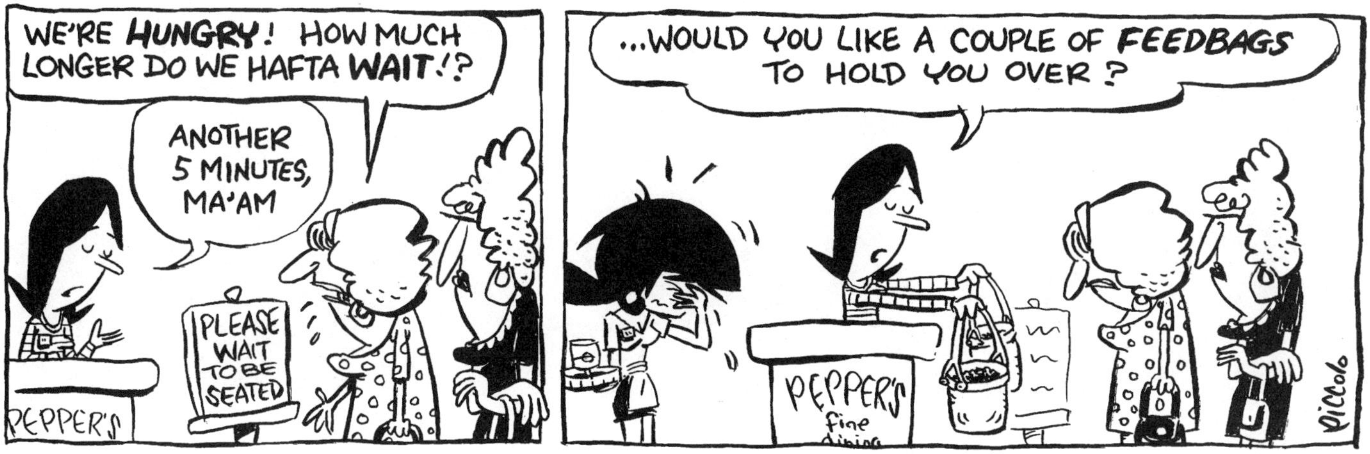
WE'RE HUNGRY! HOW MUCH LONGER DO WE HAFTA WAIT!?
ANOTHER 5 MINUTES, MA'AM
PLEASE WAIT TO BE SEATED
PEPPER'S
...WOULD YOU LIKE A COUPLE OF FEEDBAGS TO HOLD YOU OVER?
PEPPER'S fine
piccolo

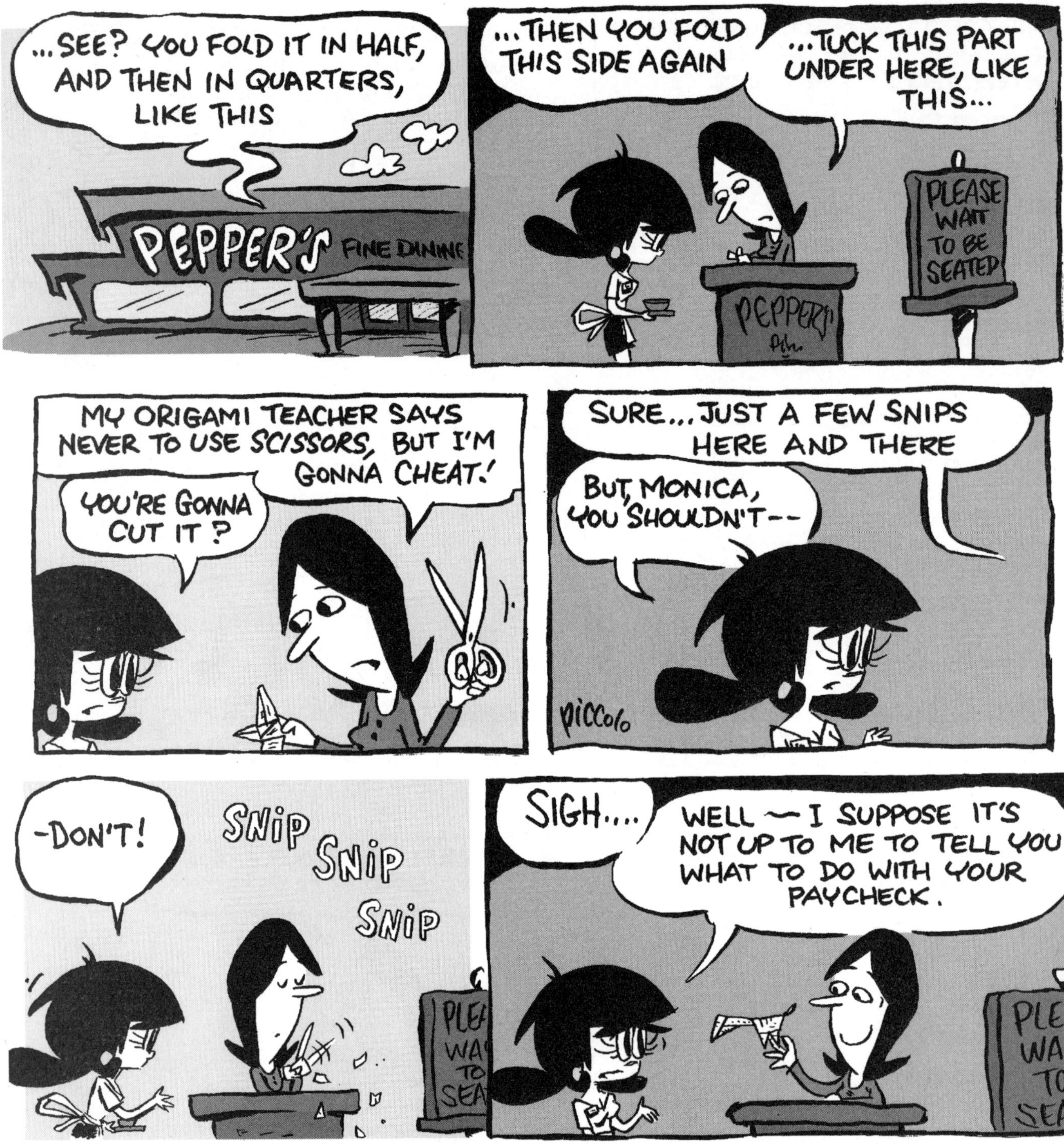
...SEE? YOU FOLD IT IN HALF, AND THEN IN QUARTERS, LIKE THIS
PEPPER'S FINE DINING
...THEN YOU FOLD THIS SIDE AGAIN
...TUCK THIS PART UNDER HERE, LIKE THIS...
PLEASE WAIT TO BE SEATED
PEPPER'S
MY ORIGAMI TEACHER SAYS NEVER TO USE SCISSORS, BUT I'M GONNA CHEAT!
YOU'RE GONNA CUT IT?
SURE... JUST A FEW SNIPS HERE AND THERE
BUT, MONICA, YOU SHOULDN'T--
piccolo
-DON'T!
SNIP SNIP SNIP
SIGH....
WELL — I SUPPOSE IT'S NOT UP TO ME TO TELL YOU WHAT TO DO WITH YOUR PAYCHECK.

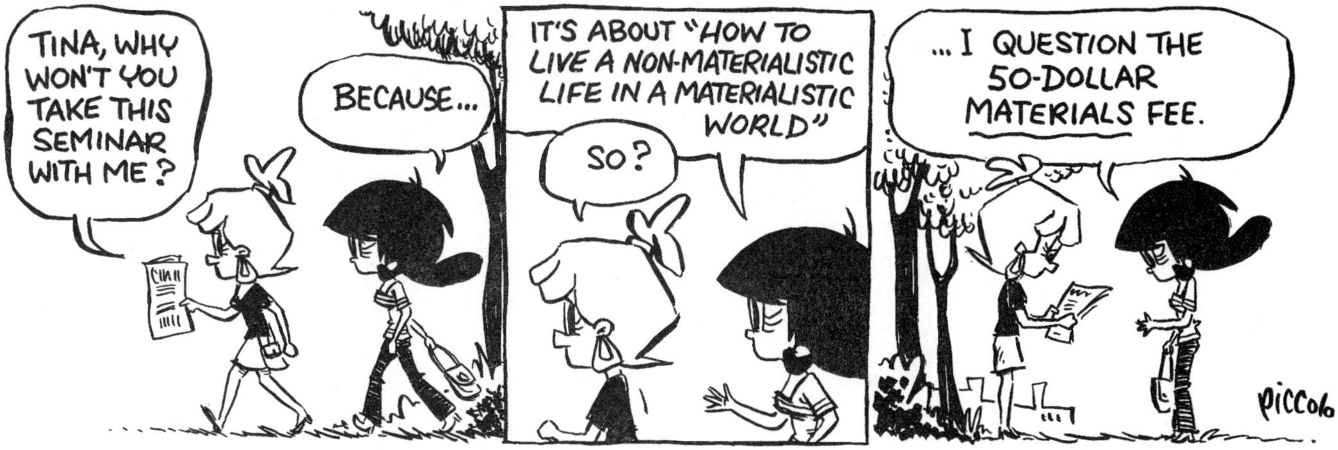
TINA, WHY WON'T YOU TAKE THIS SEMINAR WITH ME?
BECAUSE...
IT'S ABOUT "HOW TO LIVE A NON-MATERIALISTIC LIFE IN A MATERIALISTIC WORLD"
SO?
...I QUESTION THE 50-DOLLAR MATERIALS FEE.
PICCOLO

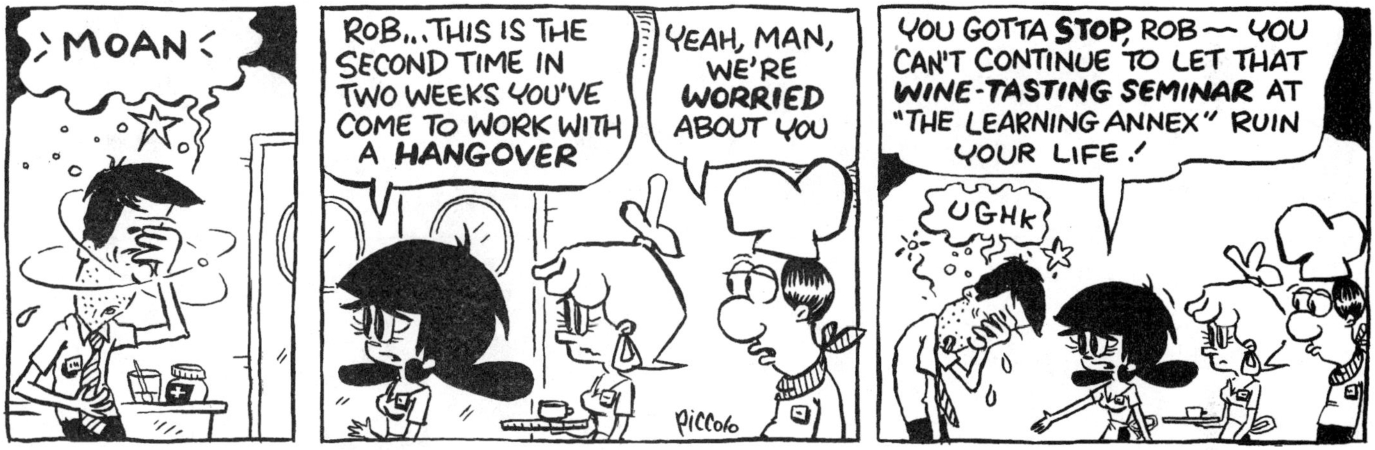
MOAN
ROB...THIS IS THE SECOND TIME IN TWO WEEKS YOU'VE COME TO WORK WITH A HANGOVER
YEAH, MAN, WE'RE WORRIED ABOUT YOU
PICCOLO
YOU GOTTA STOP, ROB — YOU CAN'T CONTINUE TO LET THAT WINE-TASTING SEMINAR AT "THE LEARNING ANNEX" RUIN YOUR LIFE!
UGHK

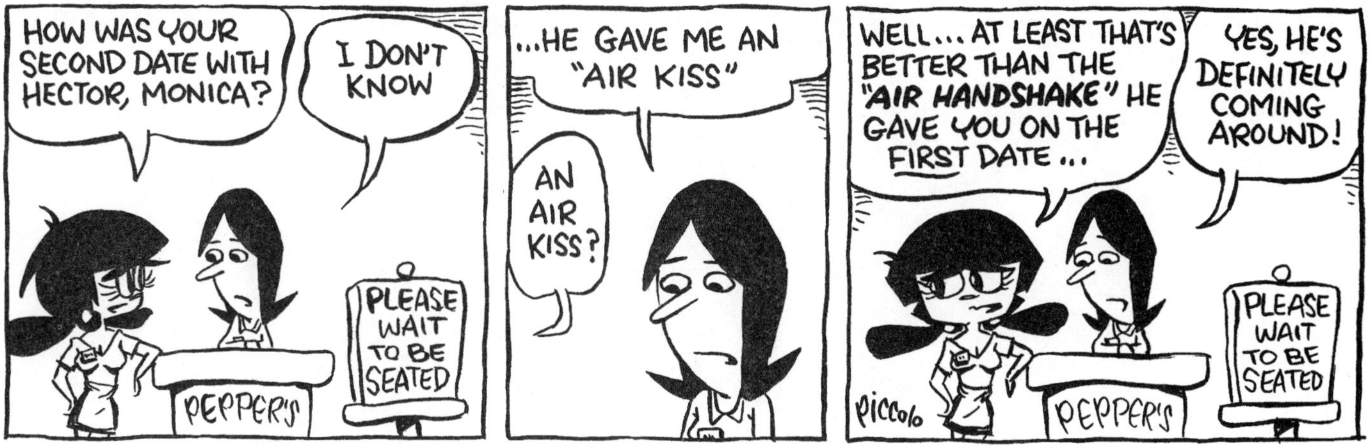
HOW WAS YOUR SECOND DATE WITH HECTOR, MONICA?
I DON'T KNOW
PLEASE WAIT TO BE SEATED
PEPPER'S
...HE GAVE ME AN "AIR KISS"
AN AIR KISS?
WELL... AT LEAST THAT'S BETTER THAN THE "AIR HANDSHAKE" HE GAVE YOU ON THE FIRST DATE...
YES, HE'S DEFINITELY COMING AROUND!
PICCOLO
PEPPER'S
PLEASE WAIT TO BE SEATED

CAN I GET MORE BUTTER, PLEASE?
PEPPER'S
FINE DININ'
I NEED MORE BUTTER...
MORE BUTTER OVER HERE, PLEASE!
piccolo
BUTTER
POOR WOMAN.....THE ONLY WAY SHE CAN GET A MEAL PAST THOSE COLLAGEN LIP IMPLANTS IS TO GREASE THE FOOD...

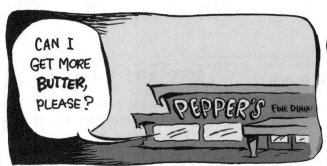

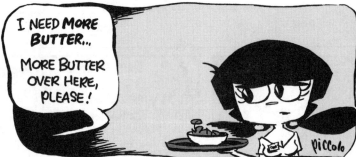

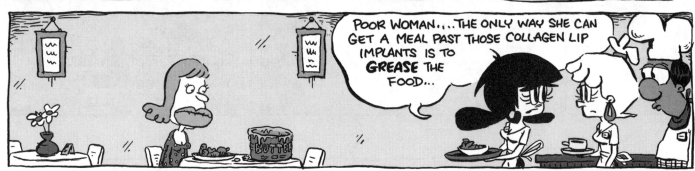

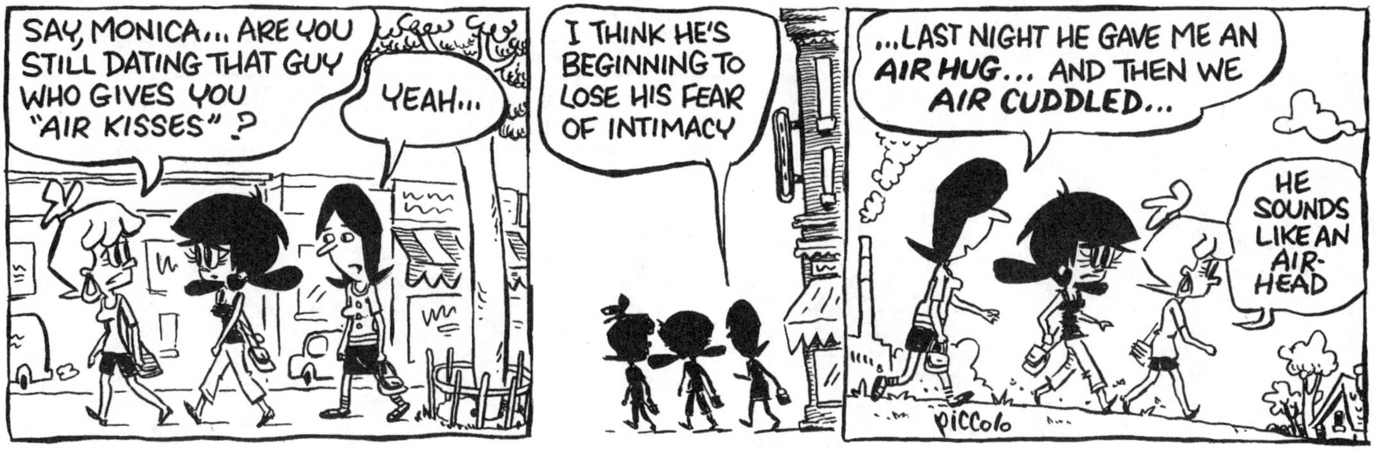
SAY, MONICA... ARE YOU STILL DATING THAT GUY WHO GIVES YOU "AIR KISSES"?
YEAH...
I THINK HE'S BEGINNING TO LOSE HIS FEAR OF INTIMACY
...LAST NIGHT HE GAVE ME AN AIR HUG... AND THEN WE AIR CUDDLED...
HE SOUNDS LIKE AN AIR-HEAD
PICCOLO

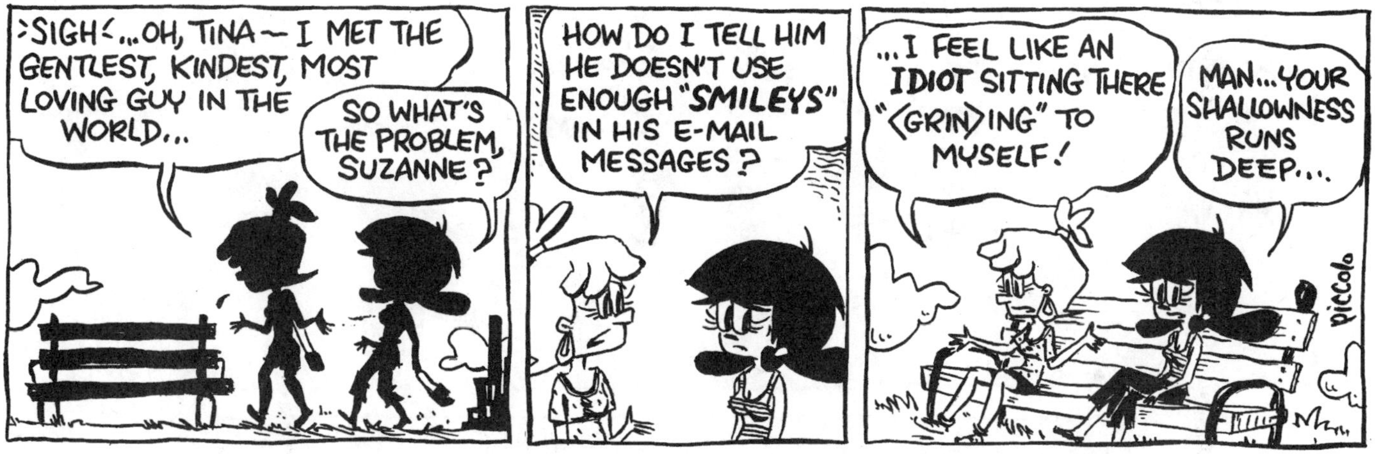
>SIGH<...OH, TINA— I MET THE GENTLEST, KINDEST, MOST LOVING GUY IN THE WORLD...
SO WHAT'S THE PROBLEM, SUZANNE?
HOW DO I TELL HIM HE DOESN'T USE ENOUGH "SMILEYS" IN HIS E-MAIL MESSAGES?
...I FEEL LIKE AN IDIOT SITTING THERE "<GRIN>ING" TO MYSELF!
MAN...YOUR SHALLOWNESS RUNS DEEP....
PICCOLO

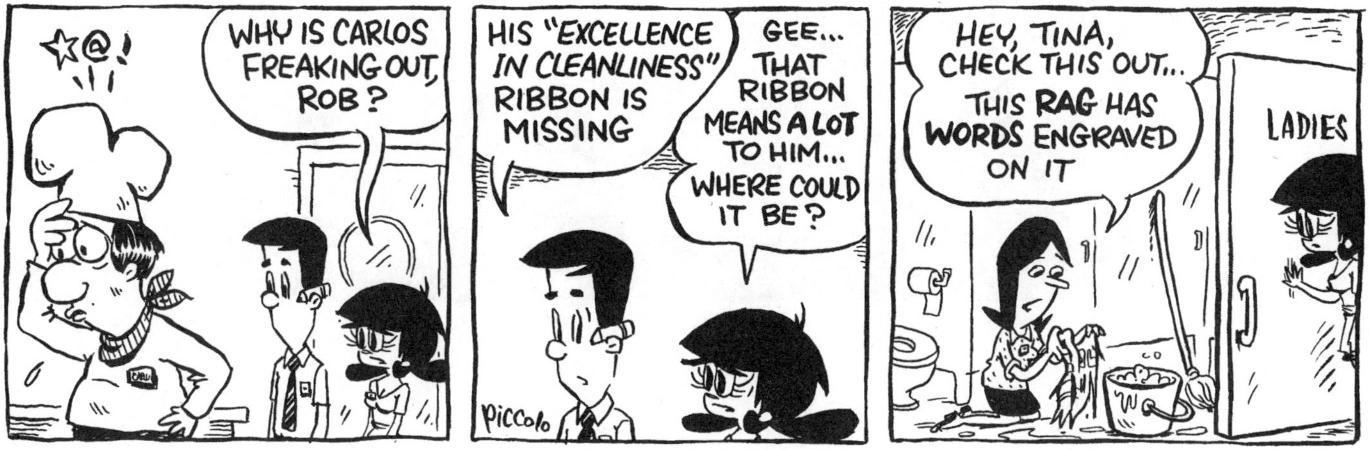
☆@!
WHY IS CARLOS FREAKING OUT, ROB?
HIS "EXCELLENCE IN CLEANLINESS" RIBBON IS MISSING
GEE... THAT RIBBON MEANS A LOT TO HIM... WHERE COULD IT BE?
PICCOLO
HEY, TINA, CHECK THIS OUT... THIS RAG HAS WORDS ENGRAVED ON IT
LADIES

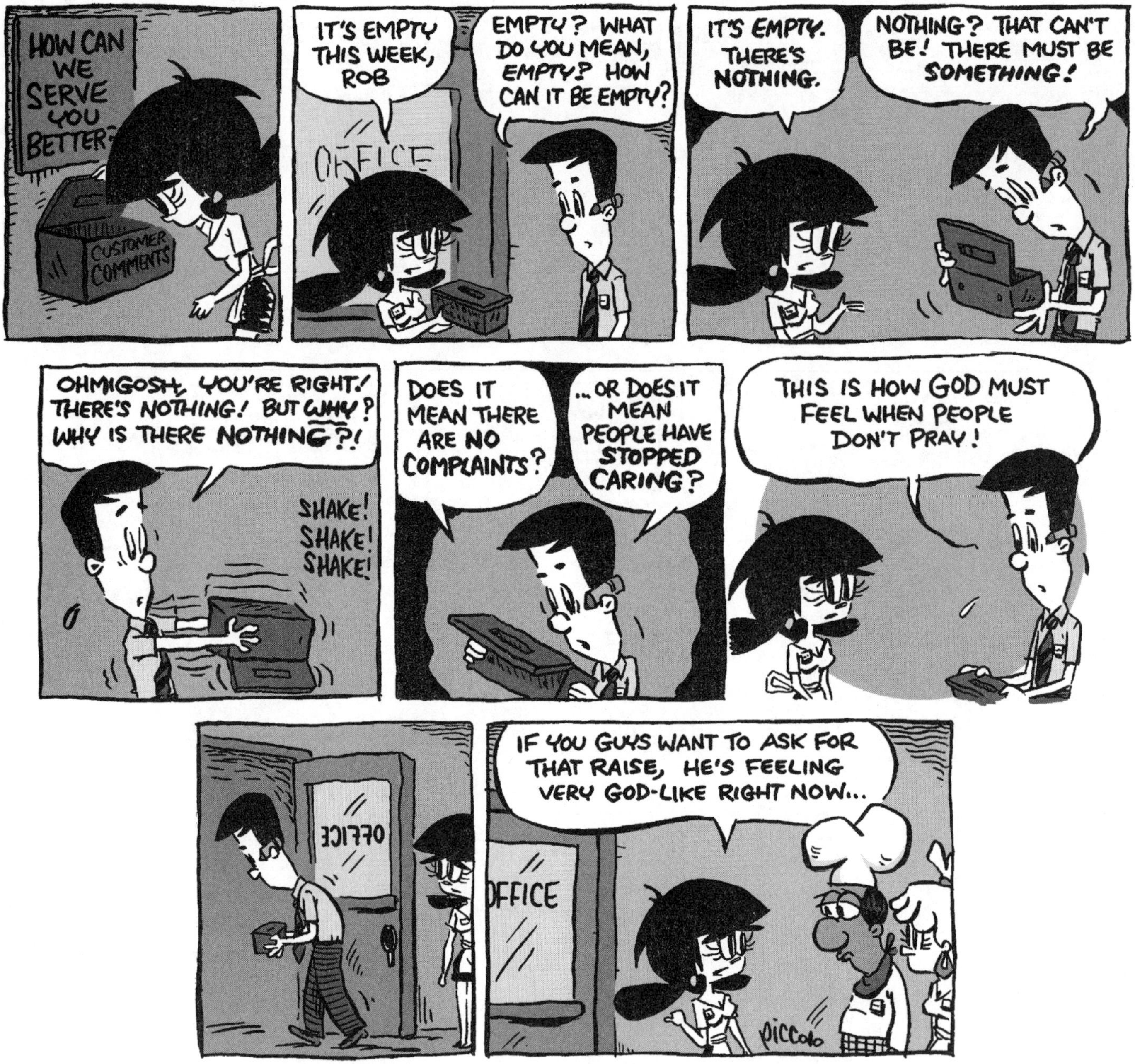
HOW CAN WE SERVE YOU BETTER?
CUSTOMER COMMENTS
IT'S EMPTY THIS WEEK, ROB
OFFICE
EMPTY? WHAT DO YOU MEAN, EMPTY? HOW CAN IT BE EMPTY?
IT'S EMPTY. THERE'S NOTHING.
NOTHING? THAT CAN'T BE! THERE MUST BE SOMETHING!
OHMIGOSH, YOU'RE RIGHT! THERE'S NOTHING! BUT WHY? WHY IS THERE NOTHING?!
SHAKE! SHAKE! SHAKE!
DOES IT MEAN THERE ARE NO COMPLAINTS?
...OR DOES IT MEAN PEOPLE HAVE STOPPED CARING?
THIS IS HOW GOD MUST FEEL WHEN PEOPLE DON'T PRAY!
OFFICE
IF YOU GUYS WANT TO ASK FOR THAT RAISE, HE'S FEELING VERY GOD-LIKE RIGHT NOW...
OFFICE
piccolo

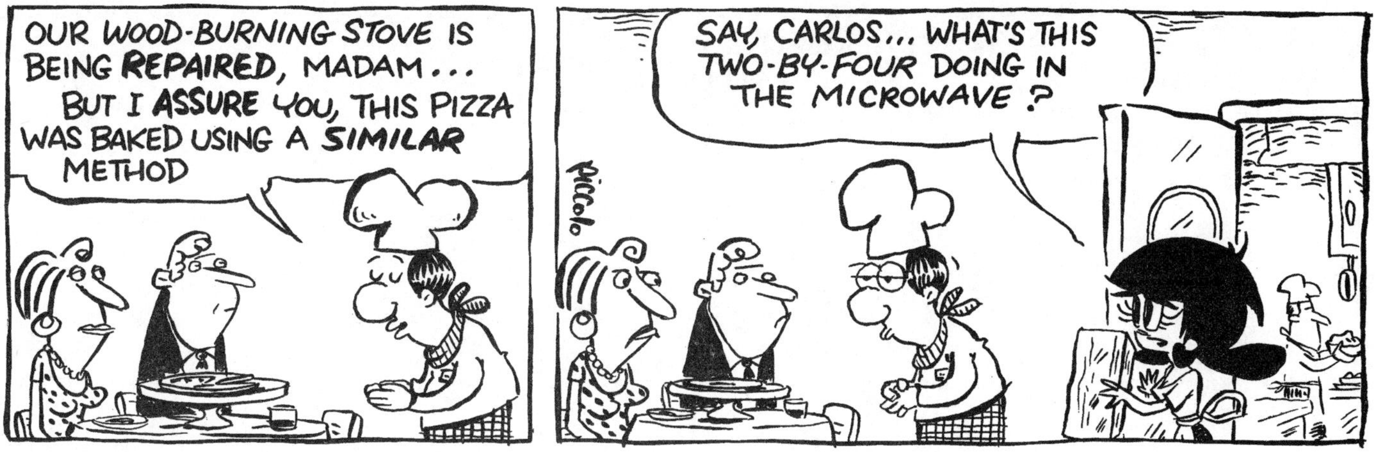
OUR WOOD-BURNING-STOVE IS BEING REPAIRED, MADAM... BUT I ASSURE YOU, THIS PIZZA WAS BAKED USING A SIMILAR METHOD
PICCOLO
SAY, CARLOS... WHAT'S THIS TWO-BY-FOUR DOING IN THE MICROWAVE ?

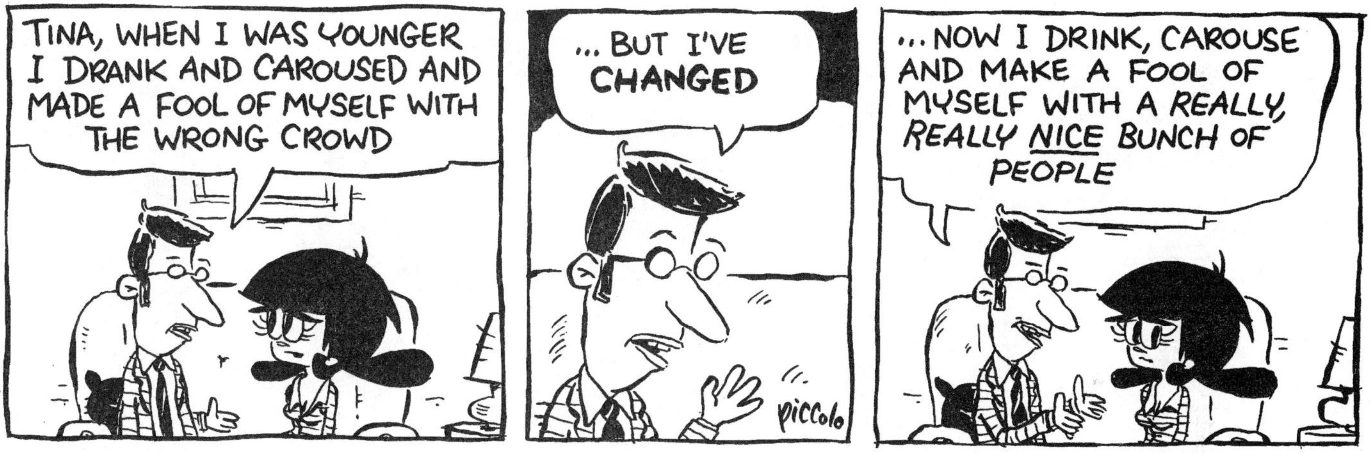
TINA, WHEN I WAS YOUNGER I DRANK AND CAROUSED AND MADE A FOOL OF MYSELF WITH THE WRONG CROWD
... BUT I'VE CHANGED
PICCOLO
... NOW I DRINK, CAROUSE AND MAKE A FOOL OF MYSELF WITH A REALLY, REALLY NICE BUNCH OF PEOPLE

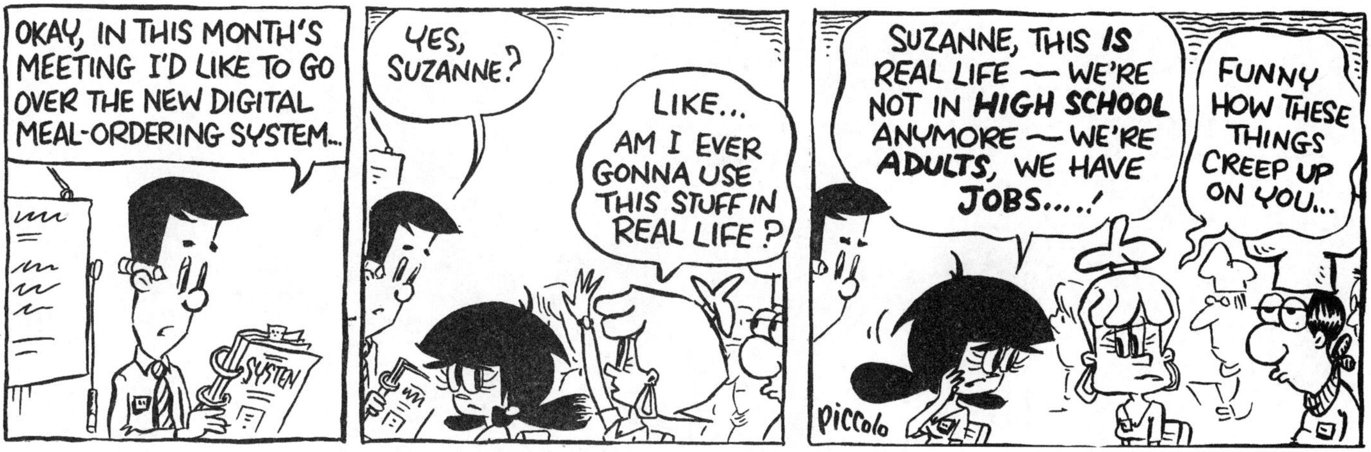
OKAY, IN THIS MONTH'S MEETING I'D LIKE TO GO OVER THE NEW DIGITAL MEAL-ORDERING SYSTEM...
SYSTEM
YES, SUZANNE?
LIKE... AM I EVER GONNA USE THIS STUFF IN REAL LIFE ?
SUZANNE, THIS IS REAL LIFE — WE'RE NOT IN HIGH SCHOOL ANYMORE — WE'RE ADULTS, WE HAVE JOBS....!
FUNNY HOW THESE THINGS CREEP UP ON YOU...
PICCOLO

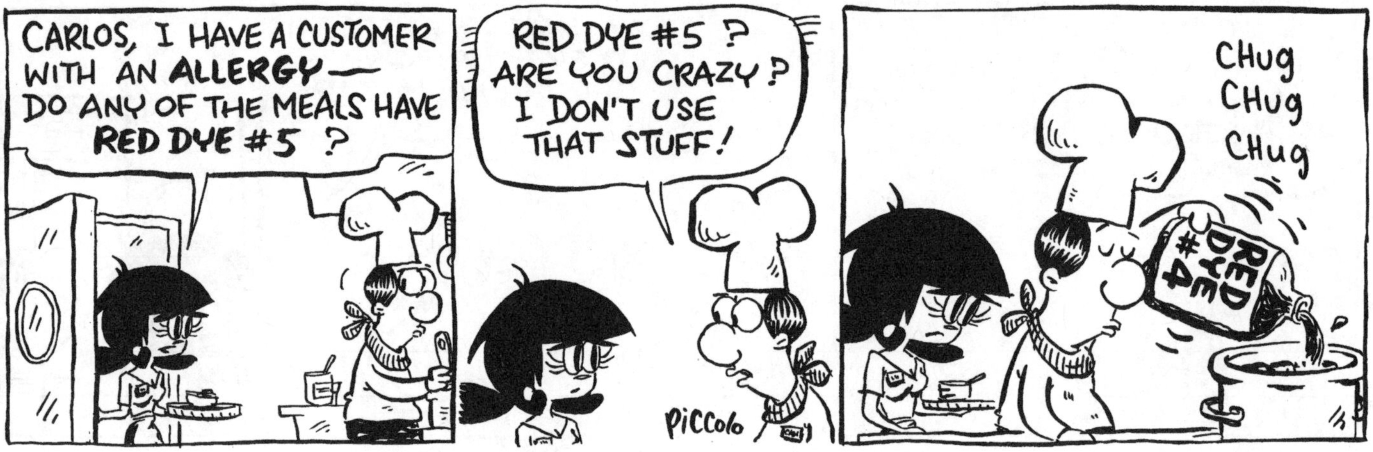
CARLOS, I HAVE A CUSTOMER WITH AN ALLERGY— DO ANY OF THE MEALS HAVE RED DYE #5 ?
RED DYE #5 ? ARE YOU CRAZY? I DON'T USE THAT STUFF!
PICCOLO
CHug CHug CHug
RED DYE #4

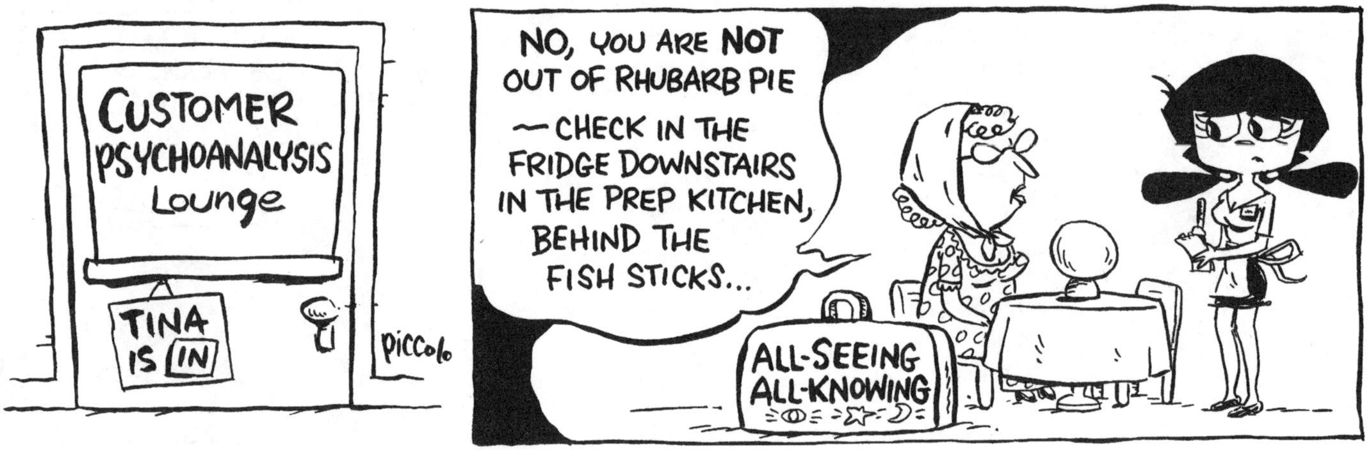
CUSTOMER PSYCHOANALYSIS Lounge
TINA IS IN
PICCOLO
NO, YOU ARE NOT OUT OF RHUBARB PIE —CHECK IN THE FRIDGE DOWNSTAIRS IN THE PREP KITCHEN, BEHIND THE FISH STICKS...
ALL-SEEING ALL-KNOWING

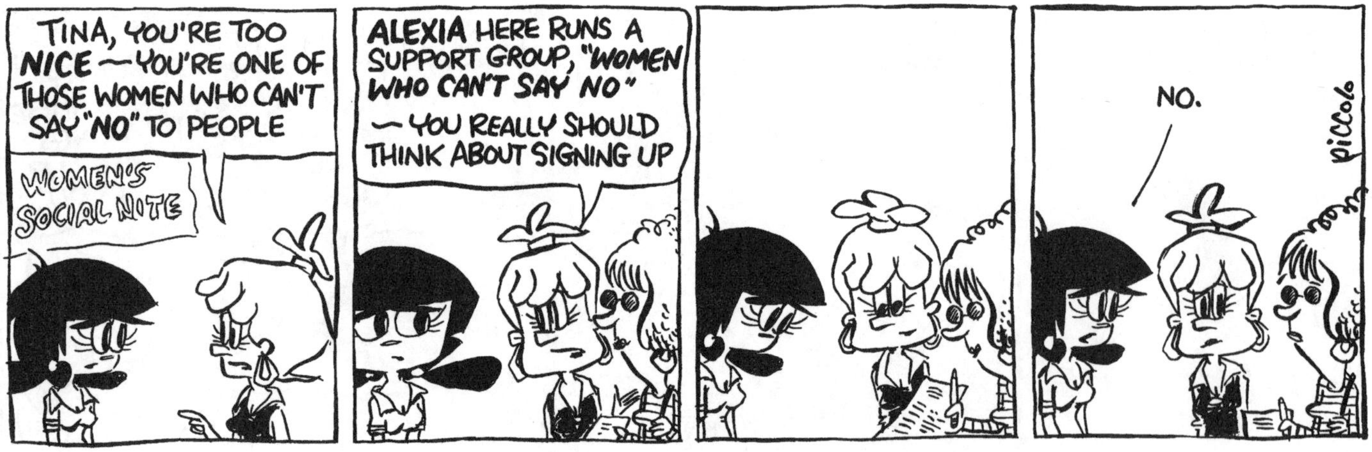
TINA, YOU'RE TOO NICE—YOU'RE ONE OF THOSE WOMEN WHO CAN'T SAY "NO" TO PEOPLE
WOMEN'S SOCIAL NITE
ALEXIA HERE RUNS A SUPPORT GROUP, "WOMEN WHO CAN'T SAY NO" —YOU REALLY SHOULD THINK ABOUT SIGNING UP
NO.
PICCOLO

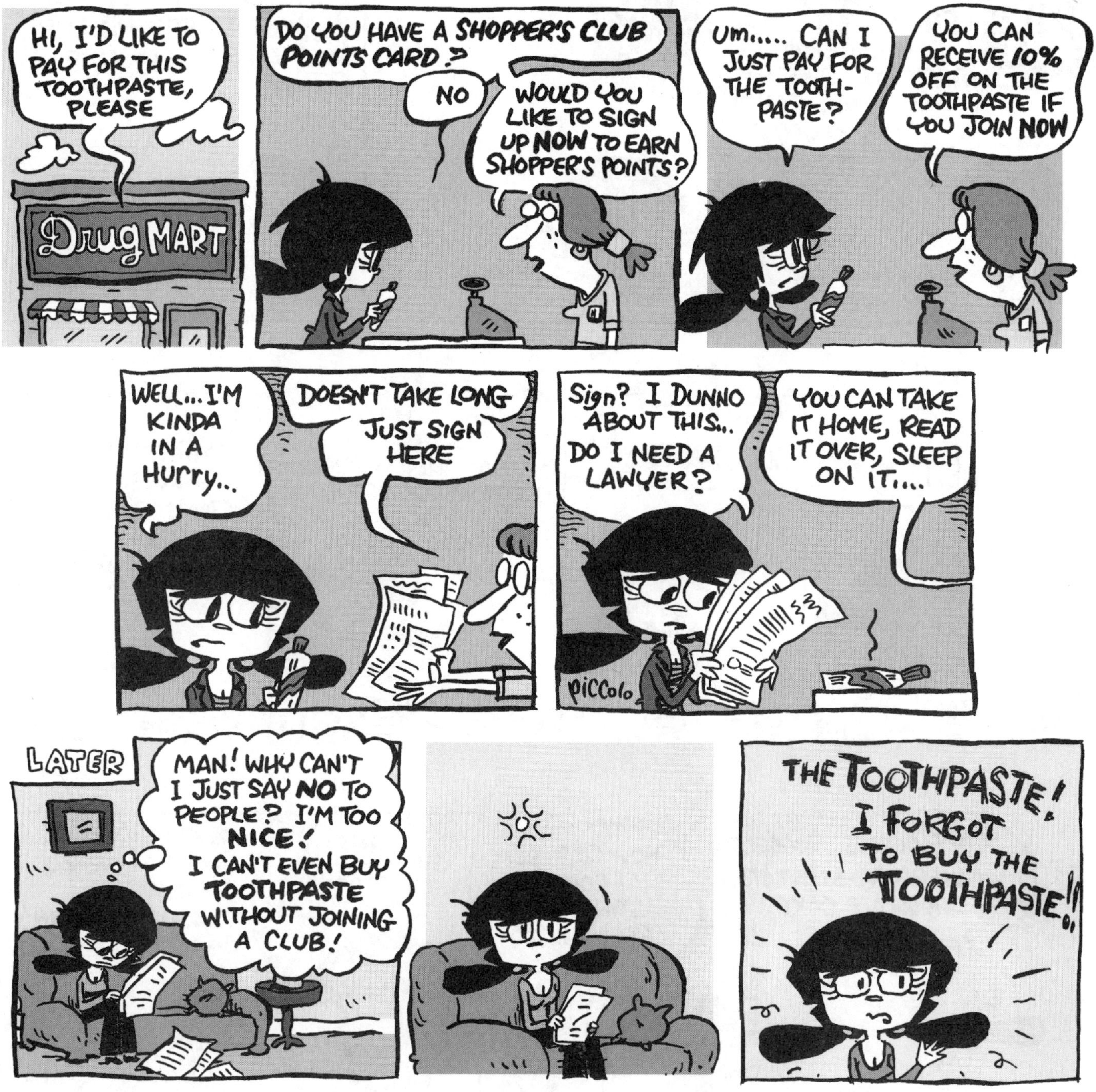
HI, I'D LIKE TO PAY FOR THIS TOOTHPASTE, PLEASE
Drug MART
DO YOU HAVE A SHOPPER'S CLUB POINTS CARD?
NO
WOULD YOU LIKE TO SIGN UP NOW TO EARN SHOPPER'S POINTS?
Um..... CAN I JUST PAY FOR THE TOOTH-PASTE?
YOU CAN RECEIVE 10% OFF ON THE TOOTHPASTE IF YOU JOIN NOW
WELL... I'M KINDA IN A Hurry...
DOESN'T TAKE LONG
JUST SIGN HERE
Sign? I DUNNO ABOUT THIS... DO I NEED A LAWYER?
YOU CAN TAKE IT HOME, READ IT OVER, SLEEP ON IT....
piCColo
LATER
MAN! WHY CAN'T I JUST SAY NO TO PEOPLE? I'M TOO NICE! I CAN'T EVEN BUY TOOTHPASTE WITHOUT JOINING A CLUB!
THE TOOTHPASTE! I FORGOT TO BUY THE TOOTHPASTE!!

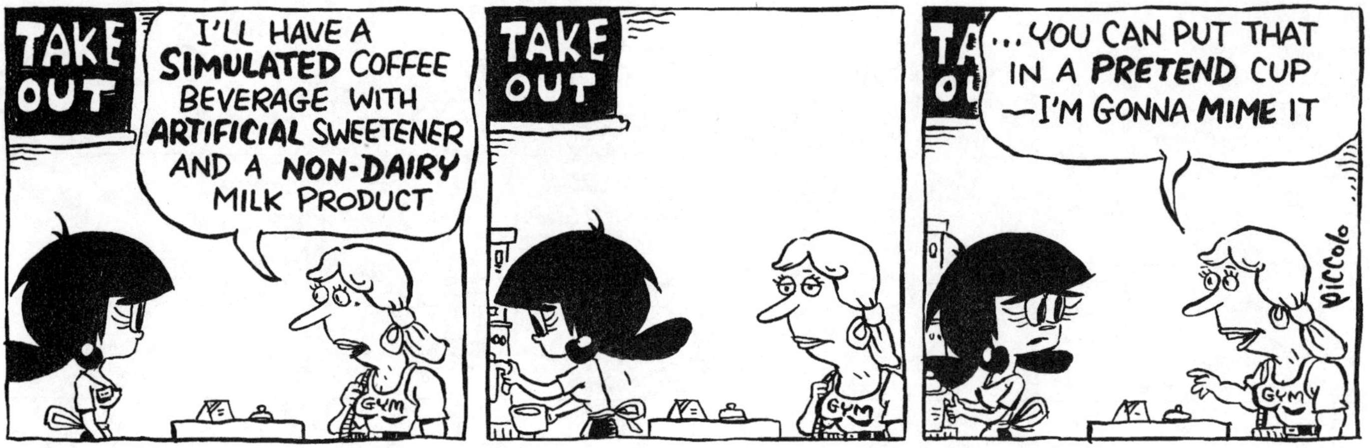
TAKE OUT
I'LL HAVE A SIMULATED COFFEE BEVERAGE WITH ARTIFICIAL SWEETENER AND A NON-DAIRY MILK PRODUCT
TAKE OUT
...YOU CAN PUT THAT IN A PRETEND CUP —I'M GONNA MIME IT
GYM
piccolo

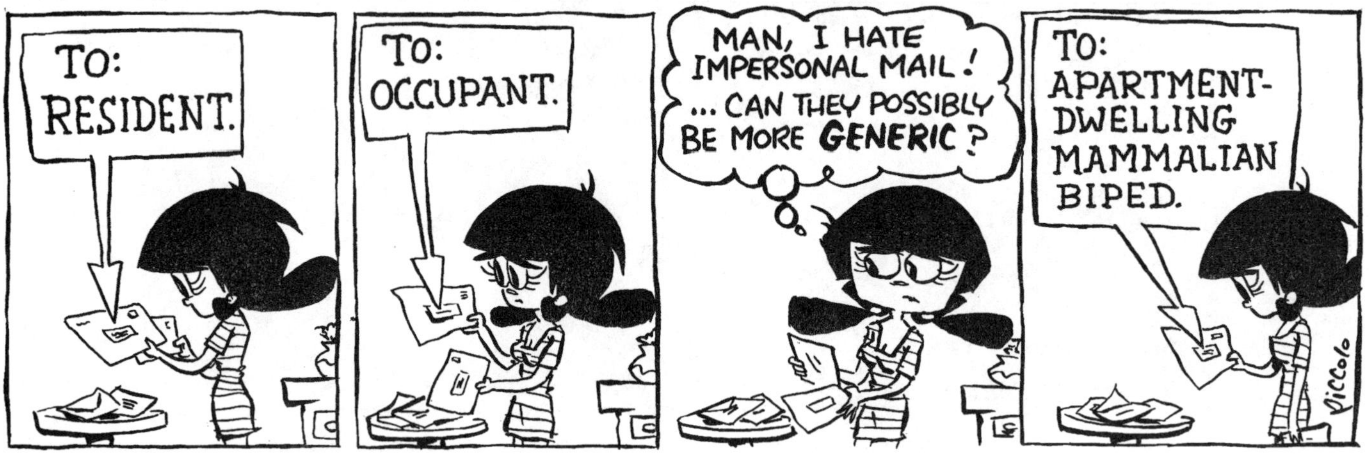
TO: RESIDENT.
TO: OCCUPANT.
MAN, I HATE IMPERSONAL MAIL! ...CAN THEY POSSIBLY BE MORE GENERIC?
TO: APARTMENT-DWELLING MAMMALIAN BIPED.
piccolo

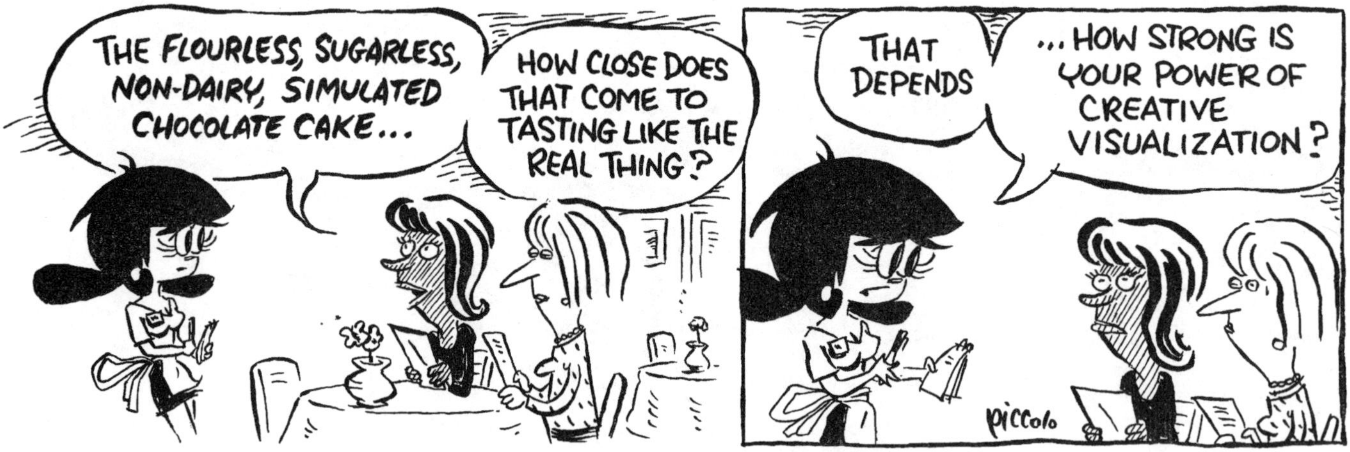
THE FLOURLESS, SUGARLESS, NON-DAIRY, SIMULATED CHOCOLATE CAKE...
HOW CLOSE DOES THAT COME TO TASTING LIKE THE REAL THING?
THAT DEPENDS
...HOW STRONG IS YOUR POWER OF CREATIVE VISUALIZATION?
piccolo

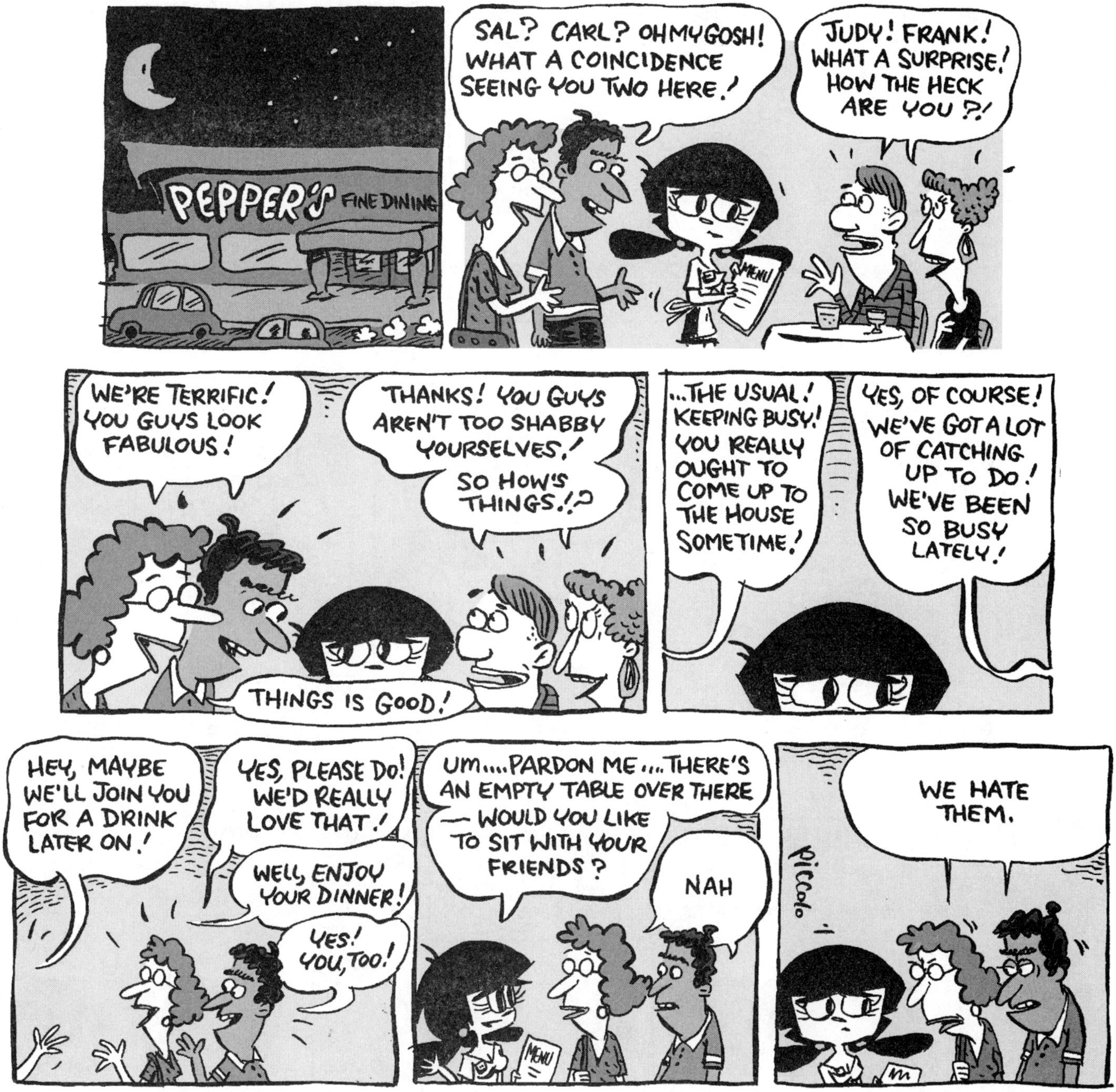
PEPPER'S FINE DINING
SAL? CARL? OHMYGOSH! WHAT A COINCIDENCE SEEING YOU TWO HERE!
JUDY! FRANK! WHAT A SURPRISE! HOW THE HECK ARE YOU ?!
MENU
WE'RE TERRIFIC! YOU GUYS LOOK FABULOUS!
THANKS! YOU GUYS AREN'T TOO SHABBY YOURSELVES!
SO HOW'S THINGS!?
THINGS IS GOOD!
...THE USUAL! KEEPING BUSY! YOU REALLY OUGHT TO COME UP TO THE HOUSE SOMETIME!
YES, OF COURSE! WE'VE GOT A LOT OF CATCHING UP TO DO! WE'VE BEEN SO BUSY LATELY!
HEY, MAYBE WE'LL JOIN YOU FOR A DRINK LATER ON!
YES, PLEASE DO! WE'D REALLY LOVE THAT!
WELL, ENJOY YOUR DINNER!
YES! YOU, TOO!
UM.....PARDON ME.....THERE'S AN EMPTY TABLE OVER THERE — WOULD YOU LIKE TO SIT WITH YOUR FRIENDS?
NAH
MENU
PICCOLO
WE HATE THEM.

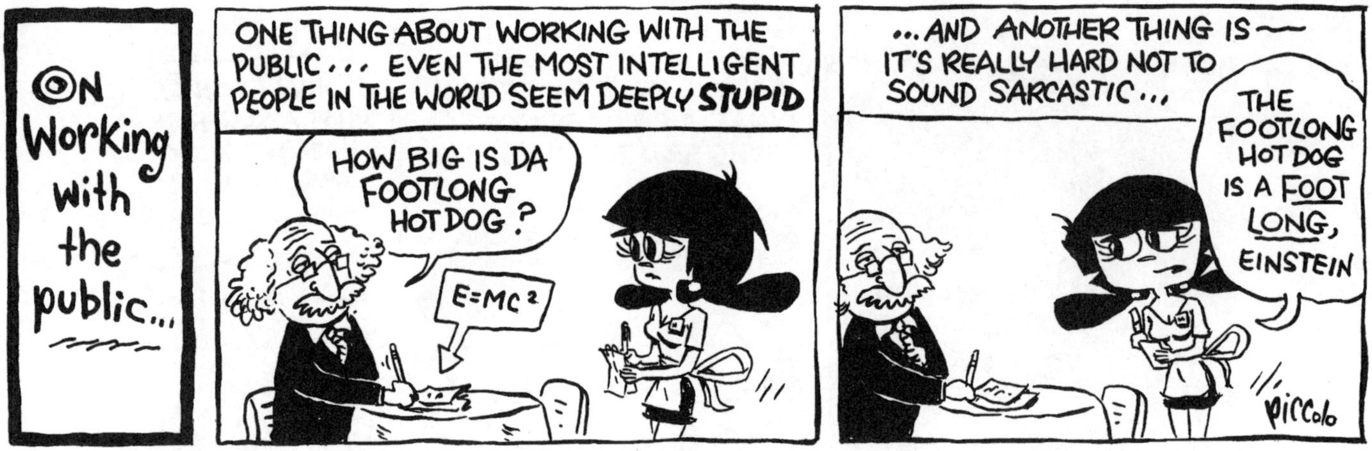
ON Working with the public...
ONE THING ABOUT WORKING WITH THE PUBLIC... EVEN THE MOST INTELLIGENT PEOPLE IN THE WORLD SEEM DEEPLY STUPID
HOW BIG IS DA FOOTLONG HOT DOG?
E=MC2
...AND ANOTHER THING IS— IT'S REALLY HARD NOT TO SOUND SARCASTIC...
THE FOOTLONG HOT DOG IS A FOOT LONG, EINSTEIN
piccolo

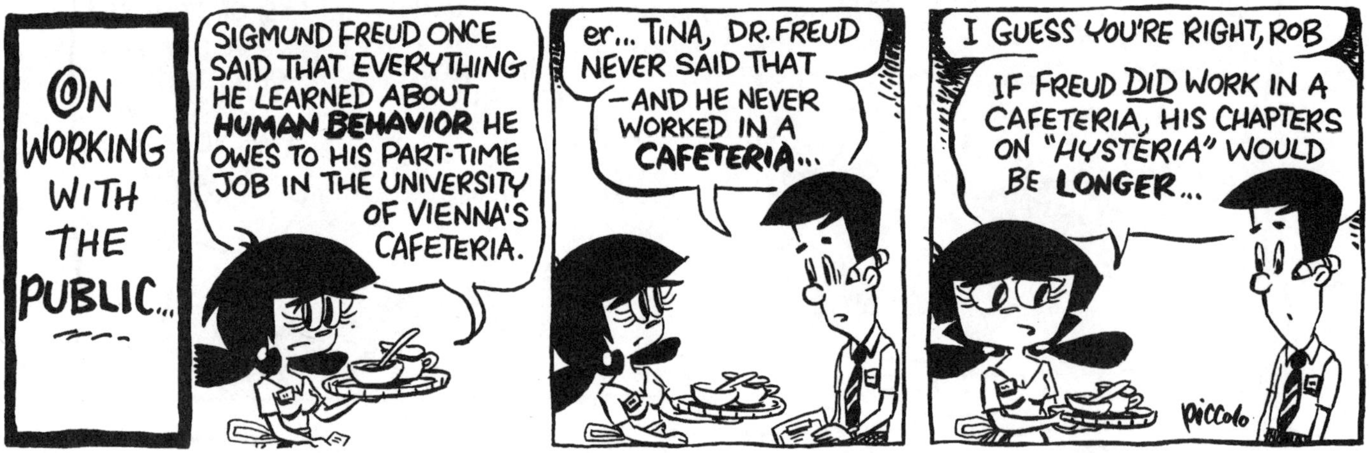
ON WORKING WITH THE PUBLIC...
SIGMUND FREUD ONCE SAID THAT EVERYTHING HE LEARNED ABOUT HUMAN BEHAVIOR HE OWES TO HIS PART-TIME JOB IN THE UNIVERSITY OF VIENNA'S CAFETERIA.
er... TINA, DR. FREUD NEVER SAID THAT
—AND HE NEVER WORKED IN A CAFETERIA...
I GUESS YOU'RE RIGHT, ROB
IF FREUD DID WORK IN A CAFETERIA, HIS CHAPTERS ON "HYSTERIA" WOULD BE LONGER...
piccolo

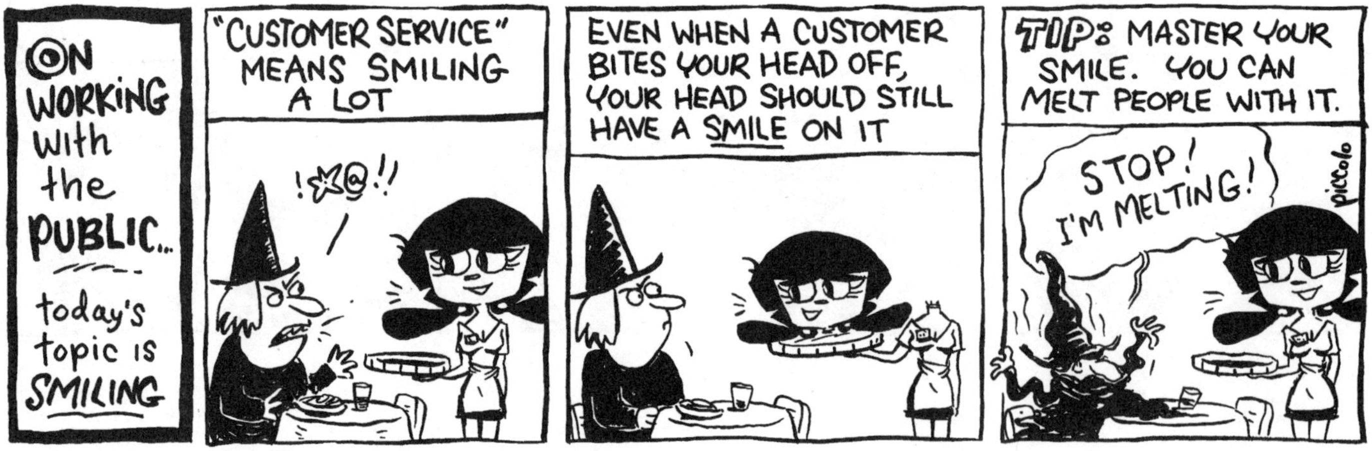
ON WORKING with the PUBLIC...
today's topic is SMILING
"CUSTOMER SERVICE" MEANS SMILING A LOT
!*@!!
EVEN WHEN A CUSTOMER BITES YOUR HEAD OFF, YOUR HEAD SHOULD STILL HAVE A SMILE ON IT
TIP: MASTER YOUR SMILE. YOU CAN MELT PEOPLE WITH IT.
STOP! I'M MELTING!
piccolo

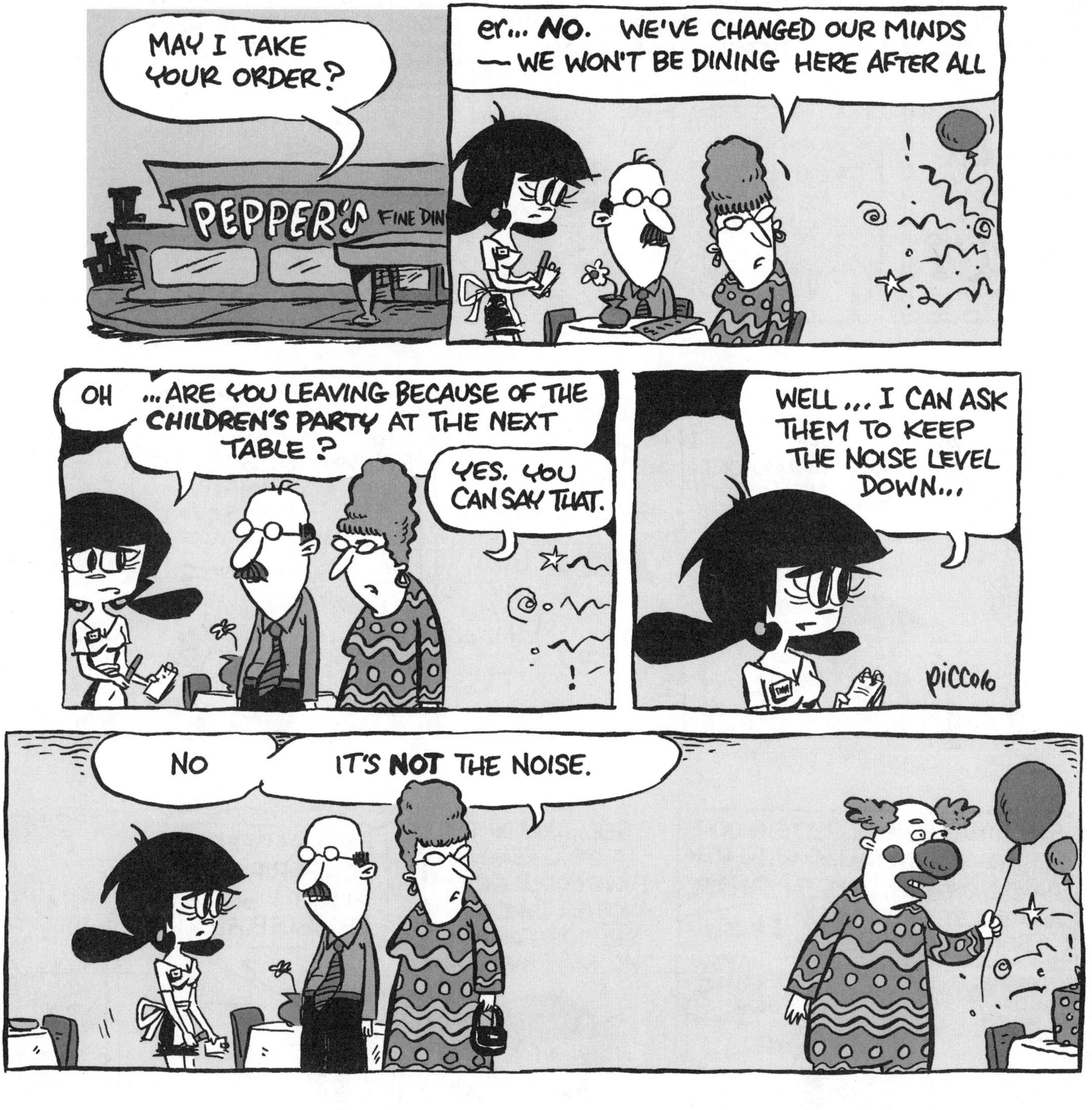
MAY I TAKE YOUR ORDER?
PEPPER'S FINE DIN
er... NO. WE'VE CHANGED OUR MINDS — WE WON'T BE DINING HERE AFTER ALL
OH ...ARE YOU LEAVING BECAUSE OF THE CHILDREN'S PARTY AT THE NEXT TABLE?
YES. YOU CAN SAY THAT.
WELL... I CAN ASK THEM TO KEEP THE NOISE LEVEL DOWN...
piccolo
NO IT'S NOT THE NOISE.

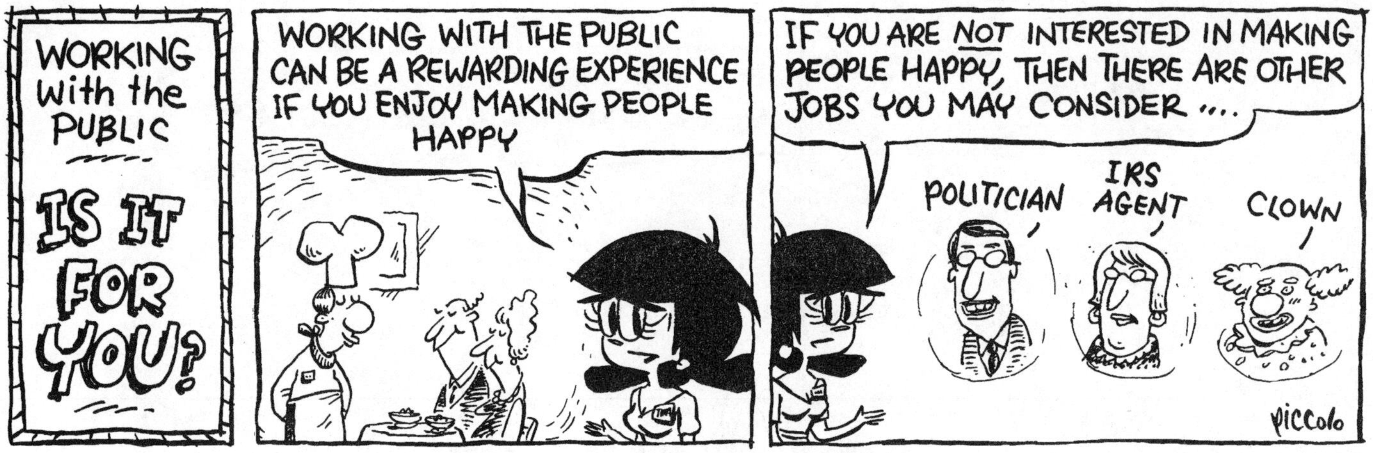
WORKING with the PUBLIC
IS IT FOR YOU?
WORKING WITH THE PUBLIC CAN BE A REWARDING EXPERIENCE IF YOU ENJOY MAKING PEOPLE HAPPY
IF YOU ARE NOT INTERESTED IN MAKING PEOPLE HAPPY, THEN THERE ARE OTHER JOBS YOU MAY CONSIDER ....
POLITICIAN
IRS AGENT
CLOWN
piccolo

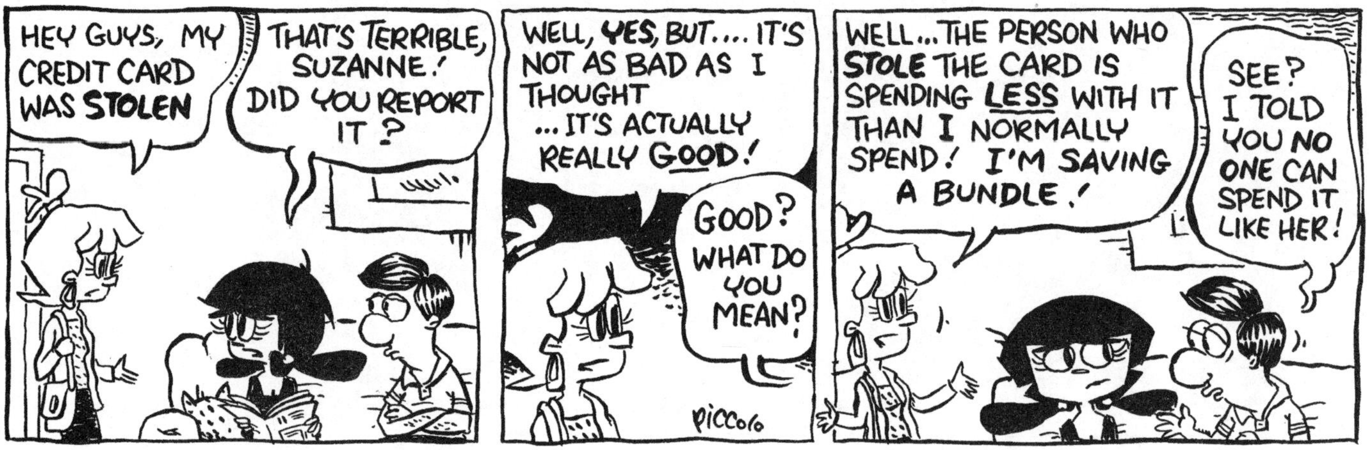
HEY GUYS, MY CREDIT CARD WAS STOLEN
THAT'S TERRIBLE, SUZANNE! DID YOU REPORT IT?
WELL, YES, BUT.... IT'S NOT AS BAD AS I THOUGHT ...IT'S ACTUALLY REALLY GOOD!
GOOD? WHAT DO YOU MEAN?
piccolo
WELL...THE PERSON WHO STOLE THE CARD IS SPENDING LESS WITH IT THAN I NORMALLY SPEND! I'M SAVING A BUNDLE!
SEE? I TOLD YOU NO ONE CAN SPEND IT LIKE HER!

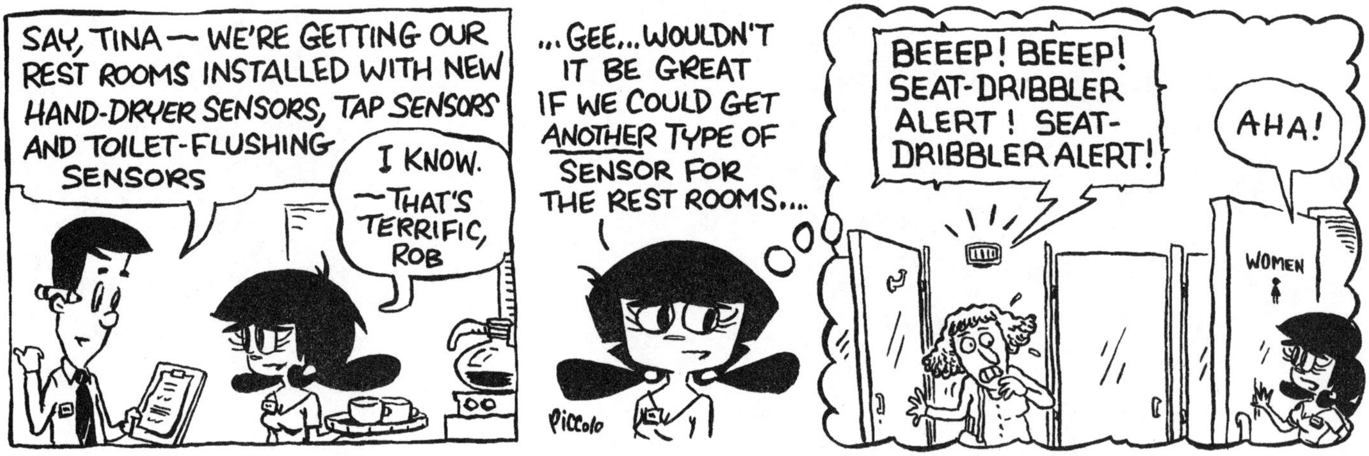
SAY, TINA — WE'RE GETTING OUR REST ROOMS INSTALLED WITH NEW HAND-DRYER SENSORS, TAP SENSORS AND TOILET-FLUSHING SENSORS
I KNOW. — THAT'S TERRIFIC, ROB
...GEE...WOULDN'T IT BE GREAT IF WE COULD GET ANOTHER TYPE OF SENSOR FOR THE REST ROOMS....
piccolo
BEEEP! BEEEP! SEAT-DRIBBLER ALERT! SEAT-DRIBBLER ALERT!
AHA!
WOMEN

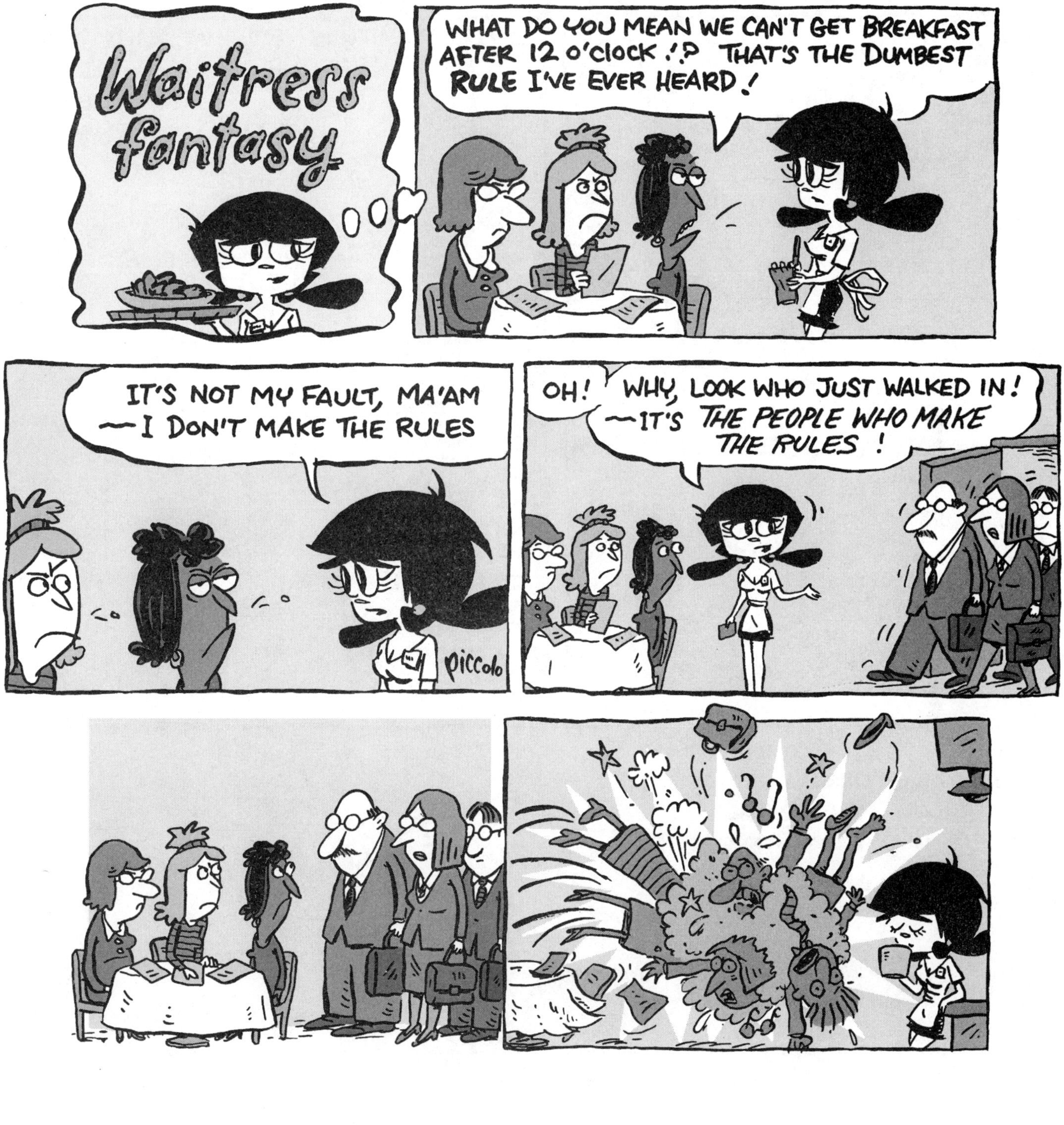
Waitress fantasy
WHAT DO YOU MEAN WE CAN'T GET BREAKFAST AFTER 12 O'CLOCK !? THAT'S THE DUMBEST RULE I'VE EVER HEARD !
IT'S NOT MY FAULT, MA'AM —I DON'T MAKE THE RULES
piccolo
OH!
WHY, LOOK WHO JUST WALKED IN! —IT'S THE PEOPLE WHO MAKE THE RULES !

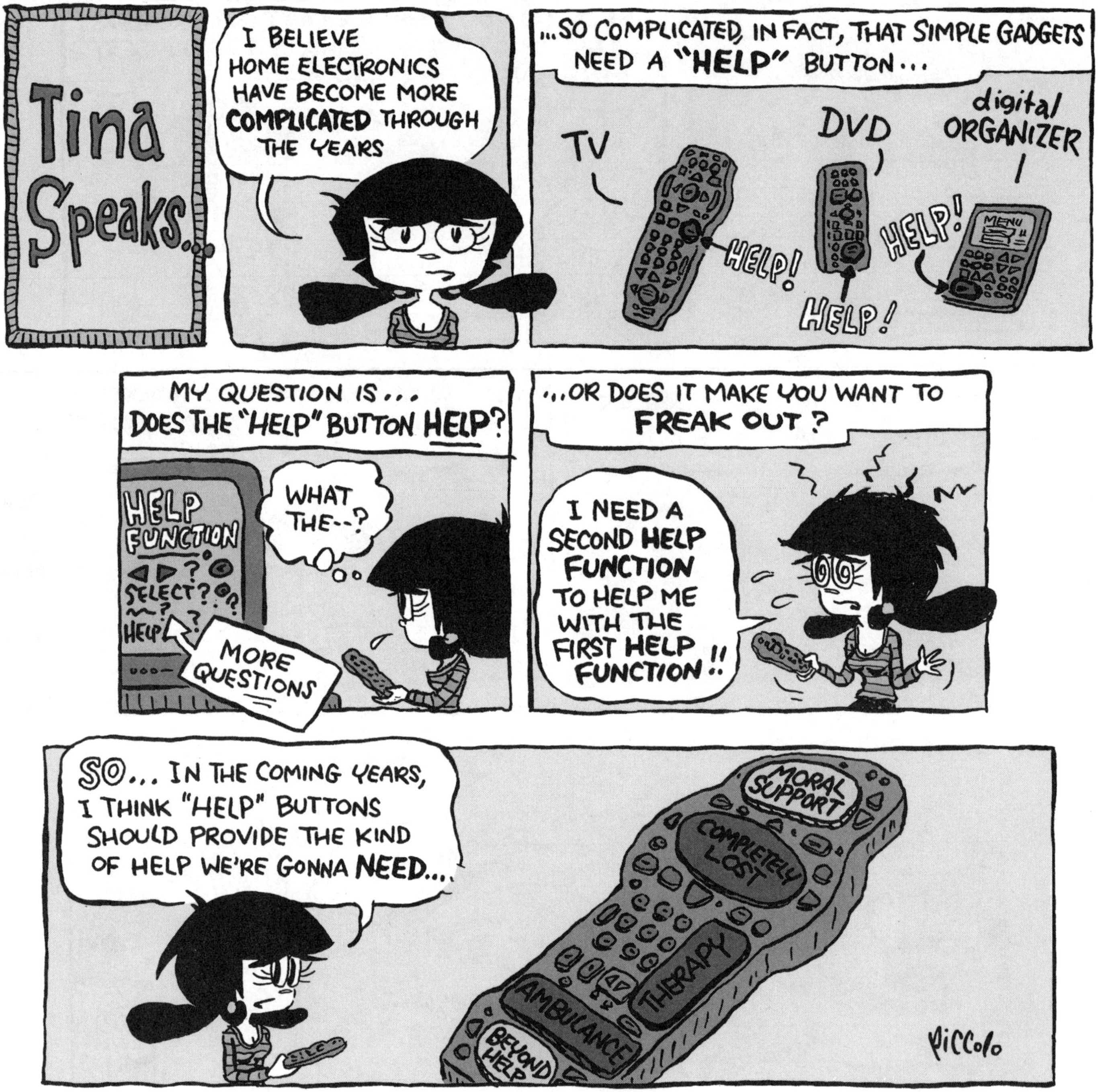

Tina Speaks...
I BELIEVE HOME ELECTRONICS HAVE BECOME MORE COMPLICATED THROUGH THE YEARS
...SO COMPLICATED, IN FACT, THAT SIMPLE GADGETS NEED A "HELP" BUTTON...
TV
DVD
digital ORGANIZER
HELP!
HELP!
HELP!
MENU
MY QUESTION IS... DOES THE "HELP" BUTTON HELP?
HELP FUNCTION
SELECT?
HELP
WHAT THE--?
MORE QUESTIONS
...OR DOES IT MAKE YOU WANT TO FREAK OUT?
I NEED A SECOND HELP FUNCTION TO HELP ME WITH THE FIRST HELP FUNCTION!!
SO... IN THE COMING YEARS, I THINK "HELP" BUTTONS SHOULD PROVIDE THE KIND OF HELP WE'RE GONNA NEED....
MORAL SUPPORT
COMPLETELY LOST
THERAPY
AMBULANCE
BEYOND HELP
Piccolo

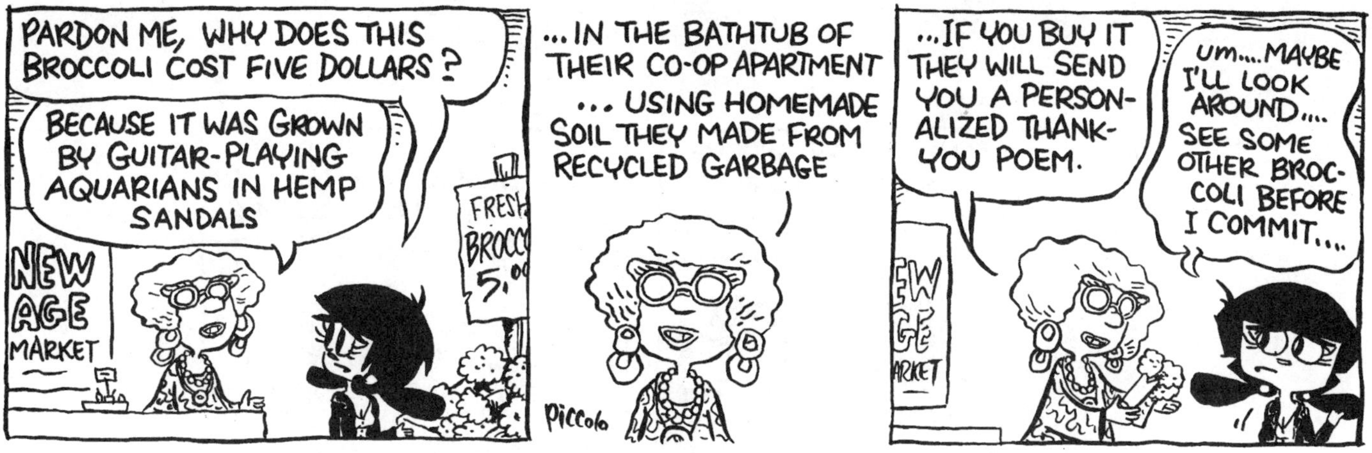
PARDON ME, WHY DOES THIS BROCCOLI COST FIVE DOLLARS?
BECAUSE IT WAS GROWN BY GUITAR-PLAYING AQUARIANS IN HEMP SANDALS
NEW AGE MARKET
FRESH BROCC 5.00
...IN THE BATHTUB OF THEIR CO-OP APARTMENT ... USING HOMEMADE SOIL THEY MADE FROM RECYCLED GARBAGE
piccolo
...IF YOU BUY IT THEY WILL SEND YOU A PERSONALIZED THANK-YOU POEM.
um.....MAYBE I'LL LOOK AROUND.... SEE SOME OTHER BROCCOLI BEFORE I COMMIT....

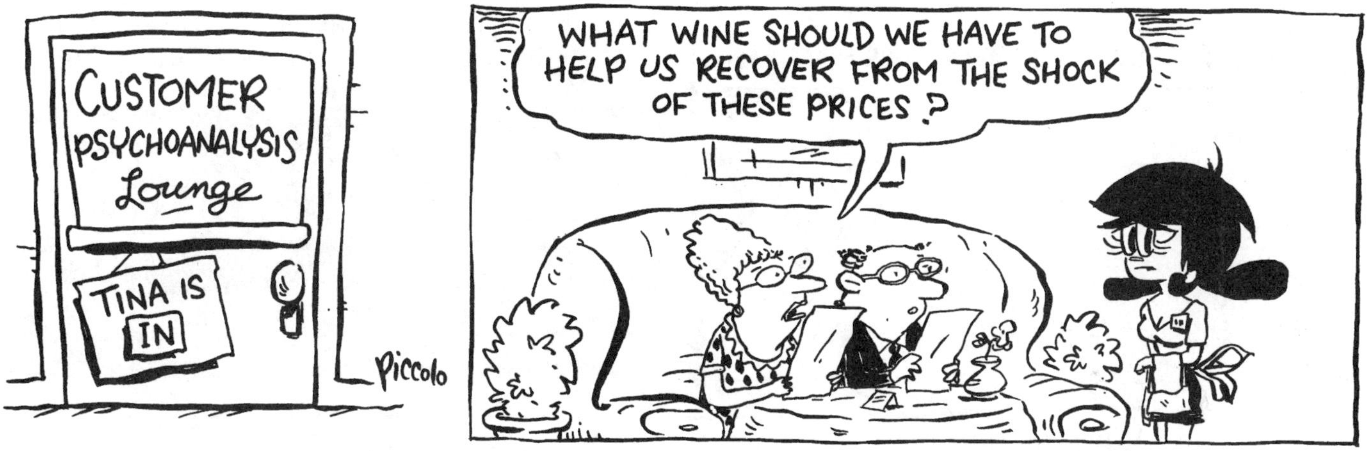
CUSTOMER PSYCHOANALYSIS Lounge
TINA IS IN
piccolo
WHAT WINE SHOULD WE HAVE TO HELP US RECOVER FROM THE SHOCK OF THESE PRICES?

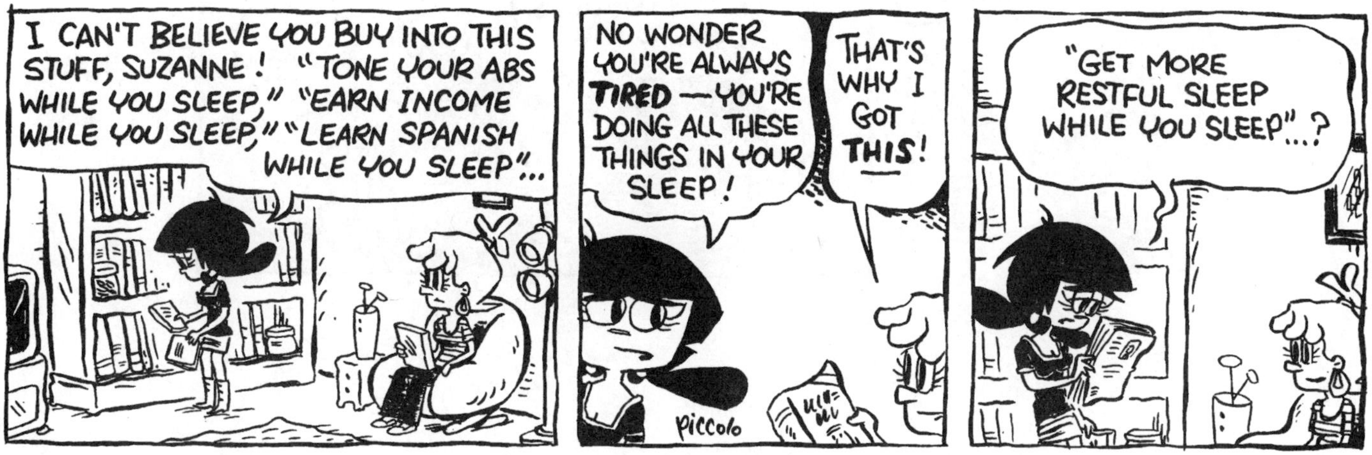
I CAN'T BELIEVE YOU BUY INTO THIS STUFF, SUZANNE! "TONE YOUR ABS WHILE YOU SLEEP," "EARN INCOME WHILE YOU SLEEP," "LEARN SPANISH WHILE YOU SLEEP"...
NO WONDER YOU'RE ALWAYS TIRED — YOU'RE DOING ALL THESE THINGS IN YOUR SLEEP!
THAT'S WHY I GOT THIS!
piccolo
"GET MORE RESTFUL SLEEP WHILE YOU SLEEP"...?

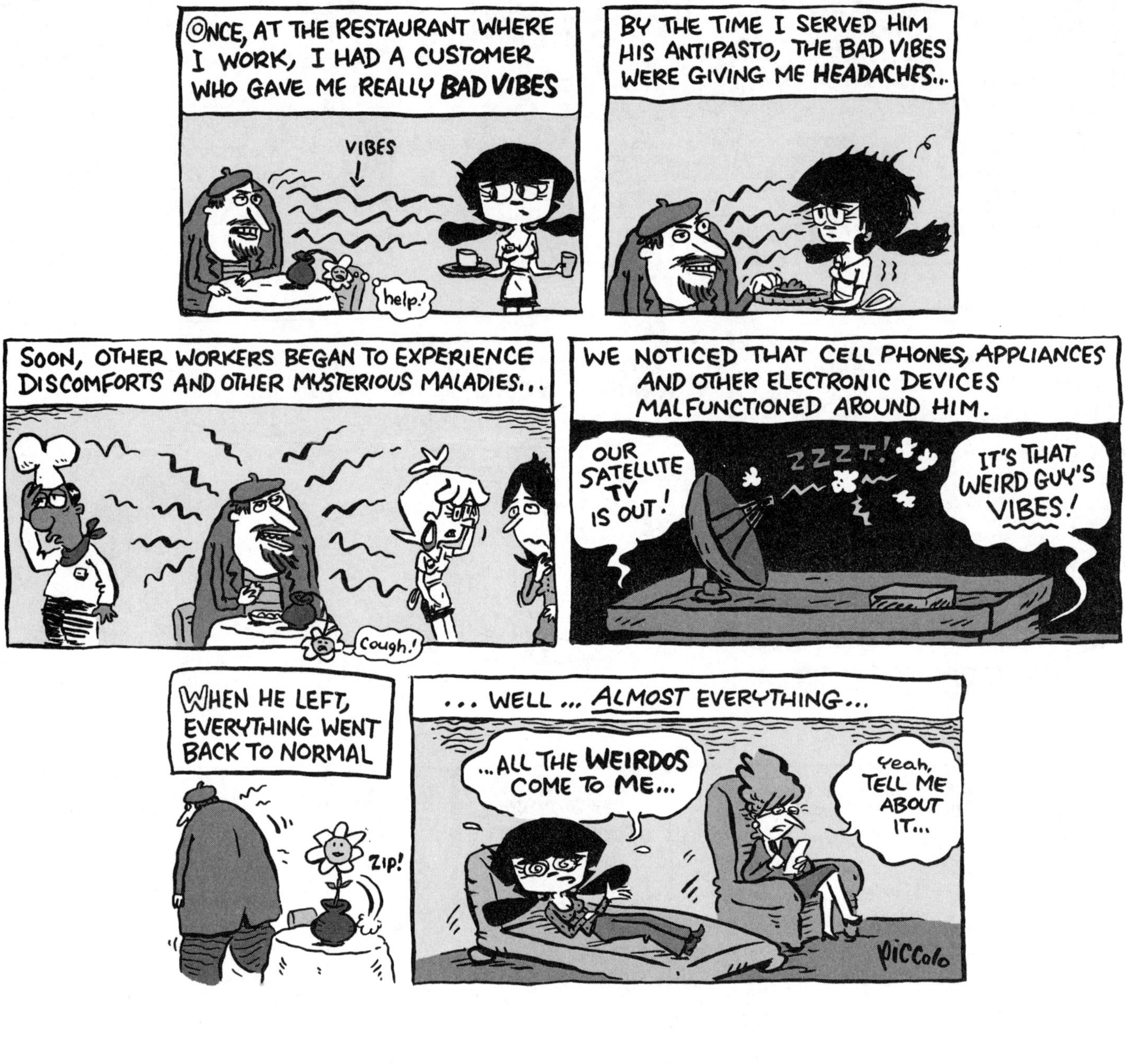
ONCE, AT THE RESTAURANT WHERE I WORK, I HAD A CUSTOMER WHO GAVE ME REALLY BAD VIBES
VIBES
help!
BY THE TIME I SERVED HIM HIS ANTIPASTO, THE BAD VIBES WERE GIVING ME HEADACHES...
SOON, OTHER WORKERS BEGAN TO EXPERIENCE DISCOMFORTS AND OTHER MYSTERIOUS MALADIES...
cough!
WE NOTICED THAT CELL PHONES, APPLIANCES AND OTHER ELECTRONIC DEVICES MALFUNCTIONED AROUND HIM.
OUR SATELLITE TV IS OUT!
ZZZT!
IT'S THAT WEIRD GUY'S VIBES!
WHEN HE LEFT, EVERYTHING WENT BACK TO NORMAL
ZIP!
... WELL ... ALMOST EVERYTHING...
...ALL THE WEIRDOS COME TO ME...
Yeah, TELL ME ABOUT IT...
piccolo

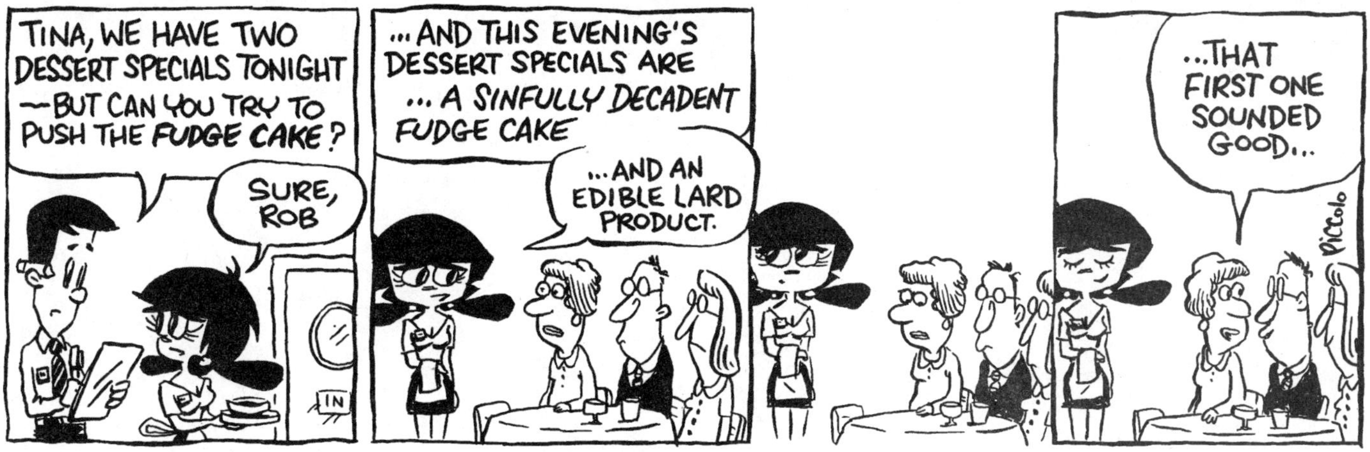
TINA, WE HAVE TWO DESSERT SPECIALS TONIGHT —BUT CAN YOU TRY TO PUSH THE FUDGE CAKE?
SURE, ROB
IN
...AND THIS EVENING'S DESSERT SPECIALS ARE ... A SINFULLY DECADENT FUDGE CAKE
...AND AN EDIBLE LARD PRODUCT.
...THAT FIRST ONE SOUNDED GOOD...
piccolo

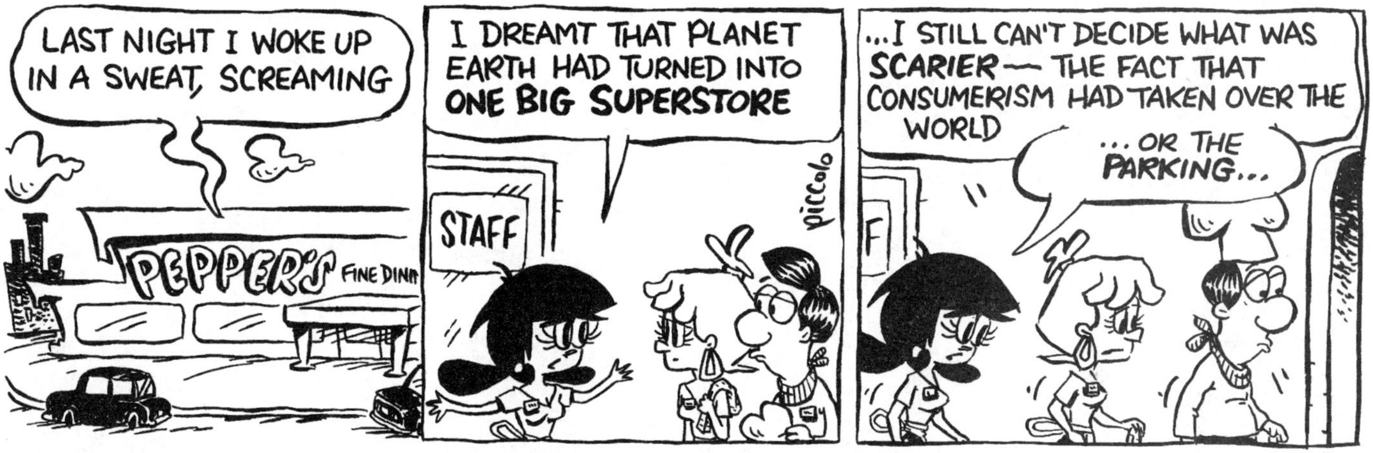
LAST NIGHT I WOKE UP IN A SWEAT, SCREAMING
PEPPER'S FINE DINI
I DREAMT THAT PLANET EARTH HAD TURNED INTO ONE BIG SUPERSTORE
STAFF
piccolo
...I STILL CAN'T DECIDE WHAT WAS SCARIER— THE FACT THAT CONSUMERISM HAD TAKEN OVER THE WORLD
...OR THE PARKING...

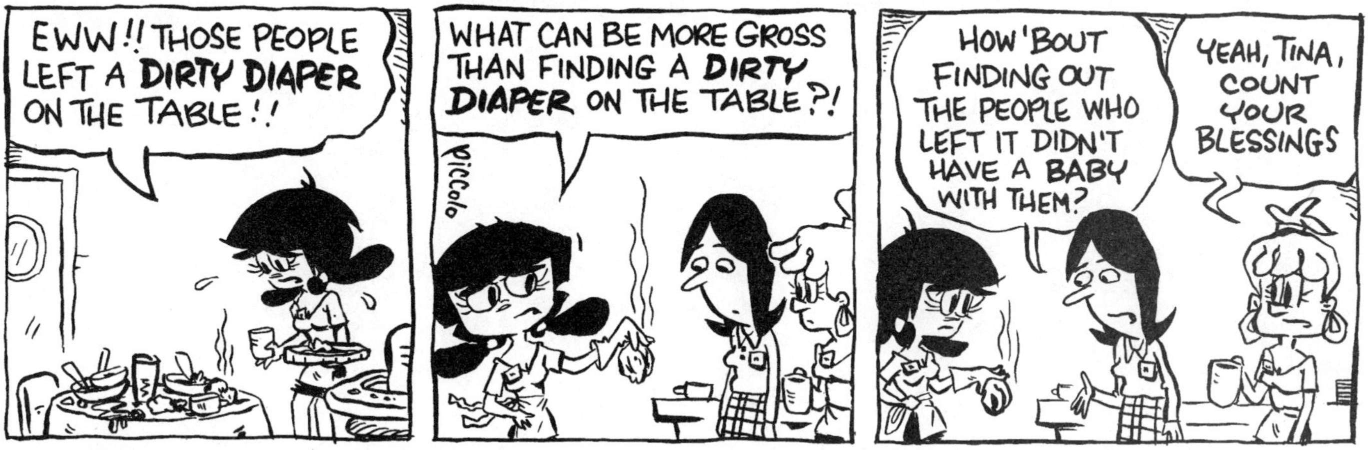
EWW!! THOSE PEOPLE LEFT A DIRTY DIAPER ON THE TABLE!!
WHAT CAN BE MORE GROSS THAN FINDING A DIRTY DIAPER ON THE TABLE?!
piccolo
HOW 'BOUT FINDING OUT THE PEOPLE WHO LEFT IT DIDN'T HAVE A BABY WITH THEM?
YEAH, TINA, COUNT YOUR BLESSINGS

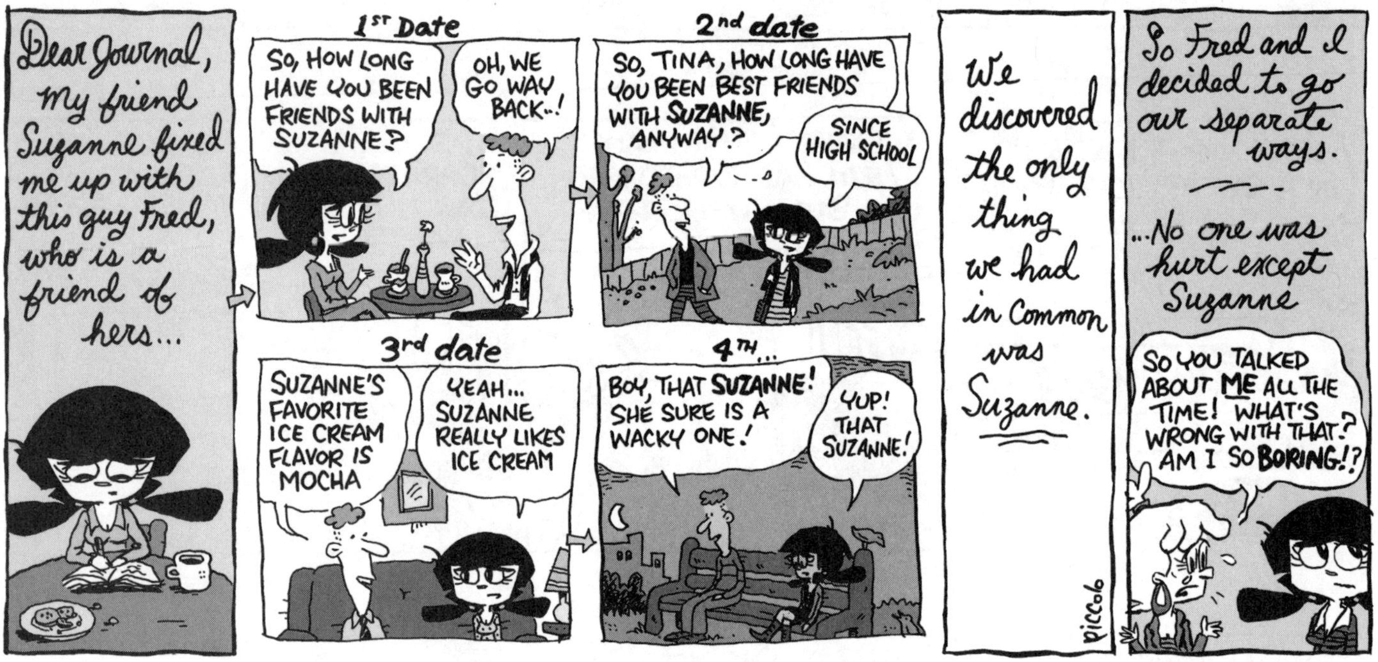
Dear Journal, my friend Suzanne fixed me up with this guy Fred, who is a friend of hers...
1ST Date
SO, HOW LONG HAVE YOU BEEN FRIENDS WITH SUZANNE?
OH, WE GO WAY BACK..!
2nd date
SO, TINA, HOW LONG HAVE YOU BEEN BEST FRIENDS WITH SUZANNE, ANYWAY?
SINCE HIGH SCHOOL
3rd date
SUZANNE'S FAVORITE ICE CREAM FLAVOR IS MOCHA
YEAH... SUZANNE REALLY LIKES ICE CREAM
4TH...
BOY, THAT SUZANNE! SHE SURE IS A WACKY ONE!
YUP! THAT SUZANNE!
We discovered the only thing we had in Common was Suzanne.
So Fred and I decided to go our separate ways.
...No one was hurt except Suzanne
SO YOU TALKED ABOUT ME ALL THE TIME! WHAT'S WRONG WITH THAT? AM I SO BORING!?
PICCOLO

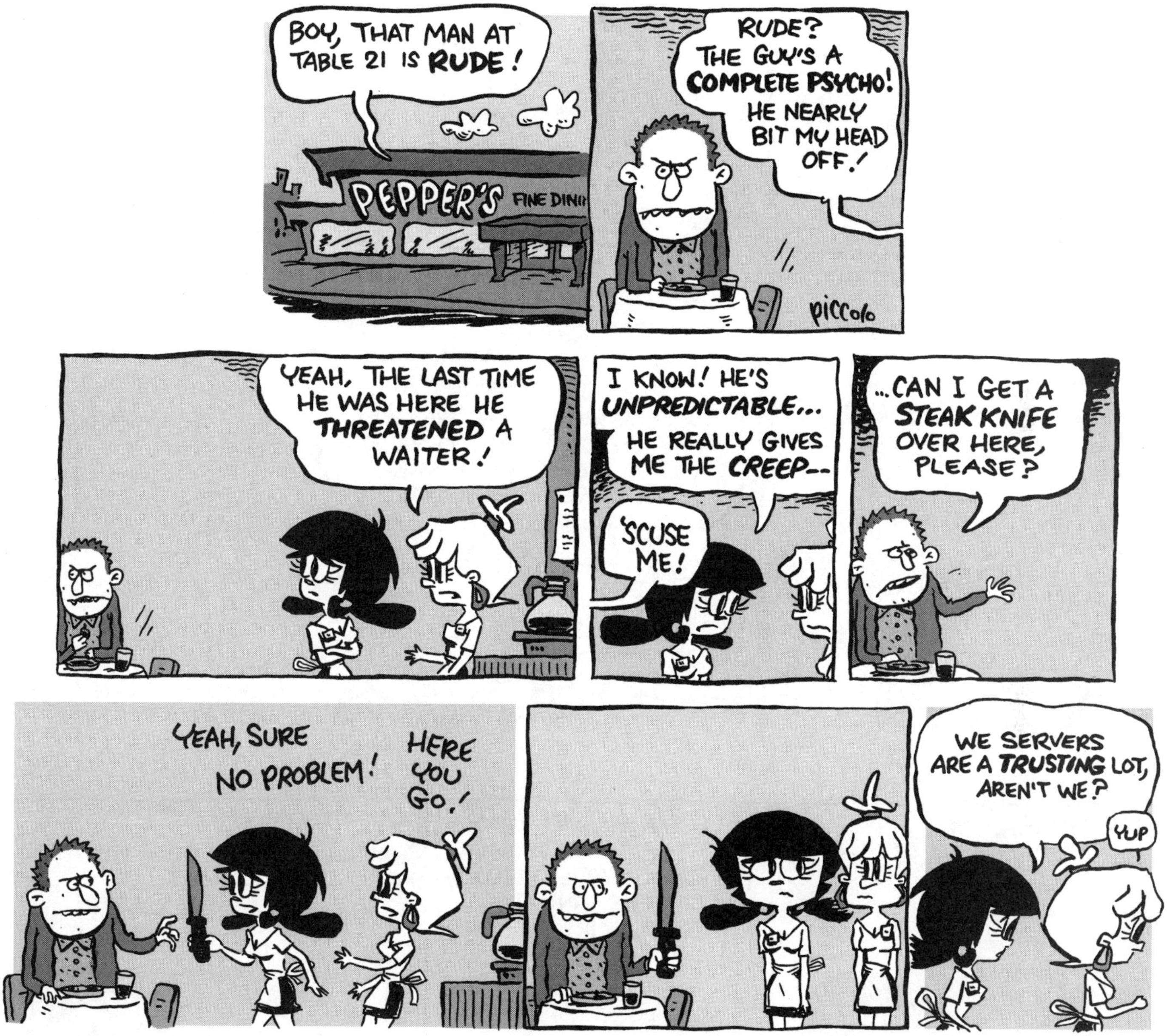
BOY, THAT MAN AT TABLE 21 IS RUDE!
PEPPER'S FINE DINI
RUDE? THE GUY'S A COMPLETE PSYCHO!
HE NEARLY BIT MY HEAD OFF!
piccolo
YEAH, THE LAST TIME HE WAS HERE HE THREATENED A WAITER!
I KNOW! HE'S UNPREDICTABLE...
HE REALLY GIVES ME THE CREEP--
'SCUSE ME!
...CAN I GET A STEAK KNIFE OVER HERE, PLEASE?
YEAH, SURE
NO PROBLEM!
HERE YOU GO!
WE SERVERS ARE A TRUSTING LOT, AREN'T WE?
YUP

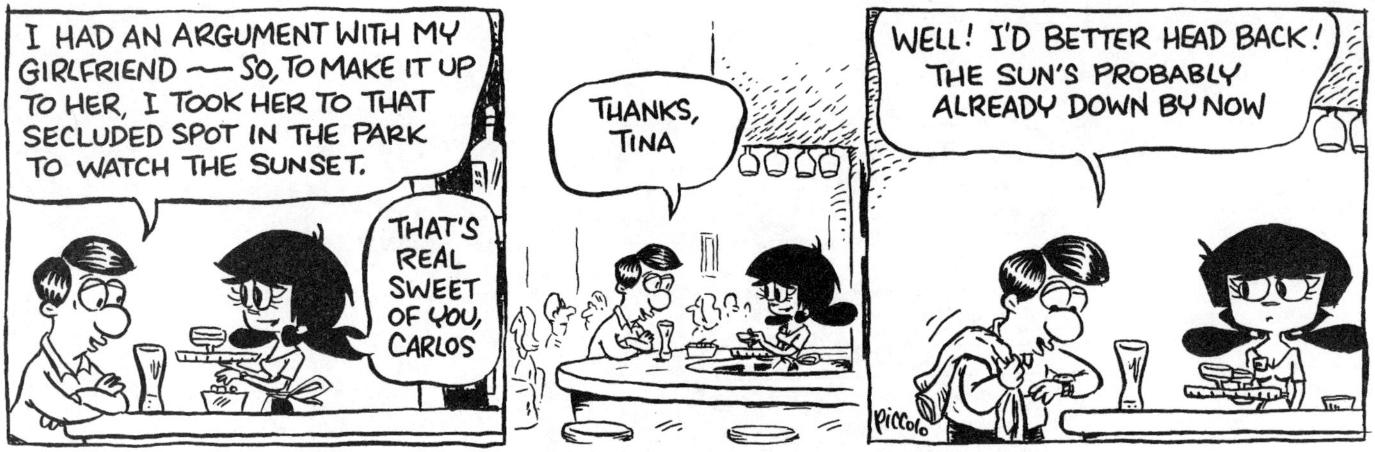
I HAD AN ARGUMENT WITH MY GIRLFRIEND — SO, TO MAKE IT UP TO HER, I TOOK HER TO THAT SECLUDED SPOT IN THE PARK TO WATCH THE SUNSET.
THAT'S REAL SWEET OF YOU, CARLOS
THANKS, TINA
WELL! I'D BETTER HEAD BACK! THE SUN'S PROBABLY ALREADY DOWN BY NOW
PICCOLO

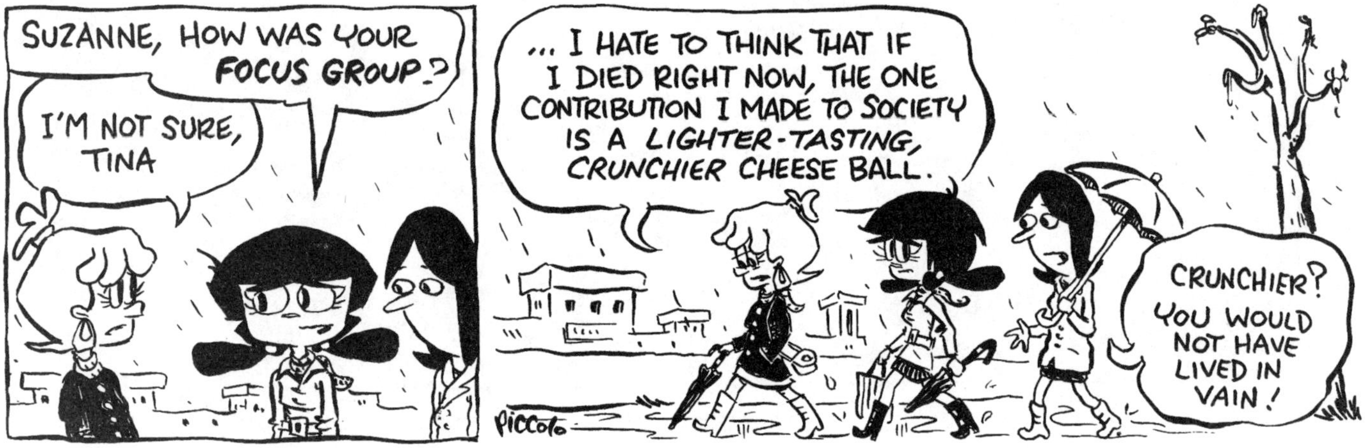
SUZANNE, HOW WAS YOUR FOCUS GROUP?
I'M NOT SURE, TINA
... I HATE TO THINK THAT IF I DIED RIGHT NOW, THE ONE CONTRIBUTION I MADE TO SOCIETY IS A LIGHTER-TASTING, CRUNCHIER CHEESE BALL.
CRUNCHIER? YOU WOULD NOT HAVE LIVED IN VAIN!
PICCOLO

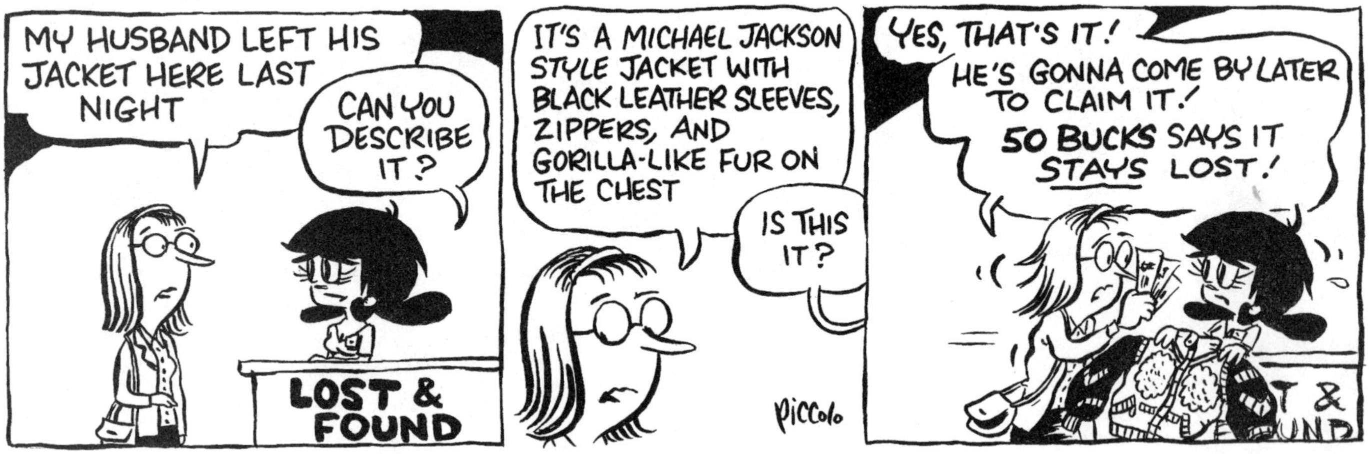
MY HUSBAND LEFT HIS JACKET HERE LAST NIGHT
CAN YOU DESCRIBE IT?
LOST & FOUND
IT'S A MICHAEL JACKSON STYLE JACKET WITH BLACK LEATHER SLEEVES, ZIPPERS, AND GORILLA-LIKE FUR ON THE CHEST
IS THIS IT?
PICCOLO
YES, THAT'S IT!
HE'S GONNA COME BY LATER TO CLAIM IT!
50 BUCKS SAYS IT STAYS LOST!

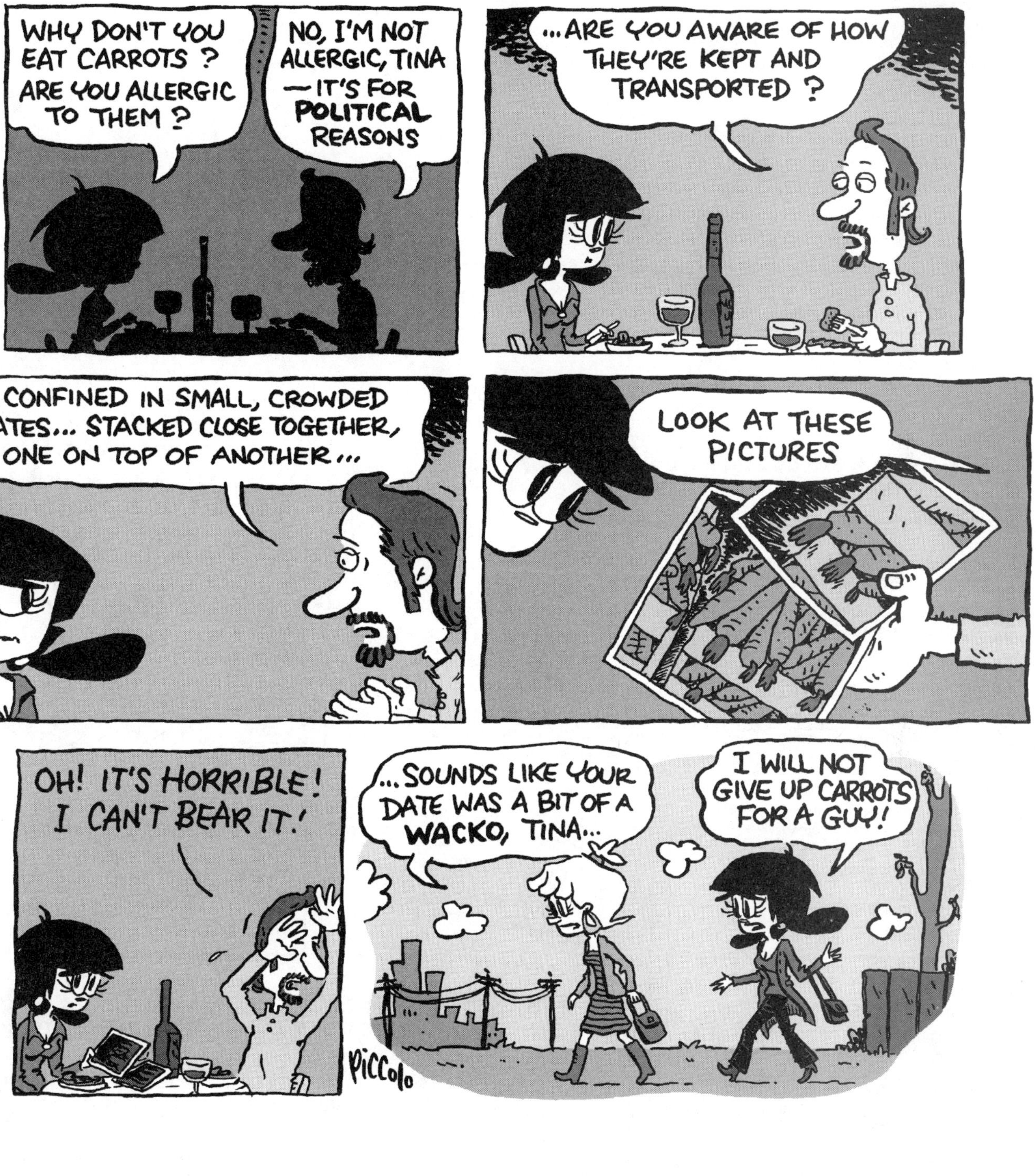
WHY DON'T YOU EAT CARROTS ? ARE YOU ALLERGIC TO THEM ?
NO, I'M NOT ALLERGIC, TINA —IT'S FOR **POLITICAL** REASONS
...ARE YOU AWARE OF HOW THEY'RE KEPT AND TRANSPORTED ?
...CONFINED IN SMALL, CROWDED CRATES... STACKED CLOSE TOGETHER, ONE ON TOP OF ANOTHER...
LOOK AT THESE PICTURES
OH! IT'S HORRIBLE! I CAN'T BEAR IT!
PICCOLO
...SOUNDS LIKE YOUR DATE WAS A BIT OF A **WACKO**, TINA...
I WILL NOT GIVE UP CARROTS FOR A GUY!

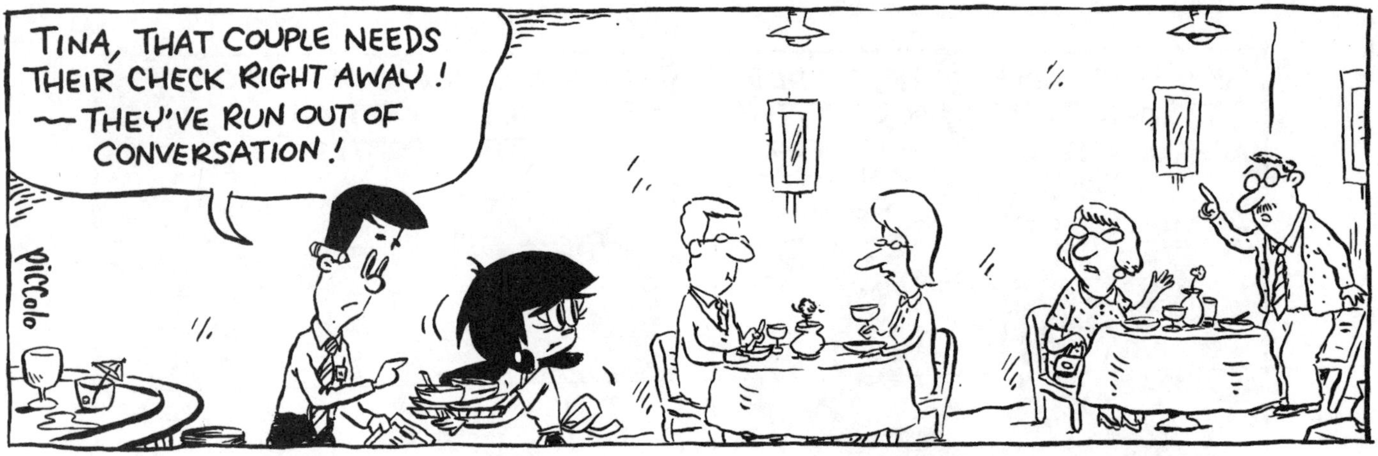

TINA, THAT COUPLE NEEDS THEIR CHECK RIGHT AWAY! — THEY'VE RUN OUT OF CONVERSATION!
piccolo

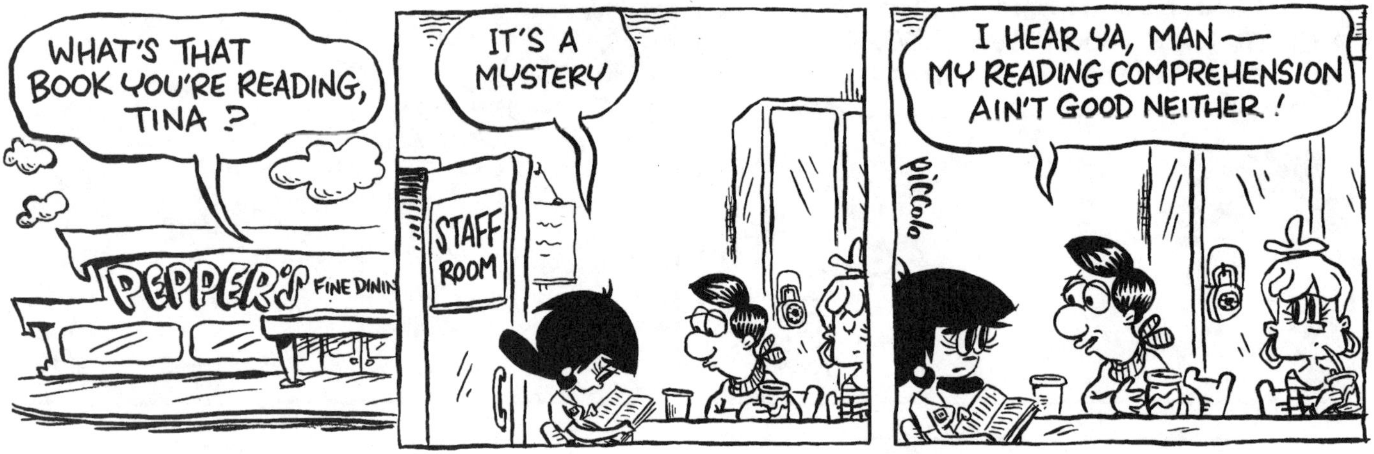

WHAT'S THAT BOOK YOU'RE READING, TINA?
PEPPER'S FINE DININ
STAFF ROOM
IT'S A MYSTERY
I HEAR YA, MAN — MY READING COMPREHENSION AIN'T GOOD NEITHER!
piccolo

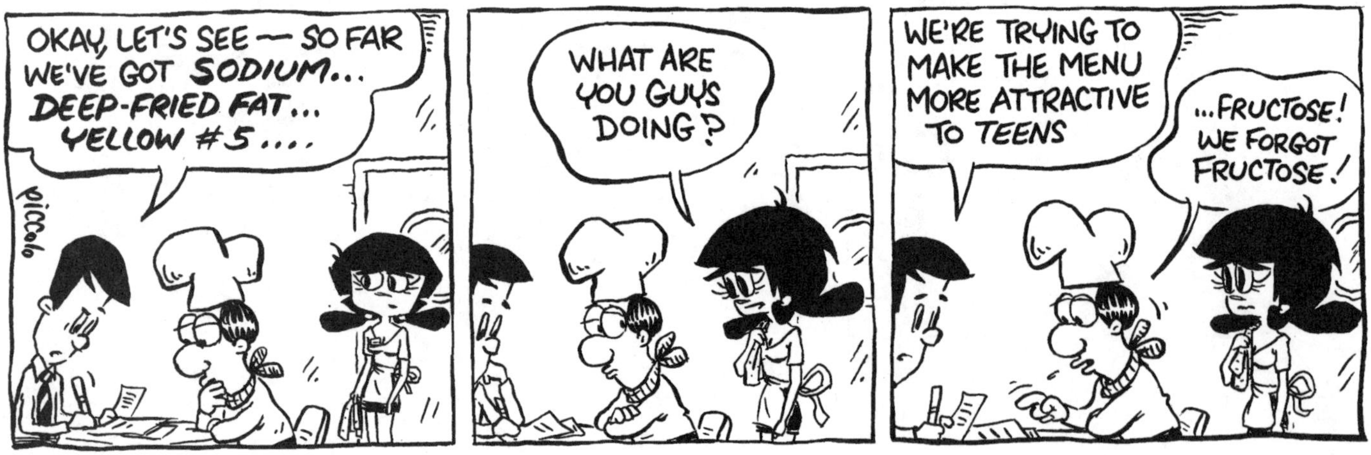

OKAY, LET'S SEE — SO FAR WE'VE GOT SODIUM... DEEP-FRIED FAT... YELLOW #5....
piccolo
WHAT ARE YOU GUYS DOING?
WE'RE TRYING TO MAKE THE MENU MORE ATTRACTIVE TO TEENS
...FRUCTOSE! WE FORGOT FRUCTOSE!

Dine & Dash ?

ONLY THE BIGGEST LOSERS DINE & DASH. WHEN A CUSTOMER LEAVES A RESTAURANT WITHOUT PAYING, IT'S NOT THE RESTAURANT THAT EATS THE COST, BUT THE **SERVER**. ~ OUT OF THEIR **OWN POCKET**.

Piccolo

Panel 1:

HEY, TINA— WE FOUND THE PERFECT PUNISHMENT FOR THAT GUY WHO TRIED TO **RUN OFF** WITHOUT PAYING HIS BAR TAB

WHAT IS IT?

Panel 2:

WE MADE HIM WORK THE **CHILDREN'S BIRTHDAY PARTY**

THE CHILDREN'S BIRTHDAY PAR--?

Panel 3:

THANK YOU FOR THE PIÑATA! ~THE KIDS LOVE IT!

OUCH

OW!

OOF!

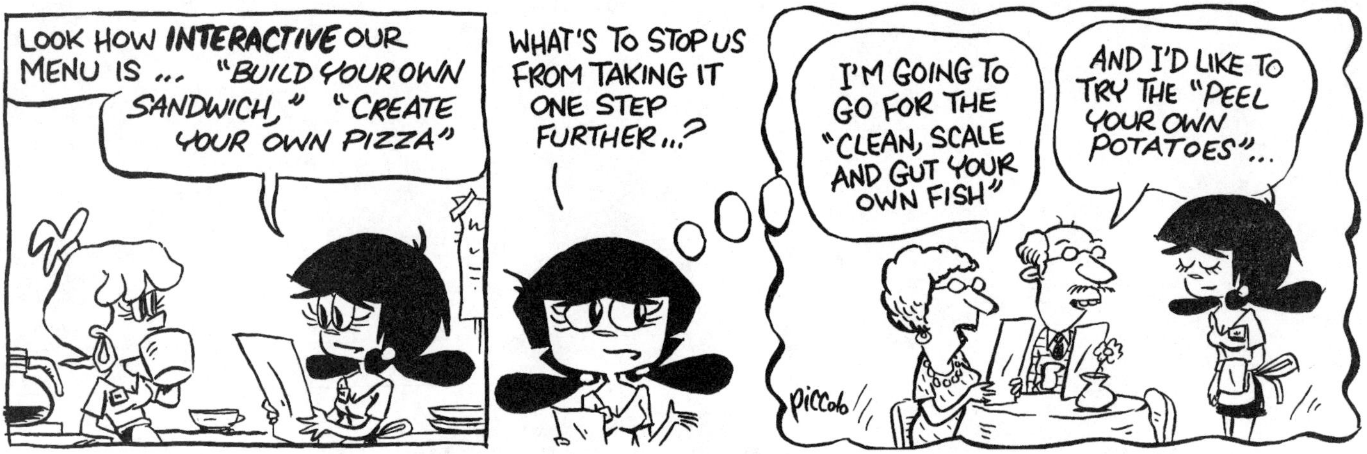
LOOK HOW **INTERACTIVE** OUR MENU IS ... "BUILD YOUR OWN SANDWICH," "CREATE YOUR OWN PIZZA"
WHAT'S TO STOP US FROM TAKING IT ONE STEP FURTHER...?
I'M GOING TO GO FOR THE "CLEAN, SCALE AND GUT YOUR OWN FISH"
AND I'D LIKE TO TRY THE "PEEL YOUR OWN POTATOES"...
piccolo

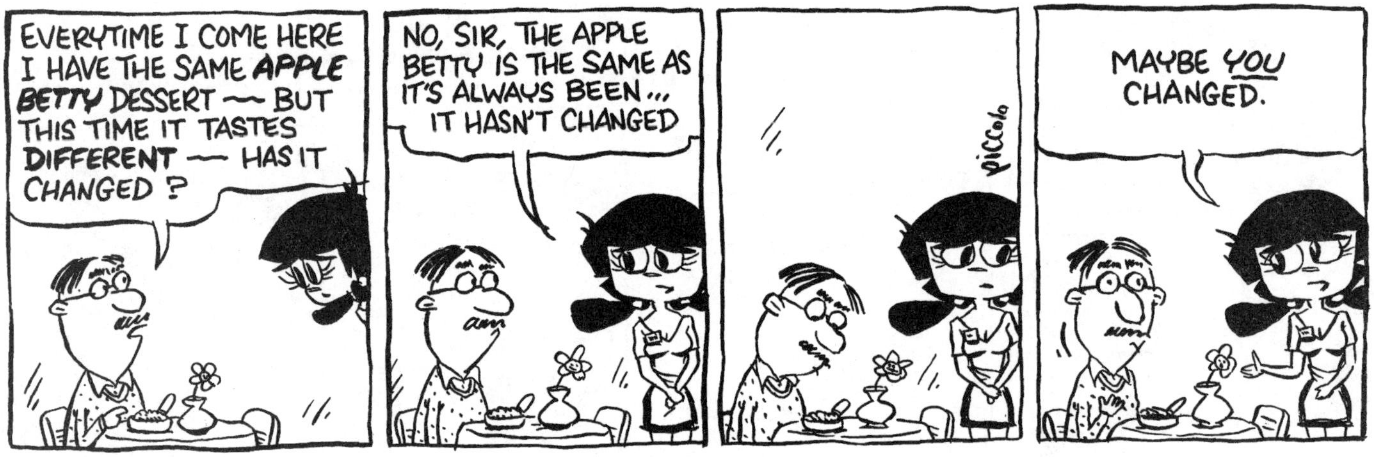
EVERYTIME I COME HERE I HAVE THE SAME **APPLE BETTY** DESSERT — BUT THIS TIME IT TASTES **DIFFERENT** — HAS IT CHANGED?
NO, SIR, THE APPLE BETTY IS THE SAME AS IT'S ALWAYS BEEN... IT HASN'T CHANGED
piccolo
MAYBE YOU CHANGED.

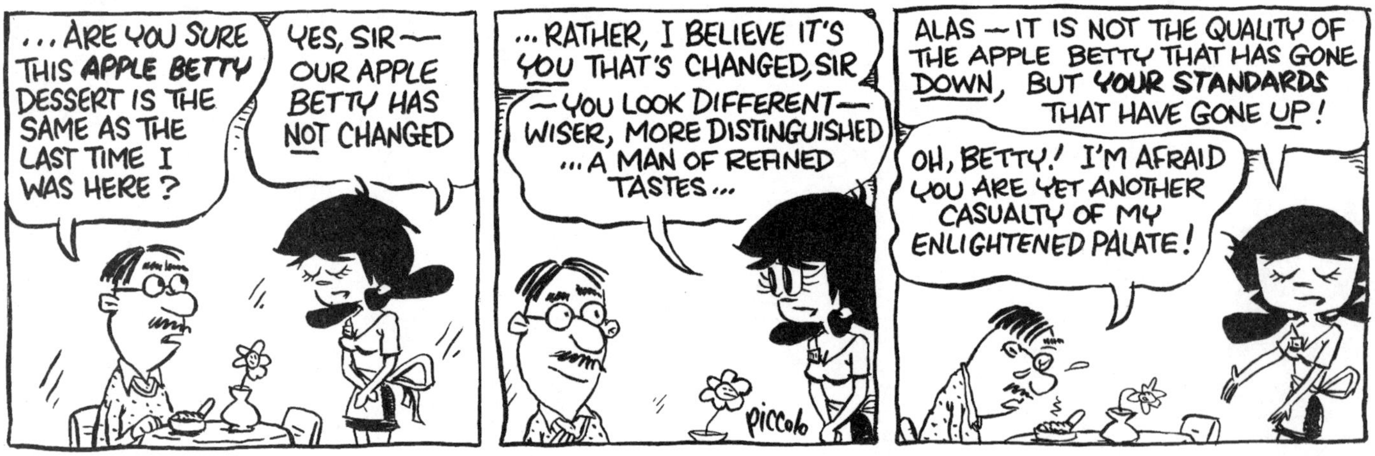
... ARE YOU SURE THIS **APPLE BETTY** DESSERT IS THE SAME AS THE LAST TIME I WAS HERE?
YES, SIR — OUR APPLE BETTY HAS NOT CHANGED
... RATHER, I BELIEVE IT'S YOU THAT'S CHANGED, SIR
— YOU LOOK DIFFERENT — WISER, MORE DISTINGUISHED ... A MAN OF REFINED TASTES...
piccolo
ALAS — IT IS NOT THE QUALITY OF THE APPLE BETTY THAT HAS GONE DOWN, BUT **YOUR STANDARDS** THAT HAVE GONE UP!
OH, BETTY! I'M AFRAID YOU ARE YET ANOTHER CASUALTY OF MY ENLIGHTENED PALATE!

Tina Speaks...
VANITY PLATES ON BIG, FLASHY VEHICLES SHOULD BE A TRAFFIC VIOLATION
MR. BIG
I MEAN, AREN'T THE VEHICLES THEMSELVES VAIN ENOUGH?
I'M SORRY, SIR, YOUR VANITY EMISSIONS EXCEED THE LOCAL TASTE LAWS!
...AND SPEAKING OF TASTE, ARE THOSE FUZZY DICE..?
IN FACT, I THINK VANITY PLATES ON BIG, FLASHY VEHICLES SHOULD BE REPLACED WITH "HUMILITY PLATES"...
I STINK
ha ha!
ha ha!
ha ha!
piccolo

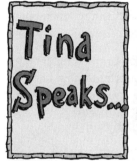

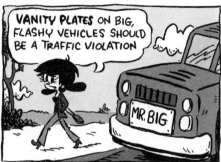

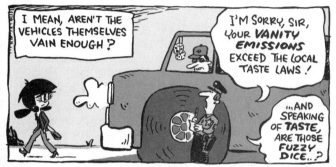

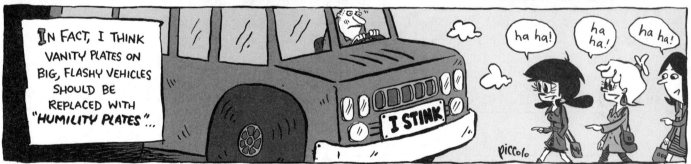

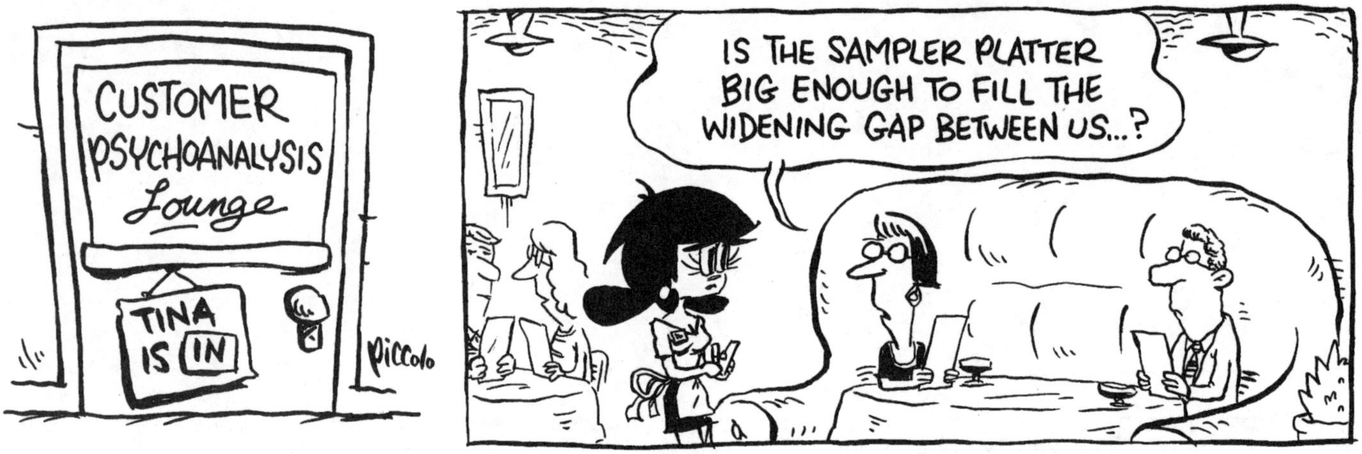
CUSTOMER PSYCHOANALYSIS Lounge
TINA IS IN
piccolo
IS THE SAMPLER PLATTER BIG ENOUGH TO FILL THE WIDENING GAP BETWEEN US...?

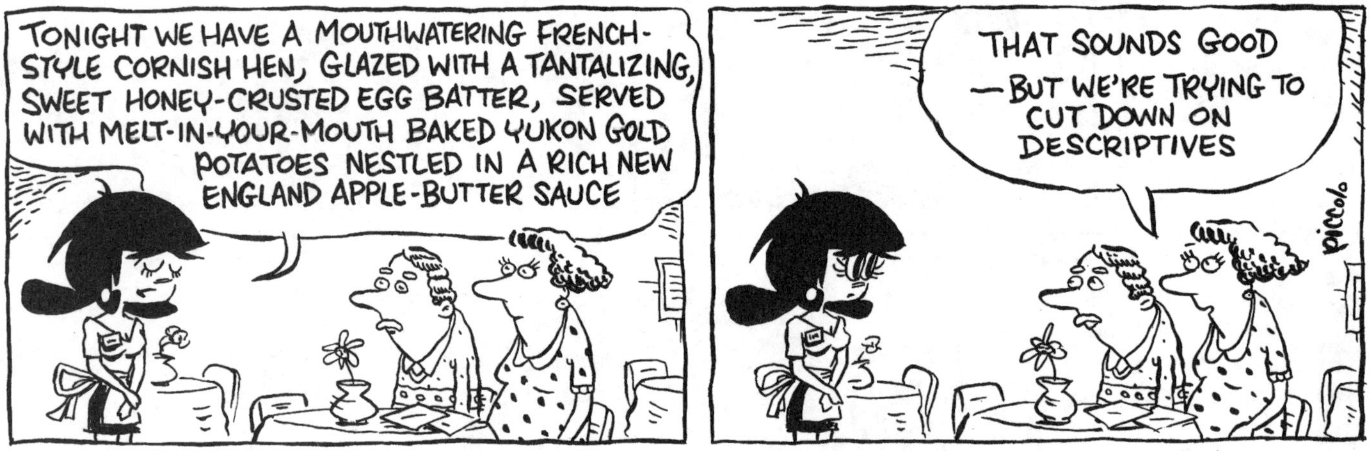
TONIGHT WE HAVE A MOUTHWATERING FRENCH-STYLE CORNISH HEN, GLAZED WITH A TANTALIZING, SWEET HONEY-CRUSTED EGG BATTER, SERVED WITH MELT-IN-YOUR-MOUTH BAKED YUKON GOLD POTATOES NESTLED IN A RICH NEW ENGLAND APPLE-BUTTER SAUCE
THAT SOUNDS GOOD —BUT WE'RE TRYING TO CUT DOWN ON DESCRIPTIVES
piccolo

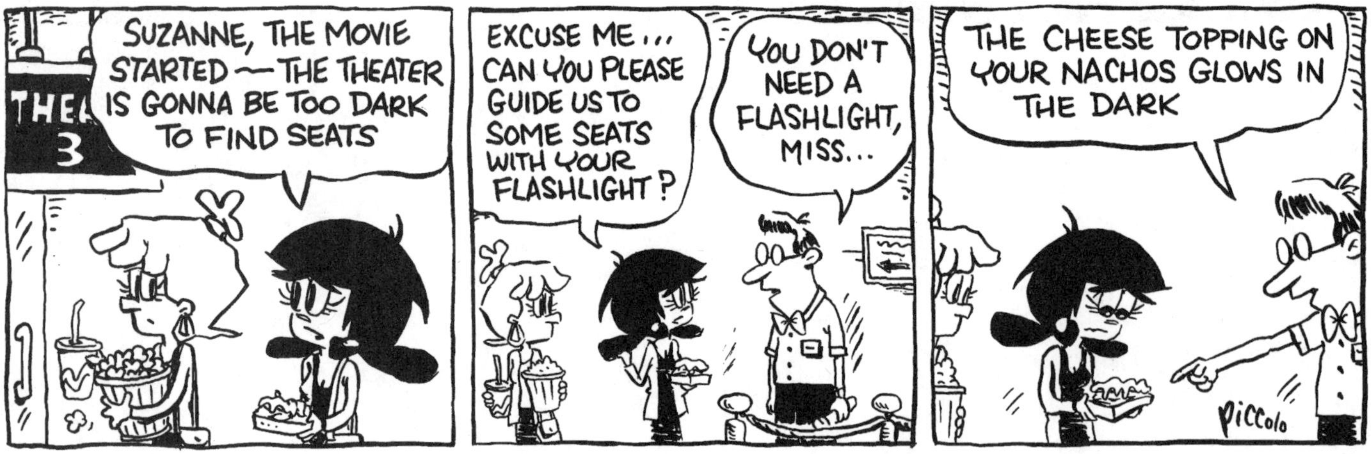
SUZANNE, THE MOVIE STARTED — THE THEATER IS GONNA BE TOO DARK TO FIND SEATS
EXCUSE ME... CAN YOU PLEASE GUIDE US TO SOME SEATS WITH YOUR FLASHLIGHT?
YOU DON'T NEED A FLASHLIGHT, MISS...
THE CHEESE TOPPING ON YOUR NACHOS GLOWS IN THE DARK
piccolo

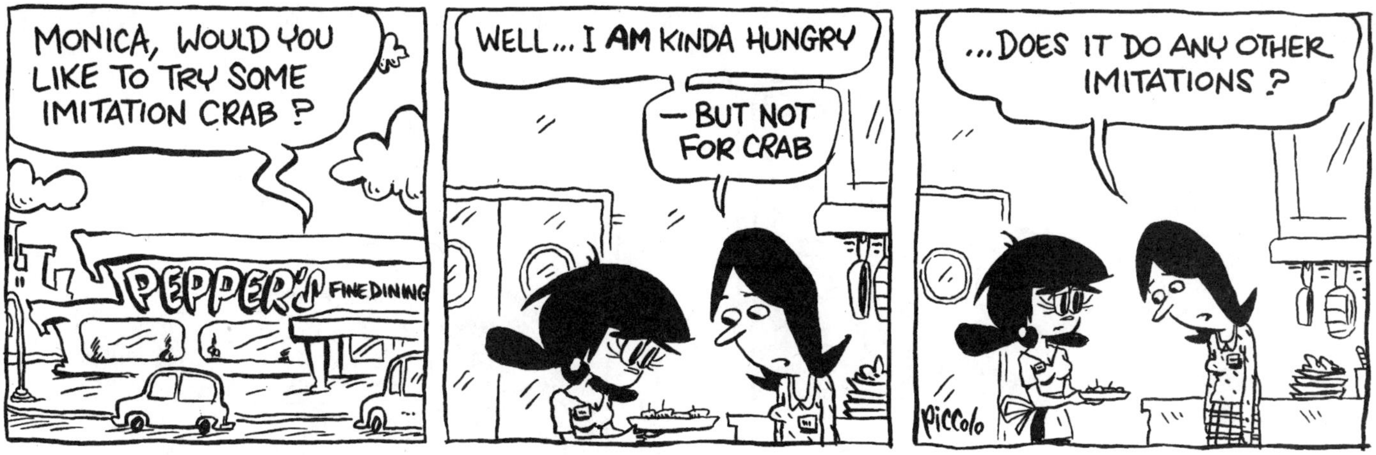
MONICA, WOULD YOU LIKE TO TRY SOME IMITATION CRAB ?
PEPPER'S FINE DINING
WELL... I AM KINDA HUNGRY
— BUT NOT FOR CRAB
...DOES IT DO ANY OTHER IMITATIONS ?
piccolo

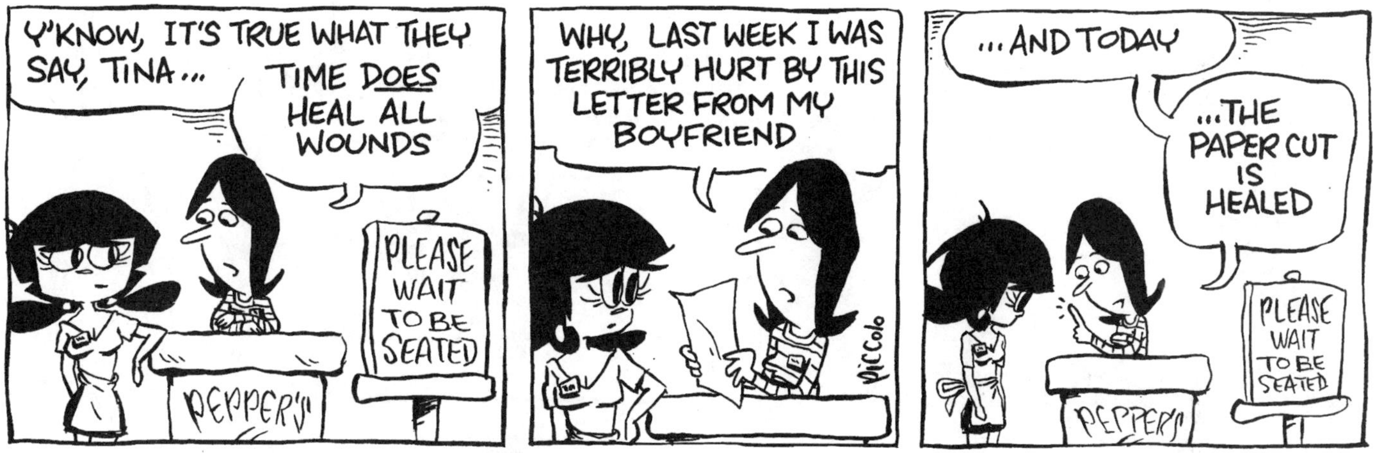
Y'KNOW, IT'S TRUE WHAT THEY SAY, TINA...
TIME DOES HEAL ALL WOUNDS
PLEASE WAIT TO BE SEATED
PEPPER'S
WHY, LAST WEEK I WAS TERRIBLY HURT BY THIS LETTER FROM MY BOYFRIEND
piccolo
...AND TODAY
...THE PAPER CUT IS HEALED
PLEASE WAIT TO BE SEATED
PEPPER'S

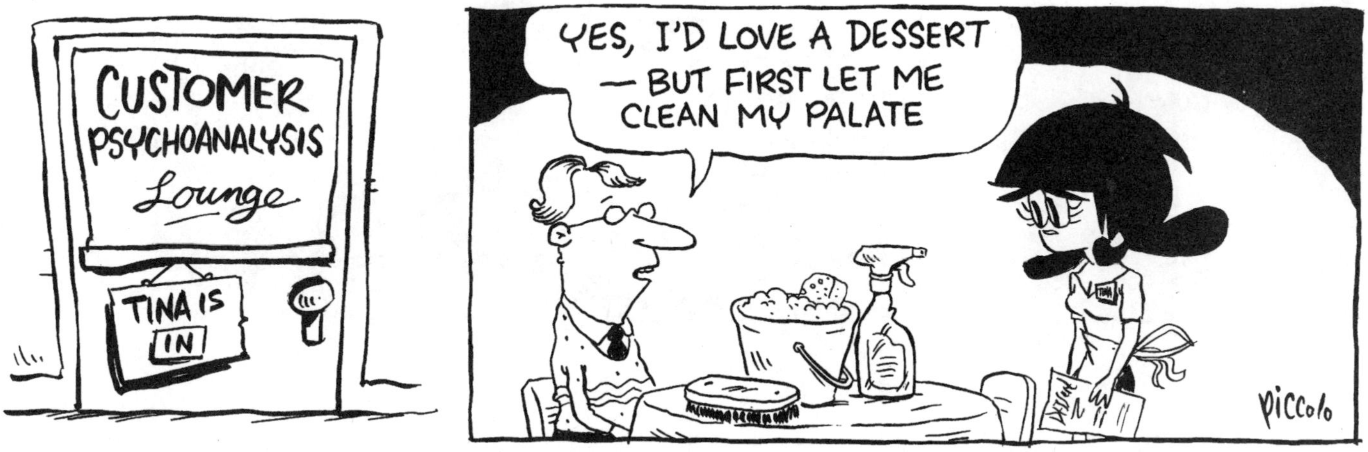
CUSTOMER PSYCHOANALYSIS Lounge
TINA IS IN
YES, I'D LOVE A DESSERT — BUT FIRST LET ME CLEAN MY PALATE
piccolo

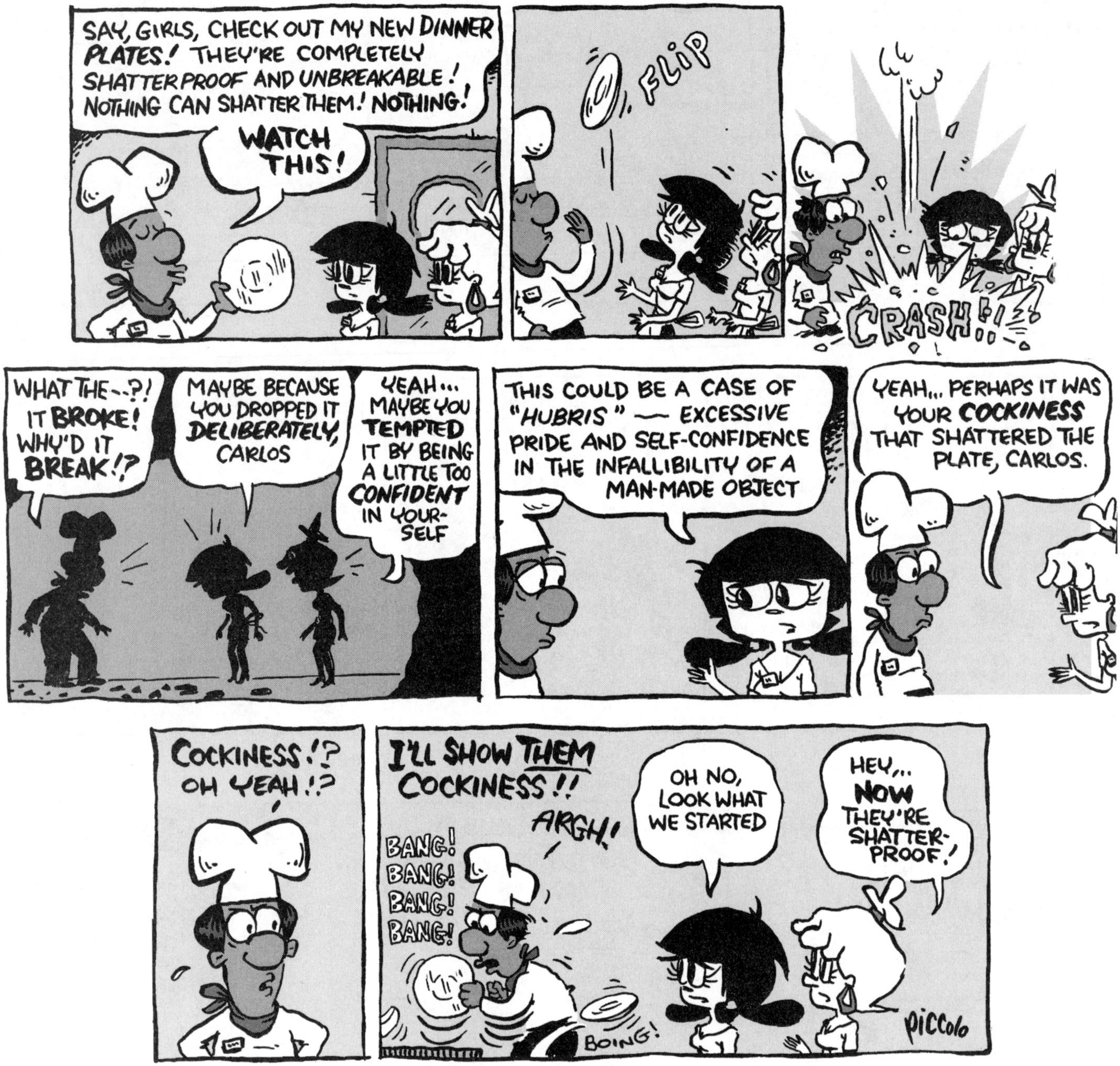

SAY, GIRLS, CHECK OUT MY NEW DINNER PLATES! THEY'RE COMPLETELY SHATTERPROOF AND UNBREAKABLE! NOTHING CAN SHATTER THEM! NOTHING!
WATCH THIS!
FLIP
CRASH!!
WHAT THE--?! IT BROKE! WHY'D IT BREAK!?
MAYBE BECAUSE YOU DROPPED IT DELIBERATELY, CARLOS
YEAH... MAYBE YOU TEMPTED IT BY BEING A LITTLE TOO CONFIDENT IN YOURSELF
THIS COULD BE A CASE OF "HUBRIS" — EXCESSIVE PRIDE AND SELF-CONFIDENCE IN THE INFALLIBILITY OF A MAN-MADE OBJECT
YEAH... PERHAPS IT WAS YOUR COCKINESS THAT SHATTERED THE PLATE, CARLOS.
COCKINESS!? OH YEAH!?
I'LL SHOW THEM COCKINESS!!
ARGH!
BANG! BANG! BANG! BANG!
OH NO, LOOK WHAT WE STARTED
HEY... NOW THEY'RE SHATTER-PROOF!
BOING!
piccolo

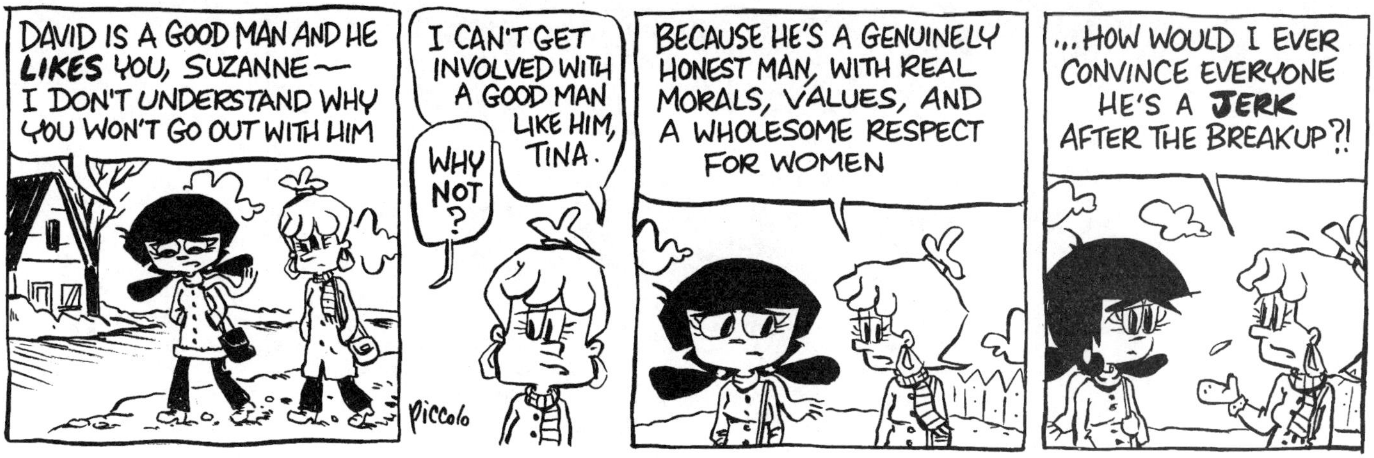
DAVID IS A GOOD MAN AND HE LIKES YOU, SUZANNE— I DON'T UNDERSTAND WHY YOU WON'T GO OUT WITH HIM
piccolo
I CAN'T GET INVOLVED WITH A GOOD MAN LIKE HIM, TINA.
WHY NOT ?
BECAUSE HE'S A GENUINELY HONEST MAN, WITH REAL MORALS, VALUES, AND A WHOLESOME RESPECT FOR WOMEN
...HOW WOULD I EVER CONVINCE EVERYONE HE'S A JERK AFTER THE BREAKUP?!

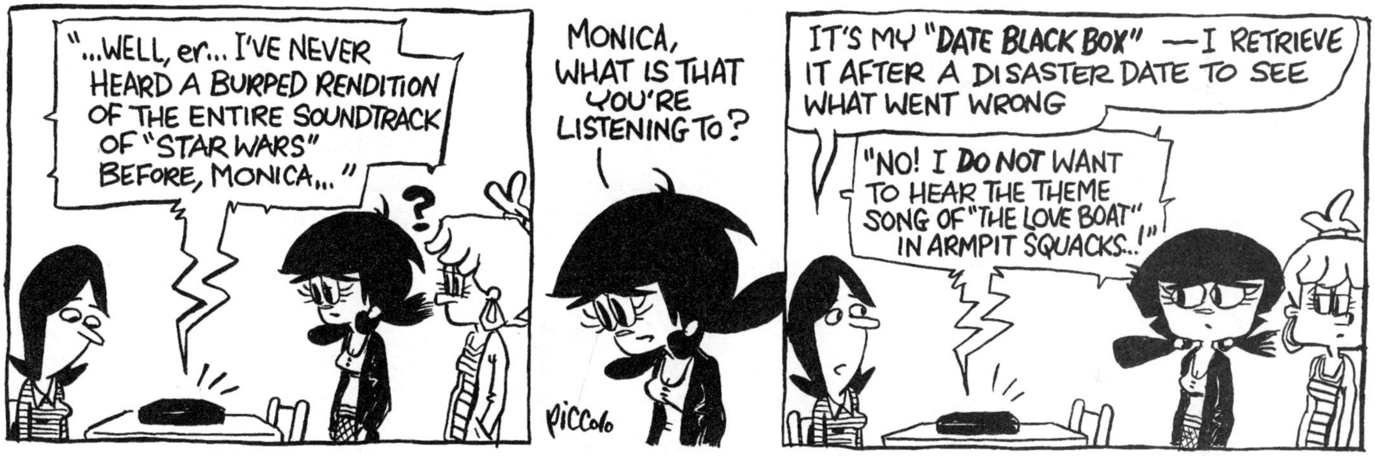
"...WELL, er... I'VE NEVER HEARD A BURPED RENDITION OF THE ENTIRE SOUNDTRACK OF "STAR WARS" BEFORE, MONICA..."
?
MONICA, WHAT IS THAT YOU'RE LISTENING TO?
piccolo
IT'S MY "DATE BLACK BOX" —I RETRIEVE IT AFTER A DISASTER DATE TO SEE WHAT WENT WRONG
"NO! I DO NOT WANT TO HEAR THE THEME SONG OF "THE LOVE BOAT" IN ARMPIT SQUACKS...!"

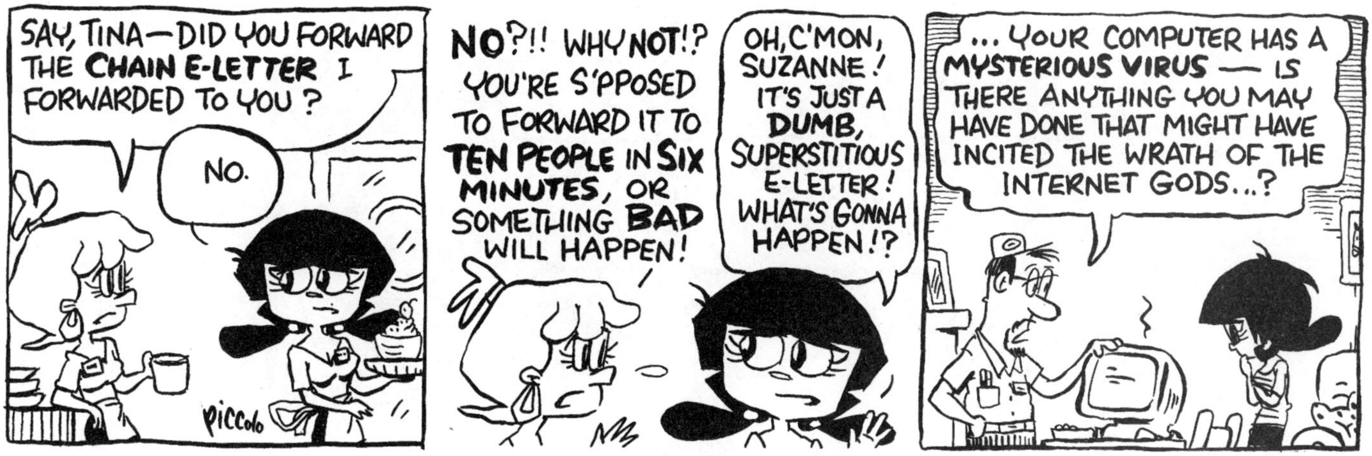
SAY, TINA—DID YOU FORWARD THE CHAIN E-LETTER I FORWARDED TO YOU?
NO.
piccolo
NO?!! WHY NOT!? YOU'RE S'PPOSED TO FORWARD IT TO TEN PEOPLE IN SIX MINUTES, OR SOMETHING BAD WILL HAPPEN!
OH, C'MON, SUZANNE! IT'S JUST A DUMB, SUPERSTITIOUS E-LETTER! WHAT'S GONNA HAPPEN!?
... YOUR COMPUTER HAS A MYSTERIOUS VIRUS — IS THERE ANYTHING YOU MAY HAVE DONE THAT MIGHT HAVE INCITED THE WRATH OF THE INTERNET GODS...?

The ITCHY SWEATER
STARRING TINA
ITCHY SWEATERS BRING OUT THE WORST IN PEOPLE
*@☆!!
?
TINA! WE'VE NEVER SEEN THIS SIDE OF YOU BEFORE!
NEVER MIND HORMONES AND PMS, AN ITCHY SWEATER CAN TAKE YOU TO THE EDGE OF MADNESS!
Y'KNOW... I BET LIZZIE BORDEN WAS WEARING AN ITCHY SWEATER WHEN SHE....
SHE'S TALKING CRAZY TALK!
piccolo
I PROPOSE A BAN ON ITCHY SWEATERS! OR AT LEAST SLAP A WARNING ON THEM!
CAUTION ITCHY SWEATER WEARER MAY SNAP
OKAY, EASY, EASY, NOW!
CAREFUL, CARLOS! IT'S A TURTLENECK!
AFTER ALL, IT'S THE TINY IMPROVEMENTS THAT MAKE THE WORLD A BETTER PLACE...
"...AND SINCE THE WORLDWIDE BAN ON ITCHY SWEATERS, THERE HAS BEEN A REMARKABLE DECLINE IN CRIME — TO SAY NOTHING OF THE SUDDEN PEACE IN THE MIDDLE EAST..."
100% SANE COTTON

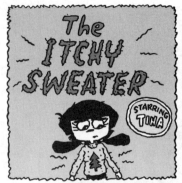

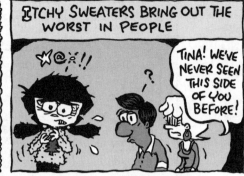

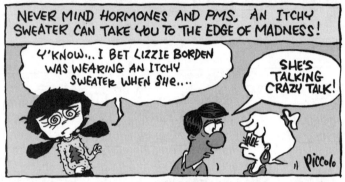

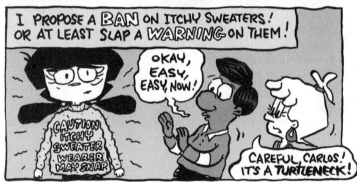

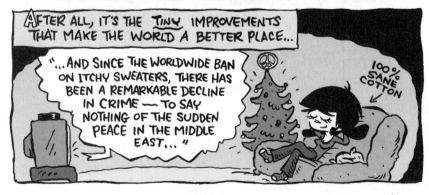

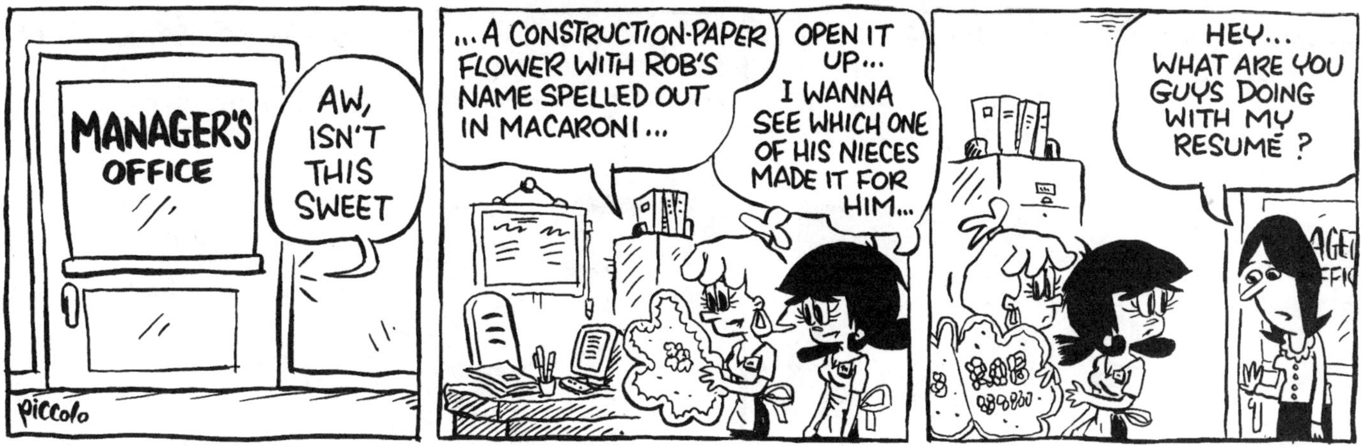
MANAGER'S OFFICE
AW, ISN'T THIS SWEET
...A CONSTRUCTION-PAPER FLOWER WITH ROB'S NAME SPELLED OUT IN MACARONI...
OPEN IT UP... I WANNA SEE WHICH ONE OF HIS NIECES MADE IT FOR HIM...
HEY... WHAT ARE YOU GUYS DOING WITH MY RESUMÉ ?
piccolo

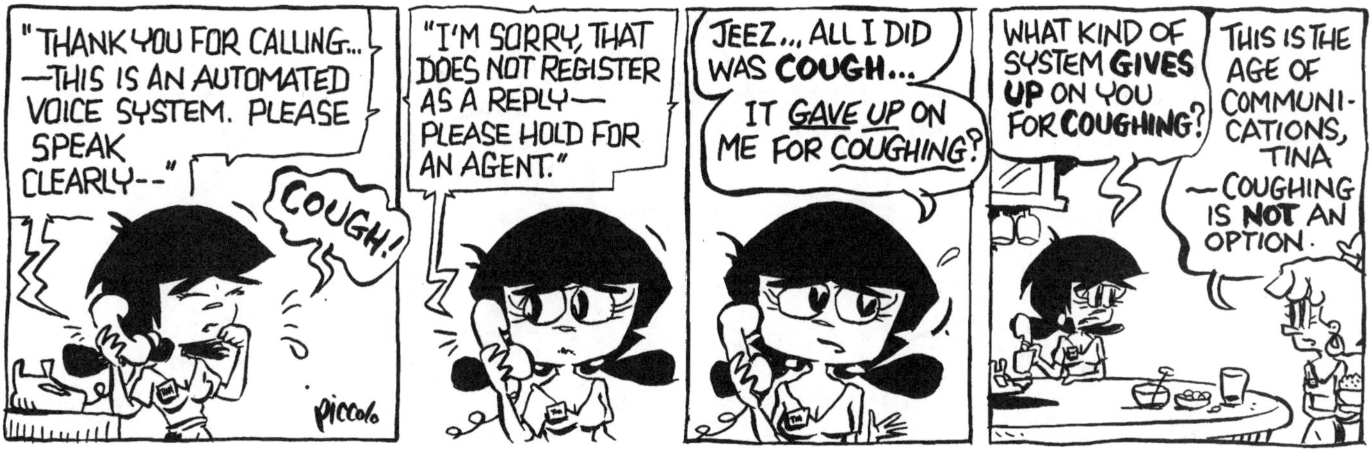
"THANK YOU FOR CALLING... —THIS IS AN AUTOMATED VOICE SYSTEM. PLEASE SPEAK CLEARLY--"
COUGH!
"I'M SORRY, THAT DOES NOT REGISTER AS A REPLY— PLEASE HOLD FOR AN AGENT."
JEEZ... ALL I DID WAS COUGH...
IT GAVE UP ON ME FOR COUGHING?
WHAT KIND OF SYSTEM GIVES UP ON YOU FOR COUGHING?
THIS IS THE AGE OF COMMUNICATIONS, TINA —COUGHING IS NOT AN OPTION.
piccolo

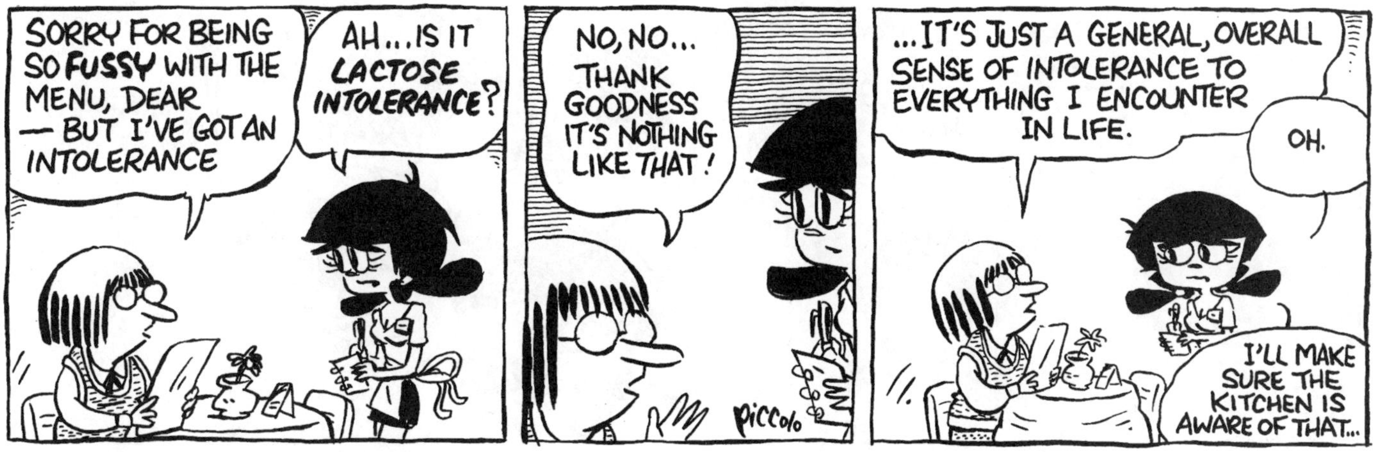
SORRY FOR BEING SO FUSSY WITH THE MENU, DEAR — BUT I'VE GOT AN INTOLERANCE
AH... IS IT LACTOSE INTOLERANCE?
NO, NO... THANK GOODNESS IT'S NOTHING LIKE THAT!
...IT'S JUST A GENERAL, OVERALL SENSE OF INTOLERANCE TO EVERYTHING I ENCOUNTER IN LIFE.
OH.
I'LL MAKE SURE THE KITCHEN IS AWARE OF THAT...
piccolo

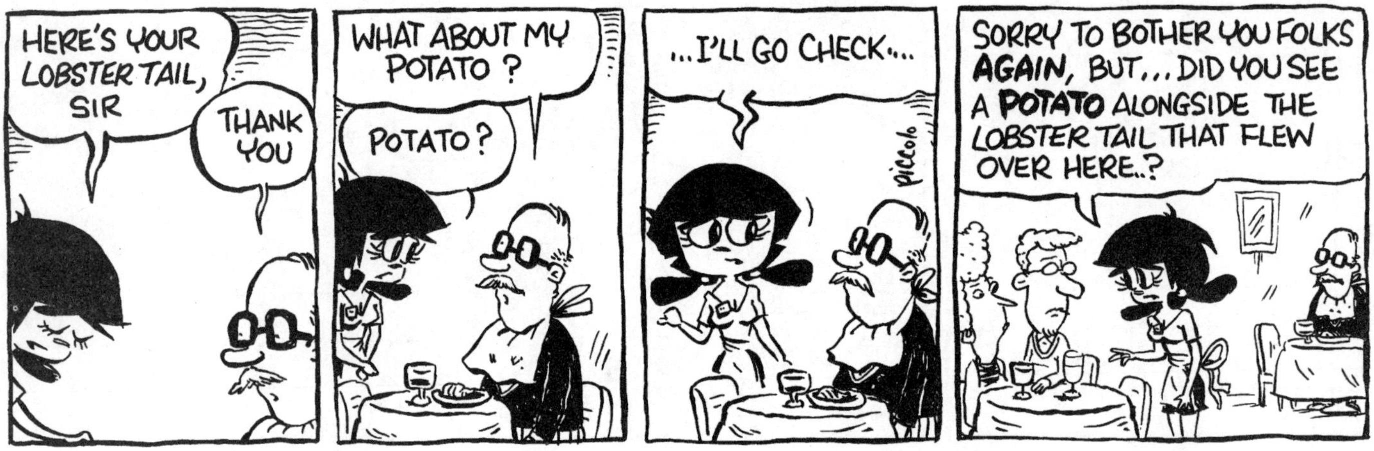
HERE'S YOUR LOBSTER TAIL, SIR
THANK YOU
WHAT ABOUT MY POTATO ?
POTATO ?
...I'LL GO CHECK....
PICCOLO
SORRY TO BOTHER YOU FOLKS **AGAIN**, BUT... DID YOU SEE A **POTATO** ALONGSIDE THE LOBSTER TAIL THAT FLEW OVER HERE..?

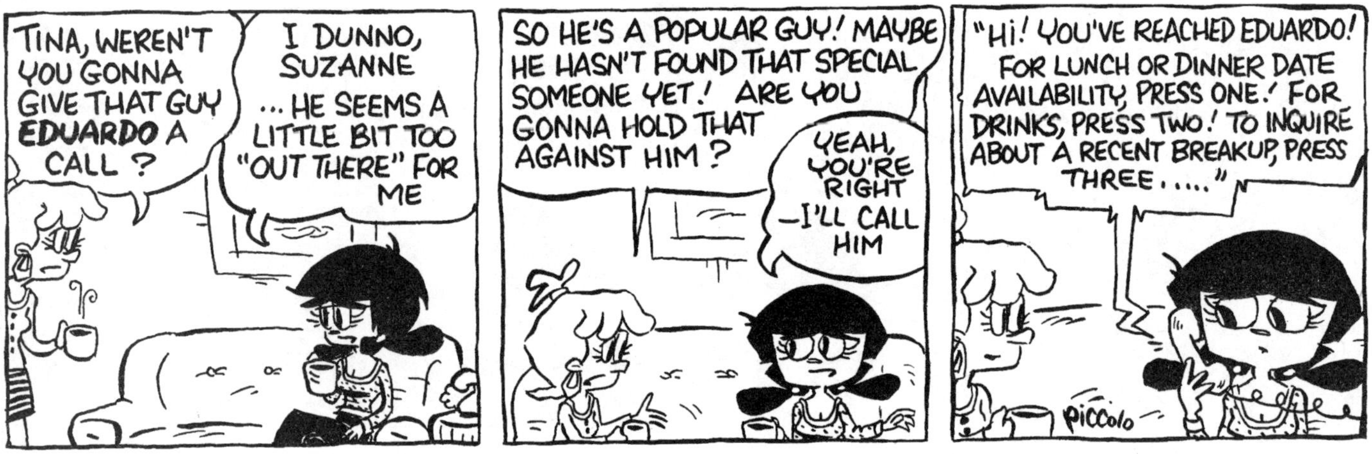
TINA, WEREN'T YOU GONNA GIVE THAT GUY **EDUARDO** A CALL ?
I DUNNO, SUZANNE ... HE SEEMS A LITTLE BIT TOO "OUT THERE" FOR ME
SO HE'S A POPULAR GUY! MAYBE HE HASN'T FOUND THAT SPECIAL SOMEONE YET! ARE YOU GONNA HOLD THAT AGAINST HIM ?
YEAH, YOU'RE RIGHT —I'LL CALL HIM
"HI! YOU'VE REACHED EDUARDO! FOR LUNCH OR DINNER DATE AVAILABILITY, PRESS ONE! FOR DRINKS, PRESS TWO! TO INQUIRE ABOUT A RECENT BREAKUP, PRESS THREE....."
PICCOLO

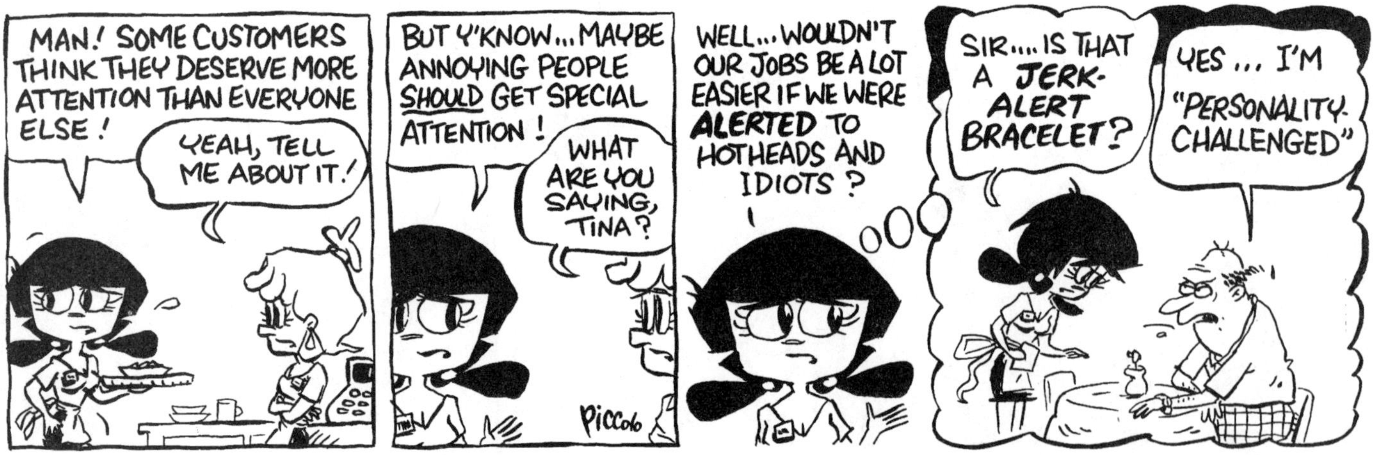
MAN! SOME CUSTOMERS THINK THEY DESERVE MORE ATTENTION THAN EVERYONE ELSE!
YEAH, TELL ME ABOUT IT!
BUT Y'KNOW... MAYBE ANNOYING PEOPLE SHOULD GET SPECIAL ATTENTION!
WHAT ARE YOU SAYING, TINA?
PICCOLO
WELL... WOULDN'T OUR JOBS BE A LOT EASIER IF WE WERE **ALERTED** TO HOTHEADS AND IDIOTS ?
SIR.... IS THAT A **JERK-ALERT BRACELET**?
YES ... I'M "PERSONALITY-CHALLENGED"

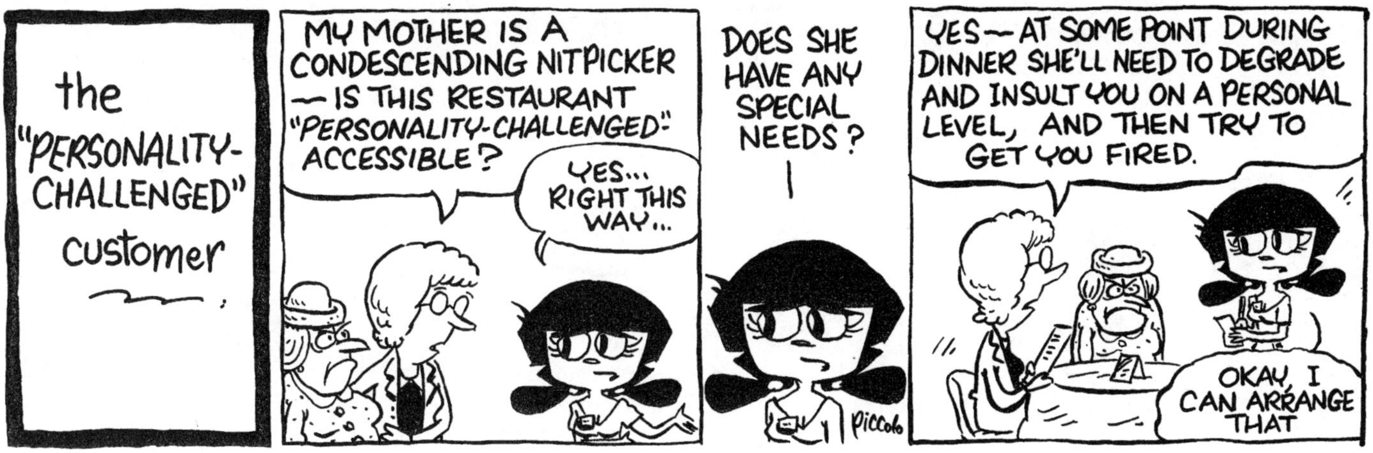

the "PERSONALITY-CHALLENGED" customer
MY MOTHER IS A CONDESCENDING NITPICKER —IS THIS RESTAURANT "PERSONALITY-CHALLENGED" ACCESSIBLE?
YES... RIGHT THIS WAY...
DOES SHE HAVE ANY SPECIAL NEEDS?
YES—AT SOME POINT DURING DINNER SHE'LL NEED TO DEGRADE AND INSULT YOU ON A PERSONAL LEVEL, AND THEN TRY TO GET YOU FIRED.
OKAY, I CAN ARRANGE THAT

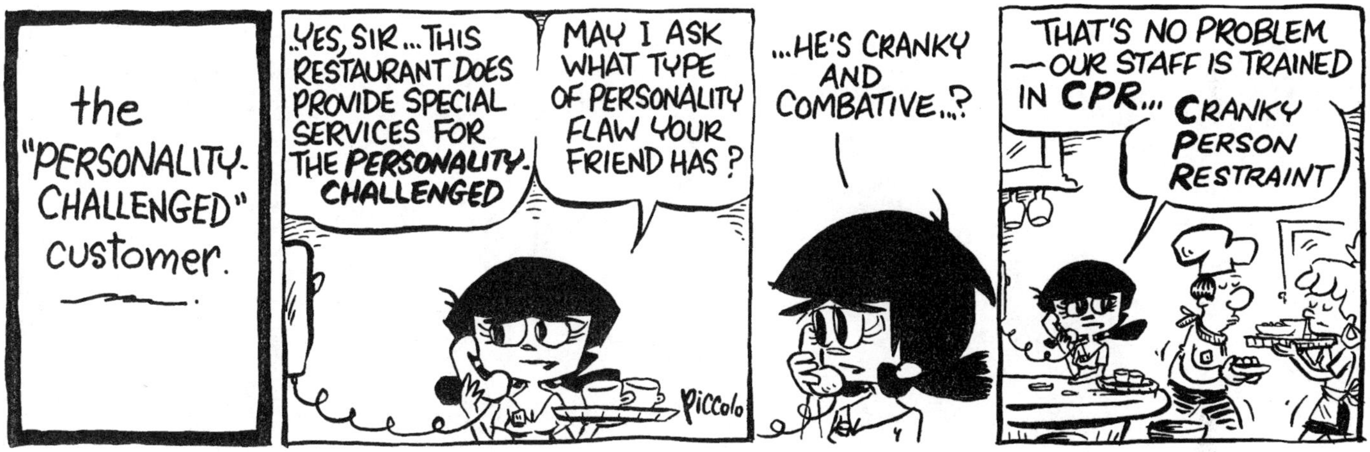

the "PERSONALITY-CHALLENGED" customer.
..YES, SIR... THIS RESTAURANT DOES PROVIDE SPECIAL SERVICES FOR THE PERSONALITY-CHALLENGED
MAY I ASK WHAT TYPE OF PERSONALITY FLAW YOUR FRIEND HAS?
...HE'S CRANKY AND COMBATIVE...?
THAT'S NO PROBLEM —OUR STAFF IS TRAINED IN CPR...
CRANKY PERSON RESTRAINT

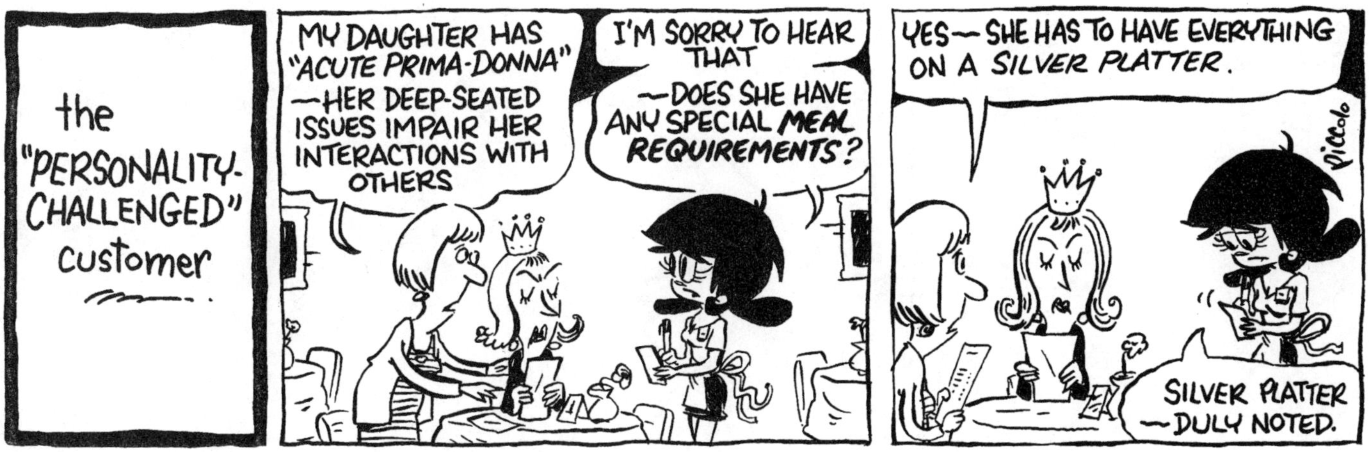

the "PERSONALITY-CHALLENGED" customer
MY DAUGHTER HAS "ACUTE PRIMA-DONNA" —HER DEEP-SEATED ISSUES IMPAIR HER INTERACTIONS WITH OTHERS
I'M SORRY TO HEAR THAT —DOES SHE HAVE ANY SPECIAL MEAL REQUIREMENTS?
YES—SHE HAS TO HAVE EVERYTHING ON A SILVER PLATTER.
SILVER PLATTER —DULY NOTED.

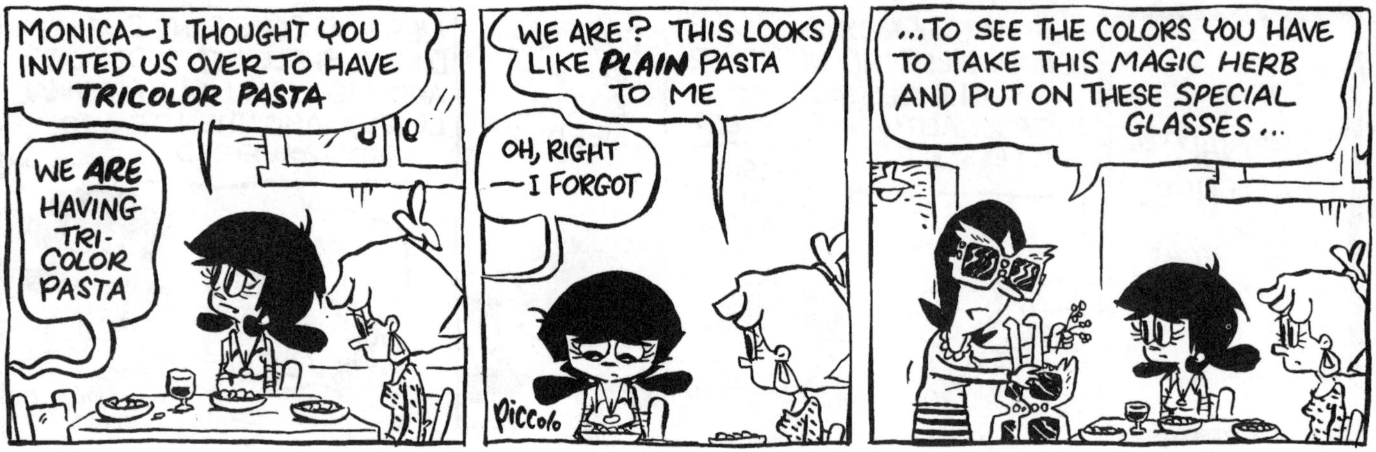
MONICA—I THOUGHT YOU INVITED US OVER TO HAVE TRICOLOR PASTA
WE ARE HAVING TRI-COLOR PASTA
WE ARE? THIS LOOKS LIKE PLAIN PASTA TO ME
OH, RIGHT —I FORGOT
PICCOLO
...TO SEE THE COLORS YOU HAVE TO TAKE THIS MAGIC HERB AND PUT ON THESE SPECIAL GLASSES...

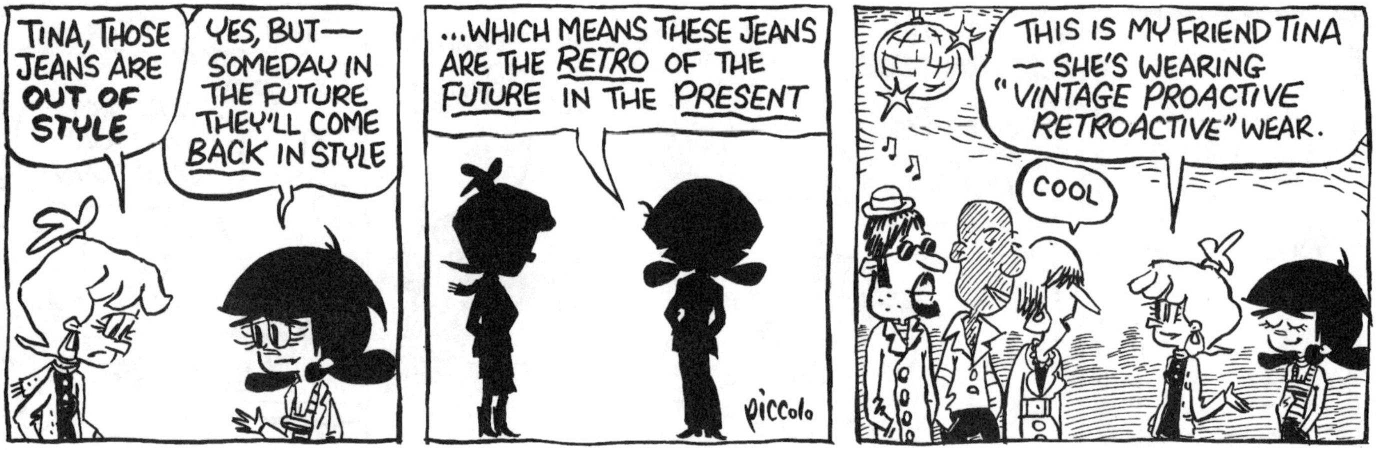
TINA, THOSE JEANS ARE OUT OF STYLE
YES, BUT— SOMEDAY IN THE FUTURE THEY'LL COME BACK IN STYLE
...WHICH MEANS THESE JEANS ARE THE RETRO OF THE FUTURE IN THE PRESENT
PICCOLO
THIS IS MY FRIEND TINA — SHE'S WEARING "VINTAGE PROACTIVE RETROACTIVE" WEAR.
COOL

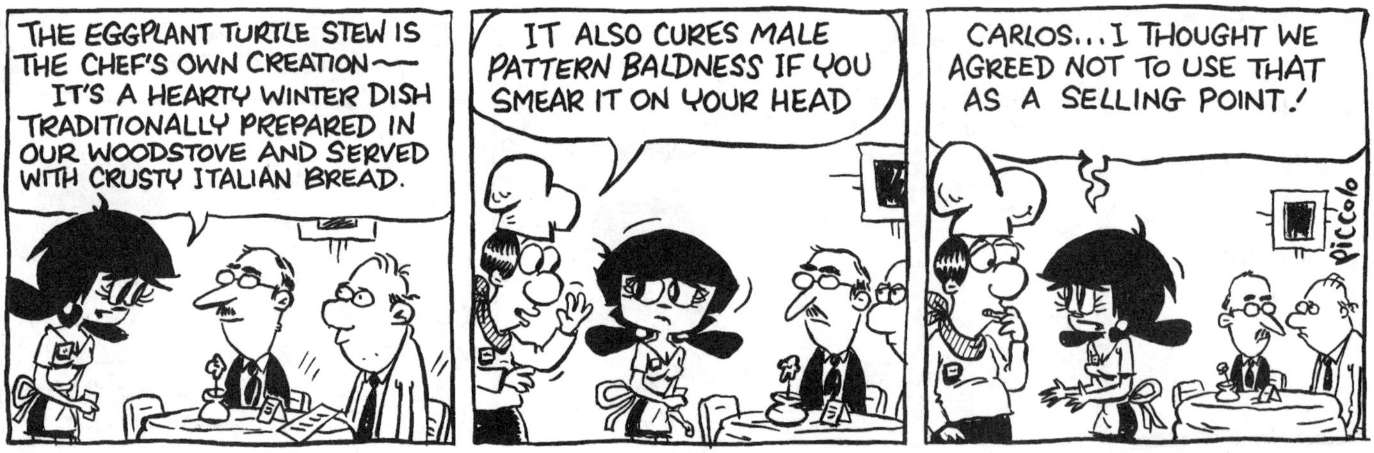
THE EGGPLANT TURTLE STEW IS THE CHEF'S OWN CREATION— IT'S A HEARTY WINTER DISH TRADITIONALLY PREPARED IN OUR WOODSTOVE AND SERVED WITH CRUSTY ITALIAN BREAD.
IT ALSO CURES MALE PATTERN BALDNESS IF YOU SMEAR IT ON YOUR HEAD
CARLOS...I THOUGHT WE AGREED NOT TO USE THAT AS A SELLING POINT!
PICCOLO

I'M NOT A SHALLOW SNOB, TINA...
I JUST DON'T WANT TO BE SEEN SHOPPING HERE AT THE "BARGAIN BARN"
SALES DESK
MORE FOR YOUR MOONY!
PICCOLO
CONGRATULATIONS, MA'AM!
?
MORE FOR
...YOU'RE OUR 10,000TH CUSTOMER...!
WE CROWN YOU QUEEN OF THE BARGAIN BARN!!
SALES DESK
SNAP!
NEWS 11
BARN QUEEN

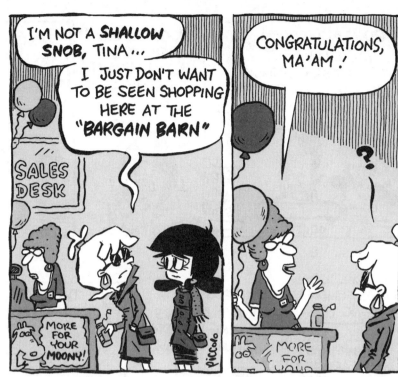

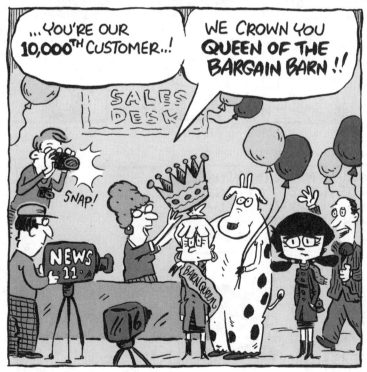

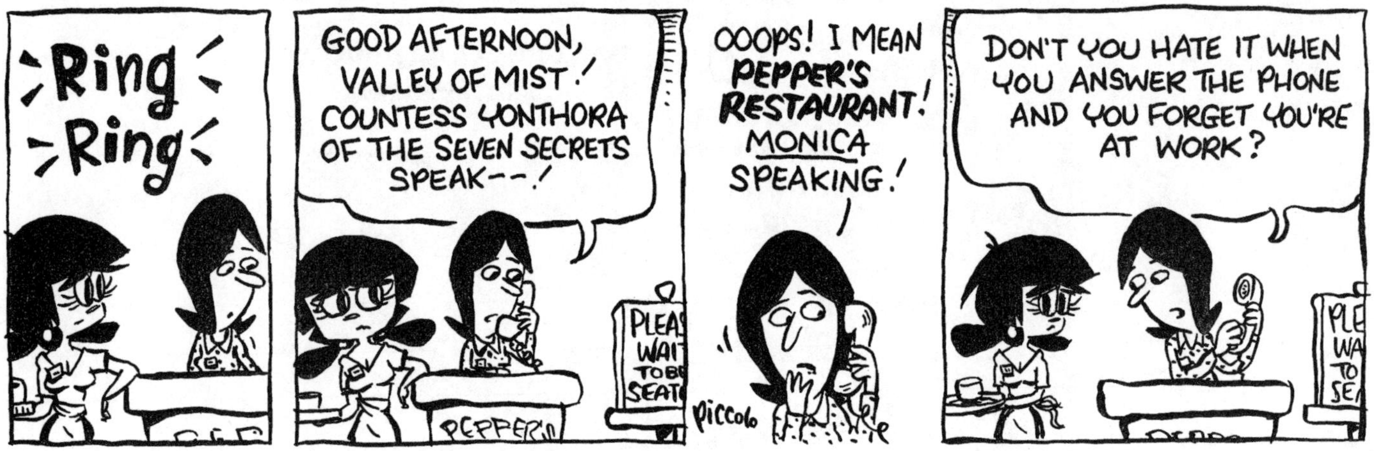
RING RING
GOOD AFTERNOON, VALLEY OF MIST! COUNTESS YONTHORA OF THE SEVEN SECRETS SPEAK--!
OOOPS! I MEAN PEPPER'S RESTAURANT! MONICA SPEAKING!
DON'T YOU HATE IT WHEN YOU ANSWER THE PHONE AND YOU FORGET YOU'RE AT WORK?

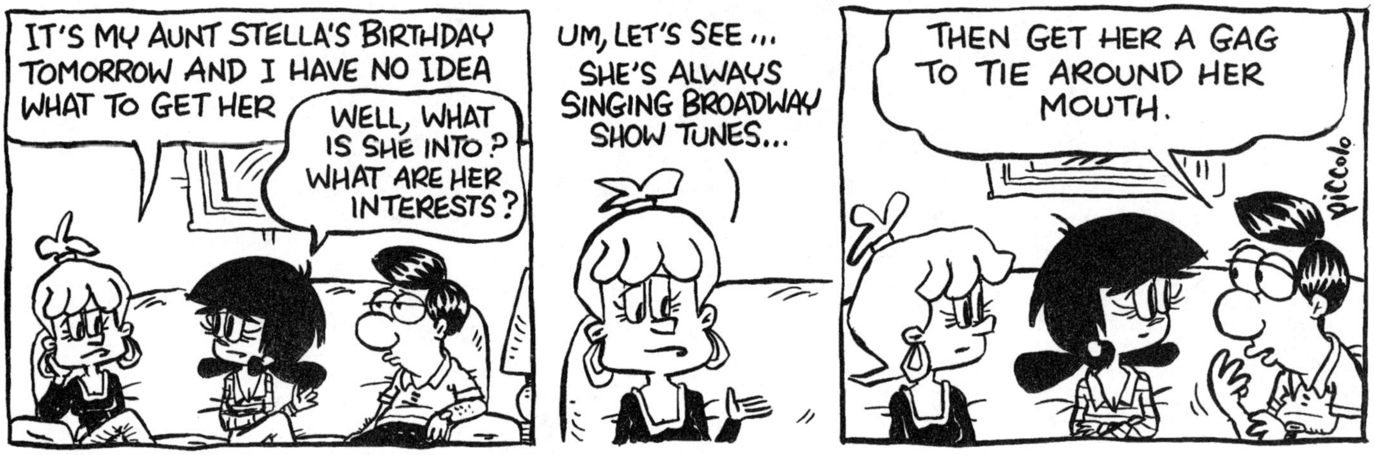
IT'S MY AUNT STELLA'S BIRTHDAY TOMORROW AND I HAVE NO IDEA WHAT TO GET HER
WELL, WHAT IS SHE INTO? WHAT ARE HER INTERESTS?
UM, LET'S SEE... SHE'S ALWAYS SINGING BROADWAY SHOW TUNES...
THEN GET HER A GAG TO TIE AROUND HER MOUTH.

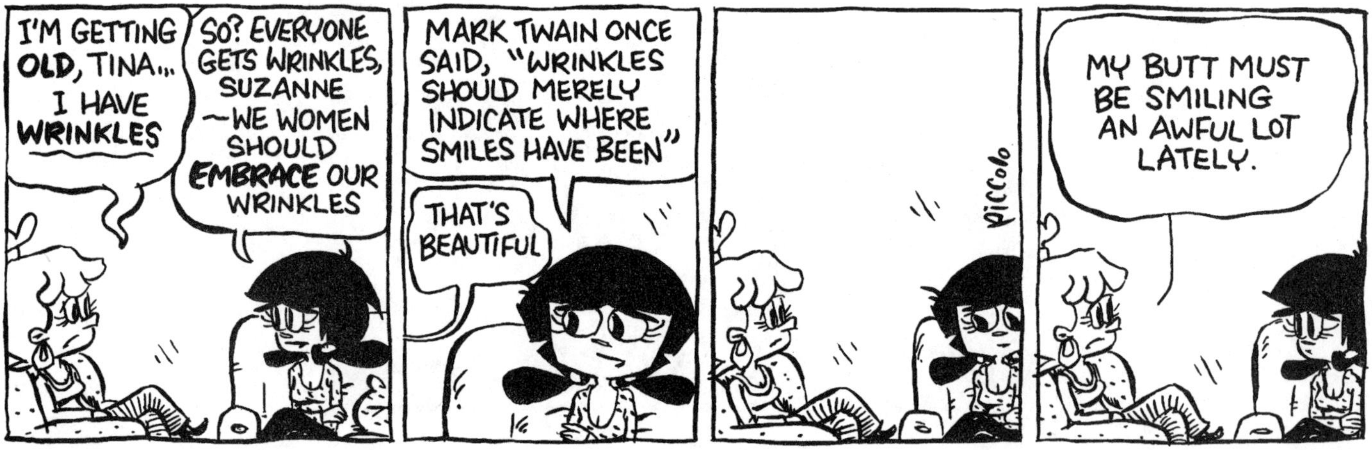
I'M GETTING OLD, TINA... I HAVE WRINKLES
SO? EVERYONE GETS WRINKLES, SUZANNE —WE WOMEN SHOULD EMBRACE OUR WRINKLES
MARK TWAIN ONCE SAID, "WRINKLES SHOULD MERELY INDICATE WHERE SMILES HAVE BEEN"
THAT'S BEAUTIFUL
MY BUTT MUST BE SMILING AN AWFUL LOT LATELY.

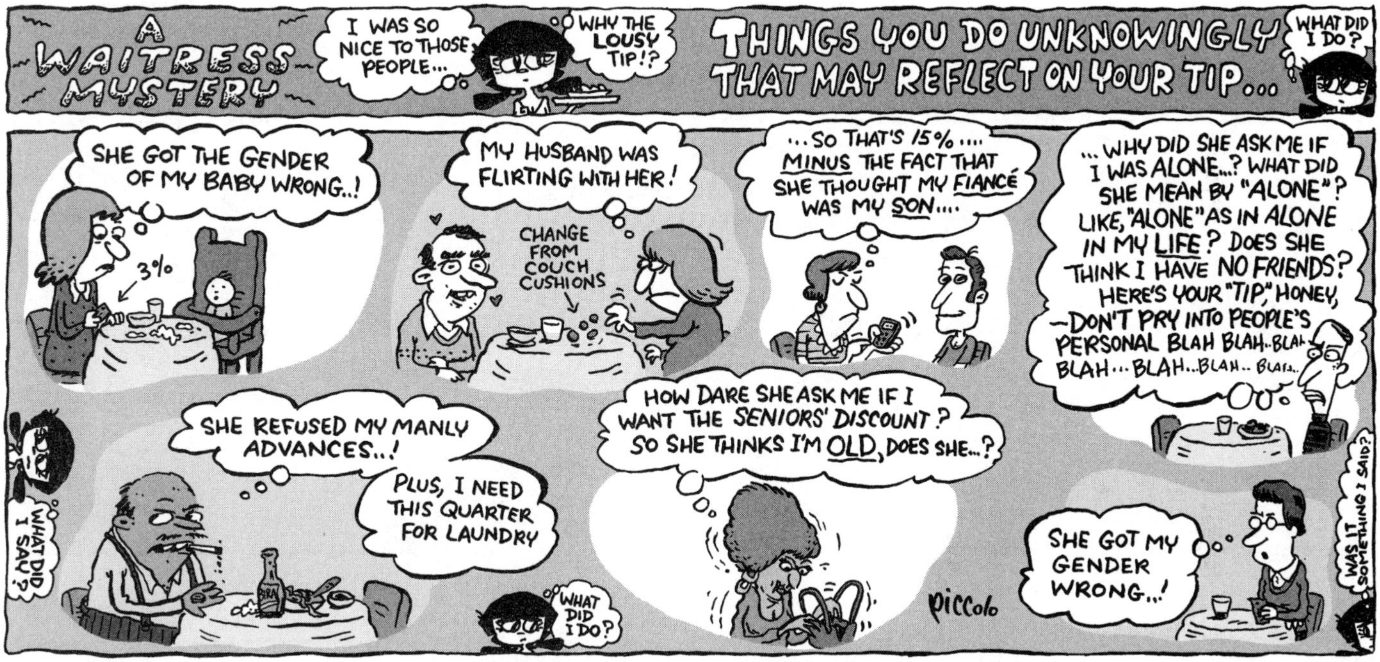
A WAITRESS MYSTERY
I WAS SO NICE TO THOSE PEOPLE...
WHY THE LOUSY TIP!?
THINGS YOU DO UNKNOWINGLY THAT MAY REFLECT ON YOUR TIP...
WHAT DID I DO?
SHE GOT THE GENDER OF MY BABY WRONG..!
3%
MY HUSBAND WAS FLIRTING WITH HER!
CHANGE FROM COUCH CUSHIONS
...SO THAT'S 15%.... MINUS THE FACT THAT SHE THOUGHT MY FIANCÉ WAS MY SON....
...WHY DID SHE ASK ME IF I WAS ALONE...? WHAT DID SHE MEAN BY "ALONE"? LIKE, "ALONE" AS IN ALONE IN MY LIFE? DOES SHE THINK I HAVE NO FRIENDS? HERE'S YOUR "TIP," HONEY, —DON'T PRY INTO PEOPLE'S PERSONAL BLAH BLAH..BLAH BLAH...BLAH...BLAH...BLAH...
WHAT DID I SAY?
SHE REFUSED MY MANLY ADVANCES..!
PLUS, I NEED THIS QUARTER FOR LAUNDRY
HOW DARE SHE ASK ME IF I WANT THE SENIORS' DISCOUNT? SO SHE THINKS I'M OLD, DOES SHE...?
WHAT DID I DO?
piccolo
SHE GOT MY GENDER WRONG..!
WAS IT SOMETHING I SAID?

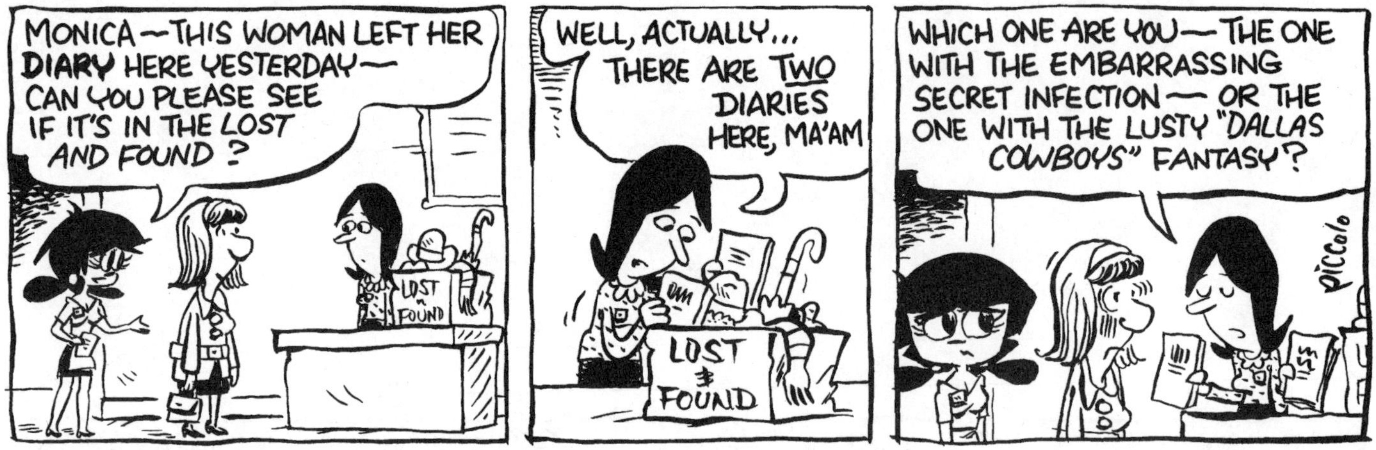
MONICA—THIS WOMAN LEFT HER DIARY HERE YESTERDAY— CAN YOU PLEASE SEE IF IT'S IN THE LOST AND FOUND?
LOST & FOUND
WELL, ACTUALLY... THERE ARE TWO DIARIES HERE, MA'AM
LOST & FOUND
WHICH ONE ARE YOU—THE ONE WITH THE EMBARRASSING SECRET INFECTION—OR THE ONE WITH THE LUSTY "DALLAS COWBOYS" FANTASY?
piccolo

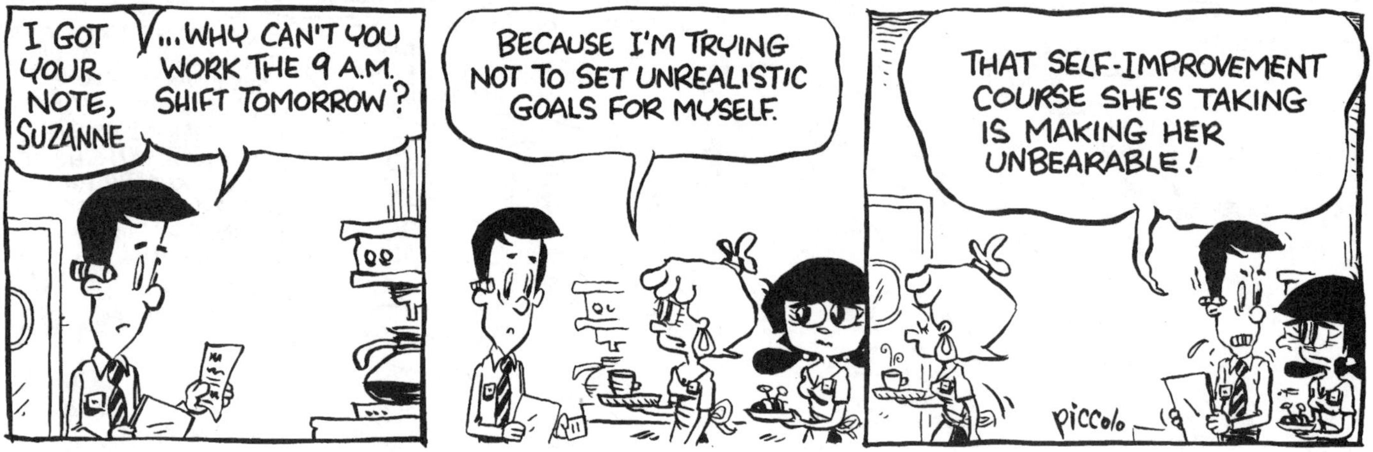
I GOT YOUR NOTE, SUZANNE
...WHY CAN'T YOU WORK THE 9 A.M. SHIFT TOMORROW?
BECAUSE I'M TRYING NOT TO SET UNREALISTIC GOALS FOR MYSELF.
THAT SELF-IMPROVEMENT COURSE SHE'S TAKING IS MAKING HER UNBEARABLE!
piccolo

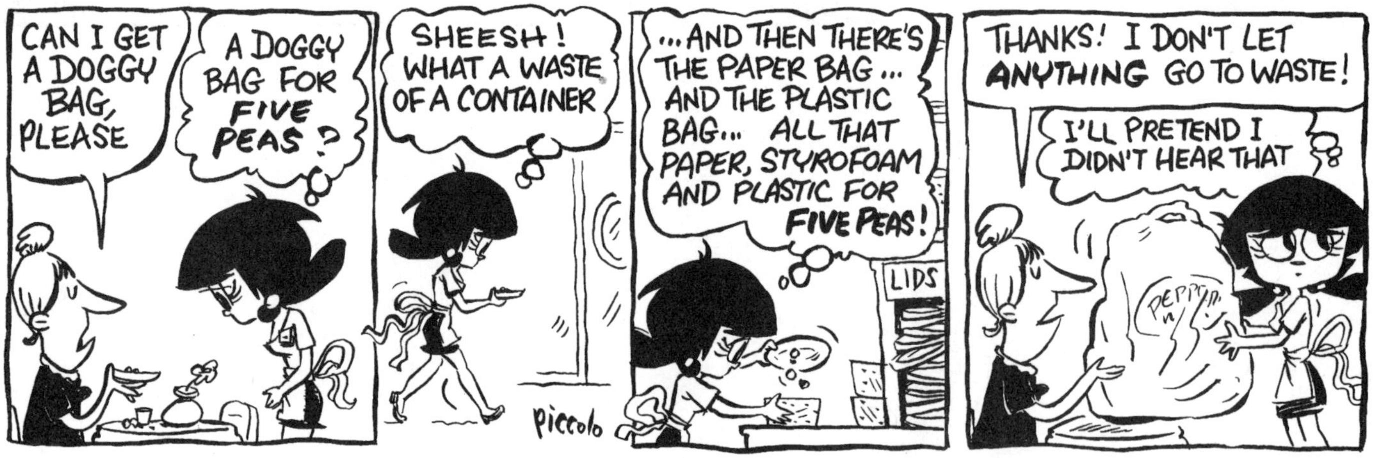
CAN I GET A DOGGY BAG, PLEASE
A DOGGY BAG FOR FIVE PEAS?
SHEESH! WHAT A WASTE OF A CONTAINER
piccolo
...AND THEN THERE'S THE PAPER BAG... AND THE PLASTIC BAG... ALL THAT PAPER, STYROFOAM AND PLASTIC FOR FIVE PEAS!
LIDS
THANKS! I DON'T LET ANYTHING GO TO WASTE!
I'LL PRETEND I DIDN'T HEAR THAT

I USED TO WORK AT A FAST-FOOD JOINT THAT HAD TABLE SERVICE
THIS EVENING WE'RE FEATURING FOOD-LIKE OBJECTS DEEP-FRIED IN AN EDIBLE OIL PRODUCT AND SERVED WITH A TOY FROM SOME DISNEY MOVIE
ONE DAY I DISCOVERED THAT THE PLACE WASN'T REALLY SUPPOSED TO HAVE TABLE SERVICE
...THE CUSTOMERS WERE JUST LAZY.
YOU'RE GONNA MAKE US WALK ALL THE WAY OVER THERE ?
THROW US SOME fries
Z Z Z
C'MERE
Piccolo

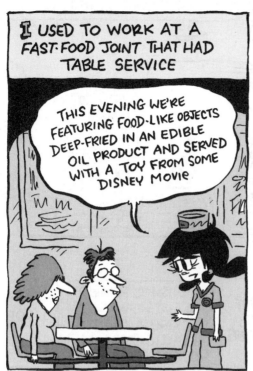

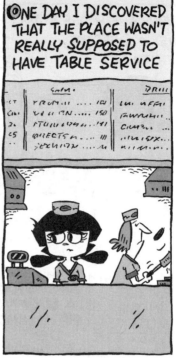

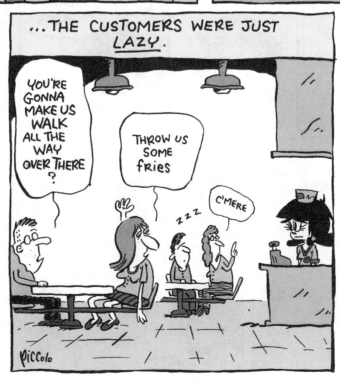

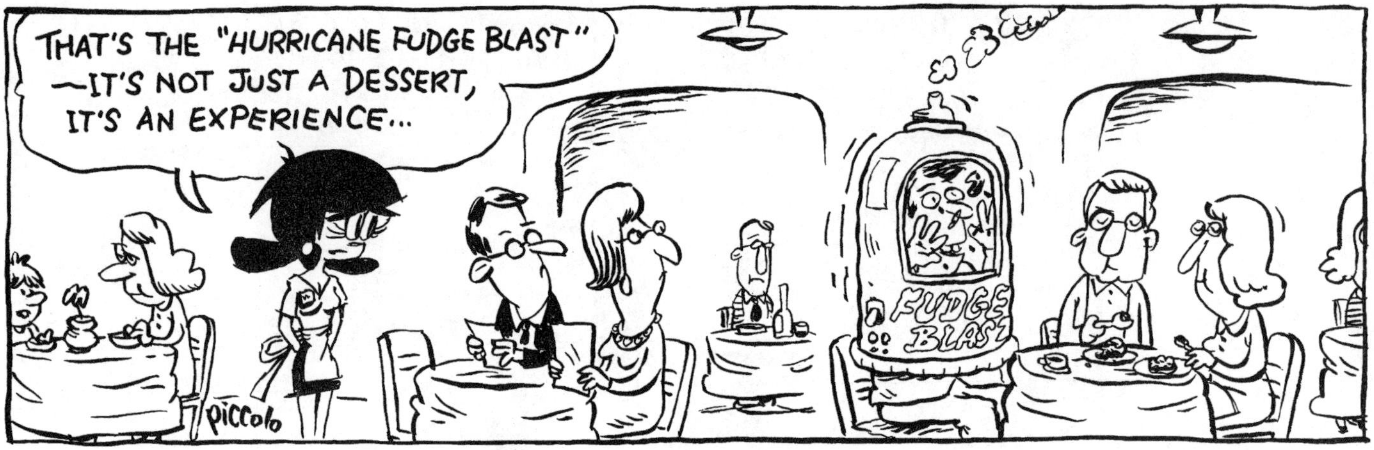
THAT'S THE "HURRICANE FUDGE BLAST" —IT'S NOT JUST A DESSERT, IT'S AN EXPERIENCE...
FUDGE BLAST
piccolo

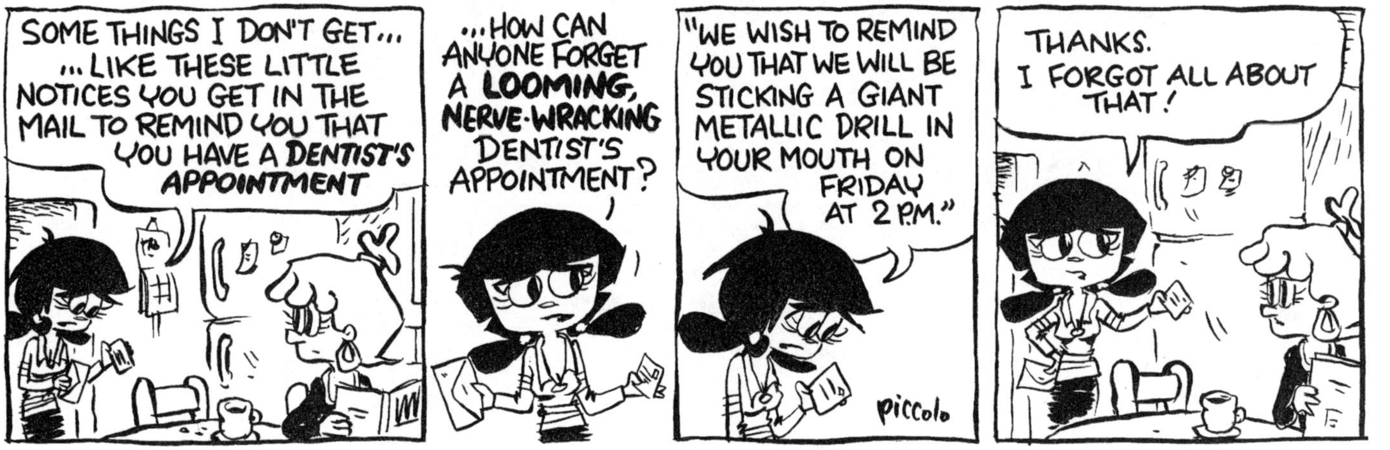
SOME THINGS I DON'T GET... ...LIKE THESE LITTLE NOTICES YOU GET IN THE MAIL TO REMIND YOU THAT YOU HAVE A DENTIST'S APPOINTMENT
...HOW CAN ANYONE FORGET A LOOMING, NERVE-WRACKING DENTIST'S APPOINTMENT?
"WE WISH TO REMIND YOU THAT WE WILL BE STICKING A GIANT METALLIC DRILL IN YOUR MOUTH ON FRIDAY AT 2 P.M."
piccolo
THANKS. I FORGOT ALL ABOUT THAT!

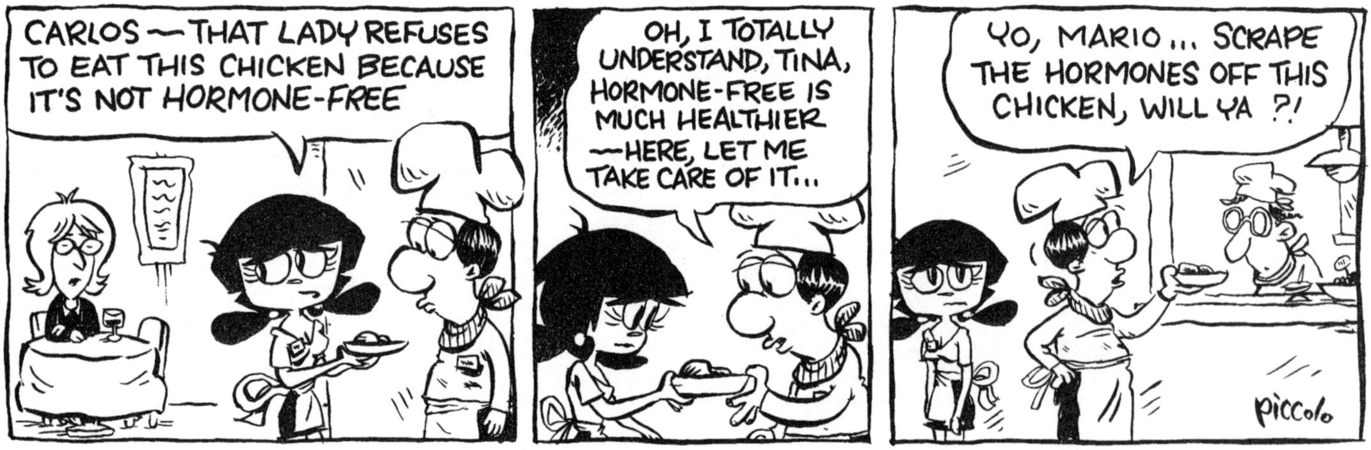
CARLOS—THAT LADY REFUSES TO EAT THIS CHICKEN BECAUSE IT'S NOT HORMONE-FREE
OH, I TOTALLY UNDERSTAND, TINA, HORMONE-FREE IS MUCH HEALTHIER —HERE, LET ME TAKE CARE OF IT...
YO, MARIO... SCRAPE THE HORMONES OFF THIS CHICKEN, WILL YA ?!
piccolo

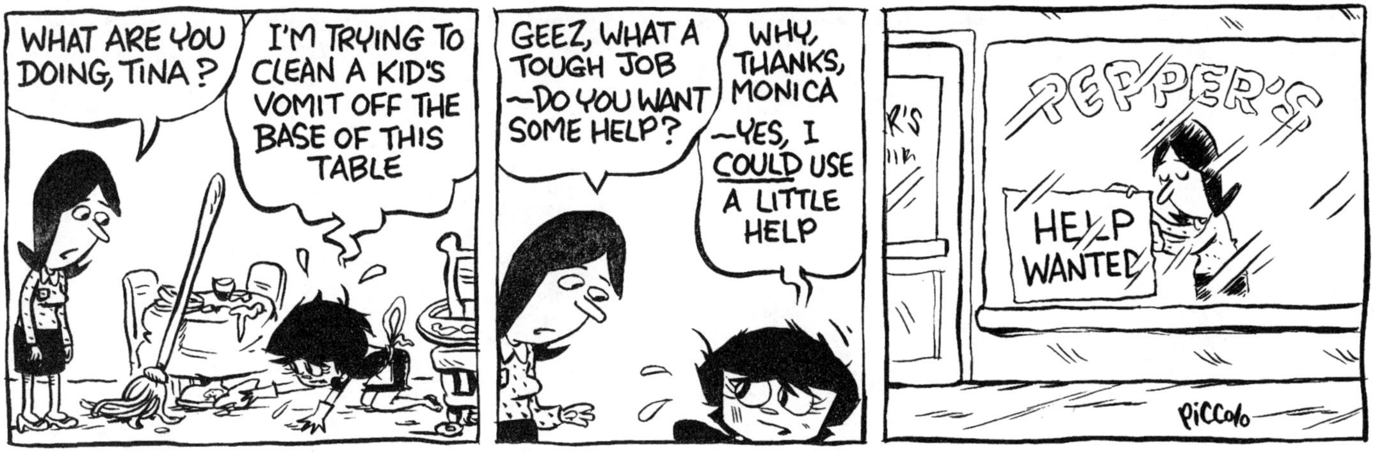
WHAT ARE YOU DOING, TINA?
I'M TRYING TO CLEAN A KID'S VOMIT OFF THE BASE OF THIS TABLE
GEEZ, WHAT A TOUGH JOB —DO YOU WANT SOME HELP?
WHY, THANKS, MONICA —YES, I COULD USE A LITTLE HELP
PEPPER'S
HELP WANTED
piccolo

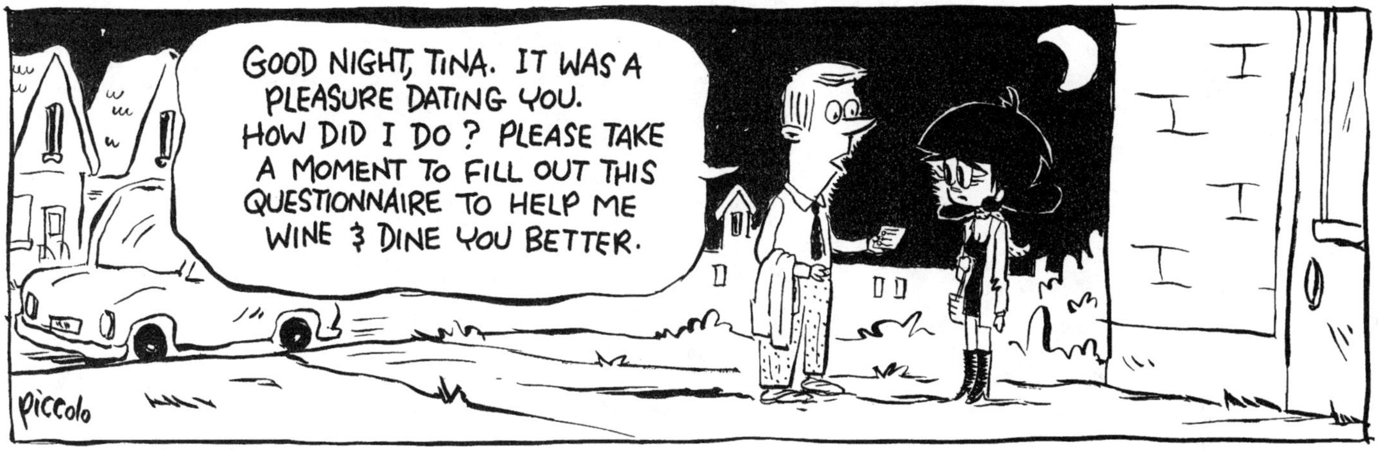
GOOD NIGHT, TINA. IT WAS A PLEASURE DATING YOU. HOW DID I DO? PLEASE TAKE A MOMENT TO FILL OUT THIS QUESTIONNAIRE TO HELP ME WINE & DINE YOU BETTER.
piccolo

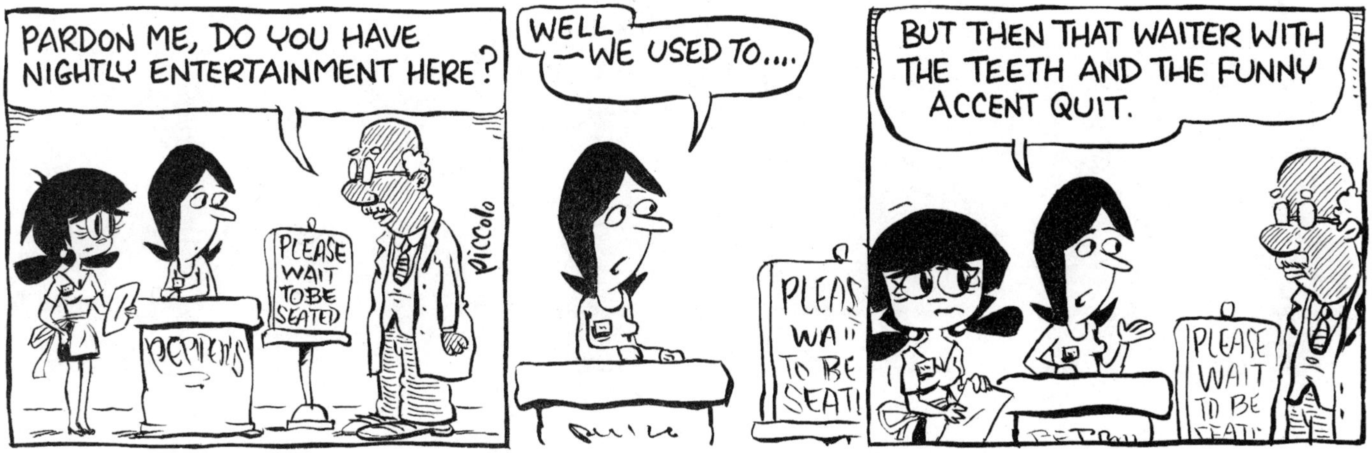
PARDON ME, DO YOU HAVE NIGHTLY ENTERTAINMENT HERE?
PLEASE WAIT TO BE SEATED
piccolo
WELL —WE USED TO....
BUT THEN THAT WAITER WITH THE TEETH AND THE FUNNY ACCENT QUIT.
PLEASE WAIT TO BE

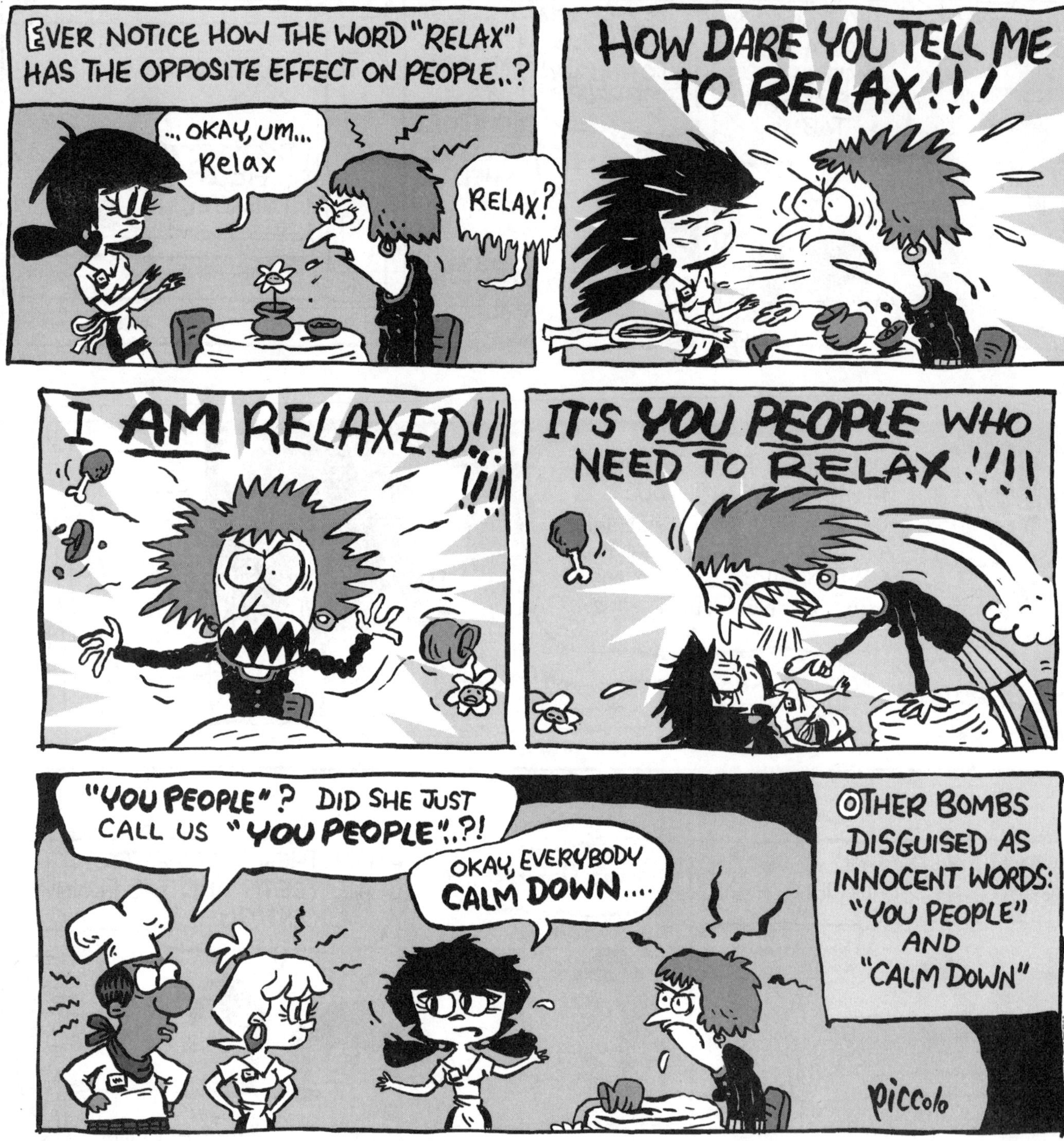
EVER NOTICE HOW THE WORD "RELAX" HAS THE OPPOSITE EFFECT ON PEOPLE..?
...OKAY, UM... Relax
RELAX?
HOW DARE YOU TELL ME TO RELAX!!!
I AM RELAXED!!!!!!!
IT'S YOU PEOPLE WHO NEED TO RELAX!!!!
"YOU PEOPLE"? DID SHE JUST CALL US "YOU PEOPLE"..?!
OKAY, EVERYBODY CALM DOWN....
OTHER BOMBS DISGUISED AS INNOCENT WORDS: "YOU PEOPLE" AND "CALM DOWN"
piccolo

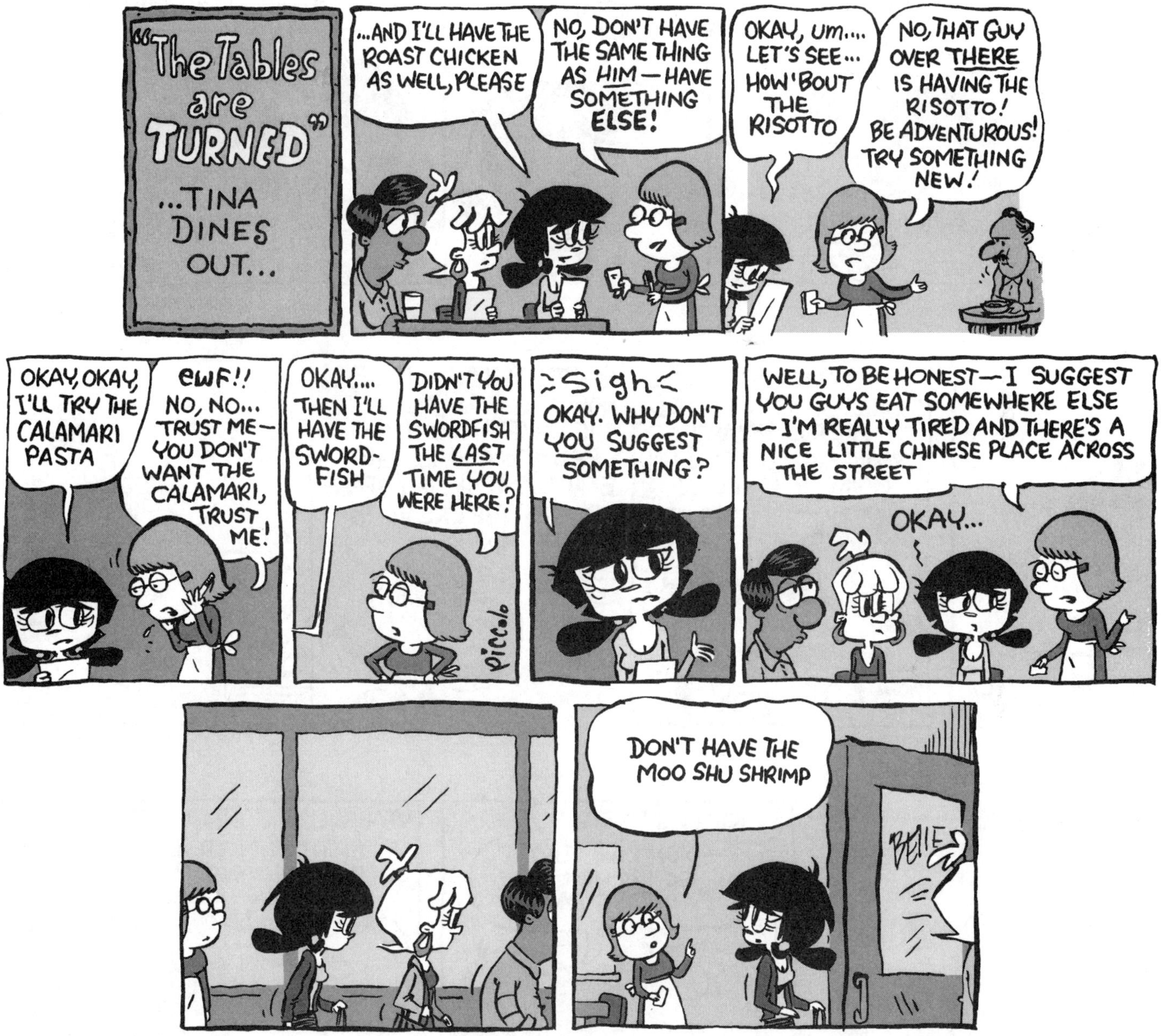
"The Tables are TURNED" ...TINA DINES OUT...
...AND I'LL HAVE THE ROAST CHICKEN AS WELL, PLEASE
NO, DON'T HAVE THE SAME THING AS HIM — HAVE SOMETHING ELSE!
OKAY, um.... LET'S SEE... HOW'BOUT THE RISOTTO
NO, THAT GUY OVER THERE IS HAVING THE RISOTTO! BE ADVENTUROUS! TRY SOMETHING NEW!
OKAY, OKAY, I'LL TRY THE CALAMARI PASTA
EWF!! NO, NO... TRUST ME — YOU DON'T WANT THE CALAMARI, TRUST ME!
OKAY.... THEN I'LL HAVE THE SWORD-FISH
DIDN'T YOU HAVE THE SWORDFISH THE LAST TIME YOU WERE HERE?
piccolo
sigh
OKAY. WHY DON'T YOU SUGGEST SOMETHING?
WELL, TO BE HONEST — I SUGGEST YOU GUYS EAT SOMEWHERE ELSE — I'M REALLY TIRED AND THERE'S A NICE LITTLE CHINESE PLACE ACROSS THE STREET
OKAY...
DON'T HAVE THE MOO SHU SHRIMP
BELLE

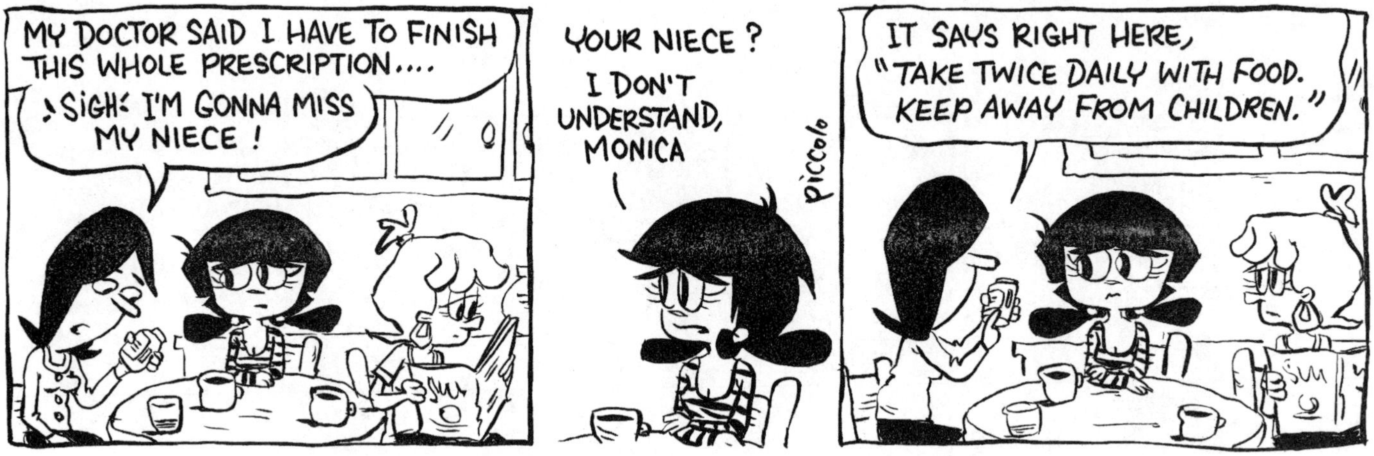
MY DOCTOR SAID I HAVE TO FINISH THIS WHOLE PRESCRIPTION....
:SIGH: I'M GONNA MISS MY NIECE!
YOUR NIECE?
I DON'T UNDERSTAND, MONICA
piccolo
IT SAYS RIGHT HERE, "TAKE TWICE DAILY WITH FOOD. KEEP AWAY FROM CHILDREN."

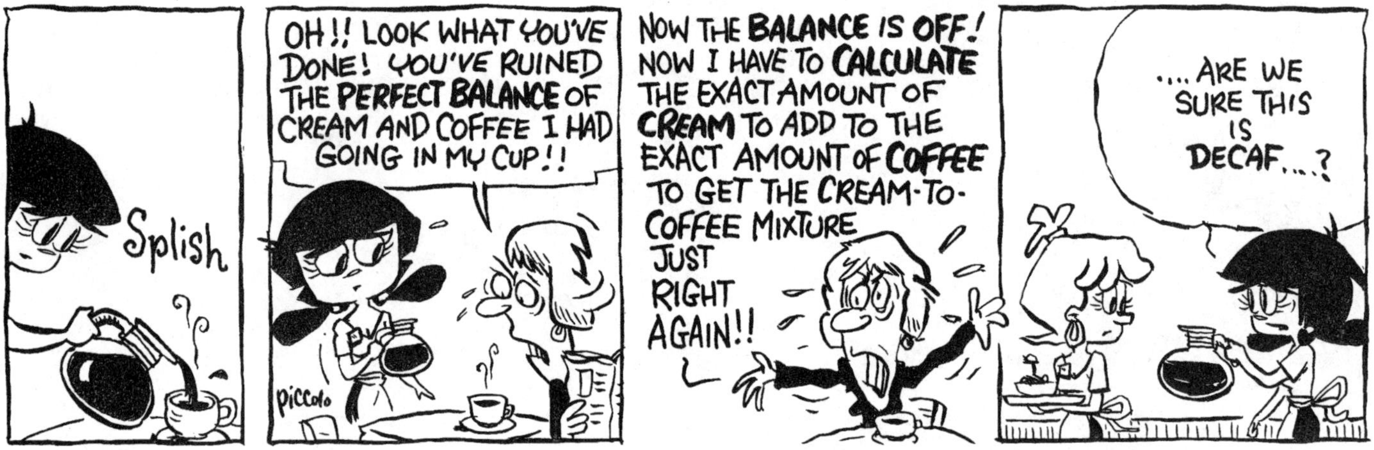
Splish
OH!! LOOK WHAT YOU'VE DONE! YOU'VE RUINED THE PERFECT BALANCE OF CREAM AND COFFEE I HAD GOING IN MY CUP!!
piccolo
NOW THE BALANCE IS OFF! NOW I HAVE TO CALCULATE THE EXACT AMOUNT OF CREAM TO ADD TO THE EXACT AMOUNT OF COFFEE TO GET THE CREAM-TO-COFFEE MIXTURE JUST RIGHT AGAIN!!
....ARE WE SURE THIS IS DECAF....?

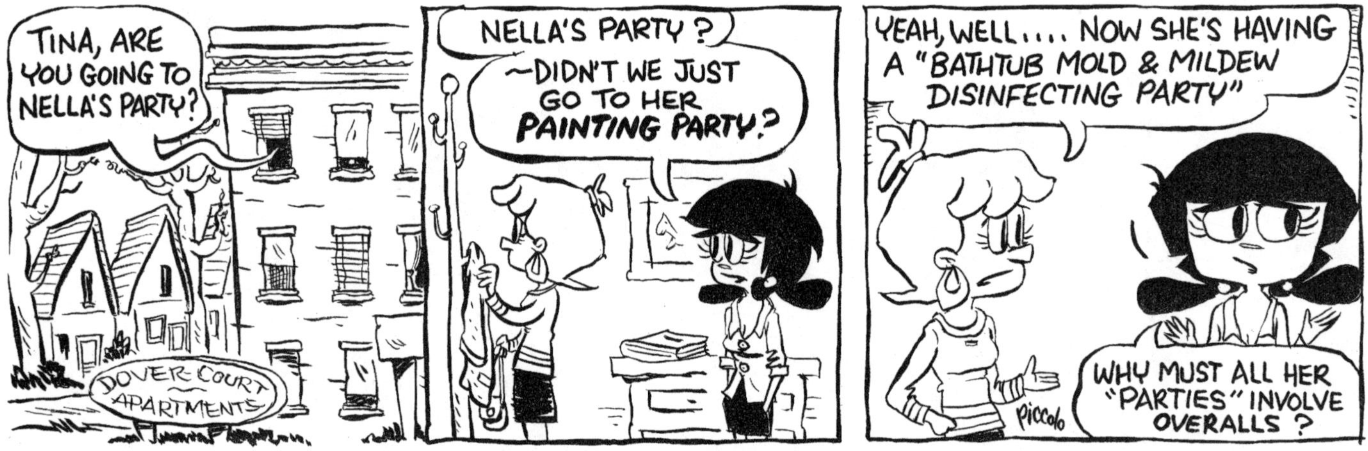
TINA, ARE YOU GOING TO NELLA'S PARTY?
DOVER-COURT APARTMENTS
NELLA'S PARTY?
~DIDN'T WE JUST GO TO HER PAINTING PARTY?
YEAH, WELL.... NOW SHE'S HAVING A "BATHTUB MOLD & MILDEW DISINFECTING PARTY"
WHY MUST ALL HER "PARTIES" INVOLVE OVERALLS?
piccolo

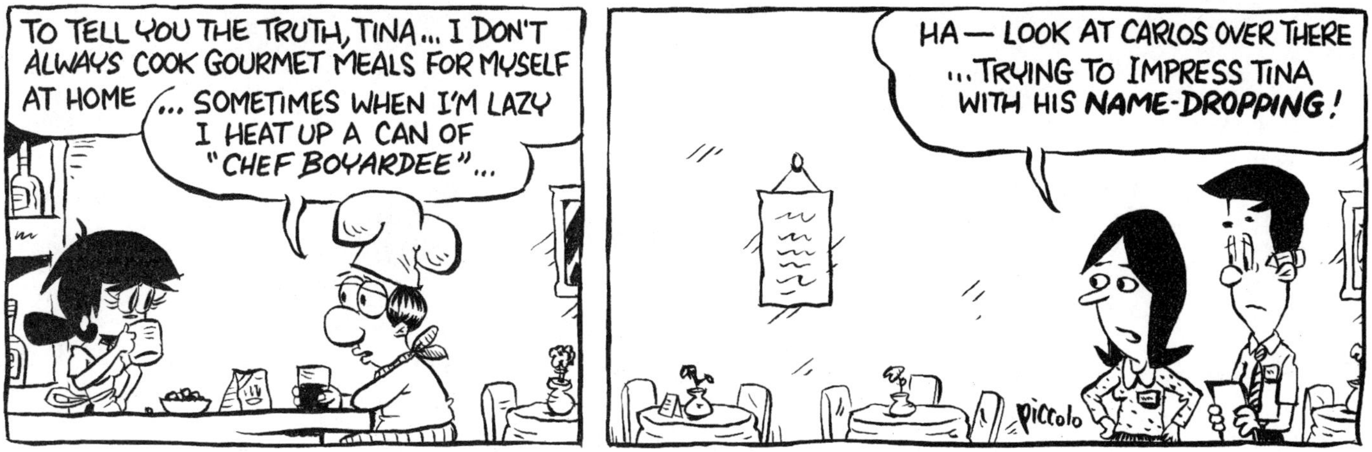
TO TELL YOU THE TRUTH, TINA... I DON'T ALWAYS COOK GOURMET MEALS FOR MYSELF AT HOME
... SOMETIMES WHEN I'M LAZY I HEAT UP A CAN OF "CHEF BOYARDEE"...
HA — LOOK AT CARLOS OVER THERE ...TRYING TO IMPRESS TINA WITH HIS NAME-DROPPING!
piccolo

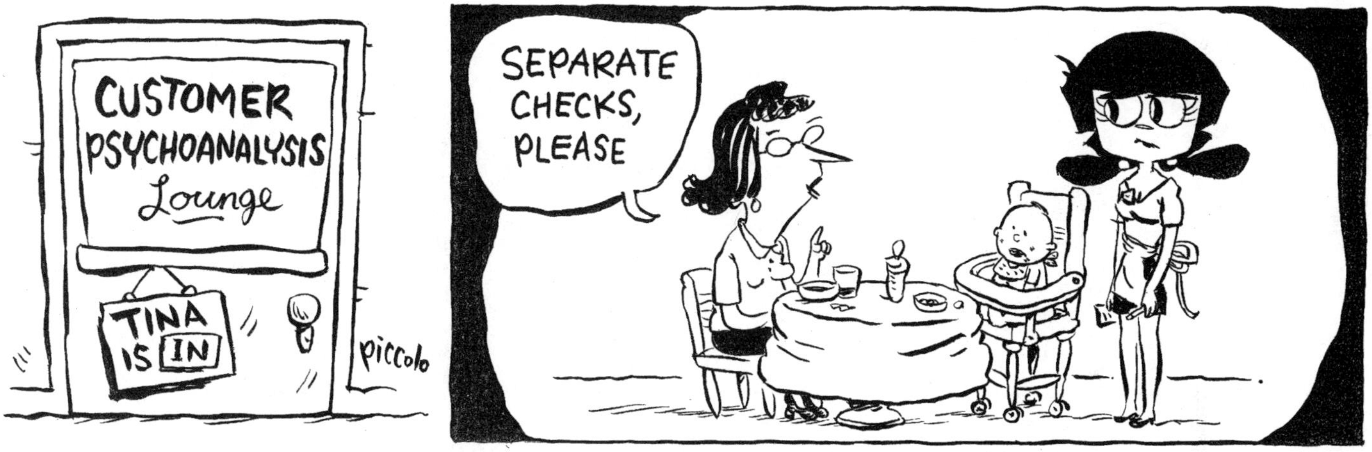
CUSTOMER PSYCHOANALYSIS Lounge
TINA IS IN
piccolo
SEPARATE CHECKS, PLEASE

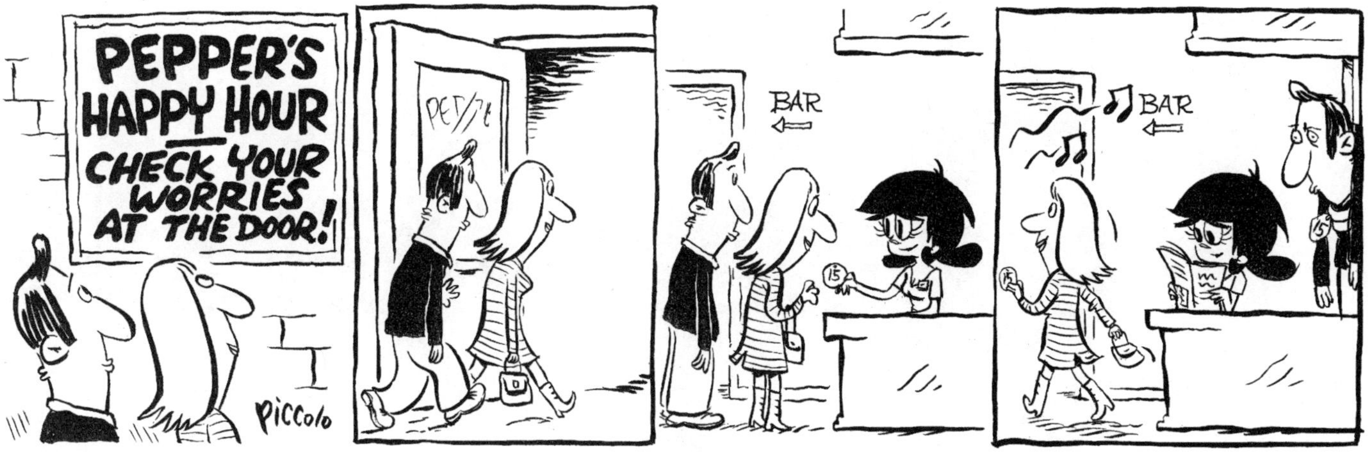
PEPPER'S HAPPY HOUR
CHECK YOUR WORRIES AT THE DOOR!
piccolo
BAR
15
BAR

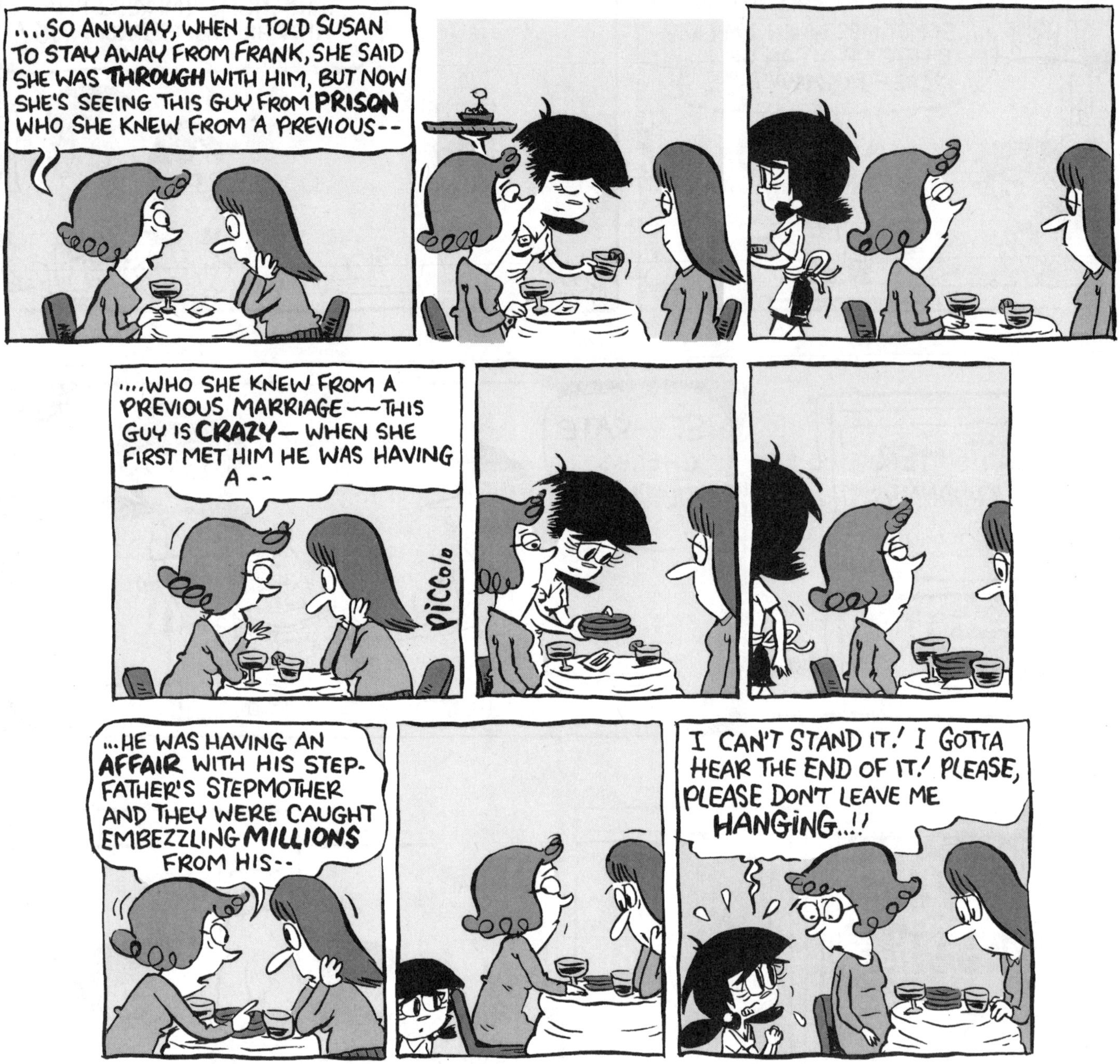
....SO ANYWAY, WHEN I TOLD SUSAN TO STAY AWAY FROM FRANK, SHE SAID SHE WAS THROUGH WITH HIM, BUT NOW SHE'S SEEING THIS GUY FROM PRISON WHO SHE KNEW FROM A PREVIOUS--
....WHO SHE KNEW FROM A PREVIOUS MARRIAGE---THIS GUY IS CRAZY-- WHEN SHE FIRST MET HIM HE WAS HAVING A--
PICCOLO
...HE WAS HAVING AN AFFAIR WITH HIS STEP-FATHER'S STEPMOTHER AND THEY WERE CAUGHT EMBEZZLING MILLIONS FROM HIS--
I CAN'T STAND IT! I GOTTA HEAR THE END OF IT! PLEASE, PLEASE DON'T LEAVE ME HANGING..!!

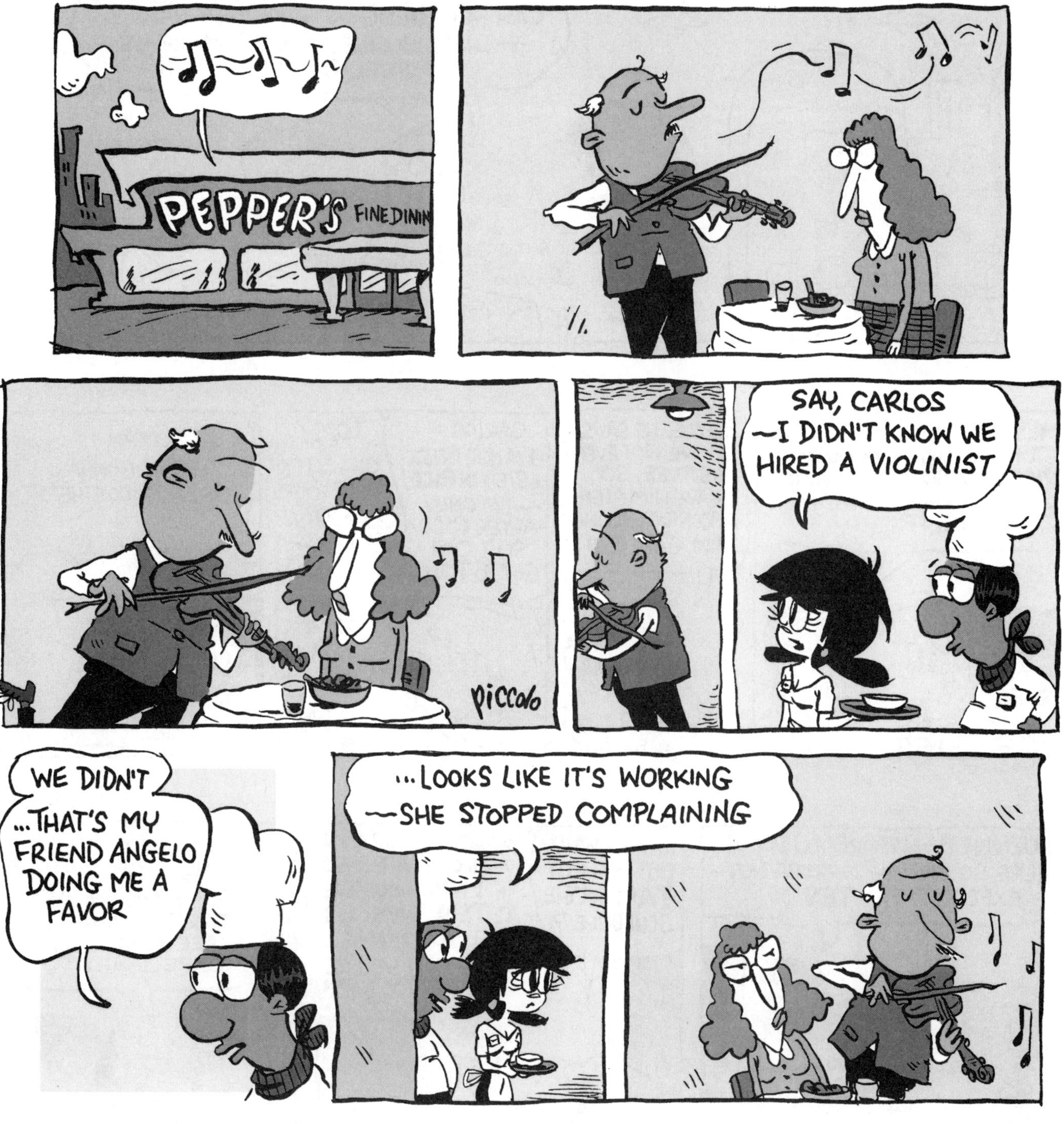
PEPPER'S FINE DININ
SAY, CARLOS
—I DIDN'T KNOW WE HIRED A VIOLINIST
piccolo
WE DIDN'T
...THAT'S MY FRIEND ANGELO DOING ME A FAVOR
...LOOKS LIKE IT'S WORKING
—SHE STOPPED COMPLAINING

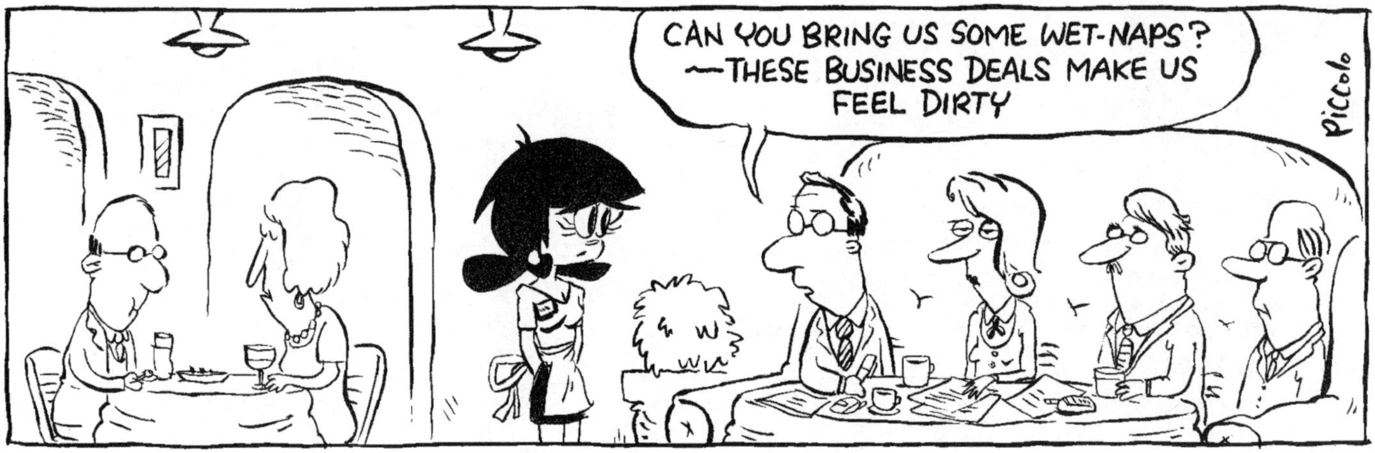
CAN YOU BRING US SOME WET-NAPS? —THESE BUSINESS DEALS MAKE US FEEL DIRTY
PICCOLO

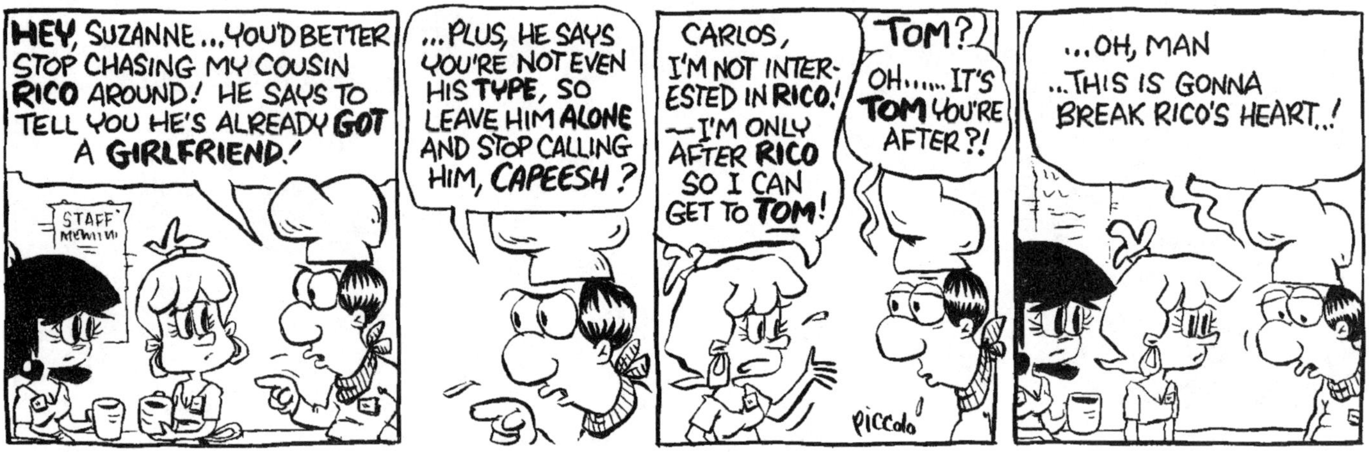
HEY, SUZANNE...YOU'D BETTER STOP CHASING MY COUSIN RICO AROUND! HE SAYS TO TELL YOU HE'S ALREADY GOT A GIRLFRIEND!
STAFF MENU
...PLUS, HE SAYS YOU'RE NOT EVEN HIS TYPE, SO LEAVE HIM ALONE AND STOP CALLING HIM, CAPEESH?
CARLOS, I'M NOT INTERESTED IN RICO! —I'M ONLY AFTER RICO SO I CAN GET TO TOM!
TOM?
OH...... IT'S TOM YOU'RE AFTER?!
PICCOLO
...OH, MAN ...THIS IS GONNA BREAK RICO'S HEART..!

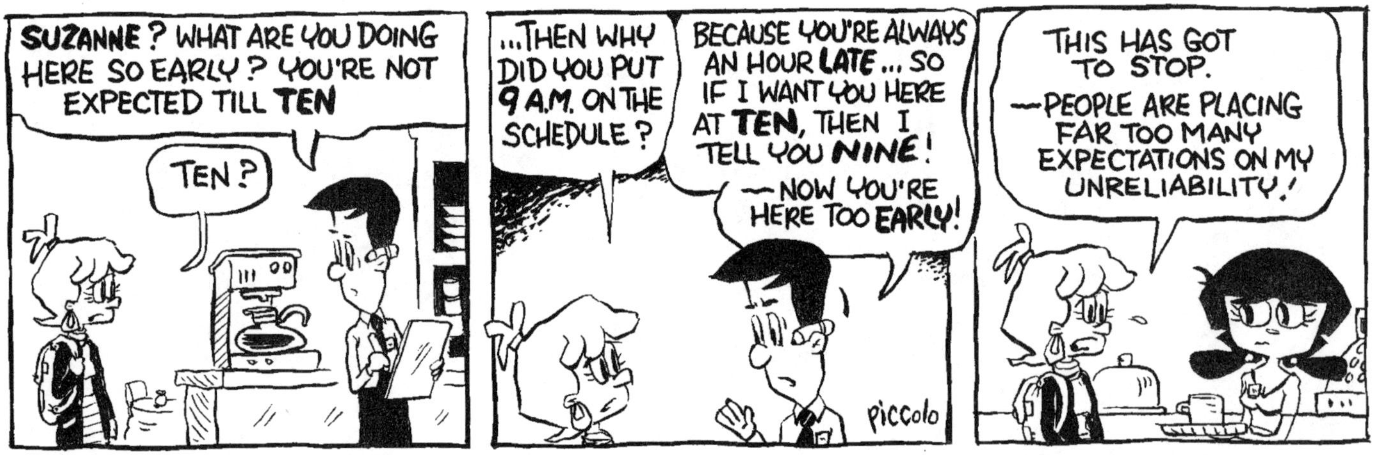
SUZANNE? WHAT ARE YOU DOING HERE SO EARLY? YOU'RE NOT EXPECTED TILL TEN
TEN?
...THEN WHY DID YOU PUT 9 A.M. ON THE SCHEDULE?
BECAUSE YOU'RE ALWAYS AN HOUR LATE... SO IF I WANT YOU HERE AT TEN, THEN I TELL YOU NINE!
—NOW YOU'RE HERE TOO EARLY!
PICCOLO
THIS HAS GOT TO STOP. —PEOPLE ARE PLACING FAR TOO MANY EXPECTATIONS ON MY UNRELIABILITY!

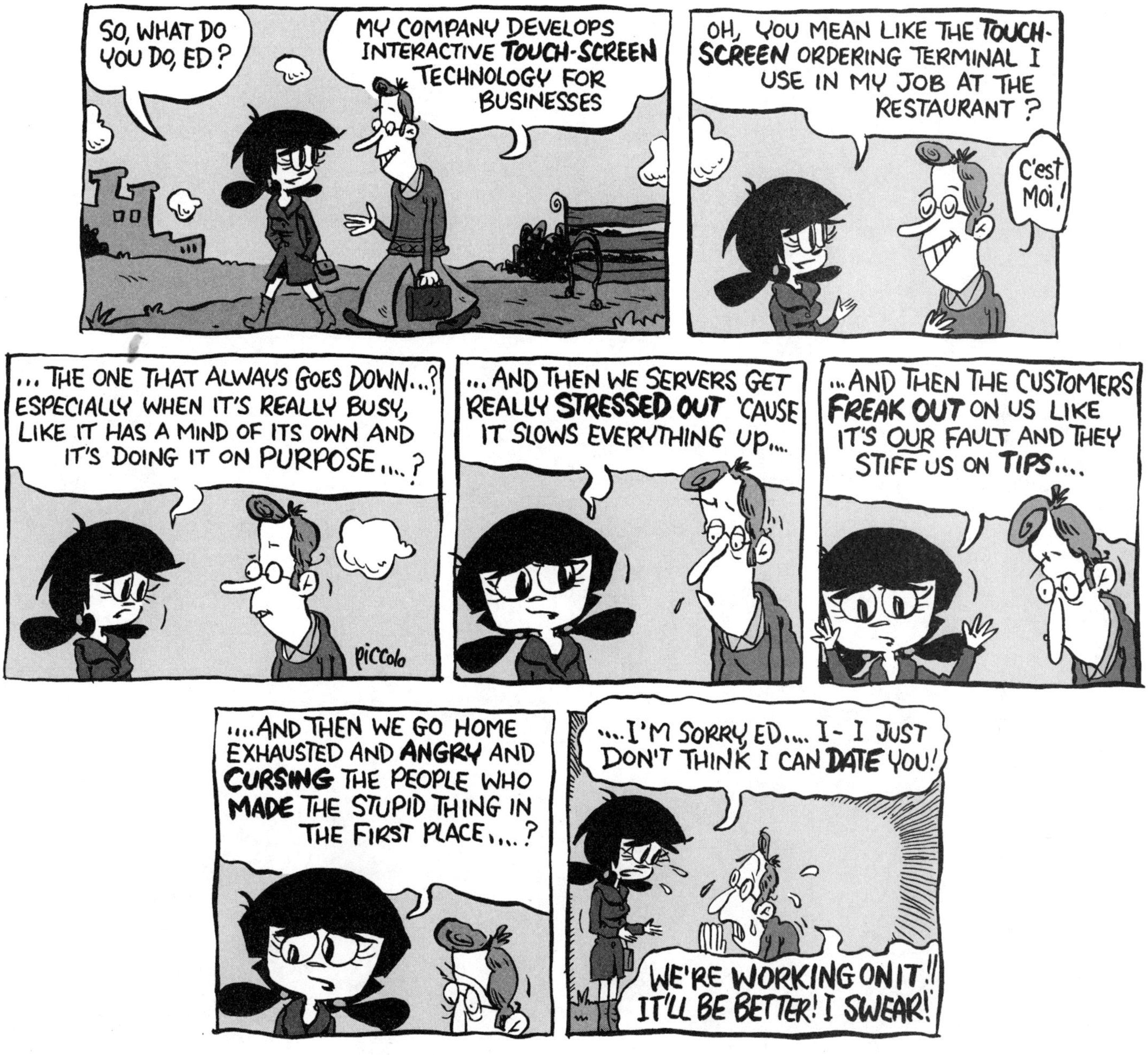
SO, WHAT DO YOU DO, ED?
MY COMPANY DEVELOPS INTERACTIVE TOUCH-SCREEN TECHNOLOGY FOR BUSINESSES
OH, YOU MEAN LIKE THE TOUCH-SCREEN ORDERING TERMINAL I USE IN MY JOB AT THE RESTAURANT?
C'est Moi!
... THE ONE THAT ALWAYS GOES DOWN...? ESPECIALLY WHEN IT'S REALLY BUSY, LIKE IT HAS A MIND OF ITS OWN AND IT'S DOING IT ON PURPOSE....?
PICCOLO
... AND THEN WE SERVERS GET REALLY STRESSED OUT 'CAUSE IT SLOWS EVERYTHING UP...
... AND THEN THE CUSTOMERS FREAK OUT ON US LIKE IT'S OUR FAULT AND THEY STIFF US ON TIPS....
.... AND THEN WE GO HOME EXHAUSTED AND ANGRY AND CURSING THE PEOPLE WHO MADE THE STUPID THING IN THE FIRST PLACE....?
.... I'M SORRY, ED.... I- I JUST DON'T THINK I CAN DATE YOU!
WE'RE WORKING ON IT!! IT'LL BE BETTER! I SWEAR!

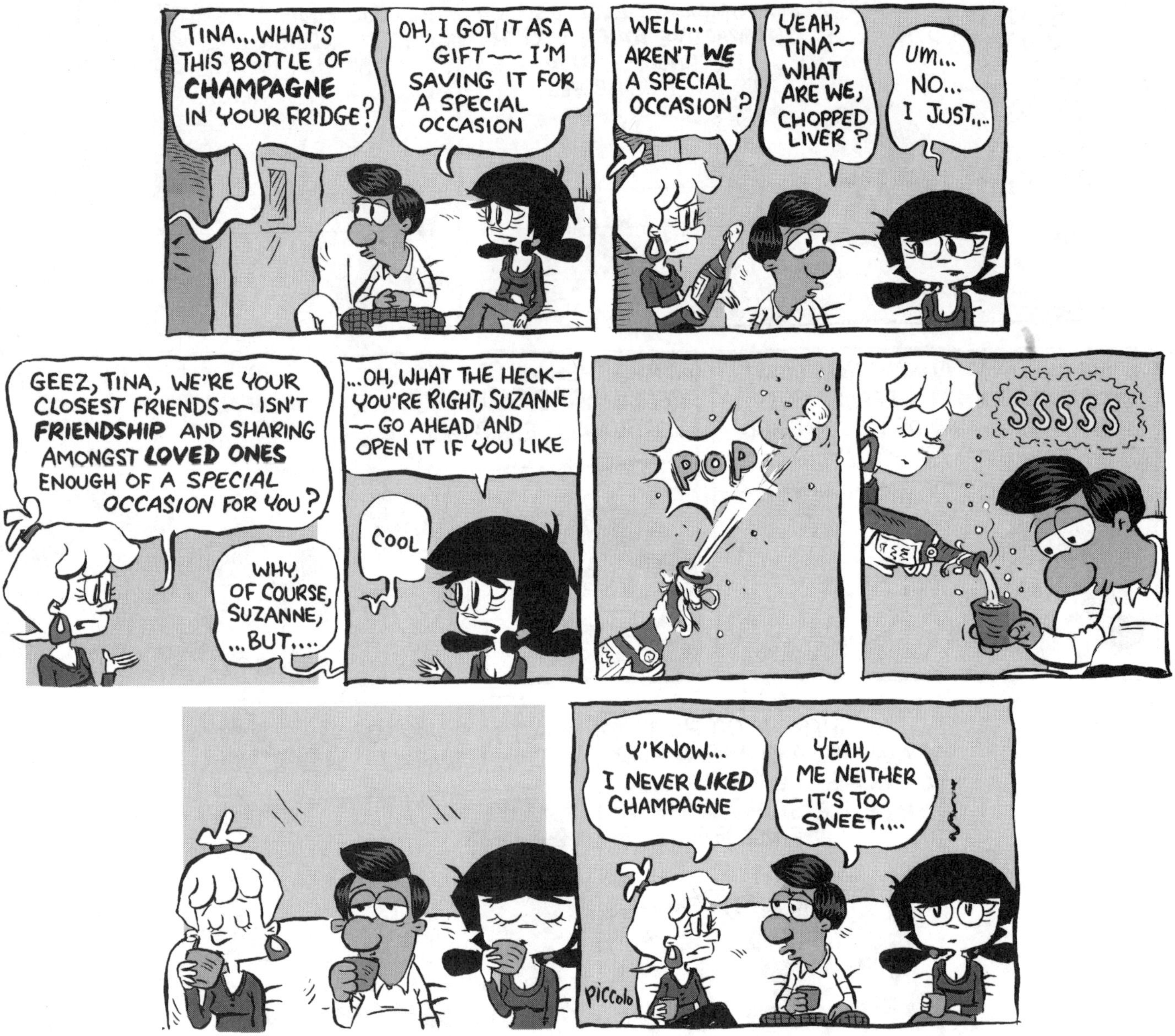
TINA...WHAT'S THIS BOTTLE OF CHAMPAGNE IN YOUR FRIDGE?
OH, I GOT IT AS A GIFT— I'M SAVING IT FOR A SPECIAL OCCASION
WELL... AREN'T WE A SPECIAL OCCASION?
YEAH, TINA— WHAT ARE WE, CHOPPED LIVER?
UM... NO... I JUST...
GEEZ, TINA, WE'RE YOUR CLOSEST FRIENDS— ISN'T FRIENDSHIP AND SHARING AMONGST LOVED ONES ENOUGH OF A SPECIAL OCCASION FOR YOU?
WHY, OF COURSE, SUZANNE, ...BUT....
...OH, WHAT THE HECK— YOU'RE RIGHT, SUZANNE — GO AHEAD AND OPEN IT IF YOU LIKE
COOL
POP
SSSSS
Y'KNOW... I NEVER LIKED CHAMPAGNE
YEAH, ME NEITHER —IT'S TOO SWEET....
PICCOLO

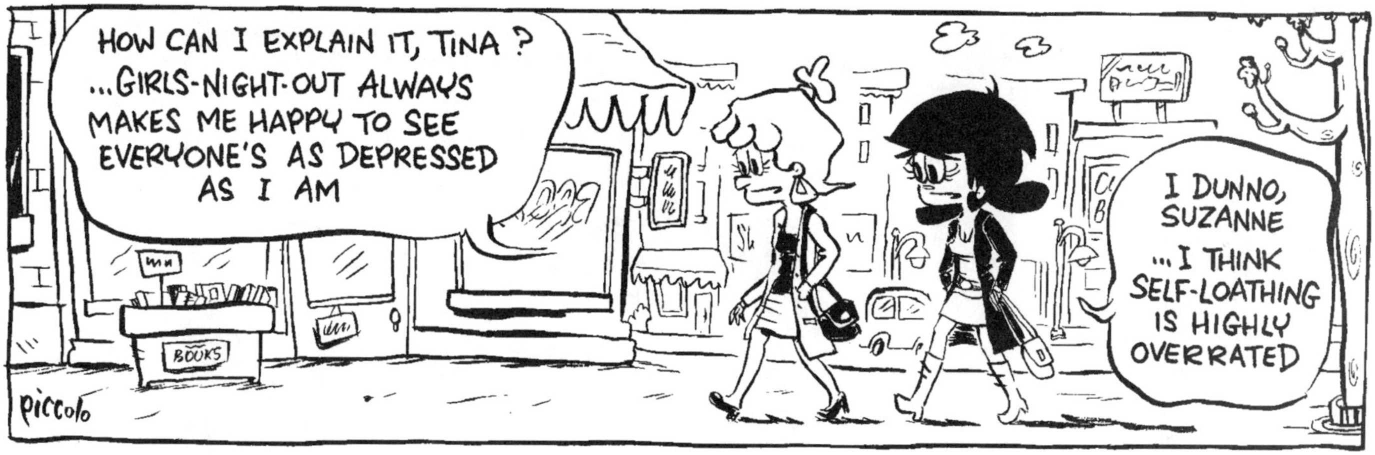
HOW CAN I EXPLAIN IT, TINA ? ...GIRLS-NIGHT-OUT ALWAYS MAKES ME HAPPY TO SEE EVERYONE'S AS DEPRESSED AS I AM
I DUNNO, SUZANNE ...I THINK SELF-LOATHING IS HIGHLY OVERRATED
BOOKS
piccolo

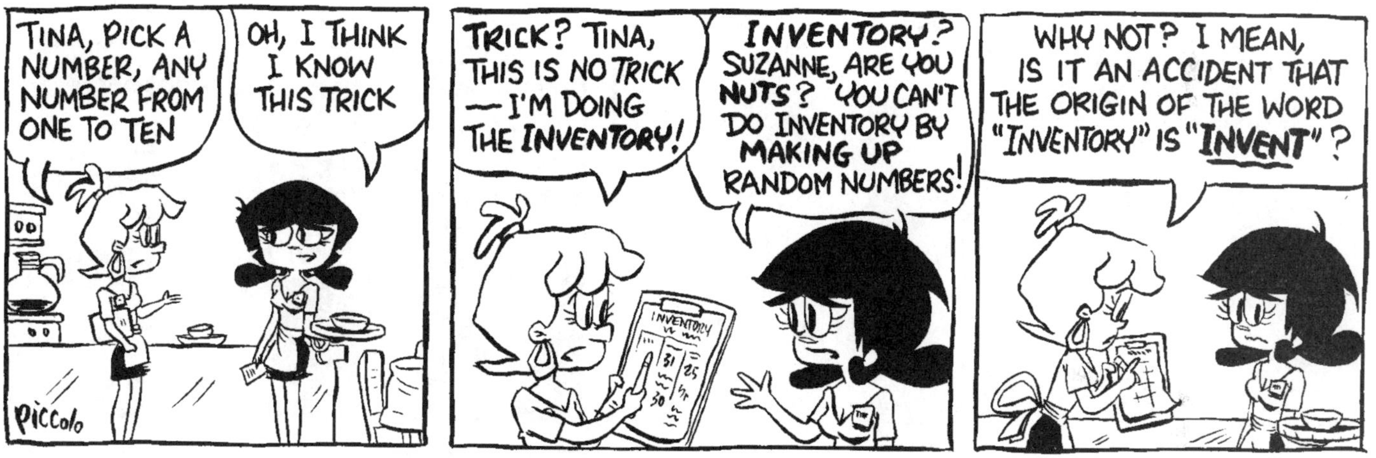
TINA, PICK A NUMBER, ANY NUMBER FROM ONE TO TEN
OH, I THINK I KNOW THIS TRICK
piccolo
TRICK? TINA, THIS IS NO TRICK — I'M DOING THE INVENTORY!
INVENTORY? SUZANNE, ARE YOU NUTS? YOU CAN'T DO INVENTORY BY MAKING UP RANDOM NUMBERS!
INVENTORY
WHY NOT? I MEAN, IS IT AN ACCIDENT THAT THE ORIGIN OF THE WORD "INVENTORY" IS "INVENT"?

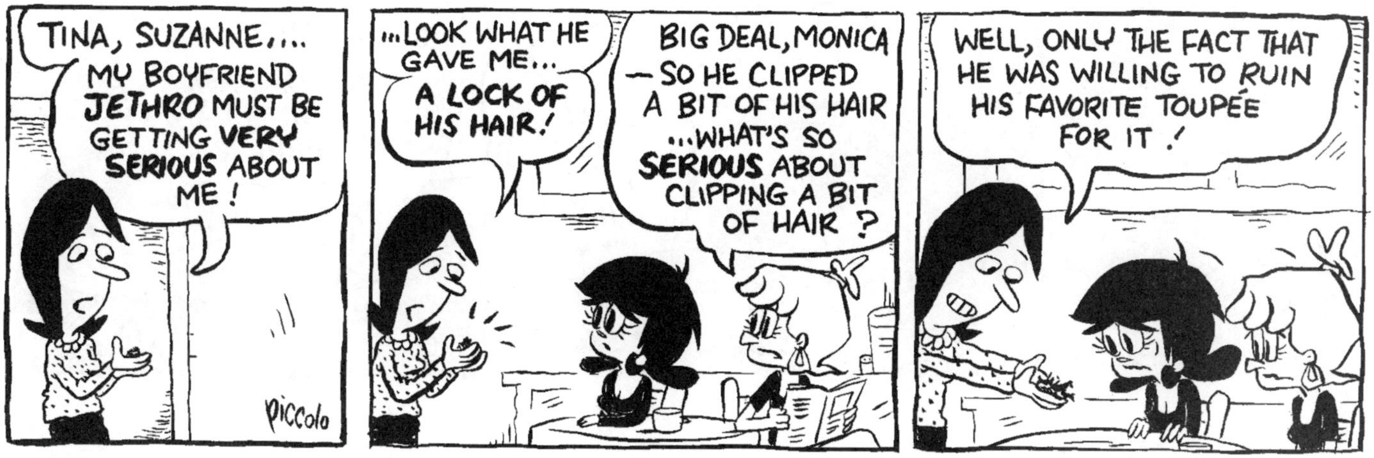
TINA, SUZANNE,... MY BOYFRIEND JETHRO MUST BE GETTING VERY SERIOUS ABOUT ME !
piccolo
...LOOK WHAT HE GAVE ME...
A LOCK OF HIS HAIR!
BIG DEAL, MONICA — SO HE CLIPPED A BIT OF HIS HAIR ...WHAT'S SO SERIOUS ABOUT CLIPPING A BIT OF HAIR ?
WELL, ONLY THE FACT THAT HE WAS WILLING TO RUIN HIS FAVORITE TOUPÉE FOR IT !

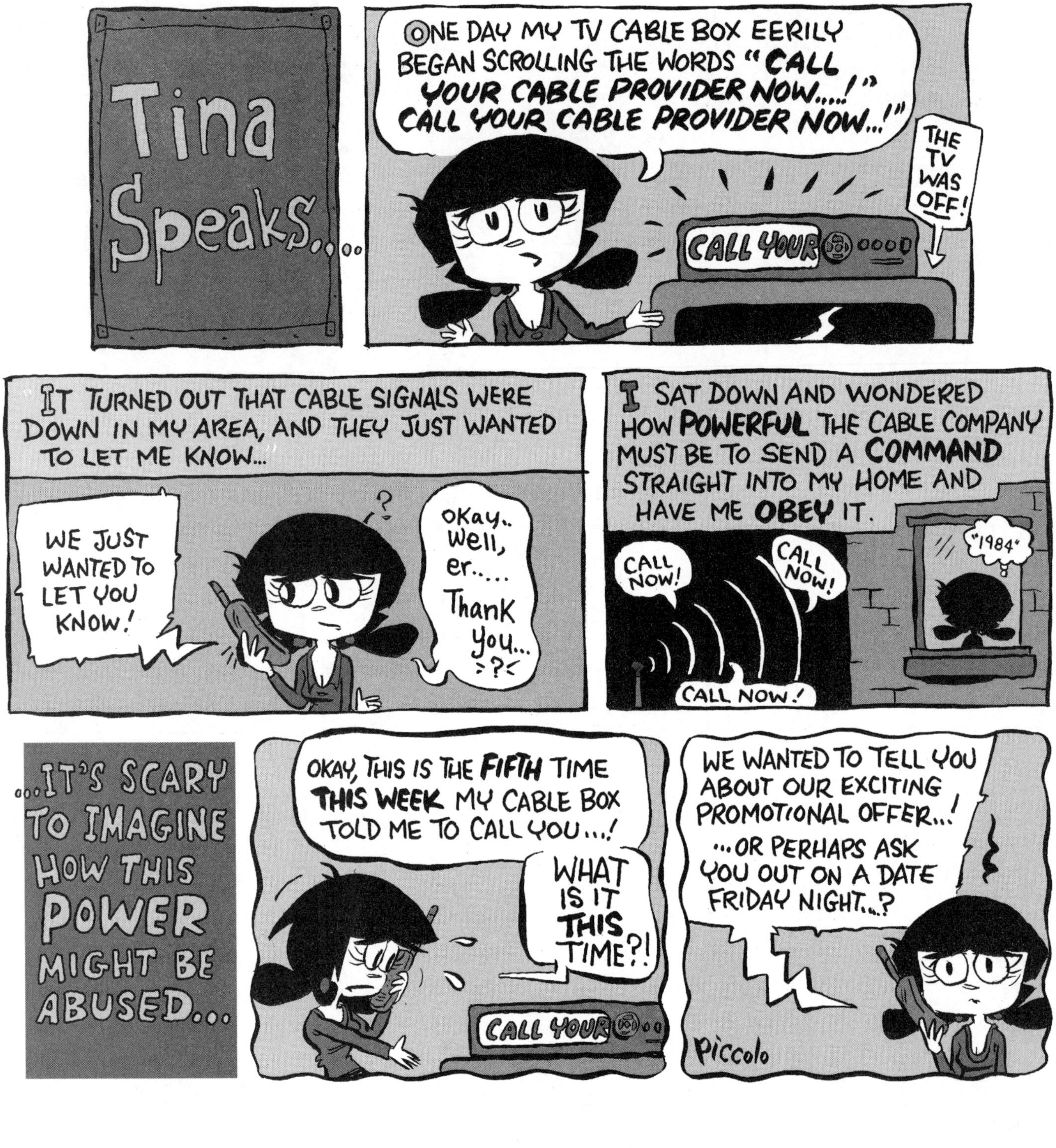

Tina Speaks...
ONE DAY MY TV CABLE BOX EERILY BEGAN SCROLLING THE WORDS "CALL YOUR CABLE PROVIDER NOW....!" CALL YOUR CABLE PROVIDER NOW...!"
THE TV WAS OFF!
CALL YOUR
"IT TURNED OUT THAT CABLE SIGNALS WERE DOWN IN MY AREA, AND THEY JUST WANTED TO LET ME KNOW..."
WE JUST WANTED TO LET YOU KNOW!
?
Okay.. Well, er..... Thank you... ?
I SAT DOWN AND WONDERED HOW POWERFUL THE CABLE COMPANY MUST BE TO SEND A COMMAND STRAIGHT INTO MY HOME AND HAVE ME OBEY IT.
CALL NOW!
CALL NOW!
CALL NOW!
"1984"
...IT'S SCARY TO IMAGINE HOW THIS POWER MIGHT BE ABUSED...
OKAY, THIS IS THE FIFTH TIME THIS WEEK MY CABLE BOX TOLD ME TO CALL YOU...!
WHAT IS IT THIS TIME?!
CALL YOUR
WE WANTED TO TELL YOU ABOUT OUR EXCITING PROMOTIONAL OFFER...!
...OR PERHAPS ASK YOU OUT ON A DATE FRIDAY NIGHT...?
piccolo

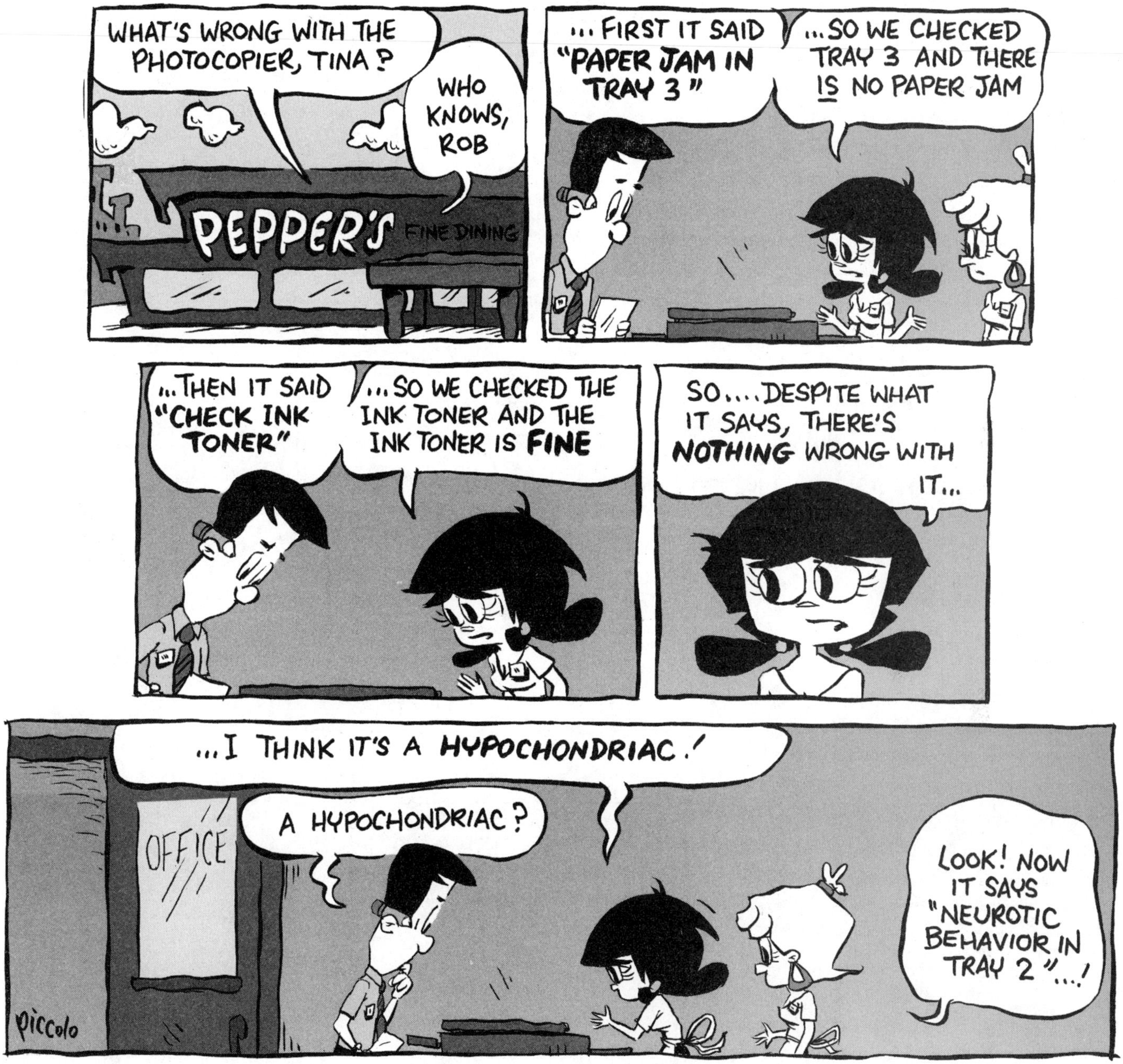
WHAT'S WRONG WITH THE PHOTOCOPIER, TINA?
WHO KNOWS, ROB
PEPPER'S FINE DINING
...FIRST IT SAID "PAPER JAM IN TRAY 3"
...SO WE CHECKED TRAY 3 AND THERE IS NO PAPER JAM
...THEN IT SAID "CHECK INK TONER"
...SO WE CHECKED THE INK TONER AND THE INK TONER IS FINE
SO.... DESPITE WHAT IT SAYS, THERE'S NOTHING WRONG WITH IT...
...I THINK IT'S A HYPOCHONDRIAC!
A HYPOCHONDRIAC?
OFFICE
LOOK! NOW IT SAYS "NEUROTIC BEHAVIOR IN TRAY 2"...!
piccolo

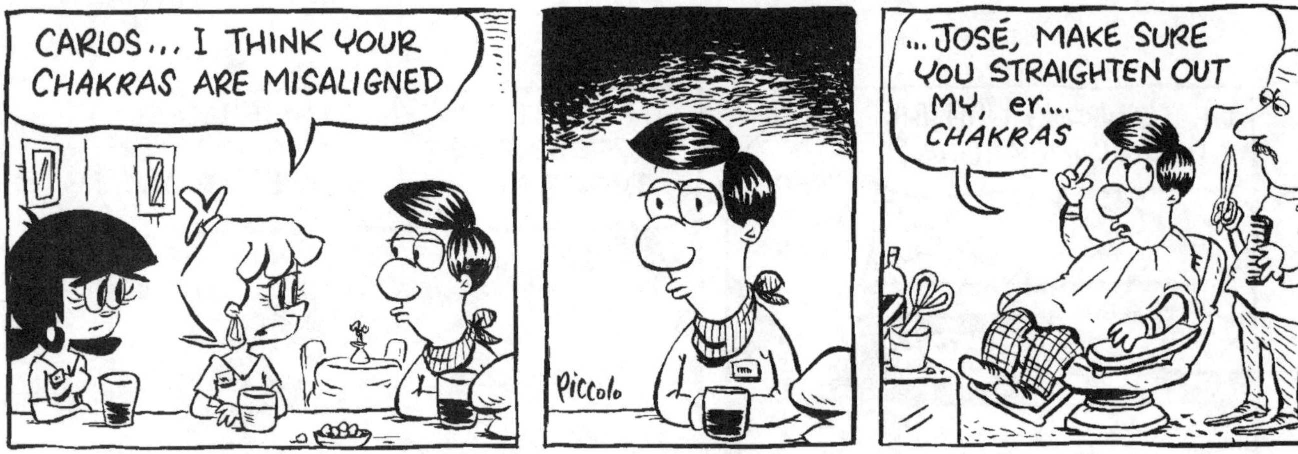
CARLOS... I THINK YOUR CHAKRAS ARE MISALIGNED
Piccolo
...JOSÉ, MAKE SURE YOU STRAIGHTEN OUT MY, er.... CHAKRAS

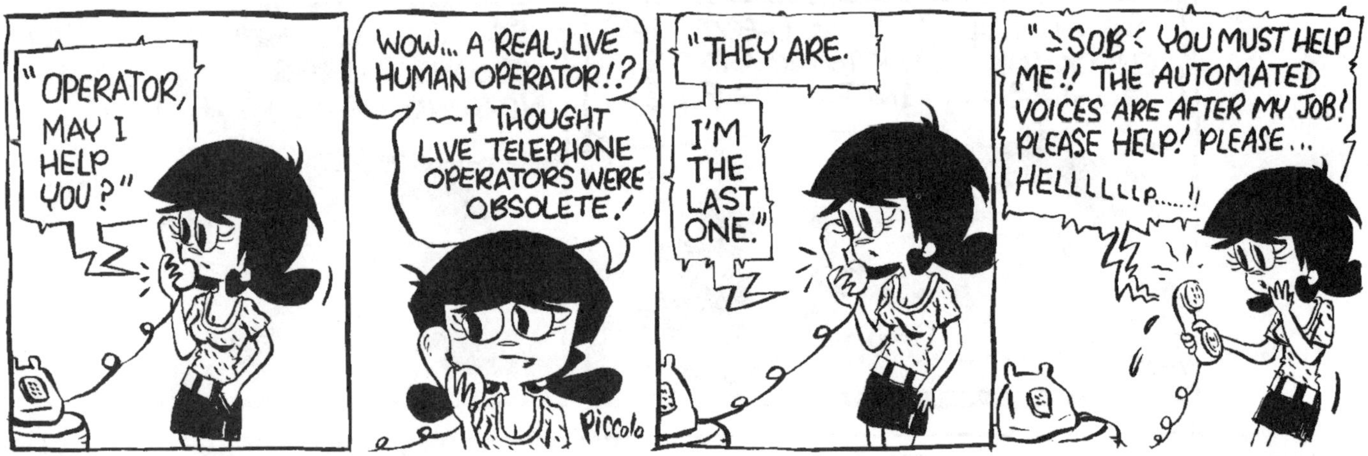
"OPERATOR, MAY I HELP YOU?"
WOW... A REAL, LIVE HUMAN OPERATOR!?
—I THOUGHT LIVE TELEPHONE OPERATORS WERE OBSOLETE!
Piccolo
"THEY ARE.
I'M THE LAST ONE."
" >SOB< YOU MUST HELP ME!! THE AUTOMATED VOICES ARE AFTER MY JOB! PLEASE HELP! PLEASE... HELLLLLLLP.....!!

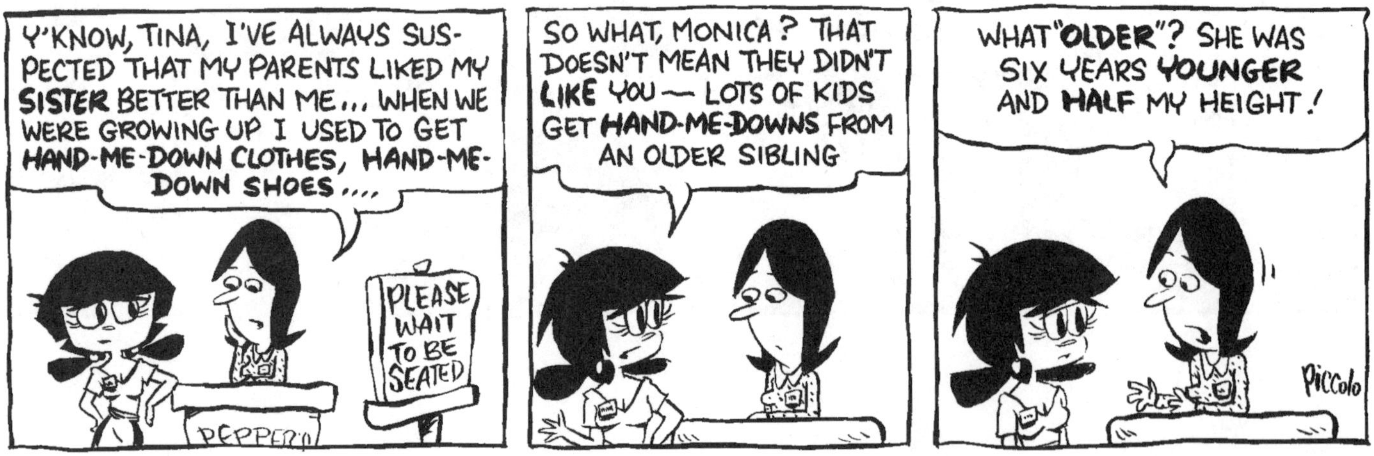
Y'KNOW, TINA, I'VE ALWAYS SUSPECTED THAT MY PARENTS LIKED MY **SISTER** BETTER THAN ME... WHEN WE WERE GROWING UP I USED TO GET **HAND-ME-DOWN CLOTHES, HAND-ME-DOWN SHOES**....
PLEASE WAIT TO BE SEATED
PEPPER'S
SO WHAT, MONICA? THAT DOESN'T MEAN THEY DIDN'T **LIKE** YOU — LOTS OF KIDS GET **HAND-ME-DOWNS** FROM AN OLDER SIBLING
WHAT "**OLDER**"? SHE WAS SIX YEARS **YOUNGER** AND **HALF** MY HEIGHT!
Piccolo

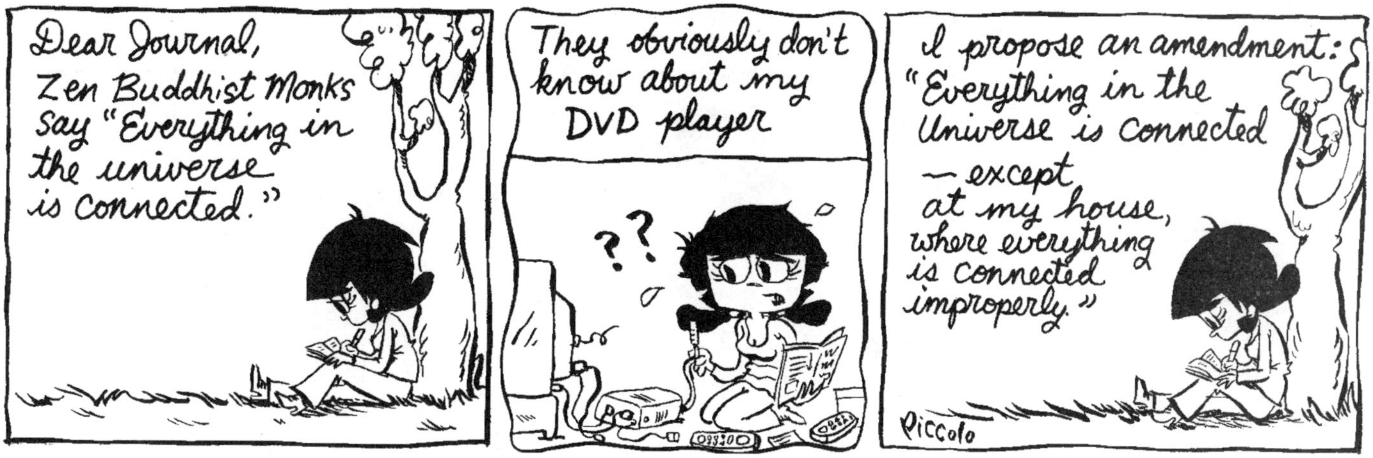
Dear Journal,
Zen Buddhist Monks say "Everything in the universe is connected."
They obviously don't know about my DVD player
I propose an amendment: "Everything in the Universe is connected — except at my house, where everything is connected improperly."
Piccolo

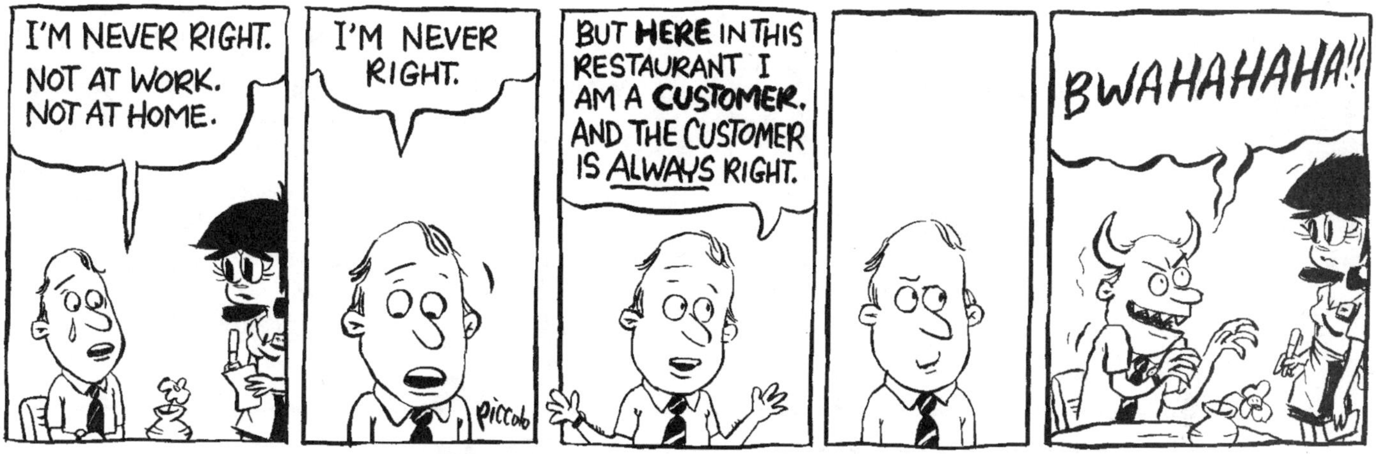
I'M NEVER RIGHT. NOT AT WORK. NOT AT HOME.
I'M NEVER RIGHT.
Piccolo
BUT **HERE** IN THIS RESTAURANT I AM A **CUSTOMER**. AND THE CUSTOMER IS ALWAYS RIGHT.
BWAHAHAHA!!

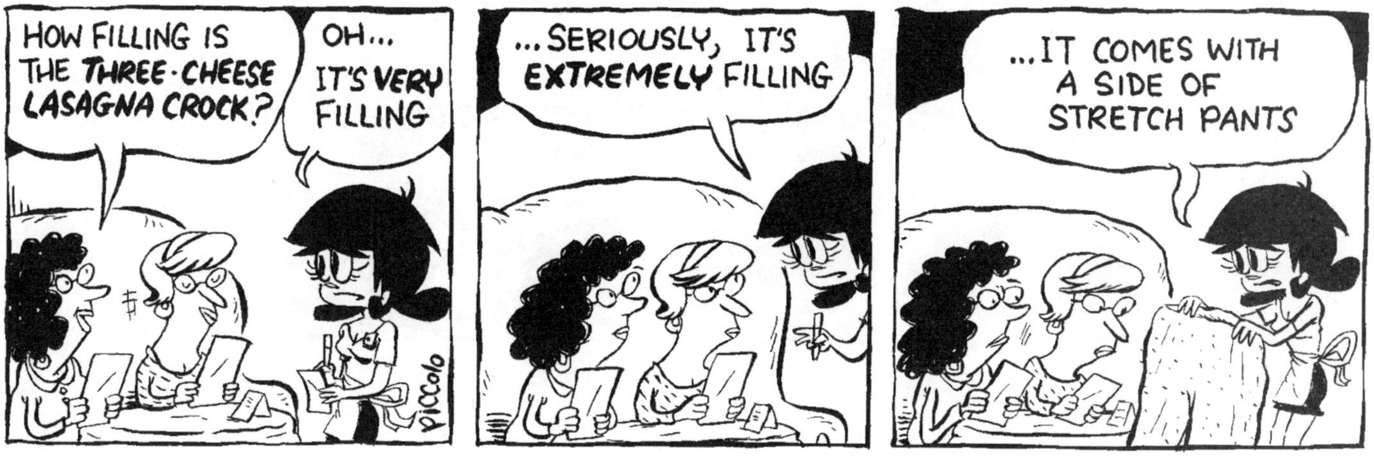
HOW FILLING IS THE **THREE-CHEESE LASAGNA CROCK**?
OH... IT'S **VERY** FILLING
Piccolo
...SERIOUSLY, IT'S **EXTREMELY** FILLING
...IT COMES WITH A SIDE OF STRETCH PANTS

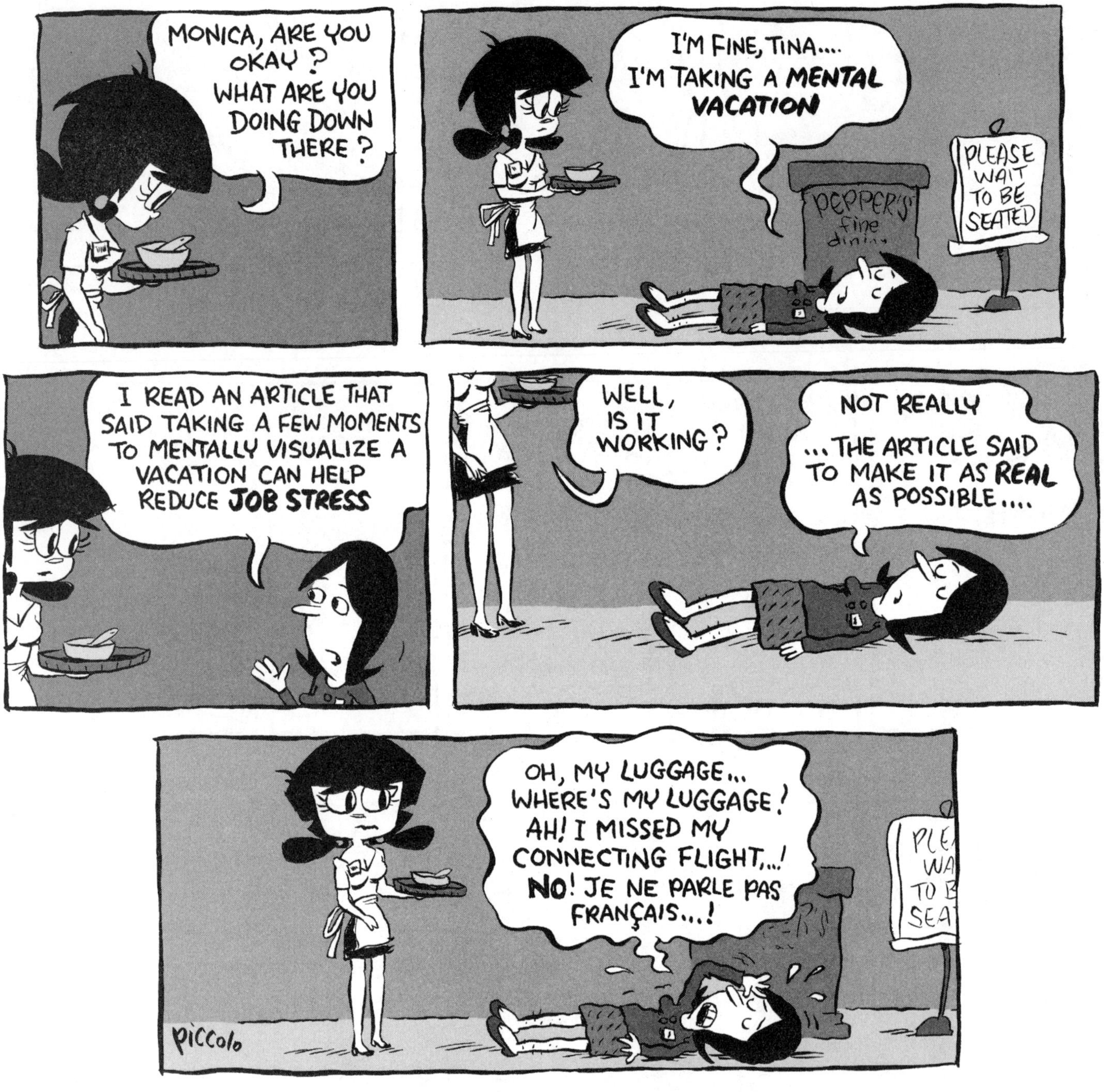
MONICA, ARE YOU OKAY? WHAT ARE YOU DOING DOWN THERE?
I'M FINE, TINA.... I'M TAKING A MENTAL VACATION
PLEASE WAIT TO BE SEATED
PEPPER'S fine dining
I READ AN ARTICLE THAT SAID TAKING A FEW MOMENTS TO MENTALLY VISUALIZE A VACATION CAN HELP REDUCE JOB STRESS
WELL, IS IT WORKING?
NOT REALLY ...THE ARTICLE SAID TO MAKE IT AS REAL AS POSSIBLE....
OH, MY LUGGAGE... WHERE'S MY LUGGAGE! AH! I MISSED MY CONNECTING FLIGHT...! NO! JE NE PARLE PAS FRANÇAIS...!
piccolo

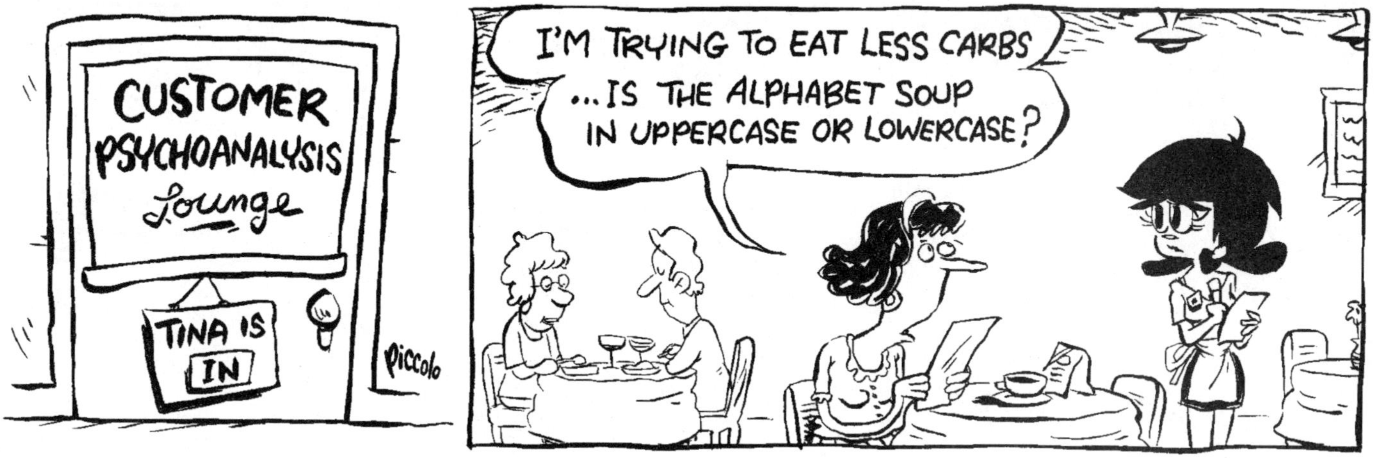
CUSTOMER PSYCHOANALYSIS Lounge
TINA IS IN
piccolo
I'M TRYING TO EAT LESS CARBS
...IS THE ALPHABET SOUP IN UPPERCASE OR LOWERCASE?

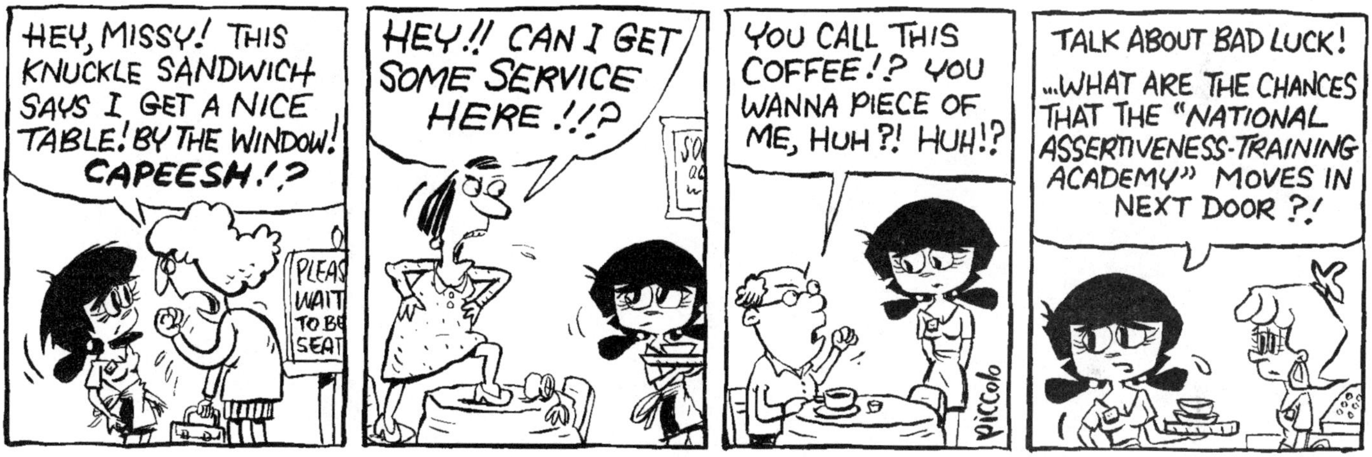
HEY, MISSY! THIS KNUCKLE SANDWICH SAYS I GET A NICE TABLE! BY THE WINDOW! CAPEESH!?
HEY!! CAN I GET SOME SERVICE HERE!!?
YOU CALL THIS COFFEE!? YOU WANNA PIECE OF ME, HUH?! HUH!?
piccolo
TALK ABOUT BAD LUCK! ...WHAT ARE THE CHANCES THAT THE "NATIONAL ASSERTIVENESS-TRAINING ACADEMY" MOVES IN NEXT DOOR?!

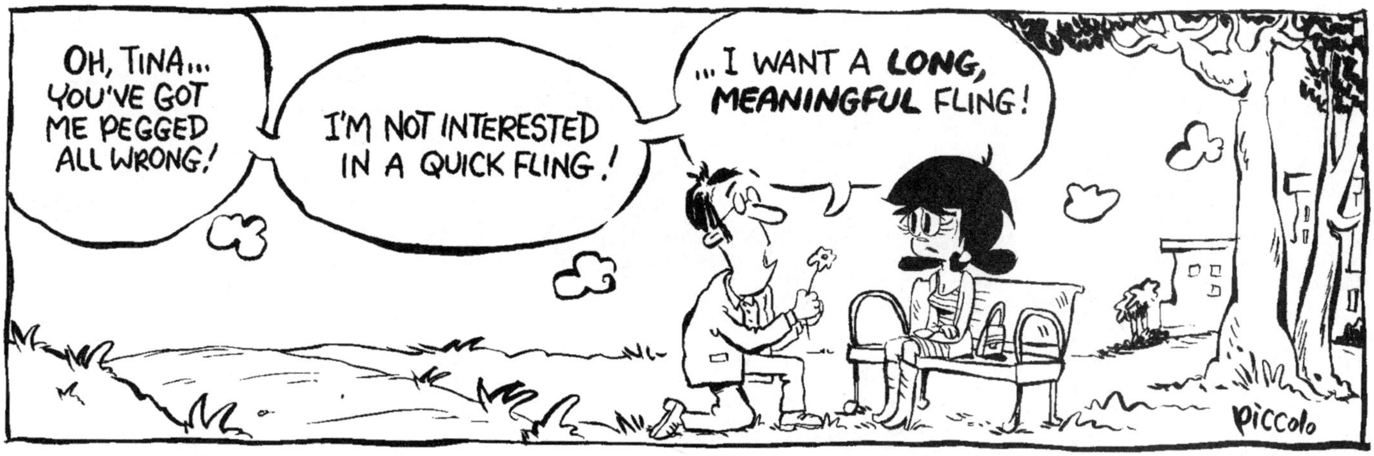
OH, TINA... YOU'VE GOT ME PEGGED ALL WRONG!
I'M NOT INTERESTED IN A QUICK FLING!
...I WANT A **LONG, MEANINGFUL** FLING!
piccolo

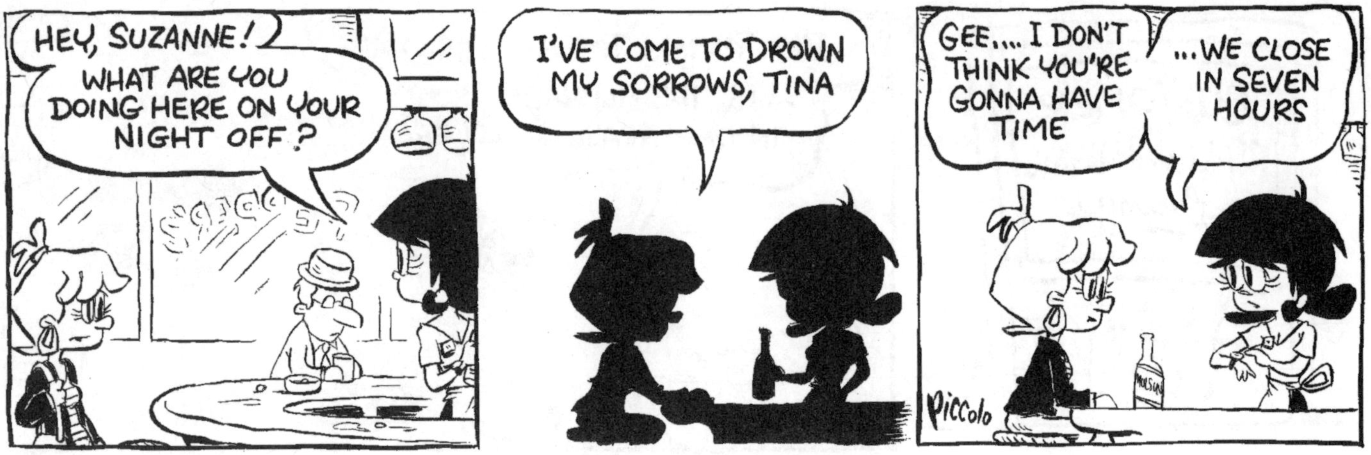
HEY, SUZANNE! WHAT ARE YOU DOING HERE ON YOUR NIGHT OFF?
I'VE COME TO DROWN MY SORROWS, TINA
GEE.... I DON'T THINK YOU'RE GONNA HAVE TIME
...WE CLOSE IN SEVEN HOURS
Piccolo

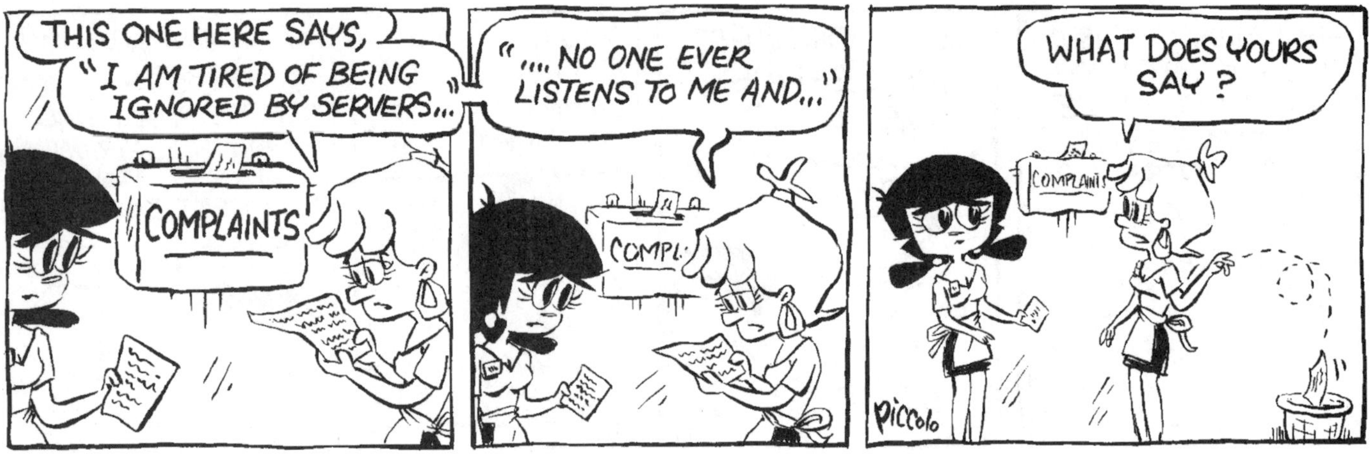
THIS ONE HERE SAYS, "I AM TIRED OF BEING IGNORED BY SERVERS..."
COMPLAINTS
"....NO ONE EVER LISTENS TO ME AND..."
WHAT DOES YOURS SAY?
Piccolo

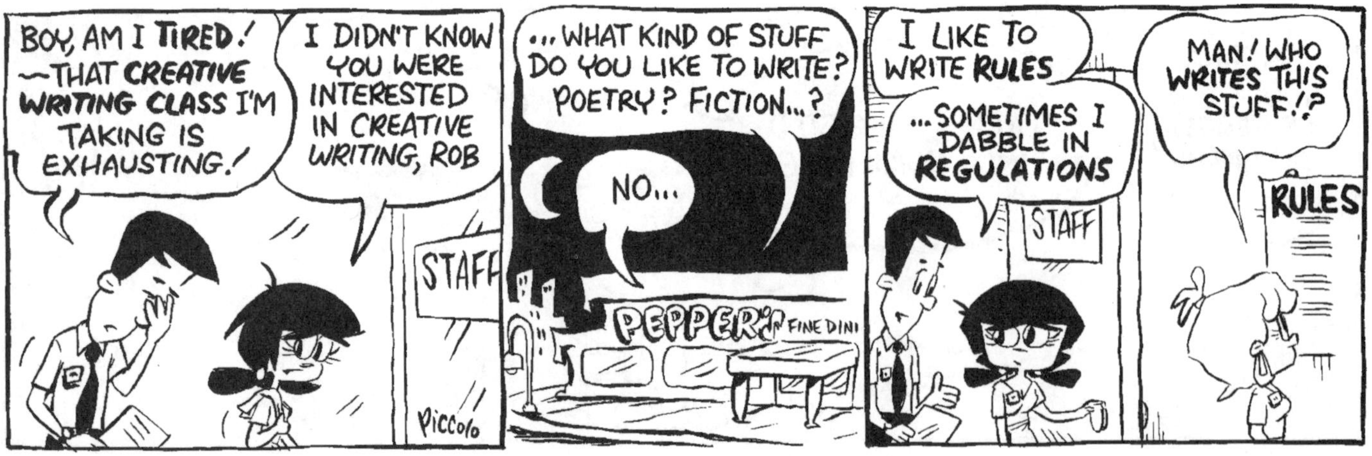
BOY, AM I TIRED! —THAT CREATIVE WRITING CLASS I'M TAKING IS EXHAUSTING!
I DIDN'T KNOW YOU WERE INTERESTED IN CREATIVE WRITING, ROB
STAFF
Piccolo
...WHAT KIND OF STUFF DO YOU LIKE TO WRITE? POETRY? FICTION...?
NO...
PEPPER'S FINE DINI
I LIKE TO WRITE RULES
...SOMETIMES I DABBLE IN REGULATIONS
STAFF
MAN! WHO WRITES THIS STUFF!?
RULES

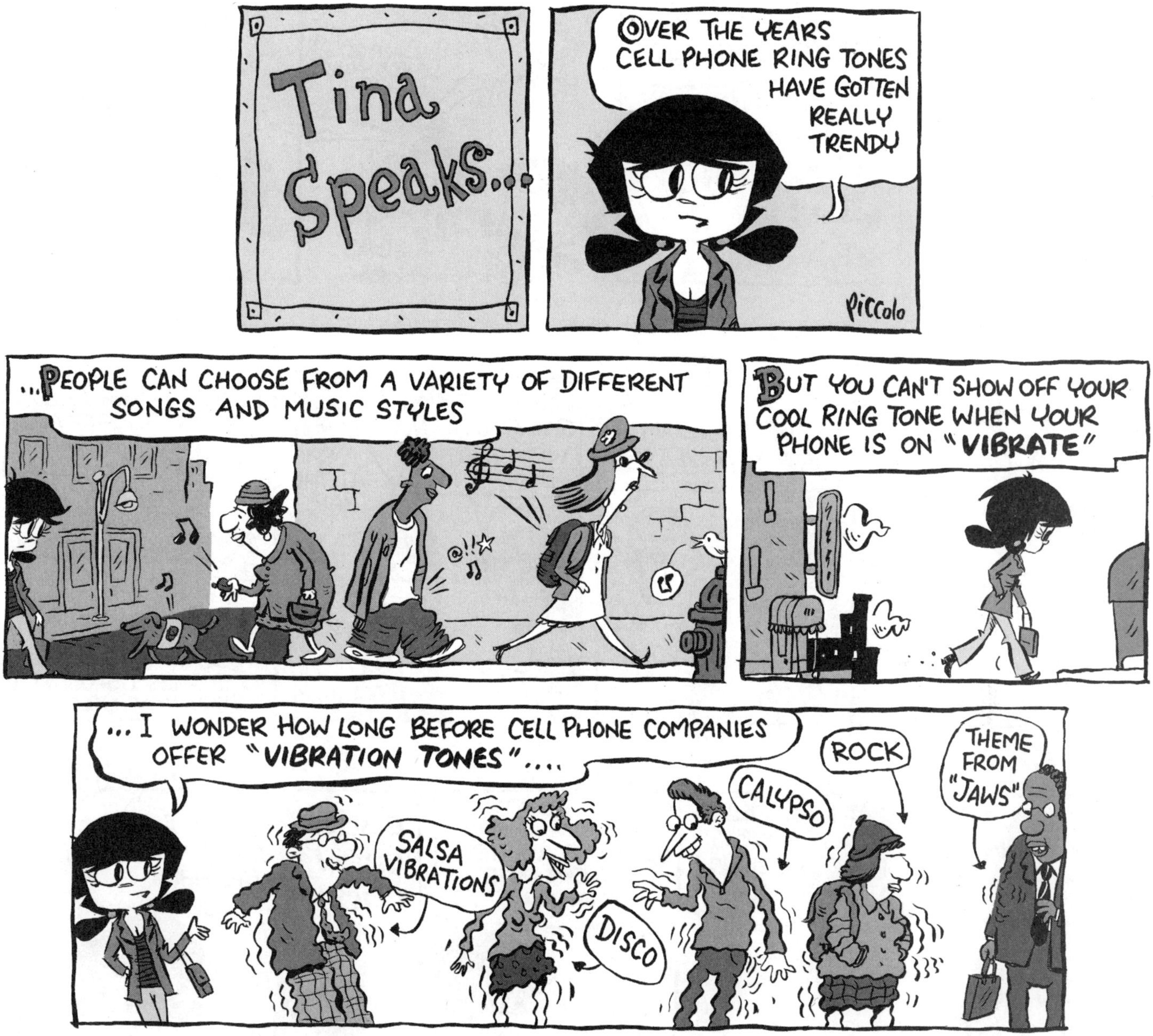
Tina Speaks...
OVER THE YEARS CELL PHONE RING TONES HAVE GOTTEN REALLY TRENDY
Piccolo
...PEOPLE CAN CHOOSE FROM A VARIETY OF DIFFERENT SONGS AND MUSIC STYLES
BUT YOU CAN'T SHOW OFF YOUR COOL RING TONE WHEN YOUR PHONE IS ON "VIBRATE"
... I WONDER HOW LONG BEFORE CELL PHONE COMPANIES OFFER "VIBRATION TONES"....
SALSA VIBRATIONS
DISCO
CALYPSO
ROCK
THEME FROM "JAWS"

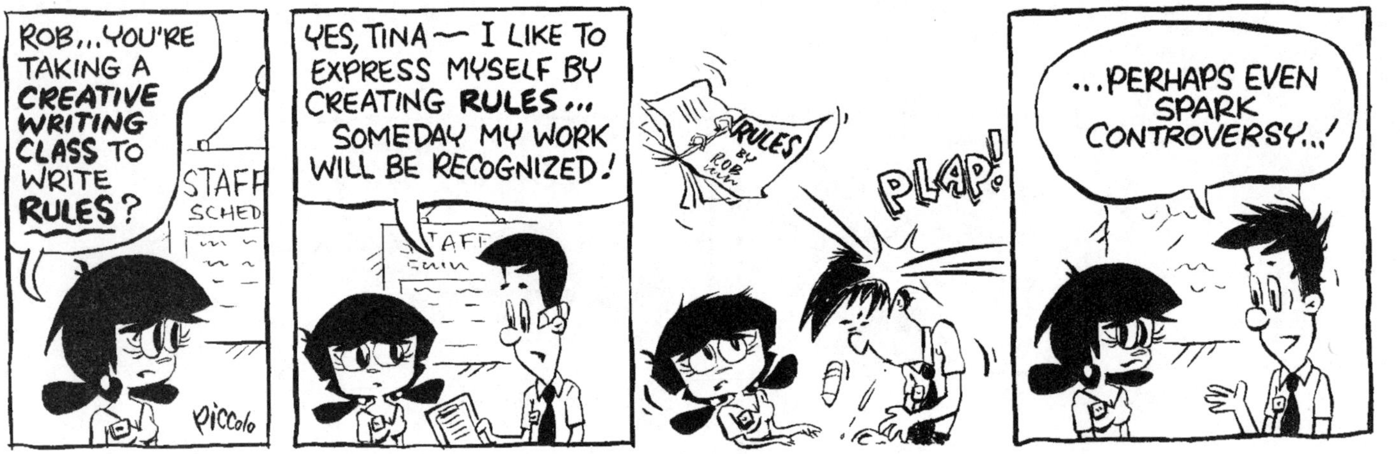
ROB... YOU'RE TAKING A CREATIVE WRITING CLASS TO WRITE RULES?
STAFF SCHED
piccolo
YES, TINA — I LIKE TO EXPRESS MYSELF BY CREATING RULES... SOMEDAY MY WORK WILL BE RECOGNIZED!
RULES BY ROB
PLAP!
...PERHAPS EVEN SPARK CONTROVERSY...!

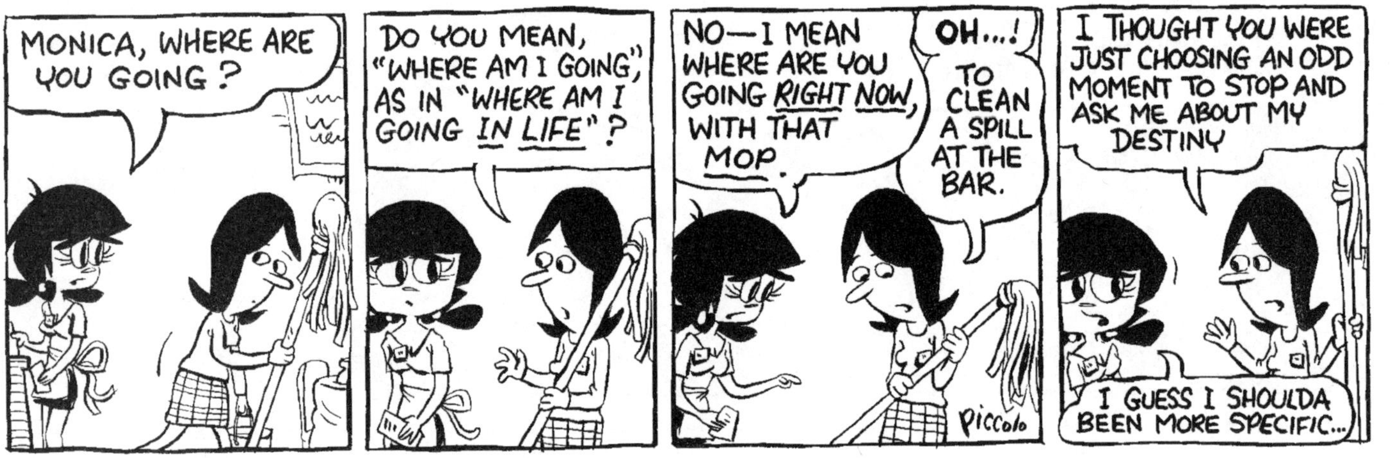
MONICA, WHERE ARE YOU GOING?
DO YOU MEAN, "WHERE AM I GOING", AS IN "WHERE AM I GOING IN LIFE"?
NO — I MEAN WHERE ARE YOU GOING RIGHT NOW, WITH THAT MOP.
OH...! TO CLEAN A SPILL AT THE BAR.
piccolo
I THOUGHT YOU WERE JUST CHOOSING AN ODD MOMENT TO STOP AND ASK ME ABOUT MY DESTINY
I GUESS I SHOULDA BEEN MORE SPECIFIC...

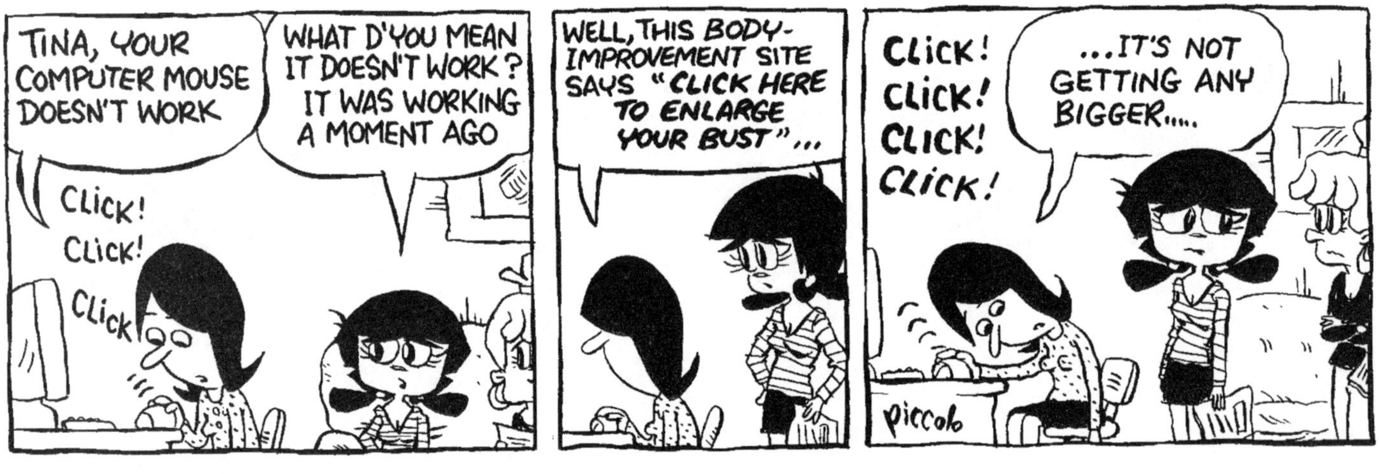
TINA, YOUR COMPUTER MOUSE DOESN'T WORK
CLICK! CLICK! CLICK
WHAT D'YOU MEAN IT DOESN'T WORK? IT WAS WORKING A MOMENT AGO
WELL, THIS BODY-IMPROVEMENT SITE SAYS "CLICK HERE TO ENLARGE YOUR BUST"...
CLICK! CLICK! CLICK! CLICK!
...IT'S NOT GETTING ANY BIGGER.....
piccolo

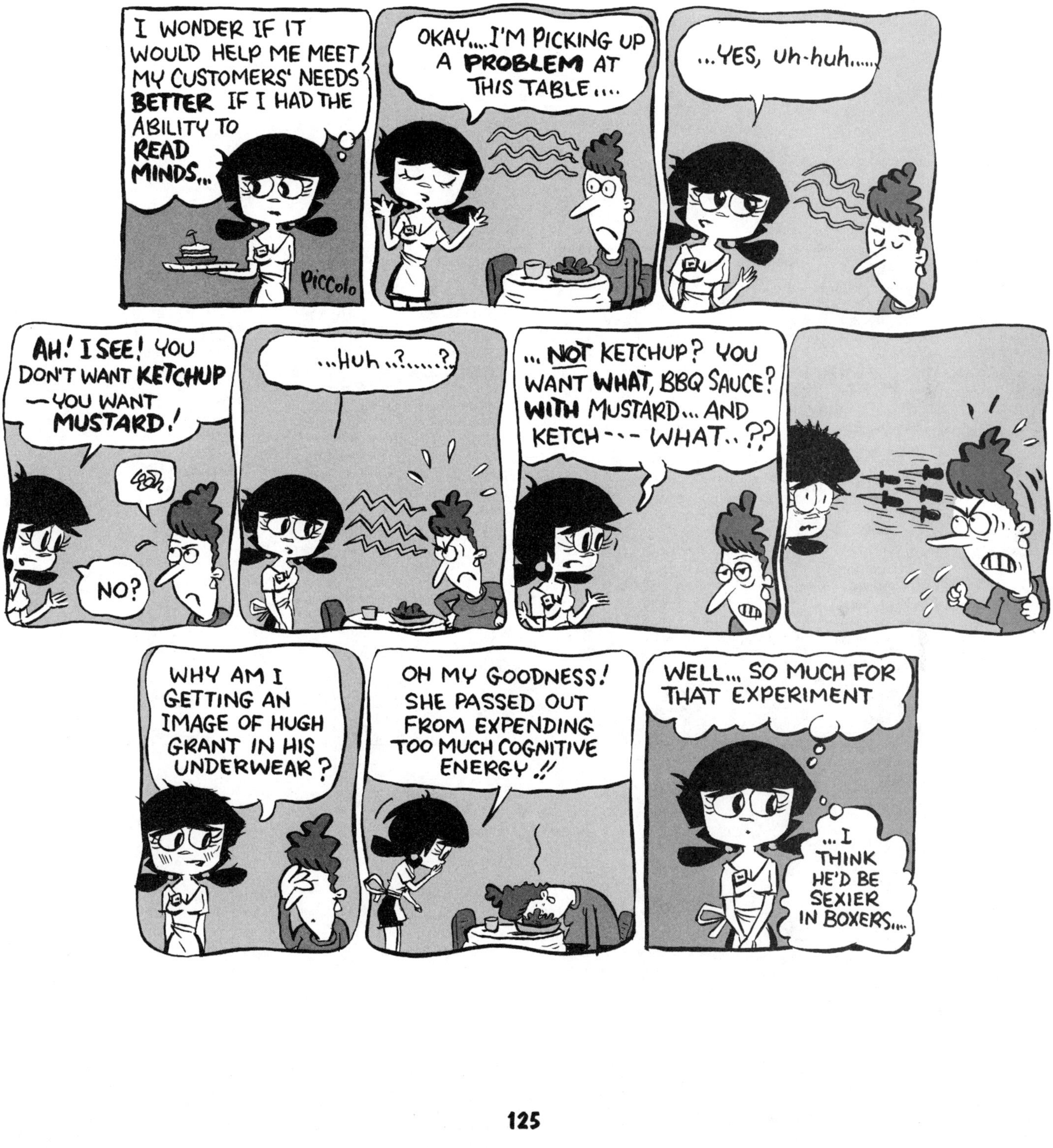
I WONDER IF IT WOULD HELP ME MEET MY CUSTOMERS' NEEDS BETTER IF I HAD THE ABILITY TO READ MINDS...
Piccolo
OKAY.... I'M PICKING UP A PROBLEM AT THIS TABLE....
...YES, uh-huh......
AH! I SEE! YOU DON'T WANT KETCHUP —YOU WANT MUSTARD!
NO?
...Huh..?.....?
... NOT KETCHUP? YOU WANT WHAT, BBQ SAUCE? WITH MUSTARD... AND KETCH--- WHAT..??
WHY AM I GETTING AN IMAGE OF HUGH GRANT IN HIS UNDERWEAR?
OH MY GOODNESS! SHE PASSED OUT FROM EXPENDING TOO MUCH COGNITIVE ENERGY!!
WELL... SO MUCH FOR THAT EXPERIMENT
... I THINK HE'D BE SEXIER IN BOXERS....

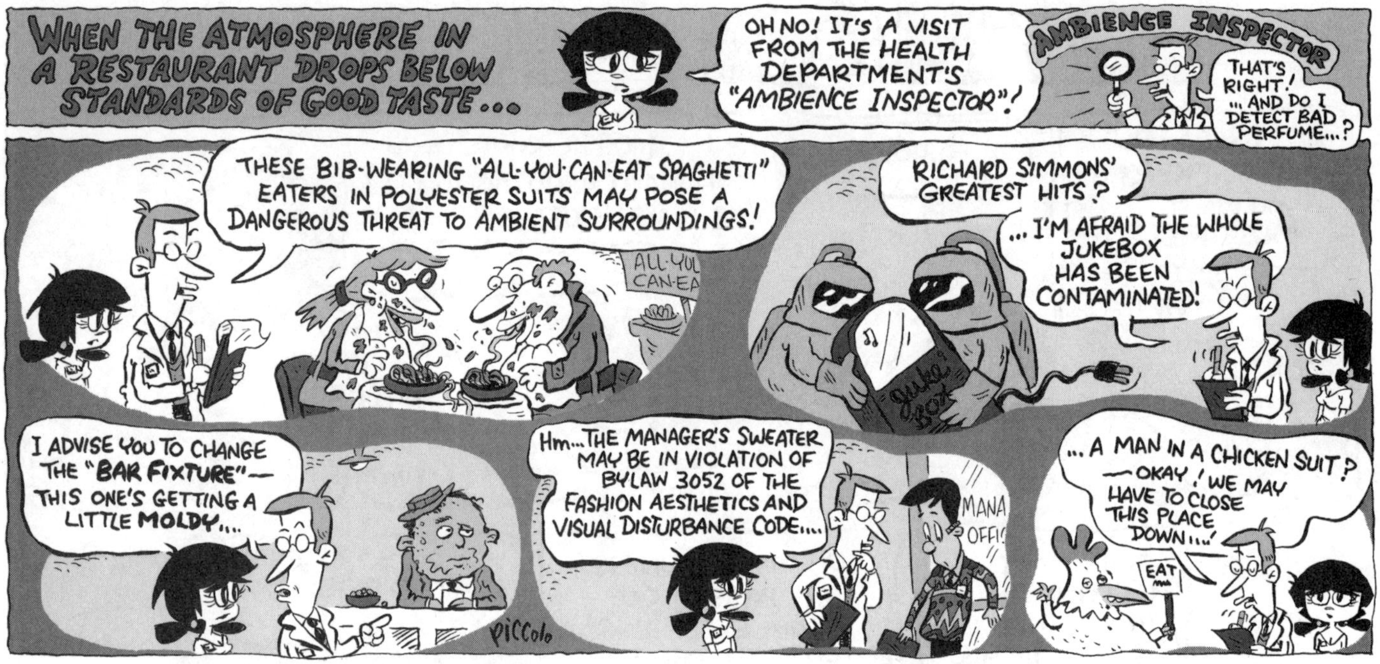
WHEN THE ATMOSPHERE IN A RESTAURANT DROPS BELOW STANDARDS OF GOOD TASTE...
OH NO! IT'S A VISIT FROM THE HEALTH DEPARTMENT'S "AMBIENCE INSPECTOR"!
AMBIENCE INSPECTOR
THAT'S RIGHT! ...AND DO I DETECT BAD PERFUME...?
THESE BIB-WEARING "ALL-YOU-CAN-EAT SPAGHETTI" EATERS IN POLYESTER SUITS MAY POSE A DANGEROUS THREAT TO AMBIENT SURROUNDINGS!
ALL-YOU CAN-EA
RICHARD SIMMONS' GREATEST HITS?
...I'M AFRAID THE WHOLE JUKEBOX HAS BEEN CONTAMINATED!
Juke Box
I ADVISE YOU TO CHANGE THE "BAR FIXTURE"— THIS ONE'S GETTING A LITTLE MOLDY....
Hm...THE MANAGER'S SWEATER MAY BE IN VIOLATION OF BYLAW 3052 OF THE FASHION AESTHETICS AND VISUAL DISTURBANCE CODE....
MANA OFFI
...A MAN IN A CHICKEN SUIT? —OKAY! WE MAY HAVE TO CLOSE THIS PLACE DOWN...!
EAT
PICCOLO

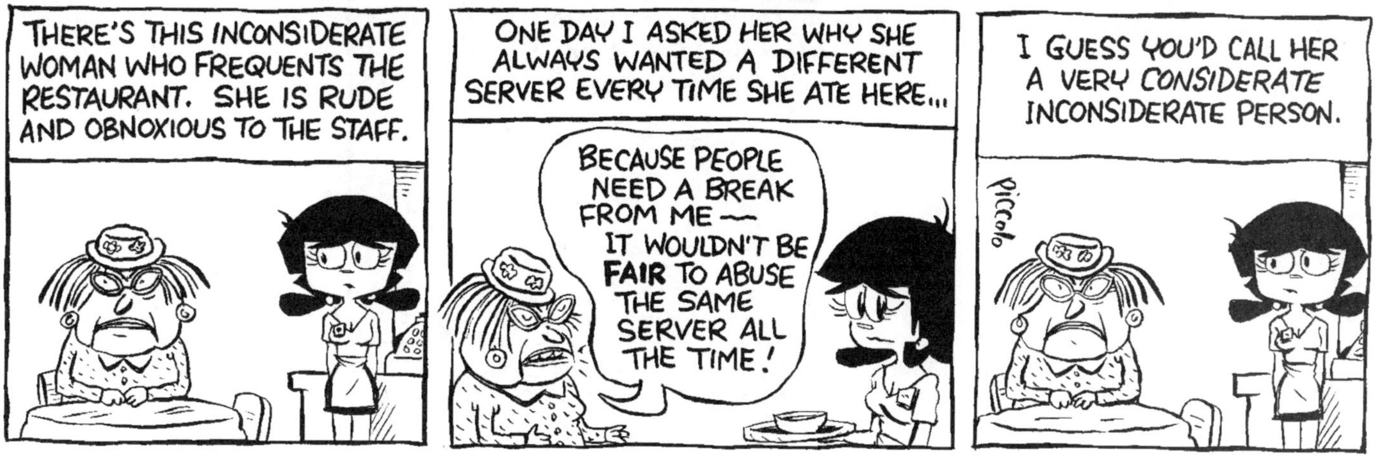
THERE'S THIS INCONSIDERATE WOMAN WHO FREQUENTS THE RESTAURANT. SHE IS RUDE AND OBNOXIOUS TO THE STAFF.
ONE DAY I ASKED HER WHY SHE ALWAYS WANTED A DIFFERENT SERVER EVERY TIME SHE ATE HERE...
BECAUSE PEOPLE NEED A BREAK FROM ME — IT WOULDN'T BE FAIR TO ABUSE THE SAME SERVER ALL THE TIME!
I GUESS YOU'D CALL HER A VERY CONSIDERATE INCONSIDERATE PERSON.
PICCOLO

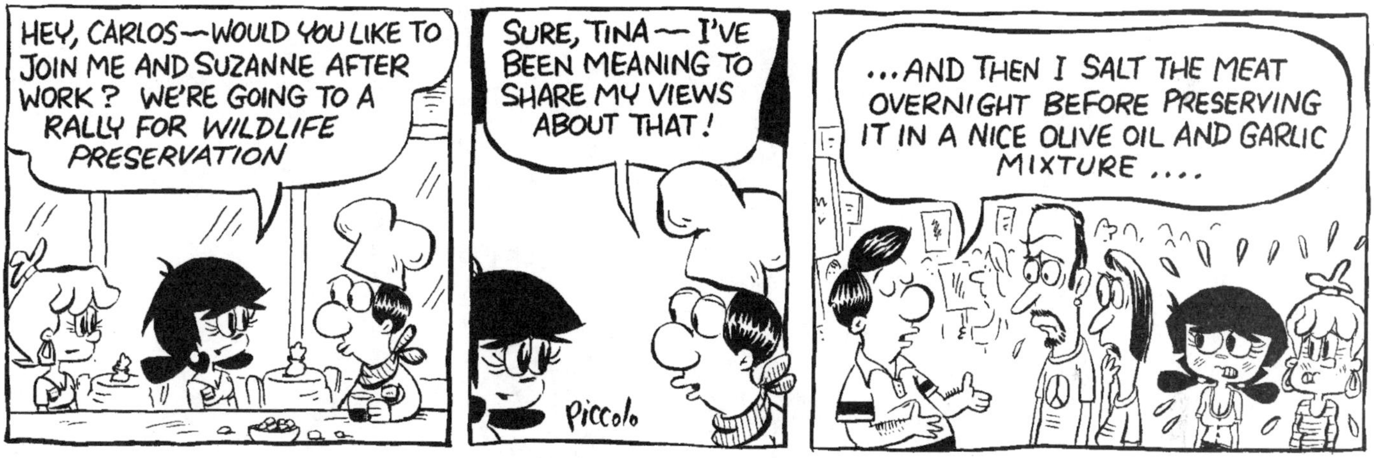
HEY, CARLOS — WOULD YOU LIKE TO JOIN ME AND SUZANNE AFTER WORK? WE'RE GOING TO A RALLY FOR WILDLIFE PRESERVATION
SURE, TINA — I'VE BEEN MEANING TO SHARE MY VIEWS ABOUT THAT!
PICCOLO
...AND THEN I SALT THE MEAT OVERNIGHT BEFORE PRESERVING IT IN A NICE OLIVE OIL AND GARLIC MIXTURE....

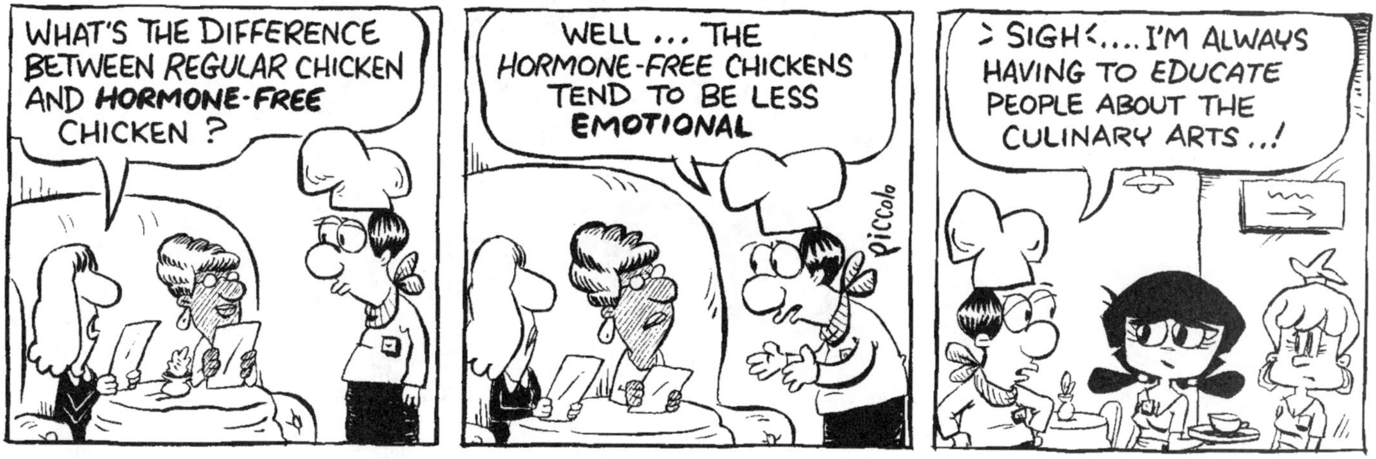
WHAT'S THE DIFFERENCE BETWEEN REGULAR CHICKEN AND HORMONE-FREE CHICKEN?
WELL ... THE HORMONE-FREE CHICKENS TEND TO BE LESS EMOTIONAL
PICCOLO
>SIGH<.... I'M ALWAYS HAVING TO EDUCATE PEOPLE ABOUT THE CULINARY ARTS..!

TINA, I HAVE AN UNUSUAL PROBLEM ...YOU KNOW HOW SOCKS GO MISSING IN THE DRYER?
Yeah?
PLEASE WAIT TO BE SEATED
"...WELL, I BELIEVE OTHER PEOPLE'S MISSING SOCKS ARE TURNING UP IN MY DRYER..."
WHAT THE--?
"...IT'S LIKE MY DRYER IS SOME KIND OF PORTAL INTO THE REALM OF LOST SOCKS"
C. 1982 DETROIT
C. 1998 TORONTO
GEEZ, MONICA, MAYBE YOU SHOULD CALL THE MAYTAG REPAIRMAN
I DID
...HE WAS VERY PLEASED TO BE REUNITED WITH HIS ARGYLE.
PLEASE WAIT TO BE SEATED
piccolo

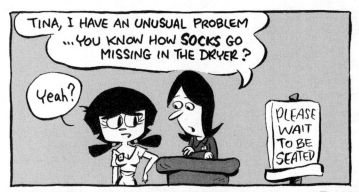

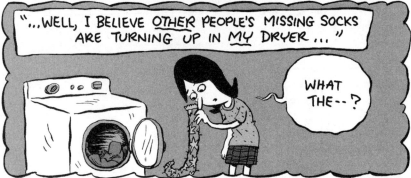

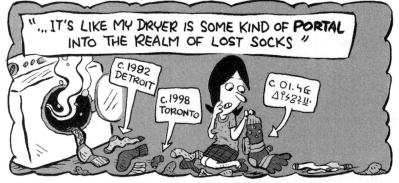

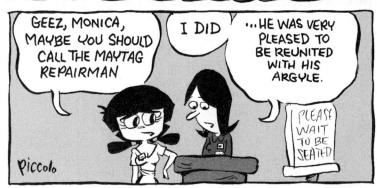